Ludovic Kennedy has been awarded honorary degrees by the Universities of Edinburgh, Strathclyde and Stirling and was knighted in 1994. A joint portrait of him and Moira Shearer by the Israeli artist Avigdor Arikha is now part of the permanent collection of the Scottish National Portrait Gallery. *Truth To Tell*, his collected writings, was published by Black Swan in 1992. He and his wife now live in Wiltshire.

# LUDOVIC KENNEDY

# IN BED WITH AN ELEPHANT

**CORGI BOOKS**

IN BED WITH AN ELEPHANT
A CORGI BOOK: 0 552 14474 6

Originally published in Great Britain by Bantam Press,
a division of Transworld Publishers Ltd

PRINTING HISTORY
Bantam Press edition published 1995
Corgi edition published 1996

Set in Garamond by Falcon Oast Graphic Art

Corgi Books are published by Transworld Publishers Ltd,
61–63 Uxbridge Road, London W5 5SA,
in Australia by Transworld Publishers (Australia) Pty Ltd,
15–25 Helles Avenue, Moorebank, NSW 2170
and in New Zealand by Transworld Publishers (NZ) Ltd,
3 William Pickering Drive, Albany, Auckland.

Reproduced, printed and bound in Great Britain by
Cox & Wyman Ltd, Reading, Berks.

*To the memory of my grandfather,*
*Sir Ludovic Grant of Dalvey*

# ACKNOWLEDGEMENTS

I have many to thank; the University of Edinburgh and Professor Peter Jones, Director of the Institute for Advanced Studies in the Humanities for a fellowship which granted me generous and much appreciated use of the facilities there; the Trustees of the Hawthornden Castle International Writers Retreat for a month's unbroken continuity of work; my researcher Fiona Morrison for three years of co-operation and companionship during which she pursued unflaggingly books and documents of mostly long ago; the librarian and staff, Edinburgh University Library, the National Library of Scotland, the Bodleian Library and the Scottish Record Office; Dr John Scally of the National Library of Scotland for reading the completed manuscript and finding fewer errors than I had anticipated; my wife Moira with her Scottish background and eagle eye for also vetting the manuscript; my nephew Richard Calvocoressi and his wife Francesca for unstinting hospitality and both stimulating and restful company at the end of many a long Edinburgh day; Ursula Mackenzie my editor at Bantam Press for patiently waiting for delivery far longer than she (or I) had expected and for her sage advice in recommending what to amend, add or omit; also at Bantam Press my copy editor Jennie Bull and picture editor Celia Dearing; my friend and literary agent Gill Coleridge for her perennial encouragement and delicately executed role as go-between; my secretaries, Joyce Turnbull and Hilary Edwards; and Annie Davies whose skills at transposing my hieroglyphic jottings into something fit for the printer seem only to improve with the years.

For a variety of other services rendered I wish to thank Michael Ancram, Eric Anderson, Peter Balfour, Geoffrey Barrow, Julian Black, David Brown, Iain G. Brown, John and Jane Buccleuch, Menzies Campbell, Angelika Cawdor, the late Hugh Cawdor, Alan Clark, Ann Davies, Deborah Devonshire, Sandy Dunbar, Alastair M. Dunnett, Owen Dudley Edwards, Andrew Fisher, Antonia Fraser, Ken Gelder, Darby and Bernadette George, Norman Gillies, Ian Gilmour, Neil Gow, Nigel Grant, Peter and Margaret Greenhalgh, the late Laura Grimond, Dawyck Haig, Ian Hamilton, Malcolm Innes, Robert Kee, Mary Keswick, Gordon Leslie, Magnus Linklater, Elizabeth Longford, Godfrey and Claire Macdonald, John MacLeod, I.F. Maciver, Bryan Magee, Andrew Marr, Jill Marshall, Allan Massie, John Menzies, Jan Morris, Philip Newell, Henry L. Philip, David Pryce-Jones, Morar Ryton, J.W. Scott, David Steel, Elizabeth Strachan, Michael Tebbutt, Martin Tyson, Parthenope Ward, James Whyte, Elizabeth Yeo and George Younger.

Some readers will be aware of the origins of the title, *In Bed with an Elephant* – the Canadian Prime Minister, Pierre Trudeau, telling the Washington Press Club in 1969 that sharing a land mass with a neighbour richer and more powerful than oneself was like sleeping with an elephant. 'No matter how even-tempered and friendly the beast, one is affected by every twitch and grunt.' P. H. Scott has already used it for the title of his admirable Saltire Society booklet. Here I am giving it a second airing.

The publishers have made every effort to trace copyright ownership and would be grateful to learn of any unwitting copyright infringement.

'Speaking of Scotland' by Maurice Lindsay, from *Collected Poems 1940–1990*, Mercat Press, Edinburgh, 1990, reproduced by kind permission of Maurice Lindsay.

Two poems by Hugh MacDiarmid, from *Selected Poems*, Carcanet Press Ltd, 1992, reproduced with permission.

Extracts from *Boswell's London Journal 1762–1763*, Frederick A. Pottle (Ed.) © 1950 by Yale University and by Edinburgh University Press, reproduced with permission.

Extract from 'Orkney Tapestry' by George Mackay Brown, from *Portrait of Orkney*, John Murray (Publishers) Ltd, 1988, reproduced with permission.

Extracts from *The Taking of the Stone of Destiny* by Ian Hamilton, Corgi 1992, copyright © Ian Hamilton 1991, reproduced by kind permission of Curtis Brown.

Extracts from *Lord Cawdor's Room Notes* reproduced by kind permission of Cawdor Castle (Tourism) Ltd.

'The Voyeur' by Tom Leonard, reproduced by kind permission of Tom Leonard.

'Scotland' by Alastair Reid, from *Weathering: Poems and Translations*, Canongate Books Ltd, 14 High Street, Edinburgh EH1 1TE, reproduced with permission.

Breathes there the man, with soul so dead,
Who never to himself hath said,
    This is my own, my native land!

SIR WALTER SCOTT


SPEAKING OF SCOTLAND

What do you mean when you speak of Scotland?
The grey defeats that are dead and gone
behind the legend each generation
savours afresh, yet can't live on?

Lowland farms with their broad acres
peopling crops? The colder earth
of the North East? Or Highland mountains
shouldering up their rocky dearth?

Inheritance of guilt that our country
has never stood where we feel she should?
A nagging threat of unfinished struggle
somehow forever lost in the blood?

Scotland's a sense of change, an endless
becoming for which there was never a kind
of wholeness or ultimate category.
Scotland's an attitude of mind.

MAURICE LINDSAY, *Collected Poems 1940–1990*

# CONTENTS

# LIST OF ILLUSTRATIONS

Prince Charles Edward with the Irish Jacobite Antoine Walsh on the shore of Loch nan Uamh, July 1745. 'Let what will happen, the stroke is struck and I have taken a firm resolution to conquer or to die.'

Drummossie Moor, Culloden. The Final Reckoning.

Prince Charles Edward. Painted in France in about 1748. 'An Italian-born stateless refugee . . . never quite the Scottish patriot that history has painted him.'

Flora Macdonald by Allan Ramsay. Dr Johnson's epitaph: 'Her name will be mentioned in history, and if courage and fidelity be virtues, mentioned with honour.'

Kingsburgh House, Isle of Skye, where Dr Johnson slept in the same bed and shared with Boswell the same room in which the prince had slept twenty-seven years earlier.

Executions of so-called witches in the seventeenth century. Between

1560 and 1720 up to 4,500 'witches' in Scotland were hanged, strangled or burned.

Sentry at Fort George clutching a nasty-looking weapon which he called an LSW. 'I asked if it was loaded and he said it was.'

James Boswell by George Wilson, 1765. 'I have the whim of an Englishman to make me think and act extravagantly, and the sense of a Scotsman to make me sensible of it.'

Dr Samuel Johnson by Sir Joshua Reynolds 1775. 'When I find a Scotchman to whom an Englishman is as a Scotchman, that Scotchman shall be as an Englishman to me.'

Thomas Rolandson's cartoon of Boswell accompanying Dr Johnson along Edinburgh's High Street, August 1773. With effluents thrown from upper windows the High Street stank from end to end. 'I smell you in the dark,' said Johnson as they marched along.'

The 'collision' as interpreted by Thomas Rowlandson, between Dr Johnson and Boswell's father. 'They become exceedingly warm and violent. Whiggism and Presbyterianism, Toryism and Episcopacy were terribly buffeted.'

The ruined chapel and Celtic Cross on Inchkenneth where Boswell was frightened by a ghost and Dr Johnson by the sight of human bones.

Fingal's Cave, Staffa by Joseph Turner, 1832. 'The man who bought the painting, foolish fellow, complained to Turner that it was indistinct. 'Indistinctness is my forte,' Turner replied.

The skull of St Magnus, killed by an axe on the orders of Earl Hakon in the twelfth century and discovered in Kirkwall Cathedral 800 years later.

Tomb of the explorer Dr John Rae in Kirkwall Cathedral. 'Eyes shut in the manner of one enjoying a light doze after a picnic lunch. The shotgun suggests that at any moment he may be roused by a companion to continue the chase.'

The prehistoric settlement of Skara Brae in Orkney, showing dresser, beds and fireplace; 5.000 years old, yet all the furniture is still in place.

Ian Hamilton (now Q.C.) 'I had dreams of a new Scotland, alive, full of ideas . . .'

The Coronation Chair, the Stone of Destiny nestling at the base of it.

The Declaration of Arbroath, 1320. 'May it please you to admonish and exhort the king of the English, who ought to be satisfied with what belongs to him, to leave us Scots in peace . . .'

Captain James Brander-Dunbar, aka John Macnab. 'A jovial scoundrel, bloodthirsty as a stoat and cruel, but good company and a man.'

Hugh Cawdor, 5th Earl and 26th Thane. 'A black-haired, funny, buccaneering sort of Thane, half poet, half pirate.'

.

The Queen of Scotland. 'Twelve years of almost unalloyed happiness in France; seven years of turbulence and drama in Scotland; nineteen years of misery in England; a journey from sunshine through storm to blackest night.'

Henry Stuart, Lord Darnley, Mary's second husband. 'I know not, but it is greatly to be feared that he can have no long life among these people.'

The Earl of Bothwell, Mary's third husband. 'A very rough customer with cruel suspicious eyes . . . a bully who once kicked his servant in the stomach.'

Loch Leven Castle, Mary's island prison for ten months. 'For two weeks, sick, pregnant, shocked and dispirited, she remained in a semi-coma so that her jailers thought she might die.'

David Hume, by Allan Ramsay, 1766. 'It is an absurdity to believe that the Deity has human passions and one of the lowest of human passions, a restless appetite for applause.'

The meeting in Edinburgh between Burns and Scott, aged fifteen, seated far right. 'The eye alone', wrote Scott, 'indicated the poetical character and temperament. It glowed (I say literally *glowed*) when he spoke with feeling or interest.'

Robert Louis Stevenson by John Singer Sargent. 'We are a race of gypsies and love change and travel for themselves. I travel not to go anywhere but to go. The great affair is to move.'

Burns' Mausoleum in St Michael's Churchyard, Dumfries. 'Light and airy, big enough to impress but not overpowering.'

Sir Walter Scott and dog seated in the Scott monument. 'That rare creature, a Scot who loved England almost as much as Scotland.'

Professor John Wilson (Christopher North), of whom Dickens said, 'A bright, mountain-looking fellow . . . as though he had just come down from the Highlands and never in his life taken pen in hand.'

Register House Edinburgh by Robert Adam as it was until 1852 when a statue of the Duke of Wellington went up which effectively blocked this view of it.

Henry Moore's statue of King and Queen at Glenkiln, Dumfriesshire. 'Majesty, authority, and in that desolate landscape, the loneliness and isolation of office.'

Parliament Hall, with Roubiliac's statue of Lord President Forbes, where advocates meet clients and each other. 'Intelligent men,' said Stevenson, 'have been walking here daily for twenty years without a rag of business or shilling of reward.'

Mrs Thatcher addressing the General Assembly of the Church of Scotland, 21 May 1988, the Moderator presiding. 'She can use the most hackneyed language as if she had minted it that morning, and wears it like a badge of virtue.'

English political leaders wake up to an awareness of the Scottish dimension.

# In Bed With An Elephant

# PROLOGUE

*In the beginning*

IN THE BEGINNING WAS THE ICE. IN PLACES THE ICE WAS TWO MILES high. I'll say that again: *the ice was two miles high*. It covered most of the northern hemisphere, it spanned the Atlantic. In America it stretched as far south as the latitude of Washington DC, and in Britain as far as London. All of Scandinavia and of Scotland lay inert beneath it.

Over many millennia the ice began to melt and the seas to rise, and in the process the peninsula of Britain became separated from the rest of Europe by the birth of the English Channel, an event which was to determine for all time England's as well as Scotland's future. No less dramatic was the shape the retreating ice made of Scotland, a terrain surrounded by water on three, almost four sides, its northern part cleft by firths and sea lochs, at one point almost split in two. Islands formed to the west of it, more than 700, and in the far north Orkney was torn from the mainland by the raging waters of the Pentland Firth. Astride the centre rose bare and purple mountains. It was a land that differed from the future lush pastures of England in almost every way.

As the ice continued to retreat northwards, the sleeping mass that was Scotland shook itself free of hibernation and came to life.

The earth became fertile, forests of pine and birch and oak grew, eagle and cormorant flew and on the tundra that had come into being reindeer and red deer grazed. There were other animals too, wolf and elk, bear and beaver, wildcat and boar; but how they came there and learned to be fleet is part of the mystery of creation. The rivers were rich in salmon and the freshwater lochs with trout, and the bays and inlets were alive with every kind of mollusc and sea fish.

Man, as hunter and gatherer, first put in an appearance some 9,000 years ago. We know this from discoveries at the farm of Morton in Fife, near the east coast firth of Tay: stone tools for shaping wood and cutting hides, evidence of traps for catching cod, shell mountains of edible crustaceans, the bones of stranded whales which they cut up and ate. The people are without a name but are believed to have come from southern Britain. Other relics of their habitation have been found elsewhere in Scotland, though sparsely distributed; not more than a dozen or twenty people to every hundred square miles.

During the remaining millennia before Christ's birth, migrants came to Scotland from Europe and these, the first agriculturists, brought seeds and plants and destroyed parts of the huge forests, as they are doing in Brazil and Indonesia today, to make clearings for cattle and crops. Among these migrants were the Beaker people, round-headed and square-jawed, so called because they had buried with them bell-shaped beakers or drinking vessels to give them sustenance in the world beyond. Later from central Europe came the first of the Celts to populate north-eastern Scotland between the Firth of Tay and the Pentland Firth. We do not know what language they spoke nor what name they gave to themselves, but the Romans called them Picts or painted people, composed of a variety of tribes of which one of the fiercest, the Caledonians, inhabited the far north; and later Caledonia became a name to represent all Scotland. Their only legacy to mankind, and it is considerable, has been carvings on stone; exquisite designs of men and beasts, birds and fish, mythical monsters, strange symbols whose meanings elude us to this day; and after their conversion to Christianity, drawings of David and the lion, Jonah and the whale, and the unique and magnificent Celtic Cross.

The Romans came to Scotland in AD 80 and although they won an early battle against the Caledonians, they were never able to subdue them. The emperor Hadrian built his famous wall from the Tyne to the Solway to keep them out, and later a more northerly barrier called the Antonine Wall after the emperor Antoninus was erected along a 40-mile front between the Forth and the Clyde. But in the end the Caledonians broke through all the Roman defences, overran Hadrian's Wall and devastated the country to the south of it. After this the Romans, whose empire was torn by internal divisions, left Britain for good.

But then the Caledonians and the Picts faced a danger from another quarter. The tribe that was to give Scotland its name, the Scotii or Scots who lived in Northern Ireland, crossed the narrow seas that divided them from Argyll and established a kingdom there which they named after their own kingdom of Dalriada. They brought with them their language which, though it has undergone many variations in the course of 1,500 years, is basically the Erse or Gaelic that is still spoken in the west of Scotland to this day.

It wasn't long before the Scots, pushing eastwards, came into conflict with the Picts and after a series of battles the Scots prevailed against them and the king of the Scots, Kenneth MacAlpin, also became king of the Picts. There was much intermarrying between the two tribes and then the Picts, as such, are not heard of again.

There were two other tribal kingdoms in Scotland at this time. The first were the Britons, who at one time had populated southern England so that the Romans had called the country Britannia after them, but had since been driven to the west and north, and now lived in the valley of the river Clyde. The other was that of the Angles who had crossed the sea from the borders of Germany and Denmark and settled in England's east coast; their territory stretching from the Tees to the Firth of Forth. They were a warlike people and in 685 their king led an army against the Scots who heavily defeated them at the battle of Nechtanmere, after which they declined. Had they won and conquered Scotland, then the whole of Britain, from the Pentland Firth to the English Channel, would have become Angle-land or England, and Scotland as a separate entity would never have existed. But the Angles together with the Saxons who came from the same part of Europe did leave behind one priceless legacy, the English language: what they spoke then is the source of what we speak today.

Although Kenneth MacAlpin invaded Lothian six times to try and finish the Angles off, he was unsuccessful and it was left to

Malcolm II in 1018 to complete the job at the battle of Carham on the Tweed. That same year the king of the Britons died without an heir, and as there had been marriages between the royal families of the Scots and the Britons, it was agreed that the Britons of Strathclyde should become subjects of the king of the Scots which they did under Malcolm's grandson, King Duncan I.

And so it came about that with the pacification of Scotland, its frontiers with England were finally fixed; and the borders that were agreed upon then are roughly the borders of today.

There were two other influences which came to bear on the peoples of early Scotland. The first were the Norsemen or Vikings who in the ninth century began their descents on Shetland, Orkney and the western isles, appearing suddenly from over the horizon in their long ships with terrifying dragon prows, plundering plate from monasteries such as Iona whose founder Columba, together with Ninian, had brought the gospel to Scotland. In time the Norsemen changed to more peaceable ways, settling in coastal areas and marrying, instead of raping, the local women. In time too the western isles, and much later Orkney and Shetland, would be taken under the Scottish Crown.

The other influence was English. Malcolm II was succeeded by his grandson Duncan who, as is well known, was killed by Macbeth. During the seventeen years of Macbeth's reign, it was not safe for Duncan's son and heir, Malcolm Canmore, to remain in Scotland, so he was sent to London as a boy of nine and spent the next fifteen years living among the English whom he grew to like, and learning to speak their language. In 1085 he succeeded to the Scottish throne and after the death of his first wife, Ingibjorg, daughter of the mighty Thorfinn Earl of Orkney, he married the English princess, Margaret Atheling, sister of Edgar Atheling who had a claim to the English throne after the death of Edward the Confessor in 1066, but ceded it to William the Conqueror.

Margaret, who spoke no Gaelic, brought to the Scottish throne and court in Edinburgh Castle a civilizing influence it had not enjoyed before. She wanted it to adopt the richer styles of the English and European courts, and arranged for the king's courtiers, who previously had been drawn from the common people, to be superseded by the nobility dressed according to their rank. She installed expensive furnishings and tapestries in the state apartments, encouraged her ladies in waiting to practise needlework and embroidery and, it is said, had meals served at banquets on gold and silver plate. Yet she was also deeply religious and persuaded the often lax Gaelic clergy to adhere to the practices ordered by the Church at Rome, in particular the observance of the sacraments at Easter and of the Sabbath being a day of rest. She was a dedicated almsgiver who with her husband cared personally for beggars and orphans. In the century after her death she was canonized as a saint, and today the oldest part of Edinburgh Castle is the little chapel built in the twelfth century and dedicated to her memory.

During her lifetime her fame and good works spread so that many merchants, attracted by the reputation of the Scottish court, came to Edinburgh in search of trade, and many English people, not enamoured of the new Norman court, made their way there too. Three of Malcolm's and Margaret's four sons (Edgar, Alexander and David) were also to become kings of Scotland and thus were the first to be of mixed English and Scottish blood.

So began the slow process of Scotland's anglicization which was to continue unchecked for the next 800 years and is not over to this day. It received further impetus in the sixteenth century with the introduction of the first Scottish Bible being printed not in Gaelic but English; further assimilation came in 1603 with the Union of the Crowns and in 1707 with the merging of the Parliaments. And throughout the eighteenth century, so incomprehensible to most Englishmen was the Scots tongue that English tutors travelled north to give elocution lessons to Scotch traders, politicians and artists so that they might not be at a disadvantage when in London. Dr Johnson, it may be recalled, commented on Boswell's efforts to lose his Scotticisms, and when in Skye in 1773 noted with approval that lessons in the schools were being taught exclusively in English; while Walter Scott, after visiting Bath, acquired an English accent which he never subsequently lost. One consequence was that by the end of the century when there was a vacuum in English literature south of the border, it was being filled by the great Scottish writers of the Enlightenment, pre-eminent among them the philosopher David Hume, the pioneer of political economics Adam Smith, and the diarist and biographer of Samuel Johnson, James Boswell.

Coming to the nineteenth and twentieth centuries the worst features of anglicization were the exclusion of Scottish history and literature in the school syllabuses. In 1880 when Lord Rosebery was Rector of Aberdeen University, he reflected that although all

7

of Scotland's universities were older than those of England, there was not in the whole of Scotland a single Professorship of Scottish History; while as late as 1949 Lord Cooper, addressing the Scottish Historical Society, pointed out that in the capital city of Scotland it was possible for a Scottish student to take a degree in History *without any knowledge of Scottish history*. 'There was a subject called British History', he said, 'which proved on examination to be English history with occasional side glances at Scotland through English spectacles whenever Scotland crossed England's path'. Professor Nigel Grant remembers one 'British' history book which had a chapter entitled 'Troublesome Neighbours to the North'. Such attitudes reminded me of the time when I visited Nsukka University in Nigeria and was shown an English GCE exam paper which called for an essay on 'Snow' which the students at Nsukka had never seen. Trevor Royle summed it up: 'There was no essential grounding in the political facts of Scotland's past, no intellectual debate or analysis about what had happened, why it had happened and what might be done to prevent it from happening again. We knew more about the Risorgimento than we did about the Land League resistance in Skye.'

Equally regrettable was the exclusion of Scottish literature. Giles Gordon, a pupil at the Edinburgh Academy in 1955 was presented by Lord Cameron with the poems of Robert Burns as a music prize. 'I found with some puzzlement, that I couldn't with ease or pleasure – in fact only with difficulty and constant recourse to the glossary – read them. Burns was Scottish, I was Scottish, yet he didn't write in the language I'd been brought up at home and school to speak and read.' He listed some of Burns' Scotticisms and wondered whether to make the effort. 'After all, I could read Shakespeare and Scott . . . and RLS and even Chaucer and they – the Scots as well as English – wrote in English, and English was the language of English literature, wasn't it? And English literature included Scottish literature, didn't it?'

That the Edinburgh Academy should fail to teach Scottish literature he considered 'a shaming indictment of the system and of the country'. As the Scottish Centre for Economic and Social Research declared as late as 1989, 'Scottish children are probably unique in learning more about the history, literature and culture of another nation than they do of their own', and concluded, 'If Scottish education is not to be turned into a provincial and parochial version of the English, alienated from Scottish people and unresponsive to Scottish needs, then . . . it has to be under the control of the Scottish people.'

Such a policy, practised over many decades, of instilling in the minds of young Scots that their country's history and culture were considered too unimportant to be part of the syllabus, was one factor in the chronic inferiority complex in relation to the English* with which so many Scots came to be affected. And it led to the sort of lack of confidence once described to me by the headmaster of Glenalmond.

His previous appointment had been as headmaster of an English public school and I asked what differences he had noted between English and Scots boys. 'During seminars at the English school', he said, 'the boys couldn't wait to tell me their own views on the subject. But here in Scotland they sit around in silence waiting for me to tell them what they ought to think.' The inability to know what to think is also to be observed in Edinburgh audiences which, many actors and lecturers will tell you, are the stickiest in Britain; laughing at a joke comes reluctantly in case it may not be a joke after all. This is what the English obsession with uniformity has done.

Pierre Trudeau had his problems with the American elephant. Today in Scotland there are a growing and articulate number of people who feel it is time to ask the English elephant to move over or, better still, out.

The seeds of my commitment to Scotland were sown early but flowered late.

In the mid 1920s, after my father had retired from the Navy, we lived in Bedfordshire. I was barely aware of Scotland's existence.

*Which the English see as chips on the Scottish shoulder. But it has been long and persistently held. The editorial in the first ever edition of *The Scotsman* in 1817 explained the choice of title: 'We have not chosen the name of SCOTSMAN to preserve an invidious distinction, but with the view of rescuing it from the odium of servility. With that stain removed, a Scotsman may well claim brotherhood with an Englishman . . .' And just recently a report of the Broadcasting Standards Council on the views of 600 Scots teenagers on current television, said this of the comedy programme *Rab C Nesbitt*, the Glasgow layabout brilliantly played by Greg Fisher:

> There was national solidarity behind the argument that while it may be all right for Scottish people to enjoy the comedy, English people should not be given the opportunity to laugh at us.

Then, at the beginning of one summer's holiday, my mother told me that she, my father and I were going to Nairn on the Moray Firth where her father had taken a house on the seafront for August. She and I would go there on the night sleeper. My father would set off in the car a few days earlier and would meet us when we arrived.

I was greatly excited by the idea of the night sleeper and of visiting Scotland, and remember the details of the journey vividly; at Euston a gaggle of porters jostling (for this was the Depression) to take our bags, and the successful one saying, 'Where to, lady?' My mother told him and, as he led us to where the night sleeper was waiting, he said, 'Nairn portion branches off at Aviemore. Main portion to Inverness.'

Third-class sleepers in those days were primitive affairs. There were no wash-basins or sheets: all that was provided was a bare bunk, though you could hire blankets and pillows from a man on the platform. While my mother was attending to these, I went to look at the engine. Green it was and huge, with a mountain of coal at the back glistening like diamonds, the driver and fireman milling about way above me and a thin wisp of smoke drifting up from the funnel. When I thought of the distance we had to travel, more than 500 miles my mother said, I wondered how the driver and fireman would manage to stay awake.

Back in the compartment my mother had unwrapped a picnic supper and while we were tucking into this, the engine gave a succession of very quick, short puffs and then a longer, more considered one, and with that the carriage creaked and we started moving. Out of the window I saw people waving and porters and others moving towards the barrier. Then, without warning, night fell. We played a paper game and later went down the corridor to the washroom. There was quite a queue of people there and some were holding on to the handrail, for by now the train had picked up speed and was roaring and rollicking through the night. I brushed my teeth with Philips's Dental Magnesia, my mother hers with stuff called Kolynos.

Before we lay down for the night, my mother asked if I wanted to say my prayers. I didn't want to, but thought my mother would mind if I didn't. So I knelt down by the bunk and did the Lord's prayer and the God Bless Mummy and Daddy and the dog routine and make me a good boy Amen; and I urged God to see that the engine-driver didn't drop off during the night. When I was a teenager I gave up saying prayers on the grounds that no-one was listening. My father knelt to say his prayers every night of his life; including, I imagine, the night before the engagement in which he and his ship were blown to pieces by two German battleships.

I took off my shoes and coat, slipped under the blanket and laid my head on the pillow. 'Diddledy dum, diddledy dee, diddledy da,' went the wheels on the unwelded rails. 'Diddledy da, diddledy dee, diddledy . . .' By then I was asleep.

In the morning I woke early and saw a chink of light behind the blind covering the window at the foot of the bed. I lay quietly and looked at it for a while, wondering how far we had travelled, whether still in England or across the border into Scotland, and if there was any way of telling between the two. At that time I had only the haziest idea about Scotland; if asked, I would have said it was an extension of England, which is how most English people have always thought of it.

I crawled to the end of the bed and peered behind the blind. What I saw was a revelation, as vivid to me now as then: a great sea of purple sloping downwards from the track for perhaps two miles; in the distance and below it a long, thin oblong loch, flanked by purple hills and, to complete the picture, a stag trotting purposefully downhill. I fell in love with the beauty of it there and then and have remained in love with it ever since. The train, which had been labouring rather heavily, came to a halt to take on water; and on a sign by the track I read 'Summit of Drumochter 1484 feet'.

At Aviemore, as the London porter had said, our bit of the train was siphoned off and attached to a new engine to take us along the single track branch line to Nairn. We passed through Grantown on Spey where salmon fishermen were wading chest-high in the river, went on to the Dava and Forres; and at each stop I noticed the engine-driver holding what looked like a circular piece of wire with a little pouch attached and a porter on the platform putting his arm out to exchange it for another as the train slid past him to a stop. I learned later that the pouch contained a key which, so long as it was in the driver's possession, meant that no other train could be introduced onto that portion of the single-line track.

At Nairn station (little changed today) my father, wearing a bow-tie and plus-fours, was waiting on the platform to meet us. A porter took our gear across the tracks while we crossed by the iron footbridge. The car we had then was a Clyno with the registered number TM 5125 (why does one remember such things?). In it my father drove us down Seabank Road to my grandfather's rented house, Tarland, on the seafront.

When the residential part of Nairn between the town and sea was built at the turn of the century, it became a fashionable watering-place for Edinburgh families and was dubbed the Brighton of the north which, for those who knew Brighton, was pushing it. Tarland, a substantial stone house which in my grandfather's day could cater for up to a dozen guests was (and is) next to the Golf View Hotel, the gardens of both overlooking the promenade and beach and rocks which at low tide were always covered with a pale green stringy seaweed peculiar to the Moray Firth. A stone's throw from Tarland stood the big house and grounds of Newton, now a hotel, but then lived in by my contemporary the young David Thomson, who later made it and its eccentric inhabitants the subject of his brilliant, award-winning book, *Nairn in Darkness and Light* (the darkness referred to his temporary blindness). Although we must both have been in Nairn for several of the same summers, our paths never crossed (though I doubt if at that age we would have had much to say to each other if they had).

We stayed at Tarland for the next five or six Augusts, and I loved every minute of them. There was everything a boy could want to do; trout fishing and later shooting, bicycle rides, cricket matches, paper chases, deep sea fishing, trips to Invergordon to visit the fleet, and golf. Golf was the main reason why my grandfather and his brother-in-law Tom Boothby came to Nairn (they had both been captains of the Royal and Ancient); and they sometimes made up a four with a General Blair whose son Shanny, then my beach companion but later as a general himself, helped to rescue Denis Hills from the clutches of the appalling Idi Amin who had been his platoon sergeant in the war; and the Earl of Dunmore, VC, a tall, bald moustachioed man whose achievement in managing to be both an earl *and* a VC greatly impressed me.

The golf links are only a couple of hundred yards along the front from Tarland and sometimes I would accompany my grandfather to the first tee and watch him and his party drive off. Because of the Depression there was always a line of raggedy men by the starter's hut, most quite ignorant of golf but all unemployed and hoping to earn half a crown a round as a caddy. But supply invariably exceeded demand, and there were always some who had to slouch off, disappointed. It is hard to believe today but in those forelock-touching times it was the practice of the golfer driving off to indicate to his caddy where he wanted his ball placed by thumping the ground with the head of his driver. Then the caddy would draw some sand from a tin box, go down on his hands and knees and build a miniature sandcastle on top of which he perched the ball. (In the Scottish National Portrait Gallery there is a picture of a nineteenth-century caddy doing just that.) Try it today with any caddy you are lucky to find and see what response you get.

Towards the end of that first holiday at Nairn an event occurred that was to help to determine for ever my future attitude to Scotland. I was told that we were going for a picnic to a place called Culloden moor, halfway between Nairn and the Highland capital of Inverness. I asked if there was fishing to be had, as we rarely took picnics without fishing, and was disappointed when told there wasn't. The moor was a desolate-looking spot and I asked my mother why we had gone there. She said it was the site of a famous battle. I asked who the battle was between and was astonished when she said the English and the Scots (she was wrong actually, it was between the English and some Scots against other Scots). Until that moment it had never occurred to me that the Scots existed as a separate people. When I had digested this, I rather tentatively asked my mother which of the two we were — tentatively because some instinct told me that she was about to shake my belief that I, and she, were English. I was right. 'Oh, Scots of course,' she said, as though it hardly needed saying.

For a while I found this even harder to accept. In the south we talked and behaved as though we were English and I doubted if any of our English neighbours thought we were anything else. Indeed my father, whose own father lived the life of an English country gentleman, seemed to me the quintessence of Englishness; for him Scotland was a place to shoot and fish.

I mulled this over for a bit and then asked my mother why, if we were Scottish as she said, we didn't speak with Scottish accents like almost everybody else in Nairn, the maids at Tarland, the people in the shops and at the golf course? (It's a question I've been asked ever since, by many Americans and some English.) My mother said that you didn't have to have a Scottish accent in order to be Scottish. Well, in that case, I said, what was it about us that made us Scottish?

The history of our two families, she said. Her father, Sir

Ludovic Grant (Grandad to me), was a Nova Scotia baronet, because some 250 years before an ancestor, one Patrick Grant, then Scottish Attorney General, had agreed to help subsidize the colony of Nova Scotia (New Scotland) in return for which the king would grant him a baronetcy. I had been born in my grandfather's house in Edinburgh where he was professor of Public and International law at the university. His father, said my mother, had been Principal and Vice-Chancellor of the University and one of his sisters headmistress of St Leonard's at St Andrews, the leading Scottish boarding school for girls.

Why did my grandfather not speak with a Scottish accent, I asked? Because his father and mother didn't, she said, and that was because both had been educated in England as well as Scotland. What about the Kennedys then, I asked, surely they weren't ever Scottish? Oh, but they were, said my mother. The family came from the south of Ayrshire where they had been politically active from the earliest times. One had been the Scottish Lord Chancellor, another had helped to arrange the marriage of the Dauphin to Mary, Queen of Scots, for which pains he was murdered. Then, at the end of the eighteenth century, Captain Archibald Kennedy, having retired from the navy to live at No. 1 Broadway, New York, heard that by the death of a distant cousin he had inherited the earldom of Cassillis and with it the family seat of Culzean Castle, designed by the Scottish architect, Robert Adam. He had three sons. The first was a friend of William IV who created him Marquess of Ailsa. The second, Robert, was my father's great-grandfather.

'So you see,' said my mother, 'you're Highland on one side of the family and Lowland on the other.'

'Not English at all?'

'Not really, no.'

I had been English too long to accept instantaneously my metamorphosis into a Scot; and if I thought that this was going to lead to an affinity with those in Nairn who spoke with a Scottish tongue, I was mistaken. To them, as to other Scots, I was English, yet that in no way diminished their natural friendliness, for Scots the world over have always accepted people as they find them. Yet I think my mother was wrong in telling me that I was not English at all; for any Scot who has been educated in England and bears no trace in his speech of a Scottish accent, must have a degree of English in his *persona*. In fact what I was (and what my mother was, though she would have hated to admit it) was an Anglo-Scot. There are many Anglo-Scots in Scotland, for instance the whole of the Scottish hereditary peerage and many of the large landowners (who would hate to admit it too) most of whom have a degree of sophistication which is inclined to be absent in the native Scot. In thought processes, attitudes, language, outlook, terms of reference, etc., there is virtually nothing to distinguish the Englishman or woman from the Anglo-Scot, especially when they are products of English public schools. Even if they live and work in Scotland, that does not to my mind make them pure Scots. Few know much of Scottish literature or poetry (either ancient or modern) and even less of Scottish words and phrases, viz. *muckle* (big, much), *speir* (ask), *kenspeckle* (recognizable, familiar), *whigmaleerie* (a whim or fanciful notion), *hochmagandy* (fornication); and fewer still can speak Scots with other than embarrassingly awful accents. In short, the Anglo-Scot in Scotland always retains his Englishness just as the native Scot in England, and however long he stays there, always retains what Robert Louis Stevenson called 'a Scottish accent of the mind'.

There is one other major difference. Most Anglo-Scots are not in the least interested in Scotland as a political entity, being strongly pro Tory and pro Union. I on the other hand am an Anglo-Scot who is pro Liberal and pro devolution. But that is to get ahead of my story.

My mother was a hybrid: fiercely Anglo and fiercely Scots. She revered all British institutions such as Parliament and the courts and the royal family and, along with several formidable Anglo-Scottish school friends, spoke of lawst, sawft, awf and gawn until the day she died. On the other hand she adored Scotland, particularly the west coast, was an accomplished performer of Scottish reels and country dances, at which she wore first a Grant and later a Kennedy sash, sang Scottish songs like 'Caller Herrin', acted in amateur productions of Scottish plays like the *Tattie Bogle* and had a fund, as her own mother did, of Scottish stories.

Sometimes when the mood took her she sang snatches of what she called Gaelic mouth music. One went like this (every 'ch' is soft as in loch):

Soo *ull*er hun, ter *hull*er reich
Soo *ull*er hun, ter *hayen* tich
Soo *ull*er hun, ter *hull*a reich,
Arro*ch*an *toch*an *hund*er reich

At*teera vee*, hilly*oop* hilly*oo*
*Ulla* hun, ter *hayen* tich,
A*teera vee*, hilly*oop* hilly*oo*,
Arro*ch*an *toch*an *hund*er reich

When I asked my mother what all this meant she said it didn't mean anything, but sounded well in unison and as an accompaniment to weaving or dancing.

I couldn't get the accent thing out of my mind. 'Did *none* of our ancestors', I asked my mother, '*ever* speak with a Scottish accent?' She said she didn't know, but in time I discovered that until at least the beginning of the nineteenth century almost no Scot in Scotland, whatever his rank, spoke with any but a Scottish accent, and was so steeped in Scottish words and phrases that many English were hard put to understand him.

This is still the problem today and another reason why the Anglo-Scot can never become a native Scot, for not having been brought up in an exclusively Scottish environment nor learned exclusively Scottish words and idioms he is often at a disadvantage. Worse, like Giles Gordon, is his inability to come to grips with the great Scottish poets of the past – Henryson, Dunbar, Fergusson, Burns – without a glossary. And yet despite what Scottish patriots may say, these writers are partly Anglo-Scottish too; for the literature they write, in form and structure and syntax, is Anglo-Saxon-based, with some Scottish words and phrases instead of English ones. The Scottish poet Edwin Muir complained that the dilemma of the Scottish writer is that, since the demise of Gaelic, he (or she) no longer has a language he can call his own and for him, therefore, there is a dichotomy between thought and feeling.

Gaelic, even though handed down from the Irish, is the only true organic Scots tongue we have ever had, in which for a poet like Sorley Maclean, who has been translated into a dozen languages, there is no dichotomy between thought and feeling; but that is now spoken only in the western isles.

Scots writers today who seek to preserve their country's identity by continuing to write in Scots dialect, must accept that they are not speaking to the world but to each other.

Eating treacle scones and baps with marmalade at Culloden that afternoon, I persuaded my mother to tell me more about the battle, when it had taken place and who were the principal participants; and what she told me helped to propel me into accepting a Scottish identity sooner than I had expected.

My mother knew only the bare bones of the story, but for a boy as romantically inclined as myself, it seemed the most romantic story I had ever heard; not a fairy story either, but one that had happened to a real live prince on the very soil on which we were sitting.

Then, before we left Culloden moor that afternoon, something occurred to my eight-year-old *alter ego* which I had not expected and which I have never forgotten. Culloden moor today is not what it was then. Today it is but another station of the cross in the great new theme park of Scotland, with an elaborate Visitors Centre which harbours a tearoom and a video display and books by authors you'd expect, like John Prebble and Eric Linklater and Robert Burns, and those you wouldn't, like Catherine Cookson and Roald Dahl and Elizabeth David; and now there are paths criss-crossing the battlefield and signs to show you where the regiments and companies of the opposing armies were lined up, as neat and sanitized as the garden of Gethsemane in Jerusalem.

But in the 1920s it was more or less untouched, a dreich expanse of moor with only the memorial Culloden Stone and a few mounds of clansmen's graves to indicate where that bloody conflict had been. But as we were having our picnic, I heard a sound which was new to me and which, although I have heard it and variations on it many times since, I have never forgotten. It was the sound of the pipes. It was a distant sound. We could not see the piper who I think must have been in a different part of the moor. But when we heard it, we all stopped our chatter and listened.

At this distance I find it hard to convey the effect that sound had on me. Although unaware until that very afternoon that I had Scots blood in my veins, the sound roused in me some deep, atavistic emotion which I could only dimly comprehend yet which instantly brought tears to my eyes. The piper, my mother told me, was playing a pibroch, a slow, melancholy lament, each long-held note leading inevitably to its successor; for me (and I suppose for the piper) it was a lament for all those on both sides, English and Scots, who had died on the battlefield and of whose presence our pilgrimage had made me aware.

I have heard the pipes on many occasions since, and they never fail to move me. I know that many of my English friends find them risible, but when I see and hear a pipe band leading a column of marchers, it instils in me dreams of glory. When I dance a reel or strathspey to the beat of pipe music, I am filled with exhilaration. And when I see and hear again the pibroch, especially when played by the lone, floodlit piper on the ramparts of Edinburgh Castle on the conclusion of the tattoo, I am consumed by what Frank Adams has called 'the joy of grief'; not only grief for the millions of my countrymen who somehow seem to have fallen in almost every war there has ever been, many for the English, many against, but for other people and things too; for the thousands dispossessed by the savagery of the Clearances and the empty glens whose ruined dwellings bear stark witness to them, for the overwhelming beauty of the mountains and moors of the Highlands and Islands, for the reed-fringed, water-lilied lochs and lochans that grace them and for the boisterous seas that flank them; but above all perhaps for the loss of our independence, our nationhood, our psyche. If I feel those things today more than ever, I am glad that the truth of them came to me, albeit subconsciously, on Culloden moor nearly seventy years ago.

# PART 1

*The Gambler from Rome*

# CHAPTER 1

## 'Entirely an Irish Project'

THERE ARE TWO WAYS OF LOOKING AT THE STORY OF BONNIE PRINCE Charlie. The second I will come to. The first, which is how I first looked at it and how many Scots and others in the world look on it today, is that of a handsome, brave and high-spirited young man, coming from across the sea against all the odds and with only a handful of supporters, little money and few weapons to reclaim for his father the kingdom from which his grandfather James II had fled ignominiously fifty-seven years before; and which had later given way to a Hanoverian and Protestant dynasty, itself more than thirty years old. He had grown up in his father's house in Rome and listened spellbound to his accounts of the rebellions of 1715 and 1719; and from his earliest days it had never occurred to him that his manifest destiny was other than to succeed where his father had failed, regain for the Stuarts the thrones of England, Scotland and Ireland. Physically he was a fine-looking man: red-haired, brown-eyed, of good physique and carriage and invariably dressed with a blue bonnet sporting the Jacobite cockade of a white rose or feather. John Murray of Broughton who met him in Rome in 1741 and later became his secretary spoke of 'the dignity that accompanies his every gesture: there is such an unspeakable majesty diffused through his whole mien as it is impossible to have an idea without seeing'. Yet although he had grace and charm, he was of limited intelligence and had a greater familiarity with the Italian language than the English which he spoke with an Italian accent; and in English he was always an atrocious speller ('God nose', he once wrote in a letter). He loved the countryside and kept himself in trim by going on long shooting safaris with his Roman Catholic mentor, Father Vinceguerra, sleeping in the open and living off the land. The Pope, if not the kings of France and Spain, recognized the Old Pretender as Britain's king and his son the Prince of Wales as his rightful heir; and wherever he travelled in Italy Charles was treated as royalty.

By the end of 1743 relations between France and England were again deteriorating and a French fleet was being assembled to launch an invasion of England. Although forbidden to enter France because of embarrassment to Louis XV, Charles, now twenty-three, secretly made his way there in early 1744 and headed for the Channel coast. His father had approved of his departure, not as a step towards reclaiming his kingdom (which ambition he himself had now all but abandoned) but in the hope of Louis granting the boy some preferment in the army against the day when a future Pope no longer recognized or, more important, continued to subsidize the Stuart cause.

Charles saw things in a different light and when the proposed invasion fleet was wrecked in a storm, he travelled to Paris to consult with Scottish and other fellow Jacobites willing to back him. He remained unfailingly optimistic and rejected any suggestions of returning to Rome 'with the melancholy prospect of spending my life there'. Among those ready to support him were two Franco-Irish shipowners who had made a fortune in the slave trade. One was Antoine Walsh, whose father had brought back Charles's grandfather, James II, from the Battle of the Boyne, and now offered the prince his frigate *du Teillay* to go to Scotland.* Another, Walter Rutledge, promised Charles his much larger ship the *Elizabeth* of sixty-eight guns and a crew of 700 to embark

*After the defeat of James II at the Battle of the Boyne, a number of prominent Irish Roman Catholics known as the Wild Geese left Ireland to settle in France. They were ready to back Charles in his enterprise in the hope that if he succeeded in restoring the Stuarts to the British throne, that would also help to restore the Catholic ascendancy in Ireland.

broadswords for the Highlanders and a small band of mercenaries.

Early in 1745 Charles embarked in the *du Teillay* with his inner circle of companions – those who became known as The Seven Men of Moidart and included the ageing, gouty Lord Tullibardine, formerly Duke (William) of Atholl, who had forfeited his title and estates in favour of his brother James because of his participation in the two previous risings. Before sailing Charles wrote to his father, 'Your Majesty cannot disapprove a son's following the example of his father. You yourself did the like in the year '15, but the circumstances now are much more encouraging, there being a certainty of succeeding with the least help . . . Let what will, happen, the stroke is struck and I have taken a firm resolution to conquer or to die and stand my ground as long as I have a man remaining with me.'

On 5 July when running up the coast of Ireland, the two ships encountered a British man-of-war, the *Lion*, and in the ensuing engagement the *Elizabeth* was so badly damaged she had to return to France with many of her crew and passengers killed or wounded. The *du Teillay* pressed on and on 23 July reached the lovely sounding isle of Eriskay in the outer Hebrides and Charles set foot for the first time on Scottish soil. Two days later the *du Teillay* crossed the Minch and came to anchor in the broad waters of Loch nan Uamh between Arisaig and Moidart.

Word was spread among the chiefs of the Highland clans that the prince was come, and that he would raise the royal standard at Glenfinnan, 20 miles away, on 19 August. On the 18th Charles marched there at the head of his followers; and today the venue is marked by the 60-foot-high monument on top of which the effigy of a highlander looks down the narrow, wooded waters of Loch Shiel. There the prince heard the skirl of the pipes as first 700 Cameron and then 300 of Macdonald of Keppoch's men came to join those already gathered on the loch shore. This was the Highland way, the clans supporting their chiefs, the chiefs supporting their prince, heir to a long line of Stuarts who had been kings of Scotland since 1371. There was a further bond. The Reformation had hardly touched this part of Britain: they were Roman Catholics and so was he. And to them England with its Protestant German king was as foreign and far away a country as America or France. The English language was unknown to them; here they spoke the native Gaelic almost to a man.

Tullibardine, though, knew only English and in English he read the royal proclamation that King James VIII of Scotland and III of England had appointed his son, Prince Charles Edward Stuart, to claim for him as Regent the thrones of three kingdoms. The royal standard of blue, white and red silk was unfurled and the assembled company, not understanding a word but getting the general gist, threw their bonnets in the air and cheered.

From Glenfinnan the prince and his followers struck south-eastwards over the hills to avoid the British garrison at Fort William, picking up a contingent of MacDonnells at Glengarry, then heading for General Wade's military road linking Fort Augustus with Dalwhinnie which today lies just off the A9 road between Perth and Inverness. The English general Sir John Cope had intended to engage the prince's force as they came over the Corrieyairack pass but on consideration thought better of it and took his troops off to the east. The Highlanders gained more recruits as they marched south, and by the time they reached Blair Atholl they were a force of some 2,500 men. Now wearing Highland dress, Prince Charles appointed as his chief of staff Tullibardine's younger brother, the brave, brilliant and inclined to be brusque, fifty-year-old Lord George Murray, a veteran of the '15 and the '19 and the only officer with any degree of military experience.

His elder brother James, the resident duke at Blair Castle, was a Hanoverian and before joining the prince's standard, George wrote him a farewell letter, apologizing for not informing him earlier that he was 'resolved to take a step which I was certain you would disapprove of when you knew it, as it would surprise you to hear it'. Although what he was about to do might result in his utter ruin, he believed it to be right. 'My life, my fortune, my expectation, the happiness of my wife and children are all at stake (and the chances are against me) and yet a principle of (what seems to me) honour and my duty to King and Country outweighs every-thing.' He concluded, 'Suppose I was sure of dying in the attempt, it would neither deter nor prevent me.' Such a passionate expression of loyalty and commitment to the forthcoming campaign by its senior officer augured well for the success of it.

Gaining further reinforcements the prince's army continued triumphantly south, marching through Perth and Stirling with pipes playing and colours flying, and sweeping aside a force of government dragoons sent to oppose them between Falkirk and Linlithgow.

Thanks to the ineptitude of General Cope the road to Edinburgh was open and, on 17 September, the prince's army entered it. Wisely not attempting to storm the castle and its garrison, the highlanders marched to the south of the city and by Salisbury Crags, out of range of the castle's guns, made their way to the palace of Holyroodhouse. This was the ancient seat of the Stuart kings where Charles's three times great grandmother Mary Queen of Scots had briefly lived and reigned; where his twice great grandfather James VI learned that he was also king of England; where his great grandfather Charles I had been crowned King of Scotland in 1633. He had come into his own.

In the park fronting the palace the prince dismounted from his bay gelding, surrounded by people who wanted to kiss his hand. 'One would have thought the whole inhabitants of Edinburgh were assembled there,' wrote Maxwell of Kirkconnell, 'and all seemed to join in the loudest acclamations. The joy seemed universal. God Save the King echoed back from all quarters of the town.' Having entered the palace Charles, dressed in a tartan coat, blue velvet bonnet trimmed with gold lace and waistcoat and breeches of red velvet with the Order of St Andrew pinned to a blue sash on his breast, came out on a balcony to acknowledge the repeated cheers. Later he attended the Mercat Cross close to the old Parliament buildings, and heard the city Herald proclaim that James VIII of Scotland and III of England was now King of Scotland, England, Ireland and France, that his son Prince Charles Edward was Prince Regent, and for all able-bodied men between the ages of sixteen and sixty to join the king's standard (though fewer than 150 did). That night at Holyrood the prince hosted a grand ball. It was as though in one day the clock had been turned back 150 years.

Next Charles set about making arrangements for his troops, now encamped at Duddingston, to be supplied with provisions and weapons to replace the odd assortment of axes, scythes and pitchforks with which many of them had set out, though in this he was only partially successful; but he was adamant that everything taken should be paid for. Then he received news that General Cope, who had taken his force by sea from Aberdeen to Dunbar, only 20 miles away, was advancing towards Edinburgh. On the morning of the 20th more welcome reinforcements in the shape of 500 Maclauchlans, Grants and Murrays joined the royal standard; and at a council of war it was resolved to march east to engage General Cope in battle. Addressing his troops with sword unsheathed, Charles said, 'Gentlemen, I have flung away the scabbard. With God's assistance, I don't doubt of making you a free and happy people. Mr Cope shall not escape us as he did in the Highlands.' Once again the Highlanders threw their bonnets in the air and cheered; for a month they had been longing for a scrap, and now they were going to have one. To his close advisers the prince announced his intention of leading his men into battle, but was dissuaded when told that if he was killed or seriously wounded, his cause would be irretrievably lost.

On the night of 20 September the two armies were encamped within a few hundred yards of one another near the village of Prestonpans, and separated by a marshy bog. Cope thought his position was impregnable and had the prince attacked from the direction expected, it would have been. But a local man, one Robert Anderson, who used to go snipe-shooting in the bog as a boy, knew of a path through it. In the early hours of the 21st and while it was still dark, the Highlanders began threading their way along the path and even before it was fully light had worked their way round to the east of the government's troops, between them and Dunbar. There, just before dawn, they attacked, throwing off the plaids which had warmed them during the night, uttering blood-curdling cries and not wasting a moment to come into close combat, the speciality at which they excelled. Cope's men, seeing these half-naked, bearded men coming towards them, wielding their terrible broadswords with which to split their skulls, sever their arms and legs and disembowel their horses, were terrified and, after a token resistance, turned and fled. Soon the retreat became a rout, with the Highlanders chasing after the demoralized enemy for almost a mile. Riding across the battlefield after the fighting had ended, the prince was appalled at the sight of so much carnage, begged his men to leave off the killing and reminded them that Cope's troops were just as much his father's subjects as themselves. Indeed it was this that led him, according to one eye-witness, 'to have the [enemy] wounded dressed and carriages provided to take them off the field, which was executed by his surgeons with all the care and expedition imaginable . . .' Government losses were 500 killed, and 1,400 taken prisoner of whom 500 were wounded. Less than 200 got away unscathed, among them Sir John Cope who brought the news of his own defeat to Lord Mark Kerr at Berwick. The Highlanders were estimated to have lost four officers and thirty men killed and sixty or seventy wounded. Later 'Hey, Johnnie Cope!' with satirical verses became one of the best known of latter-day Jacobite songs. It had been an astonishing and unexpected victory, the only visible signs of it today being a small stone cairn hidden between the main road out of Prestonpans and the main railway line to London. 'Here was fought the battle of Prestonpans' is all it says, but no-one would find it who was not looking for it.

After the battle Charles was for pushing on to Berwick but his Council decided that time was needed for retraining and seeking reinforcements. So on Sunday 22 September the Highland army re-entered the capital with pipes playing, drums beating and the government prisoners with their captured guns and colours bringing up the rear. If there had been any doubts in Edinburgh (and there were) about the efficacy of the prince's troops when they had marched out of the city with their wild garb and strange collection of weapons two days before, there were none now. All the same the prince forbade the lighting of bonfires and other celebrations of victory, saying he was far from rejoicing at the deaths of so many of his father's subjects. Besides, many of the clansmen, having had the battle they had so long desired and seen their prince firmly settled in his palace, began drifting away north, taking booty they had retrieved from the battlefield. A call went out to the Highlands for more men and although many came, increasing the prince's army to some 5,000 foot and 500 horse, many more might have come had it not been for the staunchly Hanoverian Lord President, Duncan Forbes of Culloden, who dissuaded many of the northern clans from moving south; and who, with that other government supporter, the Duke of Argyll, raised six independent Highland companies loyal to the government which became known as the Black Watch.

In Edinburgh Charles divided his time between Holyrood and Duddingston where his troops were again encamped. At the palace a court was re-established and in the picture gallery there were a succession of balls and receptions. An observer at one noted that to the ladies of fashion who came to kiss the prince's hand, he was cool, as he was not used to women's company and was seldom at ease in it. Some of his followers chided him for complimenting the ladies on their dancing, yet not dancing himself; to which he replied, 'I have now another air to dance and until that be finished, I'll dance no other.' Other ladies, stirred both by his victory and accounts of his personal appearance, rode out to see him with his troops at Duddingston. A Mrs Hepburn wrote, 'He was sitting in his tent when I came first to the field. The Ladies made a circle round the tent and after we had gazed our fill at him, he came out of the tent with a grace and majesty that is inexpressible. He saluted the circle with an air of grandeur and affability . . . and mounting his horse, rode off to view the men . . . He was in great spirits and very cheerful . . .'

Charles had reason to be cheerful, for word having reached the French of the victory at Prestonpans, they sent three ships to Montrose and Stonehaven with much needed arms and equipment, half-a-dozen field guns to add to those captured from Cope, and a present from the French king of 4,000 guineas. Such optimism was in part justified, for in London there was some unease. Horace Walpole said that if the French general Marechal Saxe and 10,000 troops appeared approaching the capital, people would be hiring windows at Charing Cross to see them go by. He added, 'I look upon Scotland as gone.'

In the prince's camp though were many who felt they had gone far enough; and that having declared the union at an end, Charles should now regroup his army and wait for any force that cousin George might send against him. Although the union was thirty-eight years old, there was little to show from the fruits of it; indeed there were those in Scotland who bitterly resented it, and had the prince stayed put in his capital, he might have attracted huge popular support. Many of his followers had no wish to go further, saying that they had risked their fortunes and lives to put a Stuart again on the throne of Scotland, but they wished to have nothing to do with England. For Charles though, Scotland was a staging post. He had set his heart on recapturing the English throne for his father and himself, and it required all his charm, enthusiasm and powers of persuasion to make them change their minds. He assured them that the English Jacobites were only waiting to flock to his standard and that a French invasion of the south coast was imminent; and what they had achieved at Prestonpans they could achieve again.

It worked: they succumbed, though only by one vote; and on the last day of October the whole army moved to Dalkeith Palace, 10 miles away, from which on 3 November they set off south in two columns. The left-hand column under the prince and Lord George Murray would march by Lauder and Kelso, make a feint towards Newcastle where government troops under the aged Marshal

28

Wade had gathered, then turn south-westwards via Jedburgh in the direction of Carlisle. There or thereabouts they would be joined by the second column under Tullibardine and the Duke of Perth who were marching directly south by way of Peebles, Moffat and Lockerbie. On 15 November Carlisle surrendered, a hundred pipers led the prince's victorious army through the town and James III and VIII was proclaimed King of England from the Market Cross. The citizens were terrified by the thought of what the wild, kilted men of the north might do. One mother hid her only surviving child, a girl of five or six, under the bed, as she had heard that the Highlanders had a taste for eating young children. Another was bold enough to ask, 'When does the ravishing begin?' unaware that this was not an activity for which they had gained a reputation.

Marshal Wade did his best to come to the relief of Carlisle, but was defeated by thick snow and sickness among his soldiers, and retired ignominiously to Newcastle. On 20 November the prince's army pushed into Lancashire, by way of Penrith, Shap, Kendal and Lancaster, arriving at Preston a week later. His conduct attracted much praise. 'He never ate much at supper,' one follower wrote, 'used to throw himself on a bed at eleven-o-clock and was up by four in the morning. As he had a prodigious strong constitution, he bore fatigue most surprisingly well.'

Two days after leaving Preston the prince entered Manchester. Here 'the mob huzzaed him to his lodgings, the town was illuminated and the bells rung,' and at supper in a house in Market Street Lane, 'substantial people came and kissed his hand.' He was in high spirits, having just received a letter from his brother Henry who had been told by the French foreign minister, the Marquis d'Argenson 'that the king of France was absolutely resolved on the expedition into England, and that you might count upon it being ready towards the 20 December.' Everything seemed to be going his way. He had left Edinburgh only twenty-three days before and his progress south had been swift and triumphant. Already his mind was leaping forward to the following week, 'in what manner he should enter London, on horseback or on foot and in what dress?'

His army swelled by another 250 volunteers – though he had hoped for at least a thousand – Charles left Manchester on 1 December for Derby. We are told that he marched at the head of two regiments of foot, wearing a light plaid with a blue sash, a grey wig and a blue bonnet with a white cockade.

Having forded the Mersey above Stockport he arrived that night at Macclesfield. Here he learnt that a force under the command of his cousin the Duke of Cumberland, George II's corpulent younger son, had reached Newcastle-under-Lyme, only 17 miles away, and was advancing to attack. So that the duke might think that Charles was making for Wales to rally more Jacobites, George Murray took a flying column south-westwards towards Congleton. As he had hoped, he met Cumberland's advance guard who, mistaking the flying column for the whole of the prince's army, prudently fell back on Newcastle.

This manoeuvre enabled the prince to do what he wanted, get between Cumberland and London and push on with speed to Derby. He arrived there on 4 December; once again, bells were rung, bonfires lit and the royal edict proclaimed. The townspeople were impressed by the sight of the Highland chieftains, dressed in blue faced with red, and scarlet waistcoats with gold lace: 'These made a fine show, being the flower of their army.' Lodgings and provisions were found for the troops and Charles himself took up residence in Lord Exeter's town house. Here he heard further good news: that on the last day of November six French transports carrying 800 men of the Scots and Irish contingents of the French army under the command of Lord John Drummond, brother of the Duke of Perth, had landed at Montrose and Peterhead. Once again his thoughts turned to London, now only 100 miles away, and whether he should enter the city on horseback and in Highland dress or on foot in English clothes.

He would have had even greater cause for optimism had he known that the possibility of his entering London in triumph was one presenting itself with mounting unease to its inhabitants. When the news that the Highlanders had got between the Duke of Cumberland and the city reached the metropolis, wrote Henry Fielding, 'they struck a terror into it scarce to be credited'. Businesses and shops closed, and according to Fielding there was such a run on the Bank of England that to gain time they paid out in warmed-up sixpences that were too hot to handle. The king, it was said, had given orders for his personal belongings to be placed on board his yacht alongside the Tower which was to be ready to sail for the Continent at a moment's notice. Soldiers were posted in the principal squares, others assembled at Barnet and Highgate, while a detachment of the Guards pitched camp on Finchley Common. All of which encouraged the Jacobites in the capital to put up posters to welcome Prince Charles; and a fund for the cause soon raised £10,000. The king's chief minister, the Duke of Newcastle, was said to have shut himself up in his apartments for a day to debate whether he should now consider shifting his allegiance. Never did the future look more uncertain. 'England', said Marshal Wade, 'is for the first comer.'

But Charles was not to be the first comer. Waking up in his comfortable bed in Lord Exeter's house, he had expected to be soon on the march; but hardly had he put on his bonnet and ventured out when he was confronted by Lord George Murray with despondent news: all the chiefs with the exceptions of Perth and Tullibardine felt that to continue the march would be suicide: they should retire to Scotland to join Lord John Drummond and his men and there make a further plan. The shattered prince attended a council of war, which began at eight in the morning and went on until nightfall, every moment lost to them being a moment gained for government forces hastening to London's defence. At first the prince was adamant in his resolution to continue. 'Rather than go back,' he declared, 'I would rather be twenty feet under ground.'

Then Lord George put the case for the chiefs. By evening the Duke of Cumberland's force of 12,000 men would be at Stafford, the same distance from London as themselves; Marshal Wade with 10,000 men was coming after them from the north, and outside London a force of some 8,000 was assembling for its defence. English Jacobites who the prince had predicted would rise for him had not done so, at least not in any numbers, nor was there any sign of the promised French invasion. Other chiefs spoke in similar vein but on Charles they made no impression. Against all the odds and with no outside help he had come within an ace of achieving the impossible, of restoring his father to the throne of his kingdom, which one day he would occupy himself: all that was needed now was one last push. Failure would mean not only the end of an enterprise, but of his own destiny and (if he wasn't killed or captured) a return to a meaningless, lotus-like existence in Rome. Montrose's famous lines cannot have been far from his mind.

> He either fears his fate too much,
> Or his deserts are small
> That puts it not unto the touch,
> To win or lose it all.

The chiefs pointed out the dangers he faced in continuing, but he brushed them aside. 'He had no regard for his own danger,' wrote Lord George Murray, 'but pressed with all the force of argument to go forward. He did not doubt but the justness of his cause would prevail, and he could not think of retreating after coming so far; and he was hopeful that there might be a defection in the enemy's army and that several might declare for him.'

Lord George and the chiefs stood firm. And next morning after the drums had beaten 'To Arms', the prince, the chieftains and some 5,000 sullen, silent men marched out of Derby by the route they had entered.

'No one', wrote Horace Walpole, 'is afraid of a rebellion that runs away', and the army which had marched south with such high hope, greeted with bells and bonfires in every town they passed through, found only hostility. Some highlanders who had dropped out from fatigue or sickness or to secure provisions, were never seen again. In some places mobs catcalled and pelted them with stones, and all the time they knew that government forces were not far behind. Their only consolation was the knowledge that every step brought them nearer home.

Despite appalling weather resulting in wagons becoming stuck in the mud and heavy weapons being lost in the crossing of streams, the army marched north as fast as it could, reaching Lancaster on 13 December, Kendal on the 15th and Penrith on the 17th. From Penrith they made a night march to Carlisle to distance themselves from their pursuers. One of those taking part called it 'one of the darkest nights I ever saw, yet did his Royal Highness walk it on foot, and the most part of the way without a lanthorn, yet never stumbled which many of us Highlanders did often.'

At Carlisle the prince decided to leave a garrison of some 400 officers and men so that when, as he intended, he came this way again, there would be a staging post. Ten miles further on they waded across the Esk and on the prince's twenty-fifth birthday were back in Scotland. To celebrate, the pipers played a reel and the Highlanders danced to dry themselves. That night they lodged in Dumfries, the next at Drumlanrig Castle as uninvited guests of the Duke of Queensberry whose ancestor had helped to bring William of Orange to the throne after James II had vacated it, and in 1707 had been instrumental in negotiating the Union. In the light of this the Highlanders felt no compunction in taking their horses into the castle, driving many of the duke's sheep into the basement to kill and eat, helping themselves to wines and spirits in the cellars and, as a parting gesture, defacing the duke's portrait of William of Orange.

Having heard that after reaching Carlisle the Duke of Cumberland had returned to London to report to his father, the prince sent Lord George Murray on to take possession of Glasgow while he stopped off for a morning's shooting on the Duke of Hamilton's estate. The next ten days he spent in Glasgow where, though not a city sympathetic to him, 'a number of devoted Jacobite ladies ministered to his needs', and in court attire he held several formal receptions. The prolonged stay also allowed the army to be re-equipped and re-provisioned.

Morale being now much improved, the prince and his followers left Glasgow early in the New Year of 1746 and headed for Stirling; and he was much heartened by the news that far from being discouraged by the retreat from Derby, many highlanders had been so impressed by his reaching so near to London that more were ready to join him; and counting the 800 men that Lord John Drummond had brought from France together with those with him, the prince now had at his disposal more men than those who had set out from Edinburgh two months before.

These were spoiling for a fight, and it was not long in coming. Old Marshal Wade had been retired, and his place taken by the dreaded General Henry Hawley who had a reputation for extreme brutality, Horace Walpole saying that frequent and sudden executions were his rare passion. Assuming that Charles would be making for Edinburgh he moved his force of some 6,000 men there in batches, the last arriving on 10 January; and one of his first actions was to erect two sets of gallows, one in the Grassmarket, the other between Edinburgh and Leith; then he set off with his artillery to relieve the garrison at Stirling. Charles and Murray, being apprised of his approach, had drawn up the Highland army near the plain of Bannockburn where Robert Bruce had defeated Edward II 430 years before. Hawley established his troops on ground near Falkirk, some 2 miles from the Jacobites and, seeing no likelihood of any imminent action, went off to Callander House to have dinner. (Callendar was the home of Lord Kilmarnock who was fighting with the prince, and it is said that his wife managed to entertain Hawley 'with reasonable good grace'.) Around 1 p.m. a messenger arrived to say that the Highlanders were attacking. Hawley took no notice and it wasn't until a second messenger arrived that he mounted his horse and arrived among his troops without a hat and, someone said, 'the appearance of one who has abruptly left a hospitable table'. Meanwhile Lord George had ordered his troops to cross the flooded river Carron which enabled them to take up a position on the high ground of Falkirk Muir, and there await events.

At around four, in pouring rain and growing dark, Hawley's dragoons, without supporting infantry, advanced on the Jacobite army, hoping the Highlanders would open fire first and then rushing them while they were pausing to reload. But Lord George instructed his men not to fire until he gave the order; waiting until the leading dragoons were almost on top of them, he fired the first shot which was the signal for others to follow. The first wave of dragoons fell almost to a man, and for the second the Highlanders lay on the ground to thrust their dirks into the bellies of the oncoming horses and then, as the horses fell, pulled down their riders to kill them. Elsewhere Highlanders who found that in the rain they could not reload their muskets, threw them down and drew their broadswords. The government front-line troops, having already been ridden down by the retreating dragoons, fired one ineffectual volley then turned and fled; they were followed by the second and third lines. In twenty minutes the retreat had become a rout. The government casualties were reckoned as 400 killed and many more wounded, and the Highlanders fifty killed and seventy wounded. Hawley who, before the battle, had written a memorandum setting out his contempt for the Highlanders' method of fighting, now reported to Cumberland on his own troops. 'Such scandalous cowardice I never saw before', and he had thirty-one dragoons hanged on the gallows for desertion and thirty-two foot soldiers shot for cowardice.

Having retrieved from the battlefield and elsewhere a vast amount of cannon, powder, muskets, tents as well as hampers of provisions and wines, the Jacobites deliberated what to do. Some wanted to pursue Hawley's demoralized brigade into Edinburgh and reoccupy the city. But Charles, staying at Bannockburn House with a heavy cold and being nursed by his host's niece, Clementina Walkinshaw (many years later the mother of his only child), was reluctant to leave. He was persuaded to when told that the Duke of Cumberland had returned to Scotland to take over from General Hawley, and orders were given for a withdrawal to the north.

By the evening of 16 February the prince's forward troops

were within 15 miles of Inverness, whose garrison was under the command of the Earl of Loudoun. That night the prince presented himself at Moy Hall, knowing that its laird Angus Mackintosh was away fighting for the government but that he would receive a warm welcome from his wife, the spirited and beautiful twenty-year-old 'Colonel' Anne, as staunch a Jacobite as her husband was a Hanoverian and who the year before had raised many recruits for the prince's cause. He was not disappointed. Anne greeted him warmly and, despite the short notice, laid on 'a plentiful and genteel supper' for the prince and seventy-five of his retinue.

Lord Loudoun however, having heard of Charles's arrival at Moy, saw a splendid opportunity of capturing the prince alive and claiming the government award of £30,000 put on his head; and having assembled a force of more than a thousand men set out for Moy. His intentions having reached the ears of the Dowager Lady Mackintosh who was then living in Inverness, she summoned a fifteen-year-old clansman by the name of Lauchlan Mackintosh, to go immediately to Moy and warn the prince of the danger. Avoiding Loudoun's men, Lauchlan reached Moy in the middle of the night and gave the alarm. The prince was in bed but throwing on a few clothes and 'with his bonnet above his nightcap and his shoes down in the heels' he and his men slipped out of the house and made their way to the shelter of the lochside. Anne ordered the blacksmith of Moy, Donald Fraser, to take a small group of men across the moor in the direction of Inverness and await Loudoun's arrival. Presently his advance guard appeared, led by the MacLeod of MacLeod, at the sight of which Fraser and his little party opened fire. The only casualty was MacLeod's hereditary piper, the legendary Macrimmon who, before leaving Skye, had composed a lament prophesying his own death. Fraser's men now began shouting the war cries of the Highland clans which led Loudoun and his men to think that the Jacobites were in strength, and so unnerved them that he gave the orders to return to Inverness. This was but another example (and there would be more in the months ahead) of the prince's astonishing good fortune during his nearly fourteen months in Britain in escaping capture or death.

On 18 February Charles and his troops entered Inverness and captured the castle, many of Loudoun's men having deserted and he himself with the Hanoverian Lord President, Duncan Forbes, having fled from the latter's home of Culloden House, 5 miles to the east. This was taken over by Charles and his staff who were joined two days later by Lord George who had brought the other half of the army along the coast road from Aberdeen.

Yet before fleeing, and indeed ever since the day that Charles had landed at Loch nan Uamh, the Hanoverian Lord President Forbes had worked hard to undermine and ensure the failure of the Prince's cause. He had, says the introduction to the book *Culloden*, published in 1815,

> confirmed several chiefs who had begun to waver in their principles; some he actually converted by the energy of his arguments and brought over to the assistance of the government which they had determined to oppose; others he persuaded to remain quiet, without taking any share in the present troubles. Certain it is, this gentleman, by his industry and address, prevented the insurrection of ten thousand Highlanders who would otherwise have joined the Pretender; and therefore he may be said to have been one great cause of the adventurer's miscarriage.

# CHAPTER 2

## *The Not So Bonnie Prince*

THE OTHER GREAT CAUSE OF THE ADVENTURER'S MISCARRIAGE WAS himself. Nothing that I have written about him so far has been untrue, but it sees him as popular history has always seen him, as Scottish patriot, hero and exemplar. Yet that is not the whole picture, indeed in the light of the Stuart papers in the archives at Windsor Castle and in the memoirs of Lord Elcho, it's a distorted one. Many historians today see the prince as a deeply flawed character, self-centred, ignorant, stubborn, obsessive, and the whole expedition misconceived and mismanaged, a disaster which should never have been allowed to happen. With that in mind, let us retrace the events covered so far and see how the disaster came about. As to why I have not fused the two interpretations into one, I would say that the first interpretation is so entrenched in the popular mind that only the second standing on its own is in a position to correct it.

To begin with, the prince's alcoholism. It has been generally supposed that he did not become a chronic alcoholic until much later in life, but the evidence now shows that he had become addicted to heavy drinking in his youth and that it had affected his judgement. Having heard reports of his imbibing on the way to France, as well as a penchant for gambling, his father wrote, '. . . for God's sake, dear child, be on your guard as to wine and play. I hope you will never give me heartbreak to ever hear you fail in them.' The advice was not taken and before long Charles was frequenting low-class Paris taverns in the company of young MacDonnell of Glengarry, himself a well known toper. Discussing with the exiled Scottish Jacobites his plans to lead a rising, he was urged by the much respected Earl Marischal, a veteran of the '15 who his father had designated as commander-in-chief in waiting of Jacobite forces in Scotland, that no rising could succeed unless it had the support of at least 20,000 clansmen and a similar number in England. Marischal wrote to the prince, 'Beside the concern I have for your person – and do not take it amiss that I tell you with my ordinary plainness – that to go single unless you are invited by the concert of the principal people . . . would be forever the destruction of the cause, and fix perhaps for ever the family of Hanover in Britain' – prophetic words indeed.

This advice, endorsed by other leading Jacobites, both in France and Edinburgh, the prince rejected. Nor, when the ill-fated venture was at last under way, was he any wiser in his choice of companions. The famed Seven Men of Moidart (actually eight) were a motley lot. Apart from Tullibardine and Charles's banker friend, Aeneas Macdonald, most of the others were Irish; Sir Thomas Sheridan, Charles's seventy-year-old tutor, Sir John Macdonald, a cavalryman in the Irish brigade of the French army, the Revd George Kelly, a sycophantic rogue who had recently spent fourteen years in the Tower of London, Mr Murray, the prince's secretary, the shipowner Antoine Walsh, and John William O'Sullivan, a soldier of fortune with a good deal of the blarney and to whose company Charles was attached. It was the Irish, against the advice of most of France's exiled Scots, who, for their own ends, wanted to see Charles's dreams of regaining the throne come true.* 'The expedition to Scotland', said Aeneas Macdonald, 'was entirely an Irish project.'

Then again, after the withdrawal of the *Elizabeth* as a result of her engagement with the *Lion* and the loss to the expedition of both the mercenaries and the weapons designated for the landing, one or two of the prince's companions wanted him to turn back. Stubborn as ever, he would not hear of it.

*See footnote on p 22.

38

A more pressing plea to call the whole thing off was made soon after Charles's arrival at Arisaig; the most respected and influential of all the Highland chiefs, young Cameron of Lochiel, told Charles unequivocally that because he had not brought the promised money, men and weapons, there was not the least chance of success. 'He advised his Royal Highness', wrote the historian John Home, not so many years after the event, 'to return to France and to reserve himself and his faithful friends for a more favourable opportunity.' But having come thus far Charles was not going to be baulked and he rejected the advice as forcefully as Marischal's. There would never be a more favourable moment, he said, the bulk of the British army was engaged on the Continent and the few regiments raised in Scotland had never seen service: it only wanted the Highlanders to begin the war. When, despite these entreaties, said Home, Lochiel still resisted, Charles told him, 'Lochiel who, my father has often told me, was our firmest friend, may stay at home and learn from the newspapers the fate of his prince.' Such an appeal was not to be denied, and reluctantly Lochiel agreed to bring his clansmen out. 'If Lochiel had persisted in his refusal to take arms', concluded Home, 'the other chiefs would not have joined the standard without him, and the spark of rebellion must have instantly expired'. The two principal Skye chiefs, the Old Etonian Sir Alexander Macdonald of Sleat and MacLeod of Dunvegan, brothers-in-law who might have been expected to bring their clansmen out in support, did not do so.* And a year later Lochiel, for his pains, was to see the redcoats loot and burn to the ground his home of Achnacarry.

Another historian, Susan Kybett, says that it was not simple patriotism or devotion to the prince that brought out the clans so much as a blend of promises and blackmail. The prospects were never brighter, Charles assured his early supporters: the French king had promised reinforcements and money and, for those who accompanied him on this great adventure, there would be titles and preferments. Those who then 'signed' for the prince, often at the end of a euphoric drinking session, were kept to their word when they sobered up later. To renege on it would have been lese-majesty.

---

*They had opted for King George by selling a hundred of their clansmen to colonize Pennsylvania. John Prebble paints a chilling picture of how, after Culloden, they and their militia, having stayed the night in the house of Grant of Glenmoriston, in the morning burnt it and everything in it to the ground as well as other clansmen's dwellings in the glen.

As for the clansmen, they needed little encouragement to do officially what they had been doing *ad hoc* for years. In 1689 the English traveller Thomas Morer wrote, 'Once or twice a year great numbers of them get together and make a descent into the Lowlands where they plunder the inhabitants and so return and disperse themselves'. As they saw it, here was an invitation to do that once again and this time officially; and perhaps on the way having a crack at the Campbells whose chief the Duke of Argyll had represented the British government in Scotland for twenty-five years. That they might also be required, if all went well, to cross the border into England, was too remote and unlikely a prospect even to consider.

It is often said that the success of leaders in whatever field is due to their knowing how to delegate. In this respect Charles was almost totally deficient. An early mistake was to appoint O'Sullivan – a man quite lacking in military administration – as his adjutant and quartermaster-general; and *his* early mistake was to bury at the far end of Loch Eil the company's small supply of cannon, powder and ball, which the government garrison at Fort William promptly dug up. An even greater error of judgement was to order Lord George Murray – the only officer of proven military ability – to alternate command of the army with the younger and inexperienced Duke of Perth.

As the march south continued Lord George's natural authority and expertise increasingly asserted itself, but because of a clash of temperaments between them, the prince could seldom refrain from questioning and at times countermanding his decisions. This led one observer to note, 'Had Prince Charles slept during the whole of the expedition and allowed Lord George to act for him according to his own judgement, there is every reason for supposing that he would have found the crown of Great Britain on his head when he awoke.'

The first public row between them occurred on the eve of Prestonpans when Lord George, wanting to attack, found that the prince had stationed his 500 Atholl men some way behind the lines; and throwing his pistol on the ground in a rage, demanded peremptorily they be brought back. The further they marched south, the worse the relationship became. As one Scottish nobleman put it:

The Prince had a hearty dislike of Lord George Murray whom

40

he referred to as one likely to betray him, yet no one could have behaved better. He did not conceal his preference for all things Irish and for the Irish officers who had come from France and in whose company he took more pleasure than in that of the Scots. It was a distressing situation and one which did not make him popular with the leaders of his army. So suspicious was he of Lord George that he engaged two Irish officers to spy on him with orders to murder him should he show any signs of wishing to betray him, a fact he was persuaded was the case.

This comes from the memoirs of Lord Elcho, heir to the Earl of Wemyss who had known Charles both in Rome and Paris, and had brought along a body of horse guards as well as a loan of £1,500. Elcho and his fellow noblemen, who were after all sponsoring the campaign as well as risking their necks on the scaffold, were particularly incensed that even after the army had pitched camp each evening it was again the Irish officers and not themselves who were bidden by the prince to dinner. Charles liked the Irish because they toadied to him whereas the Scots, no respecters of persons, are also naturally argumentative. 'He could not bear', wrote Elcho, 'the slightest contradiction which he would put down to a lack of attachment to his person'. Thus, while the prince and the Irish drank the nights away, his Scottish supporters were isolated. 'We were never thanked for all we had done for him', concluded Elcho, 'indeed quite the reverse, and he would sometimes tell us that we had only done our duty as the subjects of his father'.

Other of the prince's deficiencies that Elcho resented were his meddling in military matters about which he knew nothing, and his 'abysmal ignorance of the history, geography, constitution and laws of the nation he had come to conquer'; and he found his respect for his former companion diminishing daily.

Charles's next blunder came at Carlisle when he ordered trenches to be dug round the castle in order to take it – a pointless exercise and one almost impossible to perform on the icy November ground. Then, at a time when Roman Catholics in Britain were still banned from holding public office, he sent the Catholic Perth rather than Murray to negotiate terms of surrender with the garrison – an action hardly likely to win him English recruits.

For Murray this was the last straw and he resigned his commission, complaining 'how little my advice as a general officer has any weight with your Royal Highness'. The prince appointed Perth in his place, but this did not suit the Highlanders who had high regard for Murray and demanded he be reinstated, which he was. To emphasize his loyalty to the prince and the cause Murray agreed to continue the march south, although he must already have realized that with the men and weapons at his disposal the venture was doomed. Just what a ragged, ill-equipped body the army had become was attested to by James Gilchrist, postmaster of Dumfries, who had joined up with the Jacobites in order to spy on them for the government. 'Now that we have seen the army,' he wrote in his report to London, 'it gives us no small concern to think that a whole kingdom should have been so shamefully intimidated with such a pack of tatterdemalions, for two thirds of them are no better and great numbers of them marching without breeches, stockings or shoes'. Another anonymous witness wrote of 'a sight worthy of ridicule to every observer and matter of joy to all lovers of their country that no better than such trumpery are come to invade us . . . my spirits were quite raised at such a comic scene as this procession . . . Had King George been with me today he would have been very merry.'

But Charles continued to live in a world of his own, utterly convinced that final victory was within his grasp and that he was in measurable distance of putting his father on the throne. That he and his Highlanders had been incredibly fortunate to have reached so far south never occurred to him; and when at Derby the chiefs were solid in their determination to retreat, Charles could hardly believe his ears. Having listened with impatience to what they had to say, wrote Elcho, 'he fell into a passion and gave most of the gentlemen that had spoke very abusive language and said they had a mind to betray him'. If such a reaction was understandable in the circumstances – for it meant the end of all his hopes – it was also that of a young man who had come to believe in his own divinity. No reputable historian today would dispute that had the prince's army pressed on south, Culloden would have been fought, not near Inverness in April of 1746 but in December 1745 on the road between Derby and London.

In his book on the campaign, Lord George Murray wrote that on the way to Derby the prince had always been first up in the morning, but that on the retreat he was one of the last to leave, thus endangering the rearguard from attack by government troops.

Irritated by the prince's previous vainglorious calls for action, Murray said to him on 16 December, 'As your Royal Highness is always for battles, be the circumstances what they may, I now offer you one three hours from this time with the army of General Wade which is only three miles behind us.'

The prince declined the offer, but a day or two later, when he thought it more prudent to be up with the advance party at Penrith, government troops in pursuit had come so close to the Jacobite rearguard that an opportunity for action presented itself. Murray, who was managing the rear, sent a messenger to Penrith to ask the prince's permission to attack. The reply came back that he was to continue the withdrawal. This led Elcho to say that while the prince had made the army halt when it was necessary to march, so now it was to march and shun fighting 'when there could never be a better opportunity got for it'. Indeed the opportunity was so good that Lord George decided to ignore the prince's instructions and attack; and in the moonlight a party of Macphersons, MacDonnells of Glengarry and Stewarts of Appin routed a force of government dragoons, killing and wounding more than forty in exchange for five casualties of their own.

The prince, in receipt of three bottles of cherry brandy at the time he heard this news, expressed himself pleased, as well he might. The same could not be said of Murray who increasingly found that the only time he could exert his authority was when the prince and his Irish cronies were addled with drink in the evenings. On one occasion he told Charles that, because of the failure of O'Sullivan to arrange transport for the cannonballs (a repetition of his failure at Loch Eil), he had had to pay men sixpence a head to carry them.

Dissatisfaction with Charles reached a head when, on reaching Carlisle, he insisted on leaving 400 men of his now much reduced army as a permanent garrison. Everyone knew it could be only a matter of time before Cumberland's troops evicted them, which ten days later they did. Some were hanged, disembowelled and quartered, a few released and others imprisoned then transported as slaves to the American plantations. From this tragic episode the song, 'The bonnie, bonnie banks of Loch Lomond' is said to have originated, those hanged taking the low road and so reaching Scotland before those spared.

But resentment at the prince's high-handedness continued, and on 6 January, the day his army entered Stirling, matters came to a head. Murray, with the agreement of the clan chiefs, submitted to the prince that there should be a standing council of war over which the prince would preside; it would determine the operations for carrying on the war, and that whatever it decided would not be changed except by the council itself: the council should be able to delegate to a committee of five or seven, and in emergency discretionary powers should be granted to those in command. This, he said, was the method of all armies. Had not a council been convened at Derby, catastrophe would have followed within two or three days; had a council been consulted as to leaving a garrison at Carlisle, they would never have agreed to it, and many brave men would not have been sacrificed.

The prince's reply, no doubt fashioned by his inner circle, could hardly have been more dismissive. 'When I came into Scotland,' it began, 'I knew well enough what to expect from my enemies, but I little foresaw what I [would] meet with from my friends.' And he went on:

> I came vested with all the authority the king could give me, one chief part of which is the command of his armies, and now I am required to give this up to fifteen or sixteen persons, who may afterwards depute five or seven of their own number to exercise it, for fear that if they were six or eight I might myself pretend to the casting vote. By the majority of these all things are to be determined, and nothing left to me but the honour of being present at their debates. This, I am told, is the method of all armies and this I flatly deny, nor do I believe it to be the method of any one army in the world.

So although the prince had delegated command to Murray and Perth, he was now proposing to exercise it himself. And in answer to Murray's reminding him that this was an army of volunteers not mercenaries, he riposted that he was often 'hit in the teeth' with the assertion and if it was so and its officers gentlemen of rank and fortune, he would have expected from them more zeal, more resolution and more good manners: 'but it can be no army at all where there is no general or, which is the same thing, no obedience or deference paid to him.'

He went on:

> Everyone knew before he engaged in the case what he was to
> expect in case it miscarried, and should have stayed at home if
> he could not face death in any shape; but can I myself hope for
> better usage? At least I am the only person upon whose head a
> price has already been set, and therefore I cannot indeed threaten
> at every other word to throw down my arms and make my peace
> with the government.

The prince could adopt this tone because he knew and the chiefs
knew that while the men could go back to their homes any time
they wanted (and every day some did) they themselves did not have
that option: they were rebels whose names were known and who, as
Murray himself was quick to point out, could only look forward to
the scaffold if ever they surrendered or were captured.

Despite, or perhaps because of Murray's brilliant success at
Falkirk, Charles was determined to show him and the chiefs
who was master. Accordingly he persisted in a demand he had
already made for the reduction of Stirling Castle and its garrison.
It was a wasteful and futile ploy, disapproved by all the chiefs and
without tactical value. The officer he entrusted to the task was a
French engineer named the Marquis de Mirabelle who so placed
the Jacobite guns as to bring down on them a rain of fire from
the defenders' guns without their making the slightest impression
on the ramparts. One witness described the pomaded de Mirabelle
as 'totally devoid of judgement, discernment or common sense, his
figure being as ridiculous as his mind'. And not before time the
project was abandoned.

Nor was Charles's acquiescence in withdrawing to the Highlands given willingly. Murray's proposal was that once there, 'we
can be usefully employed the remainder of the winter by taking
and mastering the forts in the north [Forts George, Augustus and
William] . . . and in the spring we doubt not an army of ten thousand effective Highlanders can be brought together and follow your
Royal Highness wherever you think proper'. This was making the
best of a bad job, but its effect on Charles was dramatic. Striking
his head against a wall, he cried, 'Good God! Have I lived to see
this?' In calmer mood but still living in his dream world, he wrote

to Murray, 'Should we make the retreat you propose, how much more will that raise the spirit of our enemies and sink those of our own people? What opinion will the French and Spanish have of us or what encouragement will it be to the former to make the descent for which they have long been preparing, or the latter to send us any more succours?' But this bubble had long since burst, and orders were given to move.

The army having reached Inverness and knowing that a final reckoning with government forces could not be long delayed, it seems astonishing that the Jacobites did not concentrate all their energies and the little time left to them on re-equipping and retraining their forces so as to give the best account of themselves when the time came. Instead an attack was made on the government garrison at Fort Augustus which succeeded and at Fort William which failed. In addition to Perth chasing Loudon, Lord President Duncan Forbes and MacLeod of MacLeod westwards towards Skye, Murray took time off to try and recapture the family seat of Blair Castle from his Hanoverian brother, but had to withdraw on the approach of a force of German mercenaries commanded by Cumberland's brother-in-law, Prince Frederick of Hesse. Another setback for the cause was the capture of money, stores and ammunition when the ship carrying them from France ran aground. Charles himself remained in Inverness in the house of the Dowager Lady Mackintosh and, one reads with surprise, spent some time pursuing his favourite sport of shooting and giving 'several balls to keep up the spirits of his supporters'. One of his partners was Anne Mackintosh who, it was reported to Cumberland, 'dressed as nearly as she could in Highlandmen's cloathes'.

Cumberland, having paused at Aberdeen to train his troops in bayonet drill, was now on the march north with General Hawley and some 9,000 men which, thanks to the efforts of the Duke of Argyll, Duncan Forbes and others, included men of the Royal Scots, Royal Scots Fusiliers, Campbells and other Scots loyal to the government, in all a greater number of Scots than the prince's Highlanders. Accompanying them along the coast was a train of transport and supply ships. Only one obstacle now separated Cumberland from his goal of Inverness: the river Spey, much swollen with the rains and snows of recent weeks. As they approached the river at Fochabers, they sighted a Jacobite force of 2,500 men under Perth and his brother John Drummond waiting for them on the other side. Fording the river in such conditions was not going to be easy and gave a splendid opportunity to Perth and his men to inflict heavy casualties, perhaps even to throw the government forces back. But Perth was not prepared to risk his small force against one four times greater: the prince would need to consolidate his troops in one body when the final battle came; and Cumberland was relieved to see the Jacobites retreating in the direction of Inverness. Two days later he and his army entered Nairn.

On hearing that Cumberland had pitched camp at Balblair outside Nairn, Charles gave orders for his own troops to parade and then rode out of town at their head with pipes playing and colours flying. Once again they entered the grounds of Culloden House and bivouacked. Charles sent the incompetent O'Sullivan off to choose a site for the battle, and he decided on Drummossie Moor, a flat, open piece of land ideally suited for Cumberland's artillery and cavalry. When Lord George saw it he said, 'Not one single soldier but would have been against such a field had their advice been asked . . . It was certainly not proper for Highlanders.'

That night and for the first time in weeks, Elcho supped with the prince and found him in exaggeratedly optimistic mood. This, he learned, was because for the first time in the campaign he had decided to command the troops himself.

> He had no doubts as to the issue of the conflict; he had a most exalted idea of the justice of his cause, and believed that it would be difficult to get the English soldiers to attack him; his mere presence would be sufficient to frighten them away. Those who spoke of a retreat and waiting for the 3,000 soldiers who had not as yet turned up, were not listened to, and when asked for a rendezvous in case of defeat, he answered only those who were afraid could doubt of victory. In short his boastfulness that night was unworthy of a prince.

When Murray heard the news that Charles was to take over command, he must have known that for all of them, it could be the kiss of death. Yet what could he do? He saw himself as the prince's subject, and princely orders had to be obeyed. Had he still had the spirit and energy he had shown earlier, he might have insisted on recalling the council of war, even though the prince had rejected it. Perhaps he simply felt that the time for arguments and rows had passed, that he had better resign himself to whatever cards fate had in store for him.

At six the next morning the prince's army was drawn up on the moor, awaiting the enemy's arrival. The enemy did not come and presently it was learned that as it was Cumberland's twenty-fifth birthday, he proposed to celebrate it at Nairn and postpone the battle until next day.

Now a plan was proposed that rather than wait for Cumberland to attack, the Jacobite army should march towards Nairn at dusk and, in the middle of the night, fall on the government forces as they slept. Charles, who had originated the idea, was delighted by the prospect; and as they set off east he tried to humour the sullen Murray by putting an arm round his neck and saying, 'This will crown it. You'll restore the king by it. You'll have all the honour and glory of it.' Murray, we are told, took off his bonnet, bowed coldly and said nothing.

Had the plan been properly organized, had not a quarter of the Jacobite forces drifted away into the night, had those who marched had full stomachs instead of a biscuit per man per day which was all that the prince's incompetent secretary, John Hay, had been able to procure for them,* had the weather been other than sleet and rain, the scheme might have had some chance of success. As it was, by two o'clock in the morning the hungry, exhausted, dispirited clansmen had covered only six miles, and appreciating that no attack could now take place before dawn which would be suicidal, Lord George ordered a general retreat to Culloden House. When this news was relayed to the prince he became quite hysterical, shouting that no-one could give orders but himself and that he had been betrayed.

When the clansmen reached Culloden House, they flopped down where they stood, famished with hunger, bitterly cold, battered by sleet and light-headed with lack of sleep. Charles entered the house where Duncan Forbes's servants had prepared for him a dish of roast lamb, but he said he could not eat it while his men were starving and sent a party into Inverness to forage. By now it was too late. Soon the pipes sounded to rouse the sleepers to return to

---

*A considerable quantity of corn had been amassed but by a culpable negligence no bread had been baked (Elcho: *Memoirs*).

Drummossie. Many did so, some hallucinating from lack of sleep and moving like automatons. Others either never heard the order or declined to obey it and remained where they were to be slaughtered by the redcoats at will when the battle was over. Murray, appalled by having to fight on ground so advantageous to the enemy, made a last-minute search for terrain more suitable – soft, uneven, hilly ground – where Cumberland's cavalry would have less room for manoeuvre, and found something approaching it near Dalcross Castle. But when he recommended a shift to positions there, the prince would not hear of it.

The royal army meanwhile had breakfasted at Balblair on bread and cheese and a tot of brandy, and then set out in good order for Drummossie moor, a bay gelding bearing the weight of Cumberland's eighteen stone. 'My brave boys,' he had said to them the day before, 'we have but one march more and then our labours will be at an end,' and they had all cheered him and shouted, 'Flanders, Flanders,' in honour of his participation at Fontenoy.

Although, because of the wretched condition of the Highlanders, the issue was never in doubt, they fought as bravely as always. For the first twenty minutes Cumberland's artillery, sited on firm ground, created havoc in the Jacobite ranks with ball and grapeshot. Seeing their comrades fall beside them, the clansmen waited for the cry of 'Claymore, Claymore,' the order to charge. It didn't come because the prince, whose horse had been hit and groom decapitated early in the battle, was not there to give it. By the time he was found and his approval given, the redcoats were ready for them, and the bayonet drill they had practised at Aberdeen to parry the Highlanders' broadswords proved highly effective. Yet so fierce and sustained was the Highlanders' charge that they broke through the Hanoverian lines on the right, and in hand-to-hand fighting gave almost as good as they got. Then it was the turn of Cumberland's dragoons who had taken such a pasting at Falkirk but who now charged the demoralized Highland remnants, cutting them down where they stood, sending others into flight. As with all civil war battles, the fighting was savage; orders from Hawley as well as Cumberland said there was to be no quarter. As wounded Highlanders tried to crawl out from the heaped rows of dead and dying the redcoats butchered them where they lay. They also despatched those trying to make their way to Inverness. Officers and men found hiding in huts or bothies were either taken out and shot or burned alive inside them: women found succouring the wounded were not spared either.

How many of the prince's army were killed that day nobody knows but John Prebble thinks it was at least a thousand. Some clans who did make a count found they had been almost wiped out. According to Fitzroy Maclean, of 300 Stewarts of Appin who had taken the field, ninety-three were killed and more than sixty wounded: of the twenty-one officers of Clan Chattan whose territory this was, eighteen were killed along with hundreds of clansmen; while of 180 Macleans from Mull, Morvern and Ardgour, 142 never saw the west coast again.

Of those who did survive, Lord George Murray is said to have fought with exemplary courage and skill and later went into exile in Holland. The Duke of Perth, badly wounded, remained alive long enough to embark in a ship for France, but died at sea. As for the prince, for all his trumpetings during the campaign about unsheathing his sword to lead his men into battle, there is no evidence that he took part in any battle, not even at Culloden when defeat stared him in the face. 'As soon as he saw that the left of his army had yielded and was retreating', wrote Elcho, 'the Prince lost his head and fled full speed without even trying to rally some of his troops'. He was escorted from the field by O'Sullivan and others of the Irish and it must have been at this moment that Elcho, exasperated beyond endurance, is said to have called after him, 'Run, you damned cowardly Italian'.

Four miles to the west Elcho caught up with him and found him in 'a desperate state', still paranoically obsessed with the notion that he had been betrayed. The Chevalier de Johnstone too found him 'in total prostration, lost to all hope of being able to retrieve his affairs, having his mind completely imbued with the evil counsels of Sheridan and other Irishmen who governed him at their will, and giving up every design but that of saving himself in France as soon as he possibly could'. Elcho, told the same by the prince, called it an unworthy resolution and urged him to remain as leader, for there were still 9,000 clansmen to support him, and without a leader these would disperse and fall into the vengeful hands of Cumberland. Murray had said much the same, knowing that an army in being could remain a threat to an enemy: Scotland, if not England, could still be saved. But London, not Scotland, had been Charles's goal, and whatever residual loyalty his Highlanders felt for him, was not reciprocated; and he confirmed to Elcho that he intended to seek safety in France. 'Upon which I left,' said Elcho, 'and resolved never to have anything more to do with him'. Nor did he.*

To brave beginnings it was an inglorious end. Writing a century and a half later the historian Andrew Lang said the whole world regretted that the prince did not ride back to the field of battle, even if alone, and die with glory.

Instead he and the Irish rode to a safe house some 20 miles away and there, fearing that some embittered, defeated Scot might betray him for the £30,000 reward, he sent a letter to Murray to meet him at Fort Ruthven in Badenoch. He had no intention of going to Badenoch, but by assuming his letter would be intercepted, he hoped to throw any pursuers off the scent. In fact his object now was to make his way as fast as possible to the west coast and find the French ship which had been promised him. Before this, he had received a letter from Murray, written soon after the battle and not yet aware of the prince's subterfuge. In remarkably restrained language he blamed the prince for ever having raised the royal standard without having positive assurance that the French king would give assistance 'with all his force'; blamed him for relying so much on O'Sullivan 'who committed gross blunders on every occasion of moment . . . and did not so much as visit the ground where we were to be drawn up in line of battle'; and blamed him for the trust he had put in John Hay as regards provisions – 'he neglected his duty to such a degree that our ruin might probably have been prevented; the three last days, which were so critical, our army was starved.' O'Sullivan and Hay, he concluded, had so disgusted the army that had not the battle occurred when it did, there would likely have been a mutiny.

So ended the enterprise which had begun with high hopes on the far side of Scotland only seven months earlier. Had the story ended with the battle, had the prince found a boat then and there to carry him to France, it is interesting to speculate how history might have regarded him. For it was not just the campaign that created the legend of Bonnie Prince Charlie but also its aftermath;

*Elcho also went into exile in France where, having been refused a Hanoverian royal pardon, he remained for the rest of his life. Although he never met the prince again, he attempted through intermediaries in Rome, to which Charles had returned, to obtain repayment of the £1,500 which he had loaned to Charles for the campaign; but was not successful.

and I think it inconceivable that any unbiased account of the prince's activities that stopped short at Culloden would have failed to list, indeed emphasize, his manifest shortcomings: impetuosity and lack of foresight, wretched judgement, too great a reliance on the unreliable, military incompetence, insobriety, boastfulness unsupported by resolve, massive self-delusion. It is a formidable catalogue of defects and, while in themselves they may not have been enough to affect the outcome, Scotland and the world would have gained a very different picture of the prince and his influence on the campaign.

Charles was to remain in Scotland for another five months, which could hardly have been in greater contrast to his earlier life. Born a prince and treated as such in Rome, head of an army whose members regarded him as their future king, he was now in the curious position of being a tramp with a price on his head. On the other hand he had been freed from a role and a responsibility for which, like many princes, he was quite unsuited. Here were no George Murrays to contend with, no orders to be given or countermanded, nothing to engage his attention except his own survival. Fortunately, he was of a hardy disposition. Sleeping in the open and living off the land was what he had enjoyed on shooting trips in the Italian countryside; and even Elcho had to admit, 'His qualities were physical; he could endure the greatest fatigue and was indifferent to food, clothing or lodging'. It would be said that if his mismanagement of the campaign had brought out the worst in him, his long weeks of wandering in the heather, avoiding Cumberland's redcoats, living a life of hardship, being passed from clansman to clansman, in some ways and at some times, brought out the best.

# CHAPTER 3

## Flora Macdonald
## and 'Betty Burke'

FROM THE FRASER SAFE HOUSE SOUTH OF LOCH NESS TO WHICH HE
had ridden after the battle, the prince, O'Sullivan and a few others
set out for the west coast in search of a ship. They made such good
progress that by 20 April, only four days after the battle, they had
reached Arisaig. Here they went to the house where the prince had
stayed on his arrival, that of Angus Macdonald of Borrodale, whose son
had died at Culloden. He remained a week during which Macdonald's
wife ran up for him a new set of simple Highland clothes. Had he
stayed four days longer his subsequent wanderings would have been
unnecessary, for on 30 April two French privateers, the *Mars* and the
*Bellona*, dropped anchor in Loch nan Uamh, not to rescue the prince
it transpired, but, ignorant of the failure of the rebellion, to bring
quantities of Spanish gold in order to continue it. But before their
arrival the prince received word that not far away the redcoats were
already looking for him, and in desperation he commandeered a boat
to take him and his party to the desolate, treeless outer isles.

For the next several weeks the prince was a Hebridean fugitive
mostly on Benbecula and the two Isles of Uist, scurrying from one
hiding-place to another, often evading capture by a hair's breadth.

With the Catholics he was safe, but he had a narrow escape when two Protestant ministers, the Revd Aulay Macaulay and his son the Revd John,* were thwarted by the courageous tenant of Scalpay in their attempts to organize the prince's seizure. When the tenant told the raiding party he was ready to give his life in defence of the prince and that what they were attempting was an abuse of Highland hospitality, they withdrew ashamedly.

The prince suffered much hardship, sleeping on the heather or in bothies open to the elements, experiencing hunger, exhaustion and scurvy which brought on bleeding gums and ulcerated legs; he lived in tattered shoes and sodden clothing, tormented by horse-flies and midges, despite all of which he was rarely heard to complain. Once only did he enjoy a period of tranquillity when he sheltered in a remote bothy in Glen Coradale on the island of South Uist. Here, supplied by Macdonald of Clanranald with fresh clothing, provisions and sporting equipment, he spent the time watching the English warships in the Minch looking for him (one day he counted fifteen), fishing for lythe off the rocks and shooting grouse. 'He shot dozens on the wing each day', wrote a companion, 'scarce ever making a miss', though at that time of year (June) they must have been pitifully small. Drink was also a consolation. We are told he warmed his stomach each morning with a hearty bumper of brandy and often got through a bottle a day. It was then that he tended to show the less attractive side of himself, blaming the defeat at Culloden on Murray's 'infidelity, roguery and treachery', a travesty of the truth.

Meanwhile his opponent there, Cumberland, had embarked on his brutal policy of genocide, rounding up thousands of Highland men, women and even children. Some were sent south in prison ships to meet their deserts at Tyburn on Tower Hill or be shipped as slaves to the colonies; many died on the way and along with the dying had weights tied to their legs and were thrown overboard. Huts and bothies were set ablaze, whether or not occupied. In one hamlet the women were raped and then had to watch their menfolk being shot or bayonetted in front of them. And with crops and cattle systematically destroyed, many of those living in sparse, remote glens, were dying of starvation. 'There were found last week', wrote one English officer, 'two women and four children dead in the hills

*Grandfather of the historian Lord Macaulay.

who perished through want, their huts being burned'. And a Captain Berkeley of the St George's Dragoons, writing to friends in London, told of those who refused to surrender being killed. 'We seize and divide all their goods and cattle, which is distributed among the private men by order of His Royal Highness who by his conduct has rendered himself the bravest and best of generals'.

Thus was Butcher Cumberland revered by his officers. By some in Scotland too, who to their shame gave him the chancellorship of St Andrew's university, and in the principal cities honoured him with celebratory dinners. It was a Scottish peer and British Prime Minister Lord Rosebery who painted him in truer colours: 'No blacker, bloodier page will be found in the history of any country than that which records the atrocities against a brave but vanquished enemy perpetrated at the command and under the eyes of a British monarch's son.' There is a wine bar in Edinburgh's Cumberland Street which I sometimes visit but it always reminds me of the porky duke and what he did, and I am surprised that there has been no popular demand to have it renamed. But then that is typical of the laissez-faire attitude of many of my fellow countrymen.

In south Uist meantime Charles and his companions learned that his presence there had become known to the authorities and that redcoats were combing the heather in search of him. If he was to escape, he had urgently to recross the Minch, somehow avoiding the patrolling English warships. But how? Angus Macdonald, a tenant of Clanranald, had a sister named Flora, a girl of twenty-four, who had left her home at Armadale in Skye to help her brother with the sheep and cattle on his summer shieling. Now she wanted to return to Skye, and a scheme was hatched for the prince, disguised as an Irish maid, 'Betty Burke', to accompany her; and he was fitted out in a white, blue-sprigged gown of calico, quilted petticoat, mantle of camlet and headdress run up by Lady Clanranald and Flora.

A boat and boatmen were secured, and after dark, the pair left Rossinish, where the prince had landed weeks earlier, and headed for Skye. 'The Skye Boat Song' says of the prince 'Rocked in the deep/Flora will keep/Watch at your weary head', but in fact it was Flora, exhausted by two nights of sewing, who slept in the bottom of the boat and the prince who kept watch lest any of the party stepped on her. The north of Skye was in sight at first light and, although fired on by redcoats from a clifftop, they came safely ashore near the house of Sir Alexander Macdonald of Sleat. He was away at Fort Augustus paying his respects to Cumberland, but his pretty young wife Margaret, a staunch Jacobite, was at home. She was in a state of some alarm, as word that Charles was being hunted in the islands had spread, and an officer and four militiamen were dining in an upstairs room. But her husband's factor, another Alexander Macdonald, was with her, and he volunteered to guide Flora and 'Betty Burke' to his house at Kingsburgh, 7 miles to the south.

It was an odd little procession that made their way there, the prince quite unable to act the part expected of him, striding manfully along in his bonnet and calico gown; and when a party of churchgoers passed, they expressed themselves shocked at the immodest way in which 'Betty Burke' hitched up her skirts while crossing a stream.

At Kingsburgh the factor's wife was preparing for bed when her daughter came in to say that her father had brought home Flora 'with a very odd, muckle ill-shapen up wife as ever I saw'. Peeping through the hall door she took a similar view: 'I saw such an old muckle trallup of a carlin [old woman] making lang, wide steps through the hall that I could not like her appearance at all'. When her husband explained who it was, she cried, 'The prince! O Lord, we are all ruined and undone for ever. We will all be hanged now!' She calmed down enough to prepare a meal of eggs, collops, bread and cheese, after which the prince called for brandy. 'In my skulking', he said, 'I have learned to take a hearty dram' and he and Kingsburgh sat up smoking and drinking far into the night. Then he went up to a comfortable bed – the first he had slept in for weeks – and did not wake until noon.

Later that day and so as not to alarm the servants Charles left Kingsburgh still disguised as Betty Burke, then changed in a wood into Highland dress. When he bade good-bye to Flora, he said, 'I hope, madam, we shall meet in St James's where I will reward you for all you have done'.

Charles never saw Flora again. She was arrested soon after and taken by the warship *Furnace* to the Tower of London. Charles meanwhile reached Portree and with the help of a new minder, Malcolm MacLeod, who had been wounded at Culloden, crossed over the sea to Raasay, the 15-mile-long island that lies athwart the entrance to Portree harbour. His plan was to rest here a few days while the hunt for him died down, but a party of men from the *Furnace* had been there before them and a scene of desolation met their eyes: most of the houses including the laird's, thirty-two boats, 700 sheep and 280 cattle all ruthlessly destroyed. They slept two nights in the open, MacLeod hearing the prince muttering in his sleep in Italian, French and English.

The prince now expressed a wish to go to Mackinnon country in the south of Skye, as the clan had supported him in the rising and the chief's son, John Mackinnon, was Malcolm's brother-in-law. Having agreed that Charles should pose as Malcolm's servant and walk deferentially a few paces behind him, a less taxing role than of Betty Burke, the pair set off by night up Glen Varragill to Sligachan and skirting the small garrison there, came down under the shadow of the Cuillins to the wild country north of Elgol. At daylight Malcolm noticed how frequently the prince was scratching. He was in fact lousy and when he had opened up his clothing Malcolm found him crawling with the creatures and picked more than eighty off him. Personal hygiene was not one of Charles's strong points and others had noticed his habit each night of throwing himself down fully dressed and without washing, too exhausted or befuddled to do otherwise.

At John Mackinnon's house at Elgol, Malcolm found his sister at home but her husband away. He introduced the prince as his servant. They had something to eat and then Malcolm asked a servant girl in Gaelic to wash his legs and feet which were caked in mud. Told also to wash the prince's, she at first refused, saying he was nothing but a low countrywoman's son. In the end she made such a good job of it that Charles had to ask Malcolm to tell her (who spoke no English) not to go so far up!

Presently John Mackinnon appeared, and saw his prince in a shabby kilt carrying his baby son Neil round the room and singing to him. It was too much, and he wept. Charles told him he wanted a boat to the mainland, as Loch nan Uamh was not far away and there might be a French ship.

Before Malcolm MacLeod left for Portree, the prince gave him ten guineas and a buckle in remembrance. Later that year Malcolm was arrested and like Flora taken to the Tower of London. Like her also he was released in the general amnesty of 1747 and travelled with her back to Skye. 'I went to London to be hanged', he commented, 'and returned in a post-chaise with Miss Flora Macdonald'.

After further adventures which included a chase by a boat

of militiamen in the Sound of Sleat, the prince crossed to the mainland, found the house of Macdonald of Morar burned to a shell and he and his wife living in a bothy, likewise the house of Macdonald of Borrodale where he had first stayed after landing from the *du Teillay* in Loch nan Uamh the year before. But now Loch nan Uamh was empty, and with government troops aware of his arrival in the neighbourhood and warships active off the coast, he had no option but to take once more to the heather.

For the next two months Charles and a new set of minders worked their way north, travelling only by night. Passing over the high corries they walked to the west of Lochs Arkaig and Quoich, even as far as Kinloch Hourn, seeing the camp fires of the redcoats flickering in the glens below, on still nights hearing snatches of their conversation. Often, faint with hunger, they had to crawl on hands and knees between groups of enemy sentries. Meeting the legendary Seven Men of Glenmoriston – a rebel group who had banded together to live in the hills and continue fighting the English – they were given a container of milk to revive them, and later they obtained more substantial nourishment when one of the party shot a deer. Near the burned-out ruins of Achnacarry – the home of Lochiel but for whose misguided loyalty the rising would have aborted before it began – the prince received word that Lochiel, together with other Jacobite renegades, had taken refuge in the hills between the Braes of Badenoch and Atholl, to the east of the Great Glen – not far from the pass of Corrieairyack which the prince had traversed on his march south from Glenfinnan the year before. The prince met Lochiel on the slopes of Ben Alder, and his spirits revived at the sight of his larder – mutton, beef sausages, ham, butter, cheese and an anker of twenty pints of whisky. Within a day or two he was his old self again and with the drink taken, boasting that he intended to marry the King of France's daughter whom he had never met; that his brother Henry had landed in England with 10,000 men; that he would yet regain the throne and occupy St James's Palace.

Then news came to gladden his heart: Cumberland's successor in the Highlands, the Dutch-born Lord Albemarle, having heard nothing of the prince for many weeks, had assumed he must have perished and called off the hunt for him; and, even better, two French ships, the *Hereux* and the *Prince de Conti* had come to anchor in Loch nan Uamh. The party lost little time in packing up and moving off. Ten days later they reached the shores of Loch nan

Uamh, found the ships still there and embarked for France.

At long last the great adventure was over.

Had the man the redcoats were chasing in the heather for five months been some ordinary fugitive from justice, his adventures and manifold escapes from capture in one of the most beautiful and romantic landscapes in Britain, would still have fascinated. It being a prince with a price on his head, hunted across a land he claimed to be his father's, makes it irresistible; taken with the events of the year before, it is little wonder that it caught and has retained the imagination of the world.

No less memorable was the refusal of every Highlander who was given the opportunity, to betray him, despite the £30,000 government reward, then a fortune; for each man knew that had he claimed it, he could never live with himself or his clansmen afterwards. Donald MacLeod the old boatman who had rowed the prince across to Rossinish, spoke for all when he said during interrogation on the *Furnace*: 'I could not have enjoyed it eight and forty hours . . . and though I could have gotten all England and Scotland for my pain, I would not have allowed a hair of his body to be touched if I could help it'. Such was the bond of Jacobite attachment.

Charles was a man of varied attributes; but what he never was nor ever could be was 'bonnie' if by that we mean something more than personal appearance: it is one of history's great misnomers. What saddens one most about the whole doomed enterprise was his lack of any real expression of regret for the destitution and misery which his vaunting ambition had brought to the Highland clans. This was typically Stuart. Even after the news of Culloden had reached his father, James was urging his son to 'keep our own people in a due subordination without allowing them to break your head with accusations and invectives against one another, but showing that you are Master and will act your own way . . .' and concluding that the Scots 'are people who owe us a great deal while we owe them little.'

Like father, like son. All the cold comfort that Charles could offer to those whose lives he had taken up and discarded, whose loyalty to him had brought about the destruction of their homes, crops, cattle, even the forfeiture of their estates, was that one day he would return. There can have been few who wished it; for the clan system which had shaped their lives was being destroyed with everything else. English and Lowland Scots who looked on the Highlanders as savages were glad their number was up. Yet many of the great chiefs were cultivated men who had studied the classics, travelled on the Continent and kept a good table. Writing from Scotland, Daniel Defoe said of them, 'We see every day the gentlemen born here such as the Mackenzies, McLeans, Dundonalds, Gordons, MacKays and others who are named as if they were *Barbarians*, appear at court and in our camps and armies as polite and as finished gentlemen as any from other countries or even our own . . .'

No less admirable were the ordinary clanspeople, as Adam Ferguson (in whose house in Edinburgh Robert Burns met the youthful Walter Scott) noted in 1767:

> If I had not been in the Highlands of Scotland, I might be of those mind who think the inhabitants of Paris and Versailles the only polite people in the world. It is truly wonderful to see persons of every sex and age who never travelled beyond the nearest mountain, possess themselves perfectly, perform acts of kindness with an aspect of dignity and a perfect discernment of what is proper to oblige . . . a person among the mountains who thinks himself nobly born, considers courtesy as the test of his rank. He never saw a superior and does not know what it is to be embarrassed.

And Ann Grant who married the minister of Laggan wrote of the respect in which the old people were held there. 'Treated with unvaried tenderness and veneration, [they] feel no diminution of their consequence, no chill in their affections. Strangers to neglect, they are also strangers to suspicion.'

Those of us who at some point in our lives have lived in close contact with Highlanders would affirm that the observations of Adam Ferguson and Ann Grant are still true today.

Yet the myth of Bonnie Prince Charlie remains. He has become a folk hero extraordinary. Books glorify him, songs ancient and modern celebrate or mourn for him: the Eriskay love lilt, 'Charlie he's my darling', the 'Skye Boat Song', the 'Dawning of the Day', 'The Roses o' Prince Charlie', are all threnodies for a lost leader, laments for a loss of national identity. Pictures of Charlie and Flora, tartan clad, beautified and beatified, adorn the lids of boxes of chocolate, shortbread, Edinburgh Rock.

One of the first to embrace all this was, surprisingly, that unsentimental man of Scottish letters, the poet Hugh MacDiarmid. 'I have no concern with or interest in, Charles's faults and failings as an individual,' he wrote. 'There is no minimizing the high significance of a Cause . . .' Yet when MacDiarmid and others regard the prince as the icon of present-day Scottish nationalism they forget that the prince did not see it that way either. Had he ended his march in Edinburgh, as most of the chiefs wanted, sent out a call to his countrymen to rally to the defence of Scotland, and then stood firm against whatever Wade and Cumberland might send against him, he would have gone down to history as a true Scottish hero like Bruce or Wallace. Yet it was not Scotland he wanted so much as England, Ireland, Wales as well: Scotland and the Highlanders were to be stepping stones to the British throne. Even had he attained it, there is no reason to suppose that he would have visited Scotland or shown empathy for its inhabitants any more than other Stuart kings: even on the march south his closest companions had not been Scots but Irish. In short, Charles was never quite the Scottish patriot that history has painted him. He was an Italian-born stateless Catholic refugee and the Stuart standard he raised at Glenfinnan was for him no more than a flag of convenience.

There are truer inspirational sources for Scottish independence including MacDiarmid himself:

> If there's a sword-like sang                    [song]
> That can cut Scotland clear
> O' a' the warld beside,
> Rax me the hilt o' it here,                      [reach]
>
> For there's nae jewel till
> Frae the rest of the earth it's free,
> Wi' the starry separateness
> I'd fain to Scotland gie                         [delight]

I can even forgive him for calling in aid the Jacobite white cockade or rose in this, one of the most touching poems he ever wrote:

> The rose of all the world is not for me,
> I want for my part
> Only the little white rose of Scotland
> That smells sharp and sweet – and breaks the heart.

After the '45 the government in London were taking no chances. Not only were they determined to crush the Highlanders and their way of life by fire and sword, but to nip any further risings in the bud they strengthened their existing garrisons at Fort William in the west and Fort Augustus in the centre of the Great Glen and also built a brand new one. Fort George in Inverness had been destroyed by the Highlanders before Culloden and to replace it and protect the eastern approaches to Inverness by sea and land, a site for a new Fort George was chosen on a spit of land on the southern shore of a neck of water, only a mile across, where the Moray Firth is at its narrowest.

Work on it started in 1748, the designer being the newly appointed 'Military Engineer for North Britain', William Skinner, with the contract for building being given to the famous architect William Adam and, after his death, his equally famous sons. It was a massive undertaking, covering a site of 42 acres and not finished until 1769 at a cost of £200,000, which was more than the whole of Scotland's gross national product for 1750. Although never needed for the purpose for which it was built, it could house 1,600 infantrymen and an artillery unit. James Wolfe, the victor of Quebec, called it 'the most considerable and best situated fortress in Great Britain'.

Fort George today is not on the way to anywhere and therefore not a main tourist attraction. But it is only a few miles from Culloden and well worth the ten or fifteen minutes it takes to reach it: military people say it is the finest unspoilt eighteenth-century fortress anywhere in Europe. It is flanked on three sides by the sea and protected by a ring of ramparts on which guns have been placed at strategic intervals. The east being the only direction from which a land attack could have been mounted, the fort on this side is protected by a huge sunken area covered in grass and large enough to hold a couple of football fields; and above it, both in front and behind, a series of defensive ravelins and bastions. A pedestrian bridge leads across the sunken area to the old gatehouse and guardroom which in turn opens on to the main parade ground, an area large enough to contain the whole of Edinburgh Castle. It is the scale of the place that impresses.

On the far side of the parade ground are the barracks, ten or a dozen blocks built, as you would expect from the Adam family, in the classical eighteenth-century style. The block bordering the parade ground houses the living quarters of the Scottish regiment in residence, the other contains the Regimental Museum of the Queen's Own Highlanders. At the far end is the chapel, a light, airy building with Doric columns supporting an upstairs gallery and, over the chancel arch, an inscription in Latin that reads: George III, by the grace of God, King of Great Britain, France and Ireland, 1767, a view with which few Frenchmen of the time would have agreed.

Life for a private soldier in the eighteenth century and early nineteenth century was inclined to be nasty, brutish and short, and nowhere was the brutishness more marked than in the punishments meted out to transgressors. In one of the old guardrooms at the entrance to the fort it is stated that in 1770 private soldiers had to subsist on pay of 3½d (about 15p now) a day. A breakfast roll cost ½d and a piece of cheese another ½d which left 2½d. That was the price of a glass of spirits and if a man took it to warm himself against the cold, then he would have no more food for the next 24 hours. The hunger of one soldier that year was so desperate that he pulled up some raw potatoes to eat and was caught. The punishment, not unusual for the time, was 500 lashes on the bare back. But on this occasion it backfired. After his wife had tried to intervene and was led away screaming, a group of washerwomen with bags full of stones broke ranks, drove off the supervising officers and set free the prisoner and others who were also being flogged. And according to a chronicler by the name of G. Penny, that was the end, at least in this location (though not in the Royal Navy) of what he called 'these public, inhuman and disgusting exhibitions'.

A happier story is also to be found in the old guardroom of an event in the life of Private Samuel Hutton, writing in 1760:

> I should have mentioned that one of my comrades was married to a pretty little Scotchwoman who lived in camp with him and got a good deal of money by keeping a scuttling tent for the officers.
>
> The man was killed. In such a situation the woman must not remain a widow, and with such qualifications was a prize to any man. Another comrade said to me, 'I advise you to marry Kate Keith. If you won't, I will. But there's no time to be lost, for she'll have plenty of offers.' I took a few hours to consider of it, and determined upon soliciting the hand of Kate Keith. I found that plenty had been before me, but my person and good conduct obtained me the preference; and the little black-eyed

Scotchwoman accompanied me to the chaplain of the regiment the second day after her husband had fallen.

In time my wife presented me with a son. He was saluted by cannon on his entrance to the world and the ball of one was near taking off his head. The day after he was born, we were ordered to march. I wrapped my wife and child in my cloak and placed them on a baggage wagon, and the only favour I could obtain was that of marching by the side of the baggage wagon instead of marching in the ranks.

A year or two ago, when on my way into the fort (and again on the way out), I passed a sentry in battledress standing in a sentry box. He was clutching a nasty-looking automatic assault weapon rather like those you used to see in American gangster films. I asked him what it was called and he said (I think) that it was an LSW, which didn't take things much further. Was it loaded, I asked, and he said it was. Approaching the officers' mess for lunch I noticed a sign outside the modern guardroom which said SECURITY THREAT NOW HIGH IN SCOTLAND. ENSURE YOUR CAR IS SEARCHED, REPORT ANYTHING NO MATTER HOW TRIVIAL. Beside this was another sign which said BIKINI ALERT STATE A. So at lunch I asked the CO just how high the security threat was. He said, 'Put it this way. We get certain information and we have to act on it. How reliable it is we don't know, but with the IRA you can't be too careful.' I asked if there were any circumstances in which his sentries were permitted to fire their LSWs. He said there were but declined to give details.

There is a paradox here. It was the seventeenth-century Ulster plantation by Scottish Protestant colonists that has been the root cause of our problems in Northern Ireland. You would therefore expect Scots and Scotland to be a priority target for the IRA. That they have not been is presumably because the IRA have recognized that it is not the Scots as such but the British (of whom the great majority are English) who are the occupying power. Have they also refrained from attacking Scottish, and Welsh, targets because they see us as fellow Celts who, like them, also feel alienated from British rule and seek to regain some of our long-lost independence?

# INTERLUDE

AFTER SIX BLISSFUL YEARS AT NAIRN MY GRANDFATHER LOST A SMALL fortune speculating on the Stock Exchange and could no longer afford the Tarland lease. But my parents were resolved to continue summer holidays in Scotland and so began enquiring about holiday lets. They found what they were looking for in the small ads section of *The Scotsman*, a farmhouse with enough room for the family and a couple of guests in the west coast island of Islay.

After eleven months in the flat and placid acres of the Home Counties, one of the best aspects of those Islay holidays was the excitement of the journey north by car, an entry into a new, uncluttered, spacious world. We used to spend two nights on the way, the second in Edinburgh, then head west for Loch Lomond and Loch Fyne en route to the Islay ferry at West Loch Tarbert. An hour out of Edinburgh the country opened up and we left the clutter behind. Here, when the weather was good, were vistas on an altogether vaster scale; bare mountain tops reaching to huge skies, shadows of clouds drifting across their green flanks, sea lochs without a bend in them for 20 miles, rivers with frothing brown waterfalls. It was a different matter when the weather turned, mountain tops and corries lost in weeping mists, sopping cattle and sheep standing dumbly in the sodden fields, the windscreen wipers working overtime. Yet nothing could blunt the joy of being there, of anticipating the delights ahead.

The ferry's destination was Port Askaig or Port Ellen on alternate days. Port Askaig's situation was and is dramatic, a pier, a hotel and a cluster of small houses beneath a cliff that runs down to the water's edge and looks across the narrow black Sound of Jura to the island's three Paps. The approach to Port Ellen is more tranquil, a leisurely run in open water past islets and inlets where seals bask and seabirds fly. On both routes the boat called in at the little semi-tropical island of Gigha, owned at that time by the father of a friend at school, to land mail and stores.

For me the attractions of Islay which I have visited many times since, lie in its variety of highland and lowland; moor and mountains in the south, farm land in the centre, whitewashed distilleries like Laphroaig and Lagavulin and Bunnahabhain, the neat townships of Bowmore and Port Charlotte facing each other across the waters of Loch Indaal (Bowmore with its curious circular church, permitting no corners in which to hide, it is said, for either the devil or those seeking to avoid the collection plate), the golf course at Machrie where you had to circumnavigate sheep's droppings on the greens, a mile of golden beach beside it. My mother and sisters spent much of their time looking for shells on the seashore or wild flowers inland.

My father, like myself then, thought mostly of shooting and fishing. He had given me a twenty-bore gun and on a piece of moorland on the Mull of Oa in the south-west, and with the Atlantic rolling below, we chased the elusive grouse. The upper reaches of the river Laggan, little more than a glorified burn, ran close to the farmhouse, and here, when there was a spate, we could always pull out a few sea-trout and the odd salmon.

There were several lochs to fish, some dour like Ardnave, others like Staoisha or Finlaggan where we seldom came away empty-handed. Finlaggan I particularly remember because in a field beside it my mother was chased by a bull, also because of an island at one end where stood the ruins of a medieval chapel. I never paid much attention to the chapel as a boy, but years later I learned it was part of a huge fortified set- tlement called Eilean Mor which between the fourteenth and sixteenth centuries was the headquarters of Somerled and other

Macdonald chieftains who as Lords of the Isles ruled Argyll and the Hebrides.

I went back to Finlaggan recently for a radio programme and met one of the archaeological team excavating the ruins of the settlement. We crossed to the island by a rickety plank bridge. The remains of the chapel were still there and beside them a large area of tall nettles and grasses. These would be cleared during the summer, said my guide, because underneath lay the remains of Somerled's great banqueting hall which they were going to excavate. When I commented on the distance from the sea for the headquarters of a ruler who styled himself Lord of the Isles, I was told that that was its point. A fortification on the coast could be approached and perhaps stormed from behind by an enemy landing at night. Here in remote Finlaggan they would have plenty of warning of attack.

There was however one small blight on these Islay holidays, and that was Sabbatarianism. I didn't expect to shoot on a Sunday as we didn't do that in England, but I was astonished when told I couldn't fish or play golf. There was no question of golf, said my father, as on Sundays the clubhouse was closed. (I wish I had known then that an Archbishop of St Andrews in the seventeenth century had seen nothing wrong in playing a round there after the time for church had passed.) How about fishing, I asked? My father said that someone might see me carrying a rod, would spread the word around, and the local people would be offended. I was too young to be interested in spirits or even beer, but had I been a public house frequenter, I would have found that on Sundays the doors of every pub in Scotland were shut from morning to night.

So for me Sunday was what one might call a black letter day. In the morning we attended the local episcopalian church, opened for the month of August and where, there being no resident organist, my mother had agreed to be the acting one.

In the afternoon we might go for a boring drive, taking a picnic tea if the weather was fine which was rarely. One Sunday, I remember, we drove along the south coast, past old woods and uncultivated fields like in Ireland to view the exquisite Celtic cross in the tiny churchyard of Kildalton and thought to have been made in Iona in the ninth century. My mother waxed lyrical over this but for my father and myself, thinking of the balls we might have struck and the birds and fish we might have pursued, a glance was enough. Going back there the other day, I wondered how I could have been so blind.

# CHAPTER 4

## *Calvinism and Witchcraft*

TABOOS ON SUNDAY SPORT IN SCOTLAND HAVE NOW ALL BUT DIS-
appeared. But how did they come about in the first place? For an
answer one has to go back to the Scottish Reformation of 1560, morally
and intellectually a more rigorous affair than in England: for the clergy
of the Roman Catholic church which had been Scotland's religion for
500 years and Europe's for longer, had become even more depraved
than their English counterparts. At a Council of Scottish bishops
which in 1549 and again in 1552 met – too late, as it transpired
– to discuss measures to set their house in order, it was agreed that
the rejection of the faith by so many was due to 'the corruption of
morals and profane lewdness of life in churchmen of almost all ranks,
together with crass ignorance of literature and of all the liberal arts'.
Foremost among these were David Beaton, the Cardinal Archbishop
of St Andrews, who led a life of great sexual promiscuity, and his
successor, Archbishop Hamilton who was happy to agree to medical
advice that he should undergo a ten-week course of 'carefully regulated'
sexual incontinence.

The Crown accepted all this, indeed itself contributed to the
general corruption. James IV made an illegitimate son Archbishop

of St Andrews at the age of eleven; while in 1532 James V persuaded the Pope to agree to five of his illegitimate sons, three of them babies, to be titular abbots or priors of the monasteries of Kelso, Melrose and Holyrood, thus providing the little bastards with an income at the Church's expense. Existing abbots were described as 'lewd and dull' and nuns as 'unchaste and too illiterate to write their names'.

The ordinary clergy were no better. Although in mid-sixteenth century Scotland the ratio of priests to the rest of the population was about 1 to 300, it happened that of every bastard legitimized, two out of seven were the issue of priests. There were stories of priests arriving at the altar drunk, while others, according to Archibald Hay, 'hardly knew the order of the alphabet'. Church services, conducted mostly in Latin which few understood, were travesties of what they should have been. They were in essence one-man shows: the priest mumbled through the rites of office, the congregation gawped or slept: there were no communal prayers, no responses, no singing. So people went to Mass reluctantly or not at all. The incomes of most parishes were being siphoned off to cathedrals and abbeys, so that wretchedly underpaid priests refused to bury the poor until they had received the customary cow and piece of cloth, or to administer the annual sacrament until given an Easter offering; and without funds to repair them, many good churches fell into ruin. In Berwickshire alone in 1556 twenty-two churches were partly derelict, some without walls or roofs, most lacking windows, fonts, vestments or books.

There was therefore in Scotland at this time a spiritual hunger which was largely unfulfilled. It was the entry of two books into Scotland, Cranmer's *Book of Common Prayer* in 1549 and the Geneva bible eleven years later, which for the first time opened Scottish eyes to what, after the unintelligible Latin rites of Catholicism, the Christian faith had to offer: these paved the way and helped create the climate for the monumental changes that the reformers brought about.

There could hardly have been a greater contrast to the hierarchical set-up of the Roman Catholic church with its Pope, Cardinals, Archbishops, Bishops, Monsignors, and Fathers than the austere, egalitarian structure – one of the first truly democratic organizations in Europe – of the Church of Scotland that succeeded it, the essence of it being that religion was too important a matter to be left exclusively to the clergy. First the Pope's authority in Scotland was abolished by law and the celebration of the Mass forbidden.

Then in every parish a kirk session was established in which lay elders would first appoint ministers and, as guarantee against the excesses of the Catholic priests, act in concert with them in all parish matters. At district level Presbyteries were established, composed of elders and ministers from the surrounding kirk sessions: they assumed the power formerly held by Catholic bishops of ordaining ministers. Above the Presbyteries were the Synods to which the Presbyteries sent representatives, and above the Synods the General Assembly which met in Edinburgh and was composed of delegates from kirk sessions, Presbyteries and Synods. Later a Moderator was elected annually as the Church of Scotland's head.

This structure which came into being in 1560 is still the Church of Scotland's present structure. It was largely the brainchild of that scourge of Mary Queen of Scots, John Knox, who had learned his Protestantism in Calvin's Geneva, and whose statue stands today in the forecourt of the General Assembly building in Edinburgh. Preaching and administering the Sacraments were to be a minister's main duties. But Knox also advocated – centuries before the idea became fashionable – free schools in every parish 'for the virtuous education and godly upbringing of the youth of this realm'. It would be a long time before this dream became a reality, but from it stemmed the love of, and importance attached to, learning which subsequently became such a driving force in the Scottish character.

Whether a love of discipline has also been endemic in the Scottish people or whether they embraced it as an insurance against a return to the wicked ways of Catholicism is a moot point, but from the start the kirk sessions made it clear that backsliding would not be tolerated, and as many of the kirk's elders were also the local magistrates, their word was law. Universal (i.e. parish) attendance was required at services on Sundays and weekdays. Absentees were fined, as were those caught napping during the sermon. Then the Scottish Parliament, heavily influenced by these new attitudes, took it on itself to make moral misdemeanours statutory offences. Love in a cold climate being one prerequisite for a sense of warmth and well being, the Scots, like the Finns, have traditionally sought it. 'Fornication', wrote an Englishman, Sir Antony Weldon, 'they hold but a pastime wherein man's ability is proved and a woman's fertility is discovered'. So adultery became an offence in 1563, fornication in 1567, Sabbath breaking in 1579, swearing in 1581 and drunkenness in 1617.

Fornication and adultery were regarded as the most heinous offences, for which the penalty was to stand in sackcloth, bareheaded and barefooted, first at the kirk door, then on the stool of repentance inside the kirk, every Sunday for six months and on occasions for several years. Whipping and fining were also inflicted and as a last resort offenders could be excommunicated. The frequency of these punishments seemed to indicate they were poor deterrents. A more savage punishment awaited those caught practising homosexuality: in Edinburgh all offenders, whether boys or old men, were burnt alive on Castle Hill.

Even more puritanical measures were enforced on people's liberty. At Christmas and on other traditional holidays such as Midsummer's Eve, bonfires, pilgrimages, dancing and carol singing were forbidden. At the General Assembly of 1581 elders and ministers deplored card-playing, excessive drinking and gluttony, 'gorgeous and vain apparel, filthy and bawdy speeches', and 'display and merry-making' at weddings and funerals. Parliament too decided on a stricter observance of the Sabbath, in 1579 passing a law forbidding all forms of labour, physical recreation and drinking, to which the General Assembly added dancing and travel.

A more terrible example of Scottish religious extremism had come in with the Reformation in 1560, reached its peak during the course of the seventeenth century and only ended in the first quarter of the eighteenth century not long before the years of the Scottish Enlightenment. This was belief in witchcraft, the torturing of alleged witches to persuade them to confess and the trials and executions of those found guilty. A belief in witches and warlocks as in fairies and other creatures of the supernatural ('ghoulies and ghosties and long-legged beasties/And things that go bump in the night') had been widespread in Scotland from the earliest time; but the general view was that they did no harm, were invulnerable to human influence and it was best to placate them by leaving gifts of milk or oatmeal on the moor or hillside.

It was in Europe and especially Germany that the idea first arose that Satan, who was as human to the people of that time as God himself, was in the practice of enlisting covens of witches to engage in a conspiracy against the Church. In 1484 the Pope issued a bull recommending the extirpation of sorcerers. Calvin wrote that it was God's command that all witches and enchantresses should be done away with; and in central Europe during the fifteenth and sixteenth centuries they were put to death in their thousands.

Soon Scotsmen travelling on the Continent brought the virus back home. George Buchanan approved the teaching of Moses in Exodus 22.18 that witches should not be allowed to live, while his pupil James VI (James I of England) having heard it said at the trial of a coven that Satan had preached against him at midnight in the church at North Berwick, criticized 'an impious Englishman' for denying that witches existed. John Knox joined in the general consensus that they were a social menace, and supported the prosecution at a witchcraft trial at St Andrews. To us, 400 years on, such beliefs seem as preposterous as another then only recently gone out of fashion, that disease was the consequence of sin and the only cure for it was prayer, fasting and repentance.

What had once been tolerated as a superstition, putting out libations for fairies and witches, was also now regarded as a sin and it became a kind of crusade to root witches out. The victims were mostly peasants, often wives, daughters or widows of country people, many not of the highest intelligence. They were denounced publicly in the kirk session then given over to torture to make them confess. As with police methods of interrogation today, confessions were important, for they proved that the interrogators were right in their beliefs and justified the methods they had employed to obtain them. Because witches were believed to operate in covens of thirteen, the wretched victim, herself an innocent, would sometimes be obliged to name another dozen innocents with whom she admitted, under duress, to being in collusion. Professor Smout claims that during the 150 years following the Reformation, up to 4,500 witches in Scotland were hanged, strangled or burned at the stake.

Not content with the executions of (to us) patently innocent people, the government required their next of kin to pay for the expenses incurred in killing them. In a period of six weeks in 1643 at Pittenweem in Fife, John Dawson and John Crombie had to pay £40 and £80 for the executions of their wives while Thomas Cook was obliged to hand over £60 for the costs of the execution of his mother.*

In 1662 the Privy Council of Scotland was restored and, concerned by manifest malpractices in witchcraft trials, made the use of torture to obtain confessions illegal. Thereafter charges of witchcraft

*At that time there were four Scottish pounds to the English pound.

dwindled. Yet several more were to come, and one in 1696–7 was as infamous as any.

Beyond the shores of Scotland the decade in which it occurred was rich in scientific and artistic advancement. In Russia Peter the Great reformed the Russian calendar, in England Newton calculated the speed of sound, string orchestras first came into being, the Bank of England was established, while Vanbrugh, Purcell, Dryden, Congreve, John Aubrey and Grinling Gibbons were all active.

But in parts of Scotland it was still the dark ages. The case in question was that of eleven-year-old Christian Shaw, described as 'a smart, lively girl of good inclinations', elder daughter of John Shaw, laird of Bargarran, a property in the parish of Erskine in Renfrewshire, a few miles west of Glasgow. At the end of August 1696 Christian saw one of the maids Katherine Campbell 'steal and drink' some of the household milk and told her mother of it. Taxed with the offence, the quick-tempered Katherine, a Highland girl who had come south to find work, heaped curses on the child, among them that the devil would drag her soul through hell. A few days later Agnes Naismith, an old barefoot widow woman, clad in a ragged plaid, who lived locally and was suspected of witchcraft, called at the house for alms and spoke to Christian and her sister. The next night, according to a contemporary account, 'the child went to bed in good health; but so soon as she fell asleep, began to struggle and cry, "Help! Help!" and then suddenly got up and did fly over the top of a resting bed where she was lying (her father, mother and others being in the room and to their great astonishment and admiration) with such violence that probably her brains had been dashed out if a woman standing providentially by, had not broke the force of the child's motion; who, being laid in another bed, remained stiff and insensible as if she had been dead, for the space of half an hour; but for forty-eight hours thereafter could not sleep, crying out of violent pains through her whole body; and no sooner began to sleep or turn drowsy but seemed greatly affrighted, crying still, "Help! Help!" '

These manifestations, though no-one at the time knew them as such, are symptoms of hysteria; a psychological malaise often to be found in young girls on the threshold of puberty and described by Dr David Stafford-Clark as an attempt, 'never fully conscious and frequently completely unconscious on the part of the patient, and frequently completely unconscious on the part of the patient, to obtain some advantage from the representation of symptoms of illness. The advantage may be totally illusory and the symptoms both painful and crippling, but the principle underlying the illness remains the same.'

During the next seven months other extraordinary manifestations were exhibited by Christian: at times she was rendered blind, deaf and dumb, suffered violent fits which made it impossible for any-one to hold her down, screamed and shrieked when touched, cried out that Katherine Campbell was a servant of the devil and that she and Agnes Naismith were cutting up her body; brought out of her mouth straw, balls of hair, coal cinders, hay mixed with dung, small bones and pins, stuck out her tongue so far it covered her chin or else retracted it so far she was in danger of choking, became airborne at some moments and at others so rigid that she might have been dead, and shouted out that she was being attacked by the devil's crew whom she identified by name as male and female neighbours.

The onset of attacks of hysteria is often the consequence of a seemingly trivial incident triggering off a deeply felt underlying fear. In her book on the case Isobel Adam thinks that Christian's underlying fear was that of the devil whose machinations had been brought home to her vividly and terrifyingly in sermon after sermon in her local kirk. So that when Katherine Campbell told Christian that the devil would drag her soul through hell, it must have seemed to an impressionable eleven year old that here was one of the devil's agents, a witch in person, come to hand her over to the Prince of Darkness. The unexpected encounter a few days later with the old crone Agnes Naismith, who looked the very embodiment of a pantomime witch and was indeed suspected of witchcraft, must have confirmed her worst fears.

For the remainder of 1696 Christian's torments continued. In her hallucinations she claimed that the 'crew' or coven that were persecuting her met frequently in her father's orchard, presided over by the devil. He frequently asked her to renounce her baptism (a sacred rite in those days because it signified a bonding with God) and she always refused. And she named others of the crew: an old Highlander who had called at the house for alms and one of her father's tenant farmers, John Lindsay of Barloch, a decent, God-fearing man. Her father had them both committed to prison.

74

the leading physician, Dr Matthew Brisbane. On the first visit he thought she was suffering from 'hypocondriacal melancholy'. On the second he was present when she discharged various artifacts from her mouth — feathers, white stones, lumps of candle grease and egg shells. Later he said that these and other objects were too dry ever to have been in her stomach, but he did not add the corollary that she must have put them in her mouth herself.

During this visit Christian caught a glimpse of a well-known beggar and religious blasphemer by the name of Alexander Anderson and declared that she had seen his face among the crew. He was arrested and sent to prison, as was his unkempt daughter Elizabeth, aged sixteen, who had the reputation of knowing every witch from Renfrew to the sea. Katherine Campbell tried to escape arrest by fleeing to her home in the Highlands but was found in the hovel of a prostitute who was sheltering her not far from Bargarran, and taken to the Paisley tollbooth.

Because of the growing notoriety of Christian's case, the Paisley presbytery sent to Edinburgh to ask the Privy Council to appoint a Commission to look into the whole affair; and in January 1697 a Commission of nine Renfrewshire men (three related to Bargarran) under the Presidency of Lord Blantyre, a judge of the Court of Session, came to Paisley.

One of the first tasks of the Commission was to interview Elizabeth Anderson, for under Scottish law then (and indeed now) no-one can be convicted on uncorroborated evidence, and it was thought that with her reputation as an acquaintance of witches, she might be able to confirm things that Christian had said. She denied that she knew anything about witches or had ever been one herself, but then, and no doubt to the Commission's astonishment, she admitted to having frequented witches' gatherings with her father including one in the Bargarran orchard. There she had met a number of people including her great aunt Margaret Fulton, Agnes Naismith, the brothers John and James Lindsay of Formakin and an old Highlander whose name she didn't know but described as 'bent and low in stature with a grey beard and whiskers and piercing eyes'. The old Highlander was brought up from the cells and she affirmed he was the same person; further that he and her father and the others she had named had been among Christian's worst tormentors.

Next day the prisoners set off from the Paisley tollbooth in a snowstorm to walk the 6 miles to Bargarran where they would be interviewed by the Commissioners and brought face to face with the victim of their alleged persecution. The respectable grey-haired James Lindsay with a ruddy, weather-beaten face, was determined to look his best for the occasion and had put on his Sunday suit of hodden grey and a plaid; Katherine Campbell was described as 'a handsome girl, full breasted, with strong, shapely limbs, thick, curly black hair and fierce green eyes', Elizabeth Anderson as 'scrawny with matted hair'. Only her father, Alexander, whose face had a sickly pallor and whose rags hung on him as on a skeleton, lacked any semblance of health. A consumptive, his body was wracked by bouts of coughing; in a few days he would be dead.

The Commissioners, warmed by Bargarran's peat fire in the hall and refreshed by his claret, were waiting to receive them. Lord Blantyre told the accused they were suspected of the gravest offence of which a human being was capable, that of forsaking their baptism and giving themselves body and soul to the devil. Could they deny the indictment? With one voice they said they could. Had they as servants of the devil joined in the torments of Christian Shaw? With equal vehemence they said they hadn't.

Christian was brought in, wearing a long grey dress and lace-edged cap and – to the surprise of some – with shining eyes and bright cheeks, the very picture of health. In turn the prisoners were instructed to touch her with their hands, and when most did so, the girl fell writhing to the floor.

Elizabeth Anderson repeated her story about meeting with the crew in the Bargarran orchard, adding that a black man was present, wearing a cravat and bonnet who, her father said, was the devil. They discussed how best to kill Christian, then all danced with the devil. Elizabeth spoke of attending the other covens with her father, and at one of them meeting the much respected local midwife, Margaret Lang. Of all of those accused Margaret Lang seemed the most unlikely. Described as 'a comely woman with bright pink cheeks and kind blue eyes', she had practised her profession of midwife in the parish for the past thirty years and was known to all locally as 'a good woman and a true Christian'. But she too joined the others in the tollbooth.

The report of the Commissioners was taken to Edinburgh, and the Privy Council appointed a second Commission with powers to try any of the accused against whom the evidence was compelling. Because of the long list of names put forward by Christian, Elizabeth

Anderson and others, no less than twenty-four people were indicted for the crimes of witchcraft, sorcery, necromancy and charming. If any were found guilty, they were to be 'burned or otherwise put to death'.

On 18 March an advance party of five Commissioners arrived at the council chamber in Renfrew where the remit of the Privy Council was read out. Two days later Christian Shaw, whose fits and hallucinations had continued unabated since the previous August, suffered what was to be the last of them. For her, no doubt, the arrival of the Commission meant that salvation was at hand: those who had tormented her would be brought to book and punished. At any rate, she was never troubled by hallucinations or fits or discharging artifacts from her mouth again.

The Commissioners had brought advocates for the prosecution and they reduced the list of twenty-four to seven: Katherine Campbell, Agnes Naismith, Margaret Fulton, Margaret Lang, the brothers John and James Lindsay of Formakin and John Lindsay of Barloch. Because of her age, Elizabeth Anderson was fortunate not to be included. The seven were first required to recite by heart the Lord's Prayer at which many of them stumbled, and then to undergo the ritual of 'pricking'. The accused had bandages placed over their eyes and their clothing pulled back to reveal shoulders and legs. The pricker, described as 'a thin old man with the face of a death's head' had equipped himself with cast-iron (yetlin) pins 3 inches long.

Agnes Naismith was his first victim. He pierced a brown mole, hard to the touch, on her left shoulder, then again into her right leg as far as the bone without her crying out or being aware of it. It was the same with the brothers Lindsay. While a pin thrust into Margaret Lang's shoulder could not penetrate a horn mark more than half an inch, and bent when leaned on. When the bandages were taken from the accused's eyes, they were astonished to find the pins still sticking in them and to see them withdrawn without loss of blood. Such an unnatural phenomenom, it was claimed, proved them to be witches and warlocks.

After the prosecution had outlined its case, Mr James Robertson, for the defence, attacked the flimsiness of the evidence. Stories of meeting with the devil were incapable of proof. Nor had the indictment mentioned on what days and at what times the alleged crimes had taken place, thus depriving the prisoners of the defence

77

of alibi. The best authorities had declared that witches were never to be condemned until they had confessed and even then their confessions must be corroborated by external evidence. Where was that evidence?

Francis Grant for the prosecution rose to rebut. This was not a case of hearsay evidence. Witnesses had testified at being present at meetings of witches and had seen the accused there, plotting their evil deeds. Satan, he said, had carried them there in his hurricanes. 'The experience and observation of the wisest divines, lawyers, philosophers, statesmen, judges and historians at home and abroad,' he concluded, 'beside the testimony of witches everywhere, make the apparitions of witches common and most real.'

The Commissioners found there was a case to answer, a jury of fifteen were empanelled, and the prosecution called its witnesses. The Revd Andrew Turner, the Bargarran's minister, testified how Christian in her fits had named all of the accused, particularly Katherine Campbell and Margaret Lang, and had admitted to dancing in a ring of witches. Other witnesses testified that Margaret Lang was a sorcerer and had cast spells on people. Elizabeth Anderson was also called, the formerly ill-kempt beggar girl now dressed in her Sunday best with her dark brown hair bound neatly in a snood, the very paragon of respectability. She had been at six meetings of witches, she said, and all the accused had been present.

Mr Grant made his closing speech for the prosecution and Lord Blantyre charged the jury to deliver a verdict. He does not, however, seem to have summed up. Perhaps as an educated man and one before his time, he felt that the charges should never have been brought. Unable to say so, he may have thought it better to say nothing.

Next day, the jury brought in verdicts of guilty against all the accused. 'The commissioners of Justiciary', said Lord Blantyre, 'decree and adjudge [he then named the defendants] to be taken to the gallows green of Paisley upon the second Thursday of June next being the tenth day of the month betwixt two and four in the afternoon and there to be strangled at a stake till they be dead, and their bodies immediately to be burnt to ashes upon the said place, and all their moveable goods and gear to be escheat and inbrought to his Majesty's use, which is pronounced for doom.'

*    *    *

Such was the fame engendered by the trial and conviction of the Paisley witches that early in the morning of 10 June groups of people from all over the west of Scotland began converging on the gallows green to witness their execution; from Glasgow and Ayr and Lanark they came; by ferry across the river from Dumbarton and Helensburgh. It was a warm, sunny summer's day, and many had made it a family occasion bringing their children and picnics, to while away the hours until the time appointed for the executions.

Some spectators who wanted to get an early view of the seven, took up positions in the High Street, along which the prisoners would have to pass on their way from the tollbooth to the green. Their patience was rewarded a little before 1 p.m. when a drummer followed by two bailies in beaver hats took up positions at the prison gates. The gates were opened and the little knot of prisoners guarded by soldiers and with hands tied behind their backs walked slowly out. The three Lindsays came first, all well dressed, and then the women: the old crones Margaret Fulton and Agnes Naismith who seemed oblivious of their situation, then Katherine Campbell, deathly white and with her matted hair falling over her face as she kept her eyes on the ground, and lastly Margaret Lang the midwife, thin and pale with her grey hair uncombed, but the only one of the party to hold herself upright and to walk with a steady step. So great were the crowds that the soldiers were continually having to push them back to make a pathway for the prisoners.

An even greater crowd surrounded the scaffold on the green and beside it the peat fire on which the bodies would be burnt. One observer noted how many of the crowd were women. In a good position for watching the proceedings stood three or four noblemen's coaches whose owners were entertaining their friends.

Two ministers of religion had been allotted to each of the prisoners, and as the bailies called out their names, they moved across to join them. One of the ministers appointed to attend James Lindsay was the Revd James Stirling. Indicating the gallows, he warned his charge that that was the pathway to hell. Yet it could be the pathway to Heaven. Had not the time come, he asked – and it was said as much for his own peace of mind as his charge's – to confess and ask for God's forgiveness? Such was the fear of eternal hellfire in those days that James asked his brother John whether, even in the knowledge of their innocence, they should not confess and obtain salvation.

But John was adamant: No, they were not guilty, they must never confess.

The town hangman, a chimney-sweep, led the brothers on to the scaffold and tied napkins over their eyes. The crowd expected a farewell speech and were disappointed when the pair raised their arms to show the hangman they were ready. Then, as they clutched each other's bodies in their last moments on earth, the hangman cast them over the ladder. Presently their bodies hung limp. The hangman's assistants cut them down and placed them beside the smouldering peat fire.

Next in line was John Lindsay of Barloch attended by the Revd James Hutcheson. How did he come to be in this situation, the minister asked? He had no idea, he said. He knew nothing of witchcraft, had never been to a witches' meeting nor kept company with those who had. Why, he asked, had God allowed him to be persecuted in this way? The minister said he did not know, but urged his charge to say to the crowd before he died what he had just said to him. So they mounted the scaffold together and when the drum fell silent to allow John Lindsay to speak, he said in a voice faltering with emotion that as he was about to face his maker, he was guiltless of the crimes held against him. Then he too was launched into eternity.

But his words had made the crowd uneasy. He had been the only one of the condemned not to have been found guilty unanimously. Was it possible that he had been speaking the truth? Had they witnessed a miscarriage of justice, as had happened at the trials of witches in the past? If not, why had the Revd James Hutcheson supported him so openly?

Speculation ended when the first of the two old women, Margaret Fulton, mounted the scaffold. By this time her mind seemed to have gone. Asked by her ministers to make the choice between heaven and hell, she only laughed. In Elfland, where the fairy folk were about to take her, there was no talk of such places. It was as if she could not get there soon enough. The hangman launched her from the ladder and her emaciated body, like her mind, was at once bereft of life.

Now it was the turn of Agnes Naismith whose white hair, wrinkled face and bent form wrapped in tattered plaid seemed almost a replica of the woman who had preceded her. But unlike Margaret Fulton and the Lindsays, Agnes was determined to give the crowd a piece of her mind. 'Stay your hand, sir,' she said to the hangman, 'for I hae that to say to the fine leddies and gentlemen and the folk come here to see me dee, that they will mind in fear and sorrow till the end of their days.'

She was but a poor widow woman, she said, obliged to beg for her bread for many years and who had been shown little mercy by God or man. People had grudged the alms they had given her, and she had been turned away from many a kitchen door. All that she had left was her life and now they were going to take that too. Well, there had been many times when she had wished to die, but never so much as now when she could put a dying woman's curse on so great a gathering. 'May you drag out your days in dread of the wrath to come and may the devil cast you into the lake of everlasting fire.' As she was cast over the ladder, a solitary crow flew out of a blue sky, alighted on the gallows for an instant and was gone. Some said it was the devil come for his own.

There remained only two to go: Katherine Campbell aged twenty and Margaret Lang, more than sixty. Months in prison had reduced Katherine from a strong, sturdy Highland girl to a pale and sickly-looking wench. But she still had fight in her, throwing herself against the hangman and screaming insults. He beckoned to an assistant to tie the noose around her neck, and then someone in the crowd shouted, 'Let her speak!'

She did, and many of those present, aghast that one so young and far from home had to die, would remember for years to come what she said and how she said it; 'Oh, sirs,' she cried, 'would you stand by and see a young lass hanged?' What had they taken from the old women who had gone before but a year or two of pain and misery? But from her they were taking her youth and strength, the husband and children she might have had.

In a high, wailing voice she made plain her grief to all. 'Now I maun sing my ain coronach [funeral lament] alane amang strangers. Woe on the day I left my home and my kin and sought the cruel Lowlands, where a chance word in anger to a lady's child can bring trouble and death to the poor and friendless. Oh, that I could be a bird, to fly away and never tire till I perched on my ain rooftree.' Some in the crowd were weeping undisguisedly. 'Keep your tears,' she cried to them, 'they'll do no good for you or me. Let me go free and I promise you, you'll never see hint nor hair of me again.'

There were murmurings in the crowd and one or two scuffles, as though some wanted to grant the poor girl her request. Before it could get out of hand one of the bailies instructed the hangman to go ahead; and seeing him coming, Katherine let out a hideous scream. And then a shocking thing happened. As the wretched girl was thrown over the ladder, the scream dying in her mouth, she caught hold of the side of it so that her head became wedged between two of the rungs. There was a gasp of horror from the crowd, then the hangman threw her clear. But for many of the spectators the ordeal of Katherine Campbell had been altogether too much; several fainted and had to be laid on the grass.

Lastly it was the turn of Margaret Lang. The Revd Andrew Turner had known and admired her all his life, indeed their paths had crossed in many homesteads when he arrived to baptize the infant she had just delivered. He still believed she was here because of some dreadful mistake, and so could not bring himself to ask her to confess to something he knew she hadn't done. His colleague however beavered away in his efforts to save her soul. 'Ask and it shall be given you,' he said, 'knock and it shall be opened unto you.' Even now it was not too late.

His pleas were cut short by the summons of the hangman. The ministers helped Margaret on to the scaffold, and she turned to address the crowd.

It was not seemly, she said, for a woman to speak in public, but her case was extraordinary. When she was young she had committed 'the unnatural sin' (sodomy?) and given herself to the devil, a commitment she had never renounced because of her great fear of him. But as to the charge which had brought her here, that of renouncing her baptism in Bargarran yard, entering into a new covenant with the devil and receiving his mark, that she absolutely denied.

Then she prayed; for Bargarran's family and her own and for the prosperity of the Church and its ministers; and as a sinner herself she exhorted the young to beware of all sin, 'especially the scandalous and lustful'. Her final words were, 'I'll walk through this last step of death by faith and dependence on Jesus Christ.' Then the hangman seized and despatched her.

If awe, pity, horror had been some of the emotions felt by the spectators that sunny June afternoon on the gallows green of Paisley, there was one other predominant – unease, coupled with disappointment. They had come to the gallows green not only to see the wicked punished but to hear them confess, hear from their own lips of the wickedness they had practised and would no more, thus enabling the living to sleep easier in their beds at night.

In court their guilt had been proved beyond doubt, so why hadn't they confessed? Why choose hellfire and the bottomless pit when a confession and repentance could bring them to the portals of Heaven and God's forgiveness, to the means of grace and the hope of glory? It seemed so unnatural. They did not ask themselves a further question which was why it should matter to them whether the seven confessed or not. The answer to that was too uncomfortable to entertain. Could it be that the seven were innocent? Had there been a terrible mistake?

If such thoughts were occupying the minds of those present, they were given further emphasis by the enactment of the last of the day's rites. For the bodies of the seven had been thrown on to their funeral pyre and covered in tar to make them burn quicker; and soon to the nostrils of those who had not already left the field came the sweet, sickly, unforgettable stench of roasting human flesh.

Yet the majority of those who wended their way home that evening believed they had seen a good job done: witches were evil creatures, the devil's own, and these had been given their just deserts, as the Bible said they should. Who among them could have prophesied that, within the lifetimes of many, witches, like Auld Clootie himself, would be seen as no more than figments of a fanciful imagination, and the execution of the seven, as the English saw it at the time, as a glaring example of Scottish backwardness and bigotry.

The last witchcraft trial in Scotland took place in 1727 when the sheriff-depute of Dornoch sentenced an old woman to be strangled for turning her daughter into a pony. In that same year one of Scotland's greatest sons, the young David Hume, himself as committed a non-believer as the itinerant beggar Alexander Anderson, was about to embark on his brilliant philosophical career.

There was some relaxation of Sabbatarianism when James VI restored the Scottish episcopacy (and the Archbishop of St Andrews played his round of golf) but under Cromwell came new and fiercer restrictions. No-one on the Sabbath was permitted to frequent taverns, to dance, to listen to profane music, to wash, to brew ale, to bake bread, to travel or to do any worldly business. These laws had the full backing of burgh authorities and kirk sessions, some of which tried to go one better, as for instance when a kirk session in Fife punished children for playing on the Sabbath and later gave a public warning against carrying in water, sweeping the house or putting out ashes.

Some ignored these restrictions with impunity; the nobility at one end of the social scale and the vagrants at the other, the Highlanders who in their fastnesses were a law unto themselves and took a dram or two with their ministers on a Sunday; and fishermen, millers and farmers whose livelihood depended on them treating the Sabbath the same as any other day. Gradually, as the seventeenth century gave way to the eighteenth, the most extreme of the measures forbidding Sunday activities were either repealed or fell into disuse. But the lesser of them lingered on into the twentieth century, so that observance of the Lord's Day in Scotland became more marked than anywhere in Europe, and it was the last vestiges of it that I encountered in pre-war Islay. Osgood Mackenzie in his book *A Hundred Years in the Highlands* tells how in Wester Ross the farm-hands on the Sabbath thought it immoral to load turnips for the sheep into the customary wheelbarrows, which they would then have to push, yet had no objections to carrying to the fields a few turnips at a time in their arms, thus hugely and needlessly increasing their hours of labour.

The preaching of sermons was at the heart of Presbyterianism, both the Scots tongue and the latent theatricality of the Scots character being well suited for the dire warnings as to what awaited those who transgressed. You could choose Satan, to many as real a person as Jesus, or you could choose God. If the latter, you would find yourself at journey's end in the bosom of Abraham. If you were a sinner there was time for repentance, and there was no-one the Lord loved more than a sinner eager to repent. If you chose to continue in Satan's ways, then hell-fire and damnation awaited you.

What was entirely missing in the character of the average seventeenth-century Church of Scotland minister was the sort of loving kindness towards his flock which had begun to characterize the Church of England parson of the same period, often regarded by his parishioners as mentor, comforter and friend. Most Scots clergy of the time would, I think, have been mystified by the metaphysical poems of George Herbert, rector of Bemerton in Wiltshire, especially the one entitled *Love*.

Centuries of condemnatory preaching, with its vivid imagery and dramatic and doom-laden delivery, left its mark on the Scottish character. As Professor Smout says, it tended to make people feel guilty who did not feel puritan. It also helped to breed what Smout calls 'the serious-minded strain in the Scottish character', the belief that life was a pilgrimage and that those bound for Heaven were those who on earth had exhibited personal piety, sober conduct, frugality, industriousness, fulfilment of the duties of their social position, and scrupulous observance of the sabbath. For many a Scottish middle-class male this ideal proved too exacting a burden to shoulder unaided, which is why in every major Scottish city brothels have always been available for the pious to obtain relief.

Yet although in essence repressive I believe that on balance the puritan ideal in Scotland has been beneficial, leading to thrift, diligence, intellectual integrity and sound judgement: without these attributes I doubt if Scots the world over would have achieved what they have achieved. Professor Smout goes further, believing that towards the end of the eighteenth century, the forces of Calvinism which until then had seen life as a religious journey, could now be utilized as a spur to the economic and cultural opportunities that presented themselves.

> The single-minded drive in business, farming and trade in the 18th century, and which appeared in cultural matters in men as diverse as Adam Smith, James Watt and Sir Walter Scott, is strangely reminiscent of the energy of the 17th-century elders in the kirk when they set about imposing discipline on the congregation. Calvinism thus seems to have been released as a psychological force for secular change just at the moment when it was losing its power as a religion.

Calvinism, says Smout, did not 'cause' economic growth or the Enlightenment. Rather it meant that when conditions were ready for the Scots to exploit, they were ready to exploit them. And one aspect of the Scottish character ripe for exploitation was their genius for facts and figures. It was not chance that it was Scotsmen who founded the Banks of England and of France, produced the first *Encyclopaedia Brittannica*, the first National Statistical Survey, and invented logarithms;* not chance that in matters of banking, life assurance and fund management Edinburgh was to become and has remained one of the leading financial centres of Europe.

*By Napier of Merchiston after whom a new Edinburgh university has recently been named.

We made an excursion to the west, to Fort William and
Mallaig, and sailed up from Mallaig to the Isle of Skye. I liked it
very much. It rains and rains, and the white wet clouds blot over
the mountains. But we had one perfect day, blue and iridescent,
with the bare northern hills sloping green and sad and velvety
to the silky blue sea. There is still something of an Odyssey
up there, in among the islands and the silent lochs; like the
twilight morning of the world, the herons fishing undisturbed
by the water, and the sea running far in, for miles, between
the wet, trickling hills, where the cottages are low and almost
invisible, built into the earth.

D. H. Lawrence, *Letters*

# INTERLUDE

FROM ISLAY AT THE END OF AUGUST 1939 I WENT TO SKYE, FOR A WEEK of fishing and the Portree Games and balls. Astride Skye's centre are ranged the Red Hills and the magnificent Cuillins; and matching them in scale the heavily indented coastline some of whose long sea lochs almost cut the island in two and in one of which before the war wild oysters could be gathered in their hundreds. There are dramatic things to see in Skye: the mysterious, hidden Loch Coruisk, tucked away in the lee of the southern Cuillins and immortalized by Turner, the stark granite figure of the Old Man of Storr on the north-east coast, cousin to Orkney's Old Man of Hoy, looking eastwards across the Sound of Raasay; and the view northwards from the little coast road on the southernmost peninsula that runs from Ord to Tarskavaig, in the foreground the blue waters of Lochs Slapin and Eishort and beyond the huge and naked Cuillins.

In recent years the composition of Skye's population has changed dramatically. Until well into the twentieth century the inhabitants were native born. Today less than half are, the majority being Lowland Scots or English. As native residents have moved from outlying areas into urban centres like Portree or Broadford, their houses and crofts have been acquired by southerners, either as places of retirement or to run as guest houses for the summer tourist trade; another example of Scotland's increasing anglicization. Two English-women in particular have made a success of catering in Skye. One is Claire Macdonald the wife of Lord Macdonald, 22nd hereditary chief of the Clan Macdonald, lineal descendant of Somerled Macdonald of the Isles, who live at Kinloch Lodge on the Sound of Sleat which they run as a small, successful upmarket hotel; and Claire's books on Scots cooking have won an international reputation. At the other end of the island, on the shores of Loch Bay, Margaret Greenhalgh and her husband, Peter, a middle-aged couple from Lancashire, have created what has been acclaimed the best (though also small) seafood restaurant in the west of Scotland. Why have the Scots, so talented in other fields, not also flourished in the home catering trade? A legacy of Calvinism perhaps, the belief that it is unseemly, if not immoral, to show public enthusiasm for food?

There were some 20,000 people living in Skye at the end of the eighteenth century – under half that now. Then the common language was Erse or Gaelic (today the distinguished writer on Scottish history, John Prebble, goes one better and calls it Irish!). School lessons, though, were already being taught in English, so that in time fewer and fewer people spoke only Gaelic. Today about half the native islanders speak Gaelic but there is not one who cannot speak English too; among them Sorley MacLean, arguably Scotland's greatest living poet, whose Gaelic verses have been translated into fifteen languages, including Chinese.

It was to arrest the decline of Gaelic ('languages', said Dr Johnson, 'are the pedigree of nation') that in 1976 the Scottish business man Ian Noble founded a Gaelic college, formerly the steading of a farm at Ostaig near the Macdonald estate of Armadale on the peninsula of Sleat. Its director, Norman Gillies, a Skye man himself, speaks of the college's purpose. 'Firstly to teach the history of the Highlands, who we are and where we came from. My generation was educated out of Gaelic, out of crofting. It was a shame really. Not speaking Gaelic was to help us get on, not hold us back.' A Skye woman student echoed him. 'My parents spoke Gaelic to each other but not to me. They thought it second-rate.'

'Our aim', said Norman, 'is to teach Gaelic to whoever wants to learn it, whether Scots or foreigners. To train Gaelic teachers to teach it in Highland schools. And with a long-term business course which includes accountancy, law and so on, to help to slow down the continuing emigration of Skye people to Edinburgh, Glasgow and the south.'

The business course has been highly successful, 90 per cent of the students who passed having found professional employment in the Highlands and Islands; while a doctor on a shorter course, appointed to the outer isles, said he felt his patients might be more at ease with him if able to converse in their native tongue. Others who speak no Gaelic want their children to speak it, so that every year the incidence of teaching Gaelic in the state schools in the Highlands is increasing, though the rate of increase depends on the speed at which qualified teachers can be turned out.

For any patriotic Scot it is good to know that those at Ostaig are committed to preserving and expanding the use of Gaelic, and that the broadcasting authorities in Glasgow are following suit. This does not, and should not mean that, as in Ireland, the highways and byways of Scotland will be littered with Gaelic signposts and that on all official forms and in all official business Gaelic should have the same standing as English. But that it should survive as a point of reference for our culture, as a landmark of a past that has affected us all, whether we know it or not, seems desirable. It is a tiny brake on the all-pervading tide of anglicization, it is still a part of that singularity that makes us Scots.

# PART 2

## *Dr Johnson and Mr Boswell*

# CHAPTER 5

## *London*

TWO OF THE MOST DISTINGUISHED OF PAST VISITORS TO SKYE WERE the Englishman Samuel Johnson and the Scot James Boswell; and for the history of the island towards the end of the eighteenth century one could hardly have better guides than the twin accounts of their visit there in 1773: Johnson's *A Journey to the Western Islands of Scotland* and Boswell's *The Journal of a Tour to the Hebrides*. These two books, so different in style and content – Johnson's dealing mostly in generalities, philosophical, at times rather patronizing and often quite dull, Boswell's more concerned with minutiae, particularly relationships, graphic, lively and shot through with humour – opened for the first time the eyes of many in the south as to what the Highlands and islands were like; for, as the doctor said, even to the Scottish lowlanders the Highlands were as remote as Borneo or Sumatra.

But before we join the two of them in Skye, and because Boswell, in my view, was the liveliest Scots writer of English we have ever had, because also his biography of Johnson stands unrivalled of its kind, first a word about how they met and came together and planned the Scottish trip.

The son of a Scottish judge whose family had been granted the estate of Auchinleck in Ayrshire and who took the courtesy title of Auchinleck on elevation to the bench, James Boswell was educated at Mundell's School, Edinburgh and both Edinburgh University and Glasgow University. From an early age he had a rootless, restless temperament, wanting first to be a priest then a soldier and in the end (and to ensure his father's continuing his allowance) settling for the law and living in his father's house in Edinburgh. An avid reader, he had first become aware of Johnson's fame through his prolific writings, in particular articles and reviews in *The Gentleman's Magazine* and *The Rambler* and the famous Dictionary. In these he found what he called 'delight and instruction' and supposed the author to live 'in the immense metropolis of London'.

His curiosity was aroused further in the summer of 1761 when he was twenty-one by the arrival in Edinburgh of a friend of Johnson, the Irish actor Thomas Sheridan, father of the playwright, Richard Brinsley Sheridan. He had come to give a series of lectures on the English language and public speaking, the object being to render the heavily accented speech of so many Scots comprehensible to the English so that in seeking new markets and opportunities south of the border, they could better understand and be understood. 'I was often in his company,' wrote Boswell, 'and heard him frequently expatiate upon Johnson's extraordinary knowledge, talent and virtues, repeat his pointed sayings, describe his peculiarities and boast of his being his guest sometimes till two or three in the morning.' When Boswell came to London, Sheridan assured him, he would have many opportunities of meeting Johnson at his house.

Unfortunately for Boswell, when he did visit London the following year, he found that Sheridan and Johnson had quarrelled and were no longer on speaking terms. Happily another friend of Johnson, the actor Thomas Davies who kept a bookshop in Covent Garden, came into Boswell's life and promised to effect an introduction. Davies had collected many of the doctor's sayings and, said Boswell, was one of the best of the many imitators of his voice and manner. 'He increased my impatience more and more to see the extraordinary man whose works I highly valued and whose conversation was reported to be so peculiarly excellent.'

The long-awaited meeting took place on 16 May 1763 when Johnson came into Davies's bookshop where Boswell was taking tea in the back parlour with Davies and his pretty actress wife.

Through the glass window separating the living quarters from the shop, Boswell recognized the doctor's figure from the portrait painted by his friend, Sir Joshua Reynolds. Davies, said the nervous Boswell, 'announced his awful approach' in the manner of Horatio announcing to Hamlet the approach of his father's ghost – 'Look, my lord, it comes'.

Davies introduced them. 'I was much agitated,' said Boswell, 'and recollecting his prejudices against the Scotch, of which I had heard much, I said to Davies, "Don't tell him where I come from." ' But Davies refused to help and cried out ('roguishly', said Boswell), 'from Scotland,' which led Boswell to add weakly, 'Mr Johnson, I do indeed come from Scotland but I cannot help it.' Later Boswell tried to explain, not very convincingly, that he had not intended to denigrate his own country but as a light pleasantry to soothe the older man. But for Johnson it was an invitation to characteristic wit. 'That, sir, I find, is what a very great many of your countrymen cannot help.'

Although stunned by the retort, Boswell was still eager to make his mark. When Johnson turned to Davies to criticize the actor David Garrick for refusing him a three shilling ticket for a play, Boswell piped up ingratiatingly with, 'Oh, sir, I cannot think Mr Garrick would grudge such a trifle to you.' To which the doctor crushingly replied, 'Sir, I have known David Garrick longer than you have done, and I know no right you have to talk to me on the subject.'

Too late Boswell regretted his presumption. 'I now felt myself much mortified and began to think that the hope which I had long indulged of obtaining his acquaintance was blasted. And in truth had not my ardour been uncommonly strong and my resolution uncommonly persevering, so rough a reception might have deterred me for ever from making any further attempts.'

So Boswell, as he put it, remained upon the field, and before leaving, regrettably, for another engagement, 'ventured to make an observation now and then, which he received very civilly, so that I was satisfied that though there was a roughness in his manner, there was no ill nature in his disposition.' And when at the door he spoke to Davies of the hard blows he had received, Davies consoled him by saying, 'Don't be uneasy. I can see he likes you very well.'

A week later and with Davies's approval, Boswell called on Johnson at his chambers in No. 1 Inner Temple Lane; and (for the doctor cared nothing for externals) was much struck by the uncouthness of his apartment, furniture and dress. 'His brown suit of clothes looked very rusty; he had on a little old shrivelled unpowdered wig, which was too small for his head; his shirt-neck and knees of his breeches were loose; his black worsted stockings ill drawn up; and he had a pair of unbuckled shoes by way of slippers. But all these slovenly particularities were forgotten when he began to speak.' And, Boswell might have added, when he himself began to record. For despite the thirty-one year gap between them, gaps too in the frequencies of their meetings, this was the genesis of a relationship that was to grow closer as time went on and leave a legacy of biography and autobiography outstanding in English literature. It could be said to have been sealed when they dined together a month after their first meeting. 'Sir,' said Johnson, 'I am glad we have met. I hope we shall pass many evenings and mornings too, together.' Boswell added, 'We finished a couple of bottles of port, and sat till between one and two in the morning.'

During the next ten years Boswell was partly in Edinburgh practising (without much success) his profession of advocate, partly on travels abroad and partly in London. 'He lives among savages in Scotland,' commented Johnson, 'and among rakes in London.' Much of his London life was punctuated by drinking, often to excess, gambling and womanizing; and in his journals every vividly described fall from grace is invariably followed by expressions of guilt and remorse and resolutions to lead a worthier life in future. Yet what is remarkable about Boswell as a writer is his ability to set out in felicitous prose not only the moral, religious, intellectual and social arguments of the day, as recorded in the conversations of Johnson and others, but in equally attractive language to give accounts of sexual forays which in other hands would be crude and distasteful. This account of his night of love with Mrs Louisa Lewis, the actress, is one that my wife and I include in our regular poetry recitals: audiences, I have noticed, hang on every anticipatory word, and any applause at the end is a measure of their relief at having listened to a graphic account of sexual congress without (as they might have expected) finding it unacceptable.

Louisa and I agreed that at eight at night she would meet me in the Piazzas of Covent Garden. At the appointed hour I went there and sauntered up and down for a while in a sort of trembling suspense, I know not why. At last my charming companion appeared, and I immediately conducted her to a hackney-coach which I had ready waiting, pulled up the blinds, and away we drove to the destined scene of delight, the Black Lion Hotel. We contrived to seem as if we had come off a journey, and carried in a bundle our nightclothes, handkerchiefs, and other little things. We also had with us some almond biscuits, or as they call them in London, macaroons, which looked like provisions on the road.

On our arrival at the hotel we were shown into the parlour, in the same manner that any decent couple would be. I here thought proper to conceal my own name (which the people of the house had never heard) and assumed the name of Mr Digges. That Ceres and Bacchus might in moderation lend their assistance to Venus, I ordered a genteel supper and some wine.

We supped cheerfully and agreeably and drank a few glasses, and then the maid came and put the sheets, well aired, upon the bed. I now contemplated my fair prize. Louisa is just twenty-four, of a tall rather than short figure, finely made in person, with a handsome face and an enchanting languish in her eyes. She dresses with taste. She has sense, good humour, and vivacity, and looks quite a woman in genteel life. As I mused on this elevating subject, I could not help being somehow pleasingly confounded to think that so fine a woman was at this moment in my possession, that without any motives of interest she had come with me to an inn, agreed to be my intimate companion, as to be my bedfellow all night, and to permit me the full enjoyment of her person.

I came softly into the room, and in a sweet delirium slipped into bed and was immediately clasped in her snowy arms and pressed to her milk-white bosom. Good heavens, what a loose did we give to amorous dalliance! The friendly curtain of darkness concealed our blushes. In a moment I felt myself animated with the strongest powers of love, and, from my dearest creature's kindness, had a most luscious feast. Proud of my godlike vigour, I soon resumed the noble game. I was in full glow of health. Sobriety had preserved me from effeminacy and weakness, and my bounding blood beat quick and high alarms. A more voluptuous night I never enjoyed. Five times was I fairly lost in supreme rapture. Louisa was madly fond of me; she declared I was a prodigy, and asked me if this was not extraordinary for human nature. I said twice as much might be, but this was not, although in my own mind I was somewhat proud of my performance. She said it was what there was no just reason to be proud of. But I told her I could not help it. She said it was what we had in common with the beasts. I said no. For we had it highly improved by the pleasures of sentiment. I asked her what she thought enough. She gently chid me for asking such questions, but said two times.

In many accounts of his sexual excursions Boswell tells us whether or not he was 'armoured', i.e. wearing a contraceptive. For many years I wondered what form, in the days before vulcanized rubber, this took until a recent book on the history of medicine by Dr Richard Gordon enlightened me. It seems there were two kinds of armour: one fashioned from a sheep's bladder and which — a sporty touch — could be decorated with regimental colours; the other sort, made of linen, had to be wetted before use and afterwards could be rinsed out and cleaned for further use by a woman in St Martin's Lane. For his encounter with the fair Louisa, Boswell saw no need to don armour with the consequence that six weeks later he found, and not for the first time, that he had caught the pox (gonorrhoea). Knowing that he had had no other woman during the past two months, he taxed her with it and to his surprise found her equally assertive of innocence ('Sir, I will confess to you that about three years ago I was very bad. But for these fifteen months I have been quite well. I appeal to God Almighty that I am speaking true; and for these six months I have had to do with no man but yourself'). And yet Boswell's surgeon, Andrew Douglas, had assured him that she could not have been unaware of her condition. Would modern medical opinion, one wonders, given Boswell's self-described symptoms ('damned twinges, scalding heat, deep-tinged loathsome matter') confirm the view of Dr Douglas?*

It was Boswell's ambition, rare among Scots, to be a man of the world who might savour the delights of cosmopolitan society by blending into it as invisibly as possible; and to this end, when in Edinburgh, he took further lessons in elocution from a Mr Love,

*Apparently not. According to medical opinion today, the infection could have lain dormant within her, and she unaware of it.

a Drury Lane actor who was playing there. As a result Dr Johnson found his accent 'not offensive', though Eton-educated Sir Alexander Macdonald of Sleat in Skye sometimes took it on himself to correct it. That he never rid himself of it entirely is proof of the doctor's dictum that when a man has got the better of losing nine-tenths of his accent and realizes that it is not disagreeable, he relaxes his diligence and no longer wants his friends to tell him where he has gone wrong.

Boswell himself deplored attempts at absolute perfection, at what he called High English which to his ears sounded 'exceedingly disgusting' and which rendered those who practised it 'truly ridiculous'. One supposes he had in mind the guardians of Edinburgh middle-class gentility, the forerunners of Morningside and others who pronounce 'high' and 'boat' as 'hay' and 'bort' in much the same way as their English counterparts pronounce 'circumstance' as 'circum*starnce*' and 'golf' and 'involved' as 'goalf' and 'invoalved'.

And yet, Boswell found, Johnson's antipathy towards the Scots remained constant. In this, and particularly at this time, he was not alone among Englishmen. Pitt, the enormously popular war premier, had been displaced by Lord Bute, a Scot whose patronage in many people's views seemed to favour Scots disproportionately to the English, thus increasing the resentment southerners felt towards the increasing number of Scots seeking jobs in the south and, because of poverty, drive, and often a better education, finding them. They were crossing the border in droves, many pushily and assertively, forbears of those whom James Barrie called Scots on the make than which 'there are few sights more impressive'.

In the eyes of most Englishmen all foreigners were suspect and the Scots no exception – a race of barbarians inhabiting a wilderness to the north, a people who had once entered into an alliance with England's arch-enemy France, who throughout history had been a thorn in the sides of the peace-loving English and who in many people's lifetime and not so long ago, had sent an army into England to topple their king from his throne and replace him with their Stuart Pretender. And in 1762, as Boswell found at Covent Garden theatre, English resentment sometimes boiled over:

Just before the overture began to be played, two Highland officers came in. The mob in the upper gallery roared out, 'No

Scots! No Scots! Out with them,' hissed and pelted them with apples. My heart warmed to my countrymen, my Scotch blood boiled with indignation. I jumped up on the benches, roared out, 'Damn you, you rascals!', hissed and was in the greatest rage. I am very sure that at that time I should have been the most distinguished of heroes. I hated the English. I wished from my soul that the Union was broke and that we might give them another battle of Bannockburn.

I went close to the officers and asked them what regiment they were of. They told me Lord John Murray's and that they were just come from the Havana. 'And this', they said, 'is the thanks that we get – to be hissed when we come home. If it was the French, what could they do worse?' . . . The rudeness of the English vulgar is terrible. This indeed is the liberty they have; the liberty of bullying and being abusive with their blackguard tongues.

Although Boswell himself was spared from English strictures – Johnson and Garrick agreed he was 'the most unscottified of Scots' – to Johnson they remained 'a crafty, designing people, eagerly attentive to their own interests' and he particularly minded what he called 'the needy adventurers' who had had an English education yet who 'without talent or ambition lavished their fortunes in giving expensive entertainment to those who laugh at them'. One of their most striking characteristics, he noted (and it was all part of the pushiness), was never to take no for an answer. If, he said, an Englishman was up for election to a club and came to know that a certain member had voted against him, he would turn sulky in that member's presence and have nothing more to do with him. But if the candidate was a Scotchman, he 'though you vote nineteen times against him, will accost you with equal complaisance after each time, and the twentieth time he will get your vote.' Boswell himself was a perfect exemplar of this when, having been rebuffed twice by Johnson at their first meeting he was still determined to overcome any slights to gain his hero's attention.

The former Soviet Premier, Nikita Kruschev, once quoted a Russian proverb that every duck praises its own marsh, and it was this obsession of the Scots with the virtues of their native land combined with their clannishness that so riled Johnson. One evening a Scottish poet, the Revd John Ogilvie, was dining at the Mitre with Johnson, Boswell and others, and in the course of conversation bragged in a boring way about the richness of the soil in the neighbourhood of Edinburgh. The writer Oliver Goldsmith who was also present contested this, whereupon Ogilvie, disconcerted, shifted his ground, making the even more boring observation (and one can just hear an Edinburgh voice saying it) that at any rate Scotland had many noble wild prospects. This was too much for Johnson and the cue for the most famous of all his anti-Scots sallies. 'I believe, sir, you have a great many. Norway too has noble wild prospects and Lapland is remarkable for prodigious noble wild prospects. But, sir, let me tell you that the noblest prospect which a Scotchman ever sees is the high road that leads him to England.'

Johnson told Boswell that he was the only Scotchman he had ever met who did not keep bringing the name of another Scotchman into the conversation; and when he once did so to sing the praises of the Scottish-born English Lord Chief Justice, Lord Mansfield, Johnson would not allow Scotland any credit for it, Mansfield having been educated in England. 'Much', he added, 'may be made of a Scotsman if he be caught young.' On the whole Johnson found the Irish better mixers than the Scots and better actors too (it would be another 150 years before the Scots discovered their genius for comedy); though when the Bishop of Killaloe, Dr Barnard, told him of his fears that if ever the doctor visited Ireland, he would take as unfavourable a view of the Irish as he did of the Scots, Johnson was able to reassure him. 'The Irish', he said, 'are not in a conspiracy to cheat the world by false representations of the merits of their countrymen. No, sir. They are a fair people. *They never speak well of one another.*'

Yet most of his strictures were made in a light vein, what Boswell called good-humoured pleasantries: sallies about the Scots who emigrated to America and settled in barren parts because after Scotland, they did not realize they were barren; there being no cabbages in Scotland until Oliver Cromwell's soldiers brought them there; in the last war a French commander called Thurot plundered seven Scottish islands and came away with a total of three shillings and sixpence; the Scots lacked a sense of gaiety though he allowed Boswell to be an exception.

These remarks, said Boswell, were made in fun not anger; they came from the head not the heart. Nor were they personal. Of the six amanuenses who had helped him with his great dictionary five were Scots; two Macbeans, a Shiel, a Stewart and a Maitland. To all, said Boswell, he showed a never ceasing kindness and when they were in financial need, he saw to it that they were looked after.

At bottom it was Scots asserting their Scotchness that Johnson minded most, and he summed up his view with typical brevity and wit: 'When I find a Scotchman to whom an Englishman is as a Scotchman, that Scotchman shall be as an Englishman to me.' The English essayist Charles Lamb never found one. 'All my life,' he wrote towards the end of it, 'I have been trying to like Scotsmen, and am obliged to desist from the experiment in despair.'

But there were times when the boot was on the other foot; educated Scotsmen visiting the south had ample reasons for being equally riled. Of his time at school at Winchester, and in London in the 1730s, Lord Elcho had written:

> Nothing is baser or more pitiable than the abuse the English are in the habit of pouring on to the Scots, calling them 'beggars' because they are poorer than they, and Scotland a wretched country because it produces less wheat than England. If the same reason for despising a nation existed in Europe, the French would despise the English because England produces no wine, a beverage of which, by the way, the English are very fond.
>
> The Scots can boast of never having been conquered. They repulsed the Romans and the Danes, two nations who conquered England, as well as the Saxons and, in the last place, the Normans . . . The English cannot attack either the courage or the honesty or the intelligence of the Scots, and all other nations concede that the Scots surpass the English in gentleness and courtesy.

And in 1764 when David Hume was being lionized in Paris as a great *English* author he expressed his resentment in a letter to Gilbert Elliot, later Earl of Minto:

> I do not believe there is one Englishman in fifty who, if he heard that I had broke my neck tonight, would not be rejoiced with it. Some hate me because I am not a Tory, some because I am not a Whig, some because I am not a Christian and all because I am a Scotsman. Can you seriously

talk of my continuing an *Englishman*? Am I, or are you, an *Englishman*?*

Five years later and back in Edinburgh in semi-retirement, tranquil in the company of books and friends and, as he put it, done with all ambition, he could still write as he did to William Strahan.

> My ambition was always moderate and confined entirely to Letters: but it has been my misfortune to write in the language of the most stupid and factious barbarians in the world; and it is long since I have renounced all desire of their approbation which indeed could no longer give me pleasure or vanity.

A basinful of English stupidity was given to the Scottish novelist Tobias Smollett when he came to London in 1754 and joined a club of what would seem to have been Hooray Henries. Writing to Alexander Carlyle of his wish to be back in Scotland among friends, he went on:

> I am heartily tired of this land of indifference and Phlegm where the finer sensations of the soul are not felt, Felicity is held to consist in stupifying port and overgrown buttocks of beef, where Genius is lost, Learning undervalued . . . and Ignorance prevails to such a degree that one of our Chelsea club asked me if the weather was good when *I crossed the sea from Scotland*. Another desired to know if there were not more Popes than one inasmuch as he had heard people mention the Pope of Rome, which seemed to imply that there was a Pope in some other place. I answered that there was a Pope of Troy and another of Tartary and he seemed perfectly satisfied with the information which no person present pretended to contradict.

Always cognizant (how could he have avoided it?) that his friend was forming a wrong or at least a very one-sided impression

---

*Thirty years later Burns expressed the same view. 'Nothing can reconcile me to the common terms, "English Ambassador, English Court, etc . . ." Tell me, my friend, is this weak prejudice? I believe in my conscience such ideas as "my Country; her independence; her honour; the illustrious names that mark the history of my native land, etc." ' (Burns to Mrs Dunlop 1790).

of his country and countrymen, Boswell proposed that the doctor come to Edinburgh to meet some of its leading citizens and after to accompany him on a journey to some of Scotland's wilder and remoter parts. No doubt to his surprise the idea was favourably received, for as a boy Johnson had been given a copy of Martin's *Account of the Hebrides* by his father and, though poorly written, it had excited his curiosity. When Boswell was visiting Ferney in 1764 he spoke about the proposed trip to Voltaire who was as appalled as if the North Pole was to be their destination and hoped that Boswell would not insist on his going too. Johnson's health had prevented the journey taking place in 1772, but when Boswell was in London in the spring of 1773 a firm agreement was made for Johnson to travel north after the Court of Session had gone into autumn recess. It was on this visit that Boswell learned that he had been elected to the Literary Club, founded by Sir Joshua Reynolds and Johnson ten years earlier, and whose members included at one time or another David Garrick, Edmund Burke, R.B. Sheridan, Oliver Goldsmith, Dr Adam Smith, Sir William Hamilton, Sir John Hawkins, Sir Joseph Banks and Edward Gibbon — a company to which anyone would be proud to belong.

Thus Boswell achieved what had been a long held and deep-seated social ambition. 'It is certain I am not a great man', he had written with his usual honesty in 1764, 'but I have an enthusiastic love of great men and I derive a kind of glory from it.'

The club dined once a fortnight at one of London's West End taverns and seldom broke up until late. Boswell already knew most of the members and — another example of Scots perseverance — being determined to get in, shamelessly canvassed them. Johnson told him that that was how he was elected. 'Several of the members wished to keep you out. Burke told me, he doubted if you were fit for it; but now you are in none of them are sorry. Burke says that you have got so much good humour naturally, it is scarce a virtue.' Boswell said, 'They were afraid of you, sir, as it was you who proposed me,' to which Johnson rejoined that they knew that if they'd refused Boswell, they would probably never have got in another. *'I'd have kept them all out.'*

# CHAPTER 6

## *The Road to the Isles*

ON THE EVENING OF 14 AUGUST 1773 JOHNSON ARRIVED ON THE stagecoach from Newcastle at Boyd's Inn in Edinburgh's Canongate. His first impressions of Scotland can have done little to relieve his prejudices. Asking at the inn for his lemonade to be made sweeter, and having observed the waiter pick up a lump of sugar with greasy fingers and deposit it in his glass, he threw the drink out of the window; his travelling companion, a Mr Scott, said he thought that Johnson was going to knock the waiter down. Boswell, having had word of his arrival, went to the inn to collect him, and arm in arm they walked up the High Street, past the first high-rise flats in Europe, to Boswell's apartment in James's Court. But these were still the days of uncovered sewers and slops and effluvia being thrown into the street from six and seven storeys high, and though the magistrates had done much to curb the habit, the High Street stank from end to end. 'I smell you in the dark,' Johnson said to Boswell as they marched along. But he was good enough to admit that the breadth of the street and the loftiness of the buildings made a noble appearance.

Knowing of the doctor's partiality to tea, Boswell had arranged for his wife Margaret (a cousin to whom he had been married for four years) to have some waiting his arrival. As no man could be more polite when he chose, said Boswell, the doctor's conversation soon lulled her into a forgetfulness of his appearance. She even gave up her own bedroom to him, a sacrifice which Boswell described as one of a thousand obligations he owed her, the greatest, and despite his chronic unfaithfulness, her having agreed to be his wife.

In the journal that he was to publish of their tour Boswell gave the reader a run-down of Johnson's character and appearance: 'a sincere and zealous Christian of High Church and monarchical principles which he would not suffer tamely to be questioned; hard to please and easily offended, impetuous and irritable in his temper but of a most humane and benevolent heart; having a mind stored with a vast and various collection of learning and knowledge which he communicated with perspicuity and force in rich and choice expression.'

'He was conscious of his superiority. He loved praise when it was brought to him but was too proud to seek for it. He was somewhat susceptible of flattery. His mind was so full of imagery that he might have been perpetually a poet . . . He had a constitutional melancholy, the clouds of which darkened the brightness of his fancy and gave a gloomy cast to his whole course of thinking; yet . . . he frequently indulged himself in pleasantry and sportive sallies . . . He had a loud voice and a slow deliberate utterance, which no doubt gave additional weight to the sterling metal of his conversation . . . His person was large, robust, I may say approaching the gigantick, and grown unwieldy from corpulency . . . He was now in his sixty-fourth year and had become a little dull of hearing. His sight had always been somewhat weak; yet . . . his perceptions were uncommonly quick and accurate. His head, and also sometimes his body, shook with a kind of motion like the effects of a palsy; he appeared to be frequently disturbed by cramps or convulsive contractions of the nature of that distemper called St Vitus's dance . . . Upon this tour, when journeying, he wore boots and a very wide brown cloth great coat; and he carried in his hand a large English oak stick.'

From this description and of others of the great man, one gains the impression that sex was not a subject which had ever interested him, indeed that he was somehow above it. All the more pleasing therefore to record an occasion when the actor David Garrick had invited Johnson to spend some time in the Green Room during one of his plays. Asked how he had enjoyed it, he said he had been well entertained. Garrick said he hoped he would see him there often. 'No, David,' said the doctor, 'I will never come back. For the white bubbies and the silk stockings of your actresses excite my genitals.'

For three days the pair remained in Edinburgh, the Boswells inviting guests to meet the doctor at breakfast, dinner and supper; they included the Duchess of Douglas, Dr Robertson, the historian and Principal of Edinburgh University (or College as it was then called), Adam Ferguson, Lord Chief Baron Ordc, Sir Adolphus Oughton the deputy Commander-in-Chief in Scotland, fellow advocates of Boswell and many others; and Dr Johnson was given his first taste of grouse which, said Boswell, was then abundant and in season.

One guest who Boswell might have invited but didn't was his friend and landlord in James' Court the philosopher David Hume: this was because he knew of Dr Johnson's disapproval of Hume's views on religion, and that on one occasion in London Johnson had walked out of a dinner to which Hume had also been invited, so strongly did he feel about Hume's denials of the existence of a Creator (though it seems they had previously been fellow guests at a party given by the Royal Chaplain at St James's Palace, without Johnson taking offence: perhaps he felt that if the chaplain could stomach Hume's company, the least he could do as a fellow guest was to follow suit). Hume himself liked Boswell: called him 'very good-humoured, very agreeable, very mad.'

Conversation on a score of topics flowed; the duties of lawyers, the art of acting, witchcraft, party politics; notables such as Burke who, said Johnson, lacked wit; Wesley, Garrick, Swift, the eccentric Scottish judge Lord Monboddo who believed that men once had tails and that orang-utans could be taught to speak. When Hume's name came up and Johnson inevitably ridiculed him, Boswell must have been glad that he had kept the two Titans apart. Of one evening's entertainment Johnson wrote, 'We had such a conflux of company that I could scarce support the tumult.'

One morning Boswell conducted Johnson and others on a sightseeing tour of the capital which included Holyroodhouse ('that deserted mansion of royalty' Boswell called it), the University, the church (designated Cathedral by Charles I in 1633) of St Giles, and opposite it the Parliament House where until 1707 the Scottish Parliament had met and was now part of the Court of Session; in the vaults beneath the Records of Scotland were awaiting transfer to Register House which the Adam brothers were then completing at the east end of Princes Street. In the same building was housed the famous Advocates' Library with its extensive collection of rare books; and it was here that Boswell, perhaps inevitably, turned his thoughts to the Scotland that had passed. By the union with England, he said, 'We were no more. Our independent kingdom was lost.'

Characteristically and unequivocally (for he was, so to speak, on enemy soil) Johnson refused to let this pass. 'Sir, never talk of your independency who could let your Queen remain twenty years in captivity and then be put to death, without even a pretence of justice, without your even attempting to rescue her; and such a Queen too! as every man of any gallantry would have sacrificed his life for.' Equally unequivocally Mr James Kerr, the Keeper of the Records, who was also present, said, 'Half our nation was bribed by English money.' 'That is no defence,' Johnson replied. 'That makes you worse.' The Keeper of the Advocates' Library, a Mr Brown, deeply embarrassed, said he thought it better to let the matter rest. But Boswell's blood was up and he told the doctor that he must have been glad that in the last war the Scots had helped the English fight their battles. Not even this silenced Johnson. 'We could have had you for the same price, though there had been no Union, as we might have had Swiss or other troops.' If the Scots wanted separation, he for his part was agreeable; and those of them who had come to England *had only to go home*. For Boswell this was too near the knuckle for comfort, so he rather feebly shifted his ground by saying that the last three Hanoverian kings had all guaranteed to maintain the Presbyterian establishment in Scotland; to which Johnson said, dismissively, 'We'll give you that into the bargain.'

On the morning of 18 August the two friends set off north, Boswell noting that his wife was uneasy at seeing them go. Accompanying them were Mr Nairne, an advocate friend of Boswell and later a judge, and Boswell's servant, Joseph Ritter, 'a Bohemian, a fine, stately fellow above six feet high who spoke many languages'. On grounds of economy Johnson had not brought his own black servant, and on Boswell's advice had also left behind a pair of pistols, gunpowder and bullets, having been assured there was no danger of meeting robbers on the way. Crossing the Firth of Forth they landed briefly on the deserted island of Inch Keith where Mary Queen of Scots was remembered by an inscription carved on the abandoned fort, MARIA RE 1564, and where Johnson, said Boswell, 'stalked like a giant among the luxuriant thistles and nettles'. Johnson had a thing about small islands, and this was the first of several on the tour that he said he would like to own. 'I'd build a house, make a good landing-place, have a garden and vines and all sorts of trees. A rich man of a hospitable turn would have many visitors from Edinburgh.' If Boswell found anything bizarre in the thought of vines flourishing on an exposed island in the windy east Firth of Forth, he does not mention it.

They travelled by way of St Andrews, Leuchars and Dundee to Aberdeen where Johnson was to be given the freedom of the city. At St Andrews he held forth to the professors and others on drinking and smoking. When ale was cheap and plentiful, he said, the *decent* people in his home town of Lichfield used to get drunk every night and were not thought any the worse for it. But with the coming of wine there was less drunkenness, as a bottle lasted longer. Smoking too had gone out. 'To be sure, it is a shocking thing, blowing smoke out of our mouths into other people's mouths, eyes and noses and having the same thing done to us.' Yet he thought it strange that it had gone out, for everyone needed something to calm themselves, such as beating with their feet (which was what he, a non smoker, was in the habit of doing). He also gave a curious interpretation of Sunday relaxation. 'People may walk about but should not throw stones at birds.' At Montrose he caught another waiter using his fingers to put a lump of sugar in his lemonade, but this time merely shouted at him, 'Rascal!' As they progressed northwards Johnson was forcibly impressed by the lack of trees on the Scottish east coast. 'There are none', he said, in his typically exaggerated way, 'between Berwick and Aberdeen.' By 'none', said Boswell, he meant only a few and of no great size, an inaccuracy for which some touchy Scots took him to task later.

En route to Aberdeen they turned off the highway to dine with James Burnett, Lord Monboddo, an old friend of Boswell's father, and fellow judge Lord Auchinleck.* It was a risky venture, for once

---

*Traditionally Scottish judges were and still are given the courtesy title of lord on elevation to the bench. For a long time however the courtesy did not extend to their wives with the result that when a judge went on circuit with his wife and they checked into a hotel as, say, Lord Grampian and Mrs Macturk, explanations had to be made. Later wives were permitted to share their husband's courtesy titles, e.g. Lord and Lady Grampian.

in London Monboddo had roused Johnson's wrath by suggesting that the life of a savage was preferable to that of a Londoner, and Boswell feared there might be another altercation. But Monboddo greeted them warmly at the gates of his dilapidated house, wearing what Boswell called a rustic suit and a little round hat, saying he was now Farmer Burnett and would give them a farmer's dinner. In the event the two got on famously and afterwards Monboddo directed his black servant Gory to conduct them to the high road. 'When Gory was about to part from us,' said Boswell, 'Dr Johnson called to him, "Mr Gory, give me leave to ask you a question. Are you baptized?" Gory told him he was and confirmed by the Bishop of Durham. He then gave him a shilling.'

At Aberdeen Johnson dined with the principal of the university and the professors, was given his first helping of Scotch broth and declared he didn't care how soon he had it again. In the town hall Provost Jupp presented him with the freedom of the town and proposed his health in the presence of the magistrates; afterwards the doctor was escorted on the traditional walk with his burgess ticket (the citation for the freedom) stuck in his hat according to custom.

Their next port of call was Slains Castle situated on a headland overlooking the sea and the seat of the Earl of Errol, the Hereditary Constable of Scotland. He was away dining with a neighbour but Lady Errol insisted they stay the night. The earl's brother, a Mr Boyd, was also there: he had come out for Prince Charles in the '45, then hid in the island of Arran for a year before undergoing twenty year's exile in France. In praising the virtues of his sister-in-law, he said that she did not use fear or force in educating her children. Johnson disagreed. 'Sir, she is wrong. I would rather have the rod to be the general terror of all, to make them learn, than tell a child, if you do thus or thus you will be more esteemed than your brothers or sisters.' Such a method, he said, made brothers and sisters hate each other. Boswell was much taken by a portrait of Lord Errol by Johnson's friend Reynolds and by a collection of Hogarth prints; and by 'the unaffected affability' of the earl himself when he arrived home in the early evening; though as he candidly admitted this was in some part due to his weakness in admiring persons of high birth.

And he went to bed, content.

I had a most elegant room; but there was a fire in it which blazed; and the sea, to which my windows looked, roared; and the pillows were made of the feathers of some sea-fowl which had to me a disagreeable smell; so that by all these causes, I was kept awake a good while. I saw in imagination Lord Errol's father, Lord Kilmarnock (who was beheaded on Tower Hill in 1746) and I was somewhat dreary. But the thought did not last long and I fell asleep.

At Banff they stayed at an indifferent inn where Johnson, a fiend for fresh air, found no sash-cords to open his bedroom window and again caused offence when he published his book on the tour by assuming that this was a uniquely Scottish deficiency (if only, commented Boswell, he had allowed him to read his book before printing it). At Cullen they stopped for breakfast where Johnson took a dim view of finnan haddie. 'They set down dried haddocks broiled along with our tea,' said Boswell. 'I ate one; but Dr Johnson was disgusted by the sight of them, so they were removed.' They took the same road as that of the Duke of Cumberland's army on its way to Culloden, through Fochaber, Elgin and Forres and, said Boswell, 'on the very heath where Macbeth met the witches' Johnson recited from the play – 'What are these, so withered and so wild in their attire? . . .' etc. 'His recitation', said Boswell, 'was grand and affecting.'

They moved on to Nairn which they found a miserable place (its days as the Brighton of the North were yet to come). Here Johnson first saw peat fires and first heard the Erse language. Then on along the coast to Cawdor and its castle and manse where they were welcomed by the Revd Kenneth Macaulay, brother of the Revd John Macaulay who we last met in Benbecula and who the travellers were to meet at Inveraray later on their tour. Kenneth Macaulay was the soi-disant author of a book on the island of St Kilda, which the travellers suspected had been written by someone else. Although hospitable and helpful in suggesting an itinerary for their tour of the western isles, Macaulay turned out to be something of a bore, talking slightingly of the English clergy and their attachment to creeds and confessions, rites unknown to Presbyterian worshippers. Johnson put up a spirited defence but Macaulay would not give way which led to Johnson calling him a bigot. Yet Johnson was no less a bigot, having set his face since crossing the border against attending any Scottish church service. In Edinburgh he had refused to hear a sermon by Dr Robertson. 'I will hear him', he had said, 'if he will get up into a tree and preach; but I will not give a sanction by my presence to a Presbyterian assembly.'

From Cawdor they travelled the few miles to Fort George (see pages 62–4) where they were taken on a tour of the barracks. Never one to hide his erudition, Johnson held forth to his guides on the right proportions of charcoal and saltpetre in making gunpowder. Boswell was impressed, but later Johnson felt obliged to admit that he had talked *ostentatiously*. They were bidden to dinner by the fort's commander, the famous Sir Eyre Coote who had recently conducted a brilliant campaign against the French in India and who would later return there as commander-in-chief.

'At three', wrote Boswell, 'the drum beat for dinner. I, for a little while, fancied myself a military man and it pleased me'. The travellers took a liking to Coote and his wife who, Boswell said, 'had an uncommonly mild and sweet tone of voice.' Dinner, wine and conversation were all the travellers could have wished, and the regimental band played in the square below. Sir Eyre had been one of the first Englishmen to return home from India by the overland route, through Arabia and Egypt, and he told his guests that 'the Arabs could live five days without victuals and subsist for three weeks on nothing else but the blood of their camels, who could lose so much of it as would suffice without being exhausted.' The travellers left in a kind of glow. Johnson told Boswell that he would remember their day there with gratitude, while Boswell wrote, 'I could not help being struck with admiration, at finding upon this barren, sandy point, such buildings, such a dinner, such company; it was like enchantment.'

At Inverness Boswell was disappointed at not finding a letter from his wife, and for a brief moment longed to be back at home. However, he was cheered by a visit to Macbeth's castle and by what he called 'a romantic satisfaction in seeing Dr Johnson actually in it'. Having now, as it were, run out of highway, they hired four horses to carry them and their baggage along the tracks to the west, and two Highlanders, Hay and Vass, to guide them. Their way took them along the south shore of Loch Ness in the shade of birch trees; and Boswell was much struck by the contrast of the doctor on his horse ('jaunting about at his ease in quest of pleasure and novelty') with the London life he had left behind.

They had progressed some way down the lochside when Boswell caught sight of a little hut with an elderly woman at the door of it. Thinking that his friend might be interested in seeing Highland life in the raw, he proposed taking a look at it. They dismounted and went in. It was, he said, a wretched little hovel made of turf with a hole in the turf for a window. In the middle of the hut a peat fire was burning, the smoke going out of another hole in the roof; there was a pot on the fire and goat's flesh boiling in it.

> Dr Johnson was curious to know where she slept. I asked one of the guides who questioned her in Erse. She answered with a tone of emotion, saying she was afraid we wanted to go to bed to her. This *coquetry* or whatever it may be called, of so wretched a being, was truly ludicrous. Dr Johnson and I afterwards were merry upon it. I said, it was he who alarmed the poor woman's virtue. 'No, sir,' he said, 'she'll say, "There came a wicked young fellow, a wild dog, who I believe would have ravished me, had there not been with him a grave old gentleman who repressed him; but when he gets out of the sight of his tutor, I'll warrant you he'll spare no woman he meets, young or old." '

This sort of badinage in which Boswell was capable of giving as much as he got, was one of the grounds of their relationship. 'No, sir,' Boswell replied, 'she'll say, "There was a terrible ruffian who would have forced me, had it not been for a civil decent young man who, I take it, was an angel sent from heaven to protect me." '

Yet both Boswell and Johnson would have been a good deal less merry about the woman's attitude had they realized that it was less *coquetry* she was exhibiting than fear; for (according to Moray McLaren) not long before and in this very hut a woman had been raped and murdered by an English officer. The present woman's husband, a Mr Fraser, was at work in nearby woods; of their five children three were with him and two on an errand in Inverness. Before they left she gave Boswell and the guides a dram, saying she was as happy as any woman in Scotland. She asked for snuff, her great luxury; they did not have any, so Boswell gave her a shilling instead. 'She sent us away with many prayers in Erse'.

They stayed that night with the military governor of Fort Augustus and at breakfast two captains of the garrison who had recently served in America entertained Dr Johnson with accounts of the Red Indians. On the way to Glenmoriston they met a party of soldiers building a road and gave them two shillings to buy drinks. Later the soldiers came to the inn where they were staying to spend the money. Hearing them making merry in the barn, Johnson said, 'Come, let's go and give 'em another shilling apiece'. They did so and the soldiers all called him 'My Lord'. 'He is really generous,' said Boswell, 'loves influence and has the way of gaining it.' To Boswell he said, 'I am quite feudal, sir.' But he had overdone it. Unused to such charity the soldiers got blind drunk. 'Some of them fought,' said Boswell, 'and left blood upon the spot and cursed whisky next morning.'

The landlord of the inn, a Mr McQueen, told them that seventy men from the glen had left for America because they could not pay the rents. His own rent had just been raised from five to twenty pounds which he could not pay, so he was going to America too. That evening Johnson made one of his most celebrated *bon mots* when the talk turned to the guide, John Hay, who had once served nine months in a man-of-war. 'Why, sir,' said Johnson, 'no man will be a sailor who has contrivance enough to get himself into a jail; for being in a ship is being in a jail with the chance of being drowned.'

That night the travellers went to the shabby room they shared where Boswell concluded his diary for the day:

> After we had offered up our private devotions and had chatted a little from our beds, Dr Johnson said, 'God Bless us both, for Jesus Christ's sake! Good night.' I pronounced *'Amen'*. He fell asleep immediately. I was not so fortunate for a long time. I fancied myself bit by innumerable vermin under the clothes; and that a spider was travelling from the wainscot towards my mouth . . .

They left Glenmoriston at eight in the morning and Mr McQueen walked along the track with them. He told them he had joined the Highland army in the '45 and stayed with it until after Culloden. Boswell confessed himself much affected (just as I had been on that day on the moor 160 years later):

> As he narrated the particulars of that ill-advised but brave attempt, I could not refrain from tears . . . The very highland names or the sound of a bagpipe will stir my blood and fill me

with a mixture of melancholy and respect for courage . . . in
short with a crowd of sensations with which sober rationality
has nothing to do.

They struck north-west to the head of Glenmoriston, past the falls
of Cluanie and into Glen Shiel, with what Boswell called 'prodigious
mountains' looking down on them; the Five Sisters of Kintail on
one side and lofty Mam Ratagan on the other. On the way they
stopped at a hamlet where none of the inhabitants spoke English.
Boswell said that it was like being with a tribe of Indians. 'Yes,
sir,' said Johnson, 'but not so terrifying.' The people were Macraes
of the clan of Lord Seaforth. The women brought them two bowls
of milk, 'one of them frothed like a syllabub' and Boswell gave them
snuff and tobacco (which they had obtained at Fort Augustus) and
pieces of wheaten bread which he said they had never seen before;
and he distributed pennies to the children. Not to be outdone in
largesse, Johnson asked Boswell's servant Joseph and the guides to
give him change for a shilling, and he too gave each child a penny.

From Shiel Bridge (where they were shown the site of the
1719 rising) they turned due west and saw ahead of them the
first object of their journey – the Cuillin hills of Skye; and it was
along this track that Boswell and Johnson had (so far as I can tell)
the only truly bitter altercation in all their time together. It had
been a long hard slog of a day, for they had travelled more than 30
miles through rugged, mountainous country and the party were so
exhausted that all conversation had ceased. Johnson's sullen mood
was not improved by the guide Vass making a herd of goats jump
by whistling at them and then shouting, 'See the pretty goats!' It
had also begun to grow dark.

Seeing the doctor was well attended with Hay leading his horse,
Vass walking beside him and the servant Joseph bringing up the
rear, Boswell decided to ride on ahead to see what accommodation
was to be had at the inn at Glenelg, the crossing-point to Skye. He
had not gone far when Johnson called him back with a tremendous
shout, furious at being left behind. Boswell explained what he was
about but the doctor refused to be pacified, saying he would as soon
think of picking a pocket as doing what Boswell had done.

To compound matters, the inn at Glenelg proved even worse
than the one at Glenmoriston, the communal bedroom to which
they were shown (and where another occupant was already sleeping)

being 'damp and dirty with bare walls, a variety of bad smells and a coarse, black, greasy fir table', and there was nothing to eat or drink. But the doctor seemed quite philosophical when they lay down on the hay that was to be their bed so that Boswell, much perturbed by his friend's anger, raised the matter again and, as he said, 'endeavoured to defend it better'. Johnson would still not be pacified. 'Sir,' he said, 'had you gone on, I was thinking I should have returned with you to Edinburgh and then have parted from you and never spoken to you more.'

Not surprisingly Boswell slept badly. 'Dr Johnson's anger had affected me much. I considered that without any bad intention I might suddenly forfeit his friendship.' In the morning he told his friend how uneasy he had made him when speaking of returning to Edinburgh. By now somewhat mollified, Johnson confessed he had been in a passion and would not have done what he threatened, and that was the end of it. Much relieved, Boswell said that in future he would require advance warning of any quarrel, adding, 'It was absurd of me to believe you.' Johnson, still mildly on the offensive, said, 'You deserved about as much.'

In the rain they embarked in a boat to cross the Sound of Sleat to Armadale; and were greeted by Sir Alexander Macdonald of Sleat and his wife, then en route to Edinburgh.

Their island hopping jaunt had begun.

# CHAPTER 7

## *Skye*

THE SKYE THAT THE TWO TRAVELLERS CAME TO IN 1773 HAD HARDLY advanced socially since the prince and Malcolm MacLeod had made their way down it in 1746. Then, as before, there were no roads and therefore no wheeled transport: one journeyed on horseback or foot. Then as before there was only one alehouse on the island which also did duty as post office, at Sconser at the mouth of Loch Sligachan, the embarkation point for Raasay. Then as before the island was owned mostly by two great families, the MacLeods and the Macdonalds (with whom the travellers stayed in some comfort) and whose hundreds of tenants lived mostly in primitive huts in abiding poverty. Between them the travellers noted many things: how well appointed were the houses of their hosts, with excellent tables (apart from a lack of fresh vegetables), well-stocked libraries and the custom (which Johnson found exhilarating) of a piper playing at dinner; their enjoyment of the local breakfasts – tea or coffee, oatcakes, honey, marmalade, jams, and also sometimes cheese which Boswell didn't care for ('It often smells very strong') – and the habit of the men of the household to take a dram of whisky as a starter. Boswell's acute ear was quick to record the West Highland lilt of those who spoke English and how they addressed his companion as 'Toctor Shonson, Toctor Shonson'. The doctor was struck by the prevalence of superstition, of belief in a sturdy fairy called Browny and of Greogach, an old man with a long beard for whom libations of milk were left; the belief that seed sown at the time of the moon's increase would produce better crops, and that certain people were gifted with second sight. He also noticed a tendency of the islanders to lie, not purposely but as though exactness was something foreign to them. They were both amused by the highland custom of the chief of the clan calling himself either by the clan name or by his place of residence, i.e. Mackintosh or Raasay. The laird of Macfarlane told them he would be much put out if addressed as *Mr* Macfarlane. 'I and only I', he said imperiously, 'am Macfarlane.' The laird of Muck however understandably wished to be known as Isle of Muck rather than plain Muck.

The most memorable of their Skye visits was to the Macdonald house of Kingsburgh to which, it will be recalled, Flora Macdonald had led Prince Charles disguised as her maid 'Betty Burke' on arrival from Benbecula. After her release from the Tower of London in 1747 and journey back to Skye with John Mackinnon, she had fallen in love with and married Kingsburgh's son Allan, by whom she was to bear ten children. In 1772 old Kingsburgh died, and Allan, now the new Kingsburgh, and Flora helped his widowed mother to run the house and farm. On arrival Boswell found Allan dressed in Highland finery: 'a tartan plaid, a large blue bonnet with a knot of black ribband like a cockade, a brown short coat, a tartan waistcoat with gold buttons, a bluish philibeg [kilt] and tartan hose'; well might Boswell call him 'completely the figure of a gallant highlander with graceful mien and manly looks'. Flora he described as 'a little woman of a genteel appearance and uncommonly mild and well bred'; while Johnson saw her as 'a woman of middle stature, soft features, gentle manners and elegant presence'. She told them that she had heard on the mainland two weeks earlier that a Mr Boswell together with a Mr Johnson, 'a *young English buck*', were shortly coming to Skye. The doctor, said Boswell, 'was highly entertained with this fancy'. Nor could Boswell quite come to terms with the two of them meeting. 'To see Dr Samuel Johnson, the great champion of the English Tories, salute Miss Flora Macdonald in the isle of Skye was a striking sight.'

That night they slept in the same room and Dr Johnson in the same bed as that on which Prince Charles had lain on his flight south twenty-seven years earlier, a circumstance which made such an impression on Boswell that he confessed himself at a loss to put it into words. At breakfast, he said, Johnson declared that he would have given a good deal not to have been denied that bed. 'I owned he was the lucky man and observed that without doubt, it had been contrived between Mrs Macdonald and him. She seemed to acquiesce, adding, "You know young *bucks* are always the favourites of the ladies." '

The next year Allan and Flora, finding it difficult to make the farm pay, emigrated to North Carolina. Here, paradoxically, Allan fought for his Hanoverian king in the American War of Independence and was taken prisoner by the colonists. In 1779 Flora returned to Scotland and later, after Allan had been released, they took up residence again at Kingsburgh.

Flora died in 1790 when she was sixty-eight. In her will she asked to be buried in the linen sheet in which the prince and later Dr Johnson had slept, and this was done. By now she had become so famous that literally thousands came to her funeral. It took place in the little cemetery of Kilmuir in the northern part of Trotternish, not far from the beach where she and 'Betty Burke' had landed from the isles. On her tombstone is carved the tribute that Dr Johnson paid to her.

FLORA MACDONALD
PRESERVER OF
PRINCE CHARLES EDWARD STUART
HER NAME
WILL BE MENTIONED IN HISTORY
AND IF COURAGE AND FIDELITY
BE VIRTUES
MENTIONED WITH HONOUR

Above her tombstone rises a striking Celtic cross which looks out to the west, across the green *machair* where in May the white daisies lie like blossom, across the grey sea to the blue smudge of the islands where she was born and from which she set out on a brief adventure that was to capture the admiration of the world. It is difficult to stand on that spot today and contemplate it without emotion.

Elsewhere in Skye the travellers acted true to form, the doctor holding forth with gusto, wit and sometimes ignorance on a variety of topics, Boswell never afraid to admit to his journal his own endearing human failings. On the first evening of a visit to the Mackinnon who was laird of Corrichatachan (near Broadford) and his wife (a daughter of old Kingsburgh and therefore Flora's sister-in-law) Boswell sat up late with his host and other guests drinking punch. After the third bowl, he admitted, the company was cordial and merry to a high degree, 'but of what passed I have no recollection with any accuracy. I remember calling Corrichatachan by the familiar appellation of Corri which his friends all do'. Another bowl was produced and it was five before Boswell got to bed.

'I awaked at noon with a severe head-ache. I was much vexed . . . and afraid of a reproof from Dr Johnson. About one he came into my room and accosted me, "What, drunk yet?" "Sir," said I, "they kept me up." "No, you kept them up, you drunken dog." This he said with good-humoured English pleasantry.' Others of the party including his host came in with a bottle of brandy and a glass and insisted he take a dram to cure his headache, which it did. 'When I rose, I went into Dr Johnson's room and taking up Mrs Mackinnon's prayer-book, I opened it at the twentieth Sunday after Trinity in which I read, "And be not drunk with wine wherein there is excess." Some would have taken this as a divine interposition.'

Next day the doctor showed a charmingly unexpected side to himself.

> This evening one of our married ladies, a lively, pretty little woman, good-humouredly sat down upon Dr Johnson's knee and, being encouraged by some of the company, put her hands round his neck and kissed him. 'Do it again,' said he, 'and let us see who will tire first.' He kept her on his knee some time while he and she drank tea. He was now like a *buck* indeed. All the company were much entertained to find him so easy and pleasant. To me it was highly comic, to see the grave philosopher . . . toying with a Highland beauty. But what could he do? He must have been surly, and weak too, had he not behaved as he did. He would have been laughed at, and not more respected, though less loved.

Elsewhere the doctor banged on about the importance of the Christian religion, believed that infidels should be brought to book, approved the Church of Scotland repentance stool for fornicating women, was impressed by the learning of the few ministers he met but regretted they were Presbyterians. When Boswell riposted that David Hume 'whose writings were very unfavourable to religion' was, like Johnson himself, a Tory, Johnson tried to wriggle out of it by saying, 'Sir, Hume is a Tory by chance, as being a Scotchman; but not upon a principle of duty, for he has no principle.'

Another example of what Boswell called his friend's 'fits of railing against the Scots' occurred when they were sailing in a boat from Ulinish to Talisker. 'He owned that they [the Scots] had been a very learned nation from about 1550 to about 1650; but that they afforded the only instance of a people among whom the arts of civil life did not advance in proportion with learning; that they had hardly any trade, any money or any elegance before the Union; that it was strange that with all the advantages possessed by other nations, they had not any of those conveniences and embellishments which are the fruit of industry, till they came in contact with a civilized people. "We have taught you", he said, "and we'll do the same to all barbarous nations, to the Cherokees and at last to the Ourang-Outangs." When Johnson had stopped laughing Boswell said, "We had wine before the union." Johnson: "No, sir. You had some weak stuff, the refuse of France, which would not make you drunk." Boswell: "I assure you, sir, there was a great deal of drunkenness." Johnson: "No, sir, there were people who died of dropsies which they contracted in trying to *get* drunk." '

They visited the island of Raasay; and just as Malcolm MacLeod had transported the prince there in his boat in 1746, so he performed the same service for the famous pair in 1773. Malcolm was now sixty-two and, according to Boswell, heavily bearded and dressed in the Highland fashion with tartan hose, a purple camblet kilt, a black waistcoat, a green cloth coat and a yellowish bushy wig which supported a large blue bonnet with a gold button. 'I never saw a figure that gave a more perfect representation of a Highland gentleman and wished much to have a picture of him just as he was.' The island seemed to have recovered from the destruction wreaked on it by the men of the *Furnace*, the houses having been rebuilt and the farm land restocked with sheep and cattle. The MacLeod who was a chieftain of the clan and known as Raasay welcomed the party to his spacious house where other guests were staying. Thirty sat down to dinner and afterwards a fiddler was brought in for a dance, at which, said Boswell, 'Malcolm bounded like a roe'. Although Raasay did not have a large revenue from his estates, said Boswell, 'yet he lives in great splendour; and so far is he from distressing his people that in the present rage for emigration, not a man has left his estate.' The pair enjoyed themselves on Raasay, though Johnson was as much discomforted by the primitive sanitary arrangements (presumably a hole in the ground) as he was delighted by the company, the entertainments and the fare. As they left, Boswell (as he recorded in his original though not published journal) heard his companion say to the hospitable Raasay: 'You take very good care of one end of a man but not the other'!

Of all the landmarks of Skye, the castle of Dunvegan in the north of the island is probably the most famous; an imposing fortress set on a huge slab of rock overlooking the sea a few miles south of Loch Bay. The ancestral keep of the MacLeods of MacLeod, it is the only castle to have been lived in continuously by the same family for more than 700 years, and the estate still maintains some 45,000 acres including the Cuillin hills. It is believed to have been founded by Liotr (Gaelic *Leod*), son of one of the Norse kings who ruled part of Skye and the Hebrides in the thirteenth century.

In the public rooms of the castle are some curious relics: a much faded and tattered fragment of cloth called the Fairy Flag, now under glass and said to have been woven between the fourth and seventh centuries. Some say it was a present from the fairies, others that it was obtained in Palestine during the Crusades, and all believing that it had brought the MacLeods luck. When the 27th Chief, Sir Reginald MacLeod who didn't die until 1935, had it examined by a Mr Wace of the Victoria and Albert Museum and was told that it had probably been brought to Britain by the Norseman Harold Hardrada, he told him, 'Mr Wace, you may believe that, but *I know* it was given to my ancestor by the fairies'. To which Mr Wace replied, 'Sir Reginald, I bow to your superior knowledge.' Sir Reginald's daughter, who became Dame Flora MacLeod and the 28th Chief, was famous for hosting the annual piping competitions at the castle between the wars and among the relics are the pipes of the MacCrimmons of nearby Boreraig, traditional pipers to the MacLeods, the last of whom died in 1822.

Other heirlooms include the drinking horn of Sir Rory Mor MacLeod, the 15th Chief, which holds the equivalent of a bottle and a half of wine and which every heir to the chief on coming of age has to drink at one draught and 'without setting down or falling down' as proof of his manhood. The present and 29th Chief, John MacLeod, a grandson of Dame Flora and a professional singer, told me that he had failed at the dress rehearsal but had succeeded on the night with a time of one minute and fifty-seven seconds. Had it made him ill, I asked, and he said no, but he couldn't look claret in the face again for six months. I mentioned the lock of Prince Charles's hair and his waistcoat in the drawing-room and asked how they had been acquired, the MacLeod of that time being a Hanoverian. He said that when Flora Macdonald returned from America one of her daughters had married a bastard son of the 22nd Chief, one Alexander MacLeod of Glendale. Flora had stayed at the castle on several occasions, and it was this that had convinced him that the relics were genuine.

Also there is the portrait of Dr Johnson by Zoffany and the bread and butter letter that he wrote to the 23rd Chief on conclusion of his stay. Of all the enjoyable houses that he visited in Skye, he seems to have enjoyed Dunvegan the most. 'I tasted lotus,' he said, 'and was in danger of forgetting that I was ever to depart till Mr Boswell sagely reproached me with my sluggishness and softness,' and Boswell confirmed that his companion 'became quite joyous'. Johnson slept in an upper room of the wing known as the Fairy Tower (as did Sir Walter Scott when he visited the castle in 1814), and was entertained by Lady MacLeod (whom he had earlier known in London) and her daughters in the parlour immediately below – the only room in the castle, he said, where the chimney did not smoke. He seems to have been in capital form during the ten days' visit and held forth on a variety of subjects which included an admission that he had given up wine because he could not drink it in moderation, Edmund Burke's lack of humour, the falsity of Macpherson's Ossian, the irrationality of duelling, the decline of prize-fighting, the superiority of the English clergy over the Scottish, and of cotton over flannel, and he gave such a learned exposition on the making of coins and of beer that another guest thought he must have been brought up at the Mint and in a brewery. 'I was elated', wrote Boswell in his journal, 'by the thought of having been able to entice such a man to this remote part of the world;' while Johnson himself commented, 'I cannot but laugh to think of myself roving the Hebrides at sixty. I wonder where I shall rove at fourscore.' In London, said Boswell, there was always competition among their circle of friends as to who would be enjoying the doctor's conversation. 'We are feasting on it,' he wrote gleefully, 'undisturbed, at Dunvegan.'

The last time I visited Dunvegan was when making a radio programme on Skye, and I asked John MacLeod if we could record his favourite song. His choice could not have been more apt. It will be recalled that early in 1746 the MacLeod of the time took with him to Inverness the MacCrimmon of the time and there joined up with Lord Loudoun in the abortive attempt to capture Prince Charles at Moy. MacCrimmon, who was a Jacobite, had no wish to go but could hardly disobey his master. In the skirmish that ensued he was the only one to die. Before leaving Skye, said John MacLeod, he had composed the song prophesying his death.

It was, like much of Gaelic music, a profoundly melancholy song, and even if I could not understand the words, I found it deeply moving; for here in his keep of Dunvegan Castle, the 29th Chief of the clan MacLeod was singing a song which in the past 250 years previous MacLeod chiefs and clansmen and pipers must have sung or played before him. Like the castle and the Cuillins the song lived on, its melancholy the melancholy of the pibroch, of the mists that lie low on the waters of the Minch and cling to the sides of the hills, of the crying of the gulls and piping of the oyster-catchers on the shore.

A topic of particular interest to the travellers was what changes there had been in the Highland way of life in the aftermath of the '45. Admitting that when the Hanoverians first came to the throne, nine-tenths of the people of Britain were against them, Johnson regarded them now as universally accepted. Boswell found everywhere in Skye 'a high opinion of the virtues of the king now upon the throne and an honest disposition to be faithful subjects' while Johnson said that nowhere in the Highlands had he heard a health offered 'that might not have circulated with propriety within the precincts of the king's palace'. One of the penalties inflicted on the highlands after the '45 was that clan chiefs who had held courts to try offenders in their areas under the custom of heritable jurisdiction were no longer permitted to; the keeping of weapons, which every Highlander regarded as his birthright, had also been proscribed and this had angered members of clans who had fought for the king and Cumberland. The plaid and kilt had been prorogued and while this

Prince Charles Edward with the Irish Jacobite Antoine Walsh on
the shore of Loch nan Uamh, July 1745. 'Let what will happen, the
stroke is struck and I have taken a firm resolution to conquer
or to die.' (*Robert Harding Picture Library.*)

Drummossie Moor, Culloden.
The Final Reckoning.

THE BATTLE
OF CULLODEN
WAS FOUGHT ON THIS MOOR
16TH APRIL 1746.

THE GRAVES OF THE
GALLANT HIGHLANDERS
WHO FOUGHT FOR
SCOTLAND & PRINCE CHARLIE.
ARE MARKED BY THE NAMES
OF THEIR CLANS

Prince Charles Edward. Painted in France in about 1748. 'An Italian-born stateless refugee...never quite the Scottish patriot that history has painted him.'

Flora Macdonald by Allan Ramsay. Dr Johnson's epitaph: 'Her name will be mentioned in history, and if courage and fidelity be virtues, mentioned with honour.'

Kingsburgh House, Isle of Skye, where Dr Johnson slept in the same bed and shared with Boswell the same room in which the prince had slept twenty-seven years earlier.

The Mansell Collection.

Executions of so-
called witches in the
seventeenth century.
Between 1560 and
1720 up to 4,500
'witches' in Scotland
were hanged,
strangled or burned.

G.S. Lennox/The Military Picture Library.

Sentry at Fort
George clutching a
nasty-looking
weapon which he
called an LSW. 'I
asked if it was loaded
and he said it was.'

James Boswell by George Wilson, 1765. 'I have the whim of an Englishman to make me think and act extravagantly, and the sense of a Scotsman to make me sensible of it.'

Dr Samuel Johnson by Sir Joshua Reynolds, 1775. 'When I find a Scotchman to whom an Englishman is as a Scotchman, that Scotchman shall be as an Englishman to me.'

Thomas Rowlandson's cartoon of Boswell accompanying Dr Johnson along Edinburgh's High Street, August 1773. With effluents thrown from upper windows the High Street stank from end to end. 'I smell you in the dark,' said Johnson as they marched along.

The 'collision' as interpreted by Thomas Rowlandson, between Dr Johnson and Boswell's father. 'They became exceedingly warm and violent,' wrote Boswell. 'Whiggism and Presbyterianism, Toryism and Episcopacy were terribly buffeted.'

The ruined chapel and Celtic Cross on Inchkenneth where Boswell
was frightened by a ghost and Dr Johnson by the sight of
human bones.

Fingal's Cave, Staffa by Joseph Turner, 1832. 'The man who bought
the painting, foolish fellow, complained to Turner that it was
indistinct. "Indistinctness is my forte," Turner replied.'

The skull of St Magnus, killed by an axe on the orders of Earl Hakon in the twelfth century and discovered in Kirkwall Cathedral 800 years later.

Tomb of the explorer Dr John Rae in Kirkwall Cathedral. 'Eyes shut in the manner of one enjoying a light doze after a picnic lunch. The shotgun suggests that at any moment he may be roused by a companion to continue the chase.'

The prehistoric settlement of Skara Brae in Orkney, showing dresser, beds and fireplace; 5,000 years old, yet all the furniture is still in place.

edict was ignored by chiefs and chieftains, tenants who had been obliged to discard them were now too poor to make new ones.

One morning while Johnson and Boswell were staying at Ulinish on the west coast, Boswell went for a walk along the shore. 'I saw a ship, the *Margaret* of Clyde, pass by with a number of emigrants on board. It was a melancholy sight.' The subject of emigration runs like a thread through both their narratives. In the two years between 1763 and 1765 no fewer than 20,000 men, women and children had left the Highlands, 4,000 from Skye alone. The cause was poverty which the two travellers either chose not to see or, if they did, chose not to write about. Yet it was there all round them, as Thomas Pennant had observed when he visited the island the year before: 'The poor are left to Providence's care. They prowl like other animals along the shore to pick up limpets and other shell fish, the casual repasts of hundreds in these unhappy islands. Hundreds thus annually drag through the season a wretched life and numbers unknown . . . fall beneath the pressure, some of hunger, more of the putrid fever, the epidemic of the coasts.'

The cause of the poverty was that the available land was insufficient to maintain a population that increased by a half between 1750 and 1810. All the land was owned by the lairds whose tenants lived on the edge of destitution, the strips supporting their livestock and potatoes growing smaller and more uneconomic every year. Then, as the price of the black cattle, which the better off sent for sale on the mainland to pay their rents, increased, so the lairds increased their rents, in Johnson's view 'with too much eagerness'. Those who did not or could not pay were evicted. Boswell, anticipating the policies of the Liberal party by 150 years, wrote: 'All that [a laird] can get by raising his rents is more luxury in his own house. Is it not better to share the profits of his estate to a certain degree with his kinsman and thus have both social intercourse and patriarchal influence?' For their part the tenants had nothing to look forward to but a life of unceasing toil and perpetual poverty: they owned nothing and never would. America and Canada beckoned; and those who had preceded them sent back word of the opportunities offered.

The subject of emigration again featured on the travellers' last night in Skye which they spent at Sir Alexander Macdonald's house at Armadale before embarking for Mull. There was a company of fourteen, and in the evening they danced. One of the dances was called 'America'. 'Each of the couples . . . successively whirls round in a circle till all are in motion; and the dance seems to show how emigration catches till a whole neighbourhood is set afloat. Mrs Mackinnon told me that last year when a ship sailed from Portree for America, the people on shore were almost distracted when they saw their relations go off; they lay down on the ground, tumbled and tore the grass with their teeth. This year there was not a tear shed. The people on shore seemed to think that they would soon follow', and they did.

Long after Johnson and Boswell had returned to more urban surroundings, the exodus, along with the poverty and epidemics continued; year after year the emigrant ships plied their trade to the west. In 1817 it was reported that to stay alive some islanders were eating potato cuttings for the next year's planting, and begging Lord Macdonald's agent for meal to tide them over; and in 1852, eighty years after Johnson and Boswell's visit, an observer found whole families 'entirely destitute, having neither food nor clothes', both bed and body clothes being 'mere rags'. He told of families selling their winter and spring store of peat to survive. He had not seen so many cases of typhus in ten years, and visited one family near Portree where it had struck. 'The family consists of the father and mother and two children, a daughter about fourteen years of age and a son about ten. The house is a black hut on the moor, consisting of one small apartment. There is only one bed; in this the sick daughter lay. The father and son sleep during the night on a bunch of straw in a corner of this wretched habitation. The poor mother has not put off her body clothes for the last twelve days.' Another observer was at the quayside when the emigrants embarked:

The leave taking was the most painful scene I ever witnessed. Sturdy highlanders grasped each other by the hand, whilst the muscles of their faces and bodies quivered with emotion. Women hung on to the necks of friends and were in some cases removed by force. As the vessel steamed out of the bay, they stood on the poop, threw their arms into the air giving full vent of their grief as they gazed for the last time on the black, peaty glens and bleak rocky hills over which they had long been accustomed to roam, and to which they were so devotedly attached.

This shipload was bound, not to Canada or America where

so many Skye emigrants had already settled, but to the new colony of Australia. Yet when they reached that distant shore, their sentiments echoed those of the exiled Highland boatmen in Canada:

> From the lone shieling of the misty island
> Mountains divide us and the waste of seas,
> But still the blood is strong, the heart is highland,
> And we in dreams behold the Hebrides.

# CHAPTER 8

## Col, Inchkenneth,
## Iona and Mull

BEFORE LEAVING SKYE JOHNSON AND BOSWELL HAD MET AT TALISKER A young man called Donald Maclean, elder son of the laird of the island of Col (now spelt Coll and adjacent to Tiree) and who everyone referred to as Col, although he had not yet inherited. Having come to Skye on business, he was so entertained by the two travellers that he joined their party, was present at Boswell's drinking bout at Corrichatachan and promised to find a boat at Armadale to take them on an excursion to Eigg, Muck, Col, Tiree, Mull and Iona.

In his journal Boswell wrote with his usual candour of their last night at Armadale before embarking:

> We danced to-night to the musick of the bagpipe which made us beat the ground with prodigious force. I thought it better to endeavour to conciliate the kindness of the people of Skye by joining heartily in their amusements than to play the abstract scholar. I looked on this tour to the Hebrides as a co-partnership between Dr Johnson and me. Each was to do all he could to promote its success; and I have some reason to flatter myself, that my gayer exertions were of service to us. Dr

Johnson's immense fund of knowledge and wit was a wonderful source of admiration and delight to them. . . . I was also fortunate enough frequently to draw him forth to talk, when he would otherwise have been silent. The fountain was at times locked up till I opened the spring. It was curious to hear the Hebrideans when any dispute happened while he was out of the room, saying, 'Stay till Dr Johnson comes: say that to *him*.'

Told in the morning that the wind was still unfavourable, Johnson was heard to mutter, 'A wind or not a wind? That is the question.' The question was resolved during the course of the morning when the wind shifted to the east and the party embarked. It consisted of a Mr Simpson who owned the boat, Hugh Macdonald who skippered it with the help of two sailors, one with one eye, Col with his servant and five dogs – two greyhounds, a terrier, a pointer and a large Newfoundlander – and the doctor and his biographer. They were under way by one o'clock: Johnson soon felt sick and found a bunk below which he shared with one of the greyhounds.

During the afternoon the weather worsened, so they had to abandon their first plan of going direct to Iona, known then as Icolmkill (the island of St Columba) off the west coast of Mull and hoped by clearing the point of Ardnamurchan to find shelter in the Sound of Mull. But the wind there came dead against them and so Col decided to turn to the west and head for the harbour of Lochiern in his own island of Col. Boswell in his journal left a vivid impression of the terrors of that night. Earlier, before the storm rose, a small wherry had joined company with them and was now a little way astern.

The master [of the wherry] begged that if we made for Col, we should put out a light to him. Accordingly one of the sailors waved a glowing peat for some time . . . It was very dark and there was a heavy and incessant rain. The sparks of the burning peat flew so much about that I dreaded the vessel might take fire. Then, as Col was a sportsman and had powder on board, I figured that we might be blown up. Simpson and he appeared a little frightened which made me more so; and the perpetual talking or rather shouting in Erse, alarmed me still more. A man is always suspicious of what is saying in an unknown tongue; and if fear be his passion at the time, he grows more afraid.

> Our vessel often lay so much on one side that I trembled
> lest she should be overset, and indeed they told me afterwards
> that they had run her sometimes to within an inch of the water,
> so anxious were they to make what haste they could before the
> night should be worse. I now saw what I never saw before, a
> prodigious sea, with immense billows coming upon the vessel
> so that it seemed hardly possible to escape. There was something
> grandly horrible in the sight. I am glad I have seen it once.

Boswell's fears were understandable, for these are treacherous
waters even with modern aids to navigation. Yet this boat had
nothing, probably not even a compass; and the islands all around
them lay in darkness, for lighthouses as beacons for mariners were
not erected until later.

> Amidst all these terrifying circumstances, I endeavoured to
> compose my mind. It was not easy to do it; for all the stories I
> had heard of the dangerous sailing among the Hebrides, which
> is proverbial, came full upon my recollection. When I thought
> of those that were dearest to me and would suffer severely should
> I be lost, I upbraided myself as not having a sufficient cause for
> putting myself in such danger.

Piety, he wrote, afforded him comfort, though he was worried
by the opinions of Dr Hawkesworth and others that petitions of an
individual, or even of congregations, could in no way influence the
Deity: however, he was heartened by recalling Dr Ogden's affirmation that prayers *were* answered. Then came another example – for
me the most endearing – of his many admissions of human failing
and one that will strike a chord with many. It took place a little
before midnight as they were approaching Col.

> As I saw them all busy doing something, I asked Col with
> much earnestness what I could do [he might have added 'to be
> saved']. He, with a happy readiness, put into my hand a rope
> which was fixed to the top of one of the masts and told me to
> hold it till he bade me pull. If I had considered the matter, I
> might have seen that this could not be of the least service; but
> his object was to keep me out of the way of those who were busy
> working the vessel, and at the same time to divert my fear by

employing me and making me think I was of use. Thus did I
stand firm to my post, while the wind and rain beat upon me,
always expecting a call to pull my rope.

In the early hours of the next morning their miseries came
to an end.

The man with one eye steered: old Macdonald and Col and
his servant lay upon the forecastle, looking sharp out for the
harbour. It was necessary to carry much 'cloth' as they termed
it, that is to say much sail, in order to keep the vessel off the
shore of Col. This made violent plunging in a rough sea. At last
they spied the harbour of Lochiern and Col cried, 'Thank God,
we are safe!'

When the boat had come to anchor, Boswell went below to
see how his companion had fared. He found him quite ignorant
of what they had gone through, 'in philosophick tranquillity' and
with Col's greyhound keeping him warm.

The travellers stayed in Col longer than they intended for with
continuous rain and gales of wind they were unable to sail. Col
did his best to entertain them, but Johnson grew weary of the
enforced confinement. 'I want to be on the mainland and go on
with existence. This is a waste of life.' Another time he said it
would require great resignation to live in these islands. 'I don't
know, sir,' replied Boswell, and suggested that a life of mere
physical existence, eating, drinking, sleeping, walking about and
enjoying his own thoughts would be one that satisfied him. To
which Johnson, who knew his companion's social and carnal desires
better than he did, replied, 'Ay, but if you were shut up here, your
own thoughts would torment you. You would think of Edinburgh
and London and that you could not be there.'

Enforced confinement led the doctor to be even more combative
in conversation than usual. Visiting the local minister, one Hector
Maclean, described by Boswell as 'seventy-seven years of age, a
decent ecclesiastic, dressed in a full suit of black clothes and a
black wig like a Dutch pastor' and by Johnson as 'a fine old
man who had as much dignity in his appearance as the dean of
a cathedral', Johnson soon began a quarrel with him about the

virtues of Leibniz, Maclean calling Leibniz a great man, Johnson saying he was as paltry a fellow as he knew. This led Boswell to regret that the doctor could not accommodate himself to different sorts of people. 'Had he been softer with this venerable old man, we might have had more conversation; but his forcible spirit and impetuosity of manner may be said to spare neither sex nor age. I have seen even [his friend] Mrs Thrale stunned.' On reflection, he thought it better for his companion to be himself. 'Pliability of address I conceive to be inconsistent with that majestic power of mind which he possesses . . . A lofty oak will not bend like a supple willow.' That same day he had a ludicrous altercation with Johnson about which of them had the best curtains and bedposts in the room they were sharing. 'There is no arguing with Johnson,' Boswell wrote in his journal, 'for if his pistol misfires, he knocks you down with the butt-end of it.'

After nine days in Col the weather cleared and Col and his guests embarked for Tobermory in Mull whence they would travel south-westerly to Loch na Keal and the little island of Inchkenneth: here Col would introduce his new friends to his uncle and chief of his clan, Sir Allan Maclean. On arrival at Tobermory the spirits of both travellers perked up. 'Boswell is now all alive,' said Johnson, and Boswell confessed that after their confinement in Col, the bustle of human activity in Tobermory had given him 'much gaiety of spirit'. As for the doctor, Boswell wrote that after a dish of tea and some good bread and butter at the inn, his bad humour had gone off; and he couldn't resist telling the doctor how amused he had been hearing people on the tour say to him, 'Honest man! He's pleased with everything, he's always content.' He added, 'Little did they know!' Johnson replied, 'You rogue!'

There are three different ways of reaching Inchkenneth, the one the travellers took by way of Calgary and Ulva, the coast road to Salen then west to Gruline, and my favourite from the centre of Mull, where at the head of Loch Scridain and with the black cone of Ben More facing you, a road from the Iona–Craignure highway branches to the north. You pass through the forestry plantation of Knockroy with its ranks of boring conifers, then climb up the long escarpment that borders the south shore of Loch na Keal, beyond which stands Ulva. And then, almost without warning, you find yourself at the top of the escarpment and stretched out below the whole seaboard of western Mull from the Treshnish isles and little

Colonsay in the west to Eorsa and the Scarrisdale Rocks in the east. The last time I was there the sun was setting beyond Fladda, so that all the islands stood out like sentinels and, there being no wind, turning the sea into an expanse of pewter.

Five hundred feet below was the green and fertile island of Inchkenneth, a quarter of a mile off shore and only half a mile long: through my binoculars I could see a large house on it, the ruins of a chapel and a Celtic cross. Once the island had been a dependency of the monastery at Iona and the home of a Culdee foundation of monks. Later it became the home of the chiefs of the clan Maclean who owned much of Mull before they were dispossessed of it by the Hanoverian Duke of Argyll and his Campbells (because of siding with the Prince in the '45).

It would not have been surprising if Dr Johnson had found Inchkenneth, on account of its size, even more of a prison than Col. But they were given a warm welcome by Sir Allan Maclean (whose father knew Boswell's father) and his two daughters and were entranced by the little group of cottages 'only one story high' in which they lived. 'Our room was neatly floored and well lighted,' said Johnson, 'and our dinner plentiful and delicate'; and he found a collection of books. They spent the day walking about the island, visiting another little adjacent island (across water so clear you could and still can see the bottom), watching a fisherman pull oysters from their beds, attending family prayers and, as usual, engaging in lively conversation. Johnson said he would like to own an island like Inchkenneth (he had said the same to Lady MacLeod at Dunvegan), but it would be necessary to fortify it; otherwise 'what should hinder a parcel of ruffians to land in the night and carry off everything you have,' with the added danger of having your throat cut. Boswell suggested having a large dog, but Johnson riposted that a dog was no use except to alarm. 'I have heard him say', observed Boswell, 'that he is afraid of no dog' and had once seen an instance of it at Topham Beauclerk's house in the country. 'Two ferocious dogs were fighting. Dr Johnson looked steadily at them for a little while; and then, as one would separate two little boys . . . he ran up to them and cuffed their heads till he drove them asunder. But few men have his intrepidity, Herculean strength or presence of mind. Most thieves or robbers would be afraid to encounter a mastiff.'

Another curious trait of Johnson's was revealed when they visited the ruined chapel. Boswell found some human bones there and got hold of a spade and buried them. 'Dr Johnson praised me for what I had done, though he owned he could not have done it.' This was the third time on the tour that Johnson had shown his horror of human bones, previous occasions being at the chapel on Raasay and in the charter-room on Col where there lay a very large shin bone: 'Dr Johnson would not look at it, but started away'. Strange that one brave enough to tackle two ferocious dogs should feel queasy at the sight of inanimate bones.

In the evening Sir Allan related how he had recruited a hundred of his clansmen to take part in the American campaign; after which, said Johnson, 'one of the ladies played on her harpsichord, while Col and Mr Boswell danced a Scottish reel with the other.' Before going to bed Boswell did something which he omitted from his published journal but committed to his private one: he slipped out of the house, made his way in the dark to the ancient Celtic cross and there knelt and prayed. 'O Columbus, thou venerable saint,' (he meant Columba but may have been drunk), 'as we have all the reason that can be to believe that thou art in heaven, I beseech thee to pray to God that I may attain everlasting felicity.' Then, frightened by what he thought was a ghost and reluctant to rely on Columba's intercession, he retired speedily indoors.

The visit, though brief, had been a huge success. 'Dr Johnson here showed so much of the spirit of the Highlander,' wrote Boswell, 'that he won Sir Allan's heart' who offered to take them in his boat to their next port of call, Iona. For his part Johnson thought that the Sunday they had spent there was the most agreeable he had ever passed, and he later wrote a poem in Latin to celebrate the island. They were sad to say goodbye to Col whom they had grown fond of and who was now returning to take up his interrupted visit to Skye. Dr Johnson said of him, 'He is a noble animal. He is as complete an islander as the mind can figure. He is a farmer, a sailor, a hunter, a fighter. He is hospitable; and he has an intrepidity of talk whether he understands the subject or not. I regret that he is not more intellectual.' They were even sadder to learn, a year later, that Col had drowned when crossing from Ulva to Mull.

In Inchkenneth's long history Dr Johnson was not the only Englishman to grace it with his presence. A hundred and sixty years later the author of the words of the Skye Boat Song, Sir Harold Boulton, came to live there, not in Sir Allan Maclean's little group of cottages, but in the house I had seen from the top of the escarpment, bow-fronted, on three stories and painted white. In 1938 it was bought by an eccentric English peer, Lord Redesdale, father of the six gifted Mitford sisters and a son, Tom.

Despite or perhaps because of the isolation, Lady Redesdale adored Inchkenneth, staying each year from May to October. She farmed its 160 acres with cattle, sheep, goats, Shetland ponies and hens, kept a flower and vegetable garden and made (or rather her cook made) her own bread, butter and cheese. When a bull was needed to serve the cows, he had to swim there, a rope in the ring at the end of his nose being attached to the stern of a motor-boat.* According to her daughter, Diana, who found the island 'inconvenient to the last degree', there being no telephone or, if the sea was rough, post, her mother often felt the need of company. 'She spent a good part of each day looking through field glasses to see if any people should chance to appear on the opposite shore.' Then, if she saw a picnic party or a yacht at anchor, she would send the boatman over to invite whoever he found to come to tea.

But Lady Redesdale had a darker side. Another daughter, the oddly named Unity Valkyrie, a wayward child, twice sacked from school and something of an exhibitionist, had, while still a débutante, embraced the cause of Fascism as expounded by her future brother-in-law, Sir Oswald Mosley; and in 1933 at the age of nineteen, she attended that year's Nazi party Nuremberg Rally as the sole woman representative of the British Union of Fascists. Having fallen in love with Hitler, she returned the following year, wangled an introduction to him, and from then until the war became his devoted slave and one of his intimate (though not physically) group of supporters. On the day that war broke out in 1939, and perhaps having in mind Rupert Brooke's line about some corner of a foreign field, she took herself into Munich's English garden and with a little silver pistol shot herself – though not fatally.

On several occasions in the thirties her parents had joined Unity in Germany and they too had been infected by the Nazi virus. Indeed on the same day that Unity was attempting suicide in Munich, Lady Redesdale was driving her eldest daughter, the authoress Nancy, across Mull to catch the ferry to Oban and the London train. It

*Lady Redesdale's youngest daughter Deborah thinks it was the other way round, i.e. that the bull stayed put on Mull and the cows swam over to him.

was a glorious sunny day, rare for the West Highlands and Nancy remarked that if Hitler had not started the war, she could have stayed on at Inchkenneth to enjoy the weather. Whereupon, says David Pryce-Jones in his book on Unity, 'Lady Redesdale stopped the car and told her to apologize for such a slander on Hitler, or else lift her suitcase out of the car and walk'.

Unity meanwhile, was repatriated to England and came to stay with her mother at Inchkenneth in 1944. The bullet still lodged in her brain had greatly changed her; she was incontinent and limped; and in the ruined chapel where Dr Johnson had shrunk away from human bones and Boswell had buried them, she improvised religious services with her mother as sole congregation. Near the cross Boswell had seen one ghost. Unity experienced another:

> One day a stranger intruded on their worship. Lady Redesdale whispered to Unity to look over her shoulder, and there stood a man in a belted overcoat, with a lock of hair plastered down on his forehead, a bristle of a moustache. At the end of the service the man had vanished into thin air. They tried to trace him, they wondered whether a malicious journalist might have been impersonating Hitler, but the boatman swore that nobody had crossed the water.

In the end Unity's past caught up with her. One day in 1948 she complained of a chill, a headache and vomiting, was rushed to Oban's Cottage Hospital and died. Cause of death: Purulent meningitis as a result of an old gunshot wound.

Whenever I find myself in Mull these days I can never look across at tiny Inchkenneth without seeing in one part of the chapel Johnson and Boswell and the bones, and in another Unity and Lady Redesdale as minister and congregation – surely no other place of comparative size and remoteness has been immortalized by such a bizarrely contrasting quartet?

What Boswell called 'four stout rowers' were ready on the morning of Tuesday 19 October 1773 to convey Sir Allan Maclean and his guests to Iona. They landed for a picnic on the way, arrived at the island after dark, and slept that night in their clothes among a pile of hay in a barn with their travelling bags for pillows. When he awoke in the morning Boswell said, 'I could not help smiling at the idea of the Chief of the Macleans, the great English moralist and myself lying thus extended . . .'

After breakfast they went exploring, Johnson making notes and taking measurements of the ruins, Boswell visiting the cathedral to read a sermon aloud and 'indulge in solitude and devout meditation'. Johnson was as impressed by the island's fertility (it exported cattle and corn) as he was depressed by its inhabitants whom he called 'remarkably gross and remarkably neglected'. There was no minister and no school, only two inhabitants who spoke English and none who could read or write.

What surprised the travellers most was the esteem in which Sir Allan was held as Chief of the Macleans, although he hadn't visited the island for fourteen years and the titular owner of it was now the Duke of Argyll. Told that the man who was leading Boswell on a horse to the other side of the island had refused to send him some rum, Sir Allan said to him, 'You rascal! Don't you know I can hang you if I please?' Boswell, thinking the man had committed some capital crime, said, 'How so?' and Sir Allan replied, 'Are they not all my people?' Turning to the man, he went on, 'Refuse to send rum to me, you rascal! Don't you know if I order you to cut a man's throat, you are to do it.' The wretched fellow replied, 'Yes, an't please your honour, and my own too, and hang myself too.' Denying that he had ever refused to send any rum, the man said to Boswell after Sir Allan had gone, that he would have handed over the rum even if Sir Allan's dog had come for it. 'I would cut my bones for him,' he said. Boswell was impressed by such attachment to an absentee chief.

Unlike other great centres of religious pilgrimage, Jerusalem, Mecca, even Lourdes, Iona, being a small island, three miles long and a mile across and separated from the west coast of Mull by a narrow sound, being also of an austere, tranquil beauty, is an easy concept to master. Often I have crossed to the Atlantic shore, stood below the dunes where the white sheep crop the green *machair* and on a calm day listened to the gentle, apologetic suck of the wavelets across the shingle, and thought of that other water, 800 miles to the south whose tides were immortalized by Matthew Arnold:

> Listen, you hear the grating roar
> Of pebbles which the waves suck back, and fling
> At their return, up the high strand,

Begin, and cease, and then begin again,
With tremulous cadence slow, and bring
The eternal note of sadness in.

Near me the sea is green because of the sandy bottom, then
shelves to the dark blue of deep water. Away to the north are
the little black islands of Lunga and Staffa and Dutchman's Cap
like a battlefleet at anchor, and to the north-west the contours of
Coll and Tiree. South, beyond the thin horizon, lies the coast of
Ulster whence the royal Irishman Father Colum, already the founder
of fifteen churches there, came to found another, the greatest of all,
in his island of Icolmkill and from here conveyed the Word across
the breadth of Scotland. In 563 he came ashore in Iona with twelve
disciples, though today nobody can tell you where. Then Iona was
part of the vast Irish settlement of Dalriada which embraced all
Argyll and the Hebrides and from whose ruler Columba obtained
permission to build a monastery.

Columba is said to have been tall with brilliant eyes and
the front part of his head shaved. His biographer says he wore a
cassock of homespun, undyed wool over a linen shirt and sandals
on his feet. He and his brethren spent the day in prayer, labour
and reading and writing; and both on Iona and in Mull they
tended the sick and needy. Often at night he would wander off
to solitary places to pray alone; and he slept in his clothes on a
bed of flagstones. He recognized no episcopal authority, but liked
to entertain visiting bishops and others who came to the island,
allegedly kissing them on arrival. His biographer says that he was
much loved by the community and was as fond of animals as of
men. 'When an exhausted heron fell upon the strand, he ordered
it to be fed and tended till it was able to fly again and on the last
evening of his life he caressed an old horse which rubbed its head
against him, and blessed it.'

Iona was Columba's home for thirty-four years, though he made
many journeys to the mainland to convert the Picts to Christianity
and at least two return visits to Ulster. In the summer of 597 he knew
he was dying, and in making notes from the 23rd Psalm, he wrote at
the foot of the page, 'Here I make an end; what follows my successor
will write.' He attended the first service on Sunday morning, then
rested on his stone bed. When the bell rang for matins he made a
supreme effort and hurried to the church. His attendant Diarmait

followed and as the church was dark, called out, 'Where art thou, father?'

> A moment later the brethren bearing lanterns, as was the custom, came in to service, when they saw the saint lying before the altar. Diarmait raised him up and supported his head: all saw he was dying and began to wail. Columba opened his eyes and looked with a delighted smile to right and left. They thought he saw attendant angels. Diarmait held up Columba's right hand, and the saint moved it in benediction of those present, but could not speak; then he passed away.

In the same year as St Columba died, another saint, Augustine voyaged from Rome to Kent to bring Christianity to southern England. (It was his namesake Augustine of Hippo who prayed 'Make me chaste, O Lord, but please not yet'.) Forty years later a follower of St Columba, St Aidan, did the same for northern England by travelling from Iona to Lindisfarne in Northumbria to establish a monastery there. Later still the famous illuminated Book of Kells, now in Trinity College, Dublin, is believed to have been begun in Iona but later removed to Kells in Ireland, together with the community of Iona when the whole area was overrun by the Vikings. During the next 500 years Iona is lost to history, but around 1200 AD the island once again became a centre of religious life. From his stronghold on Loch Finlaggan in Islay Reginald, son of Somerled and his successor as Lord of the Isles permitted an abbey to be built in Iona on the site of St Columba's monastery and south of it a nunnery of the Augustinian order.

In time the monks and nuns left and both abbey and nunnery fell into disrepair: and it wasn't until the eighteenth century when communications opened up that the outside world came to know of what was there. The ruins of the religious buildings, the survival of half a dozen striking Celtic crosses, the little edifice said to have been St Columba's cell, the graveyard alleged (but now dismissed) as harbouring the tombs of the early kings of Scotland, all set in such a remote and unique location, made a vivid impression on visitors.

Among them was the poet Wordsworth whose introduction to the island was hardly a happy one which he expressed in less than happy verse:

How sad a welcome! To each voyager
Some ragged child holds up for sale a store
Of wave-worn pebbles, pleading on the shore
Where once came monk and nun with gentle stir . . .

and he was also put off by (surprisingly) so many tourists. In 1818 Keats came to Iona after trudging the length of Mull along 'the most dreary track you can think of', eased only by the voice of their guide who sang two Gaelic songs, 'one made by a Mrs Brown on her husband's being drowned – the other a Jacobin [he meant Jacobite] one on Charles Stuart.' In a letter home from Iona he related the now discounted legend of sixty-one kings being buried there, 'forty-one Scotch from Fergus II to Macbeth; eight Irish; four Norwegians; and one French'. But he was struck by the tombs of Highland chieftains, 'their effigies in complete armour, face upward, black and moss-covered', among them 'the famous Macdonald, Lord of the Isles'. He had been told that in St Columba's time the now treeless island had been covered in woods; also that there had been 300 crosses on the island but that 'the Presbyterians' had destroyed most of them. He met the schoolmaster. 'He is a Maclean and as much above four feet as he is under four feet three inches. He stops at one glass of whisky unless you press another and at the second unless you press a third.'

Yet it was the nearby island of Staffa, that extraordinary phenomenon of pillars of basalt rock like a cluster of organ pipes or the bare trunks of trees, first known to the outside world only the year before the Johnson–Boswell tour, that most excited the attention of visitors. 'The colour of the columns is black', wrote Keats, 'with a lurking gloom of purple'. For solemnity and grandeur he thought it surpassed the finest cathedrals and in a poem he called it 'the cathedral of the sea'. Wordsworth was so moved by seeing flowers in bloom on top of the columns that he also wrote a poem in which every line bore his inimitable signature ('Children of Summer! Ye Fresh Flowers that brave/What Summer here escapes not, the fierce wave/And whole artillery of the tempest blast . . .'). Sir Walter Scott was equally typical in his opening lines ('The shores of Mull on the eastward lay/And Ulva dark and Colonsay/And all the group of islets gay/That guard famed Staffa round . . .').

Yet the two who have given Staffa its most lasting fame were not poets but a composer and a painter. The composer was Felix

Mendelssohn on whom the Hebrides had made a great impression. The day his boat came to Staffa the sea was rough and many passengers were seasick: they included, wrote Mendelssohn's friend Carl Klingemann, the mother of 'two beautiful, cold daughters of a Hebrides aristocrat' and an eighty-two-year-old woman who wanted to see Staffa before she died.

> We were put out in boats and lifted by the hissing sea up the pillar stumps to the celebrated Fingal's Cave. A greener roar of waves surely never rushed into a stranger cavern – its many pillars making it look like the inside of an immense organ, black and resounding and absolutely without purpose, and quite alone, the wide gray sea within and without.

It was the sight of this, despite his seasickness, that so excited Mendelssohn that there and then the first ten or twelve bars of what was to become first 'The Hebrides' and later 'Fingal's Cave', came into his head. He wanted to try it out as soon as possible on a piano, but it was a Sunday and when he reached his lodging at Tobermory, although there was a piano there, there could be no question of music. It required the greatest diplomacy, said Klingemann, to persuade the landlord to allow the lid to be opened briefly to enable Mendelssohn to jot down what had been coursing through his mind all day. It was to be another year before the work was completed and given its first public performance; and although not greatly praised at the time, it was to become one of classical music's most enduring works. Wagner called it Mendelssohn's masterpiece while Brahms said of it, 'I would gladly give all I have written to have composed something like the Hebrides Overture'.

The painter was Turner whose canvas of Staffa was as Turneresque as Wordsworth's poem was Wordsworthian. The man who bought the painting, foolish fellow, complained to Turner that it was indistinct, to which Turner replied, truly enough, 'Indistinctness is my forte.'

For these and other travellers the relics of Iona may have impressed as a unique group of antiquities, but with every year that passed they were crumbling into decay. The island being part of the vast estates of the dukes of Argyll, in 1874 the enlightened 8th Duke authorized a programme of restoration. Twenty years later he did even better by making over the principal buildings to a Trust, a condition being that they must put a roof on the abbey and restore it for worship.

The final stage of restoration came in 1938 when the Revd George McLeod (later Lord McLeod of Fuinary) founded the Iona Community as an ecumenical Christian centre where people might come to discover, or rediscover, their faith, 'break down the barriers between prayer and politics, the religious and the ordinary.' A permanent staff under the direction of the Warden (who may be Presbyterian or Catholic, Methodist or Baptist, male or female) stay there all year round, and in summer welcome hundreds of pilgrims from all over the world who come for a week at a time. They have a busy programme, attending lectures, taking part in study groups, sharing domestic chores, creating their own entertainment.

On my last visit I was invited by the young Warden to join the current group for lunch. They were mostly middle-aged Englishwomen, some spinsters, others who had escaped from their husbands for a week, and all, it seemed to me, brimming over with vitality and enjoyment. We ate soup and homemade bread, cheese and fruit. Also present was a guest lecturer, young and bearded Father Donoghue from Galway. Not long before it had been disclosed that his bishop was the father of a seventeen-year-old son by an unmarried woman and had had to leave his see in a hurry. I wanted to ask Father Donoghue about the bishop but felt it might have embarrassed him. The women, not all Christians, were ecstatic about their visit, so different from what they were used to, and had special praise for Father Donoghue. One said, 'Father Donoghue's views on spirituality and the importance of intuition are simply *mind-blowing*.'

After lunch the Warden and I took a walk along the *machair*, and he showed me where soldiers stationed during the war had fashioned a little golf course. Of the people I had met at lunch he said, 'They all come here searching for something, though they're not sure what – a meaning to their lives perhaps but few of them would want to admit to it.' He went on, 'We're not here to convert people but to share things with each other and worship together.' He gave me a glance. 'God is here and now, you know, not out there or beyond the clouds.' I have heard others say this, but have no idea what they mean. It has always seemed to me that God as a concept is whatever you care or don't care to make of him; and there are many people who *do* think of him as being out there or up above, and why not? I asked what sort of things those on the course share. 'Tonight,' he said, 'volunteers among them are going to give us a concert. What will it be like? I don't know. Some in the past have been brilliant, some horrendous, but that's not the point. The point is that by sharing an experience in this way with comparative strangers, people are doing things they may never have done before, giving to their lives a new dimension.' I said, 'A spiritual dimension?' 'For some yes,' said the Warden. 'For some definitely.'

I made my way to the embarkation point for the Mull ferry, past the great medieval Celtic crosses of St Oran (a cousin of Columba), St John, St Martin and St Matthew, past the St Columba Hotel where the new-mown grass smelled of essence of vanilla, past St Ronan's chapel and the ruins of the nunnery, past the long trim row of cottages where live most of the island's hundred inhabitants, and so down to the ferry.

There must have been around fifty of us on that crossing, Japanese, Germans, Scandinavians, all sorts, and when we had completed the short journey and had disembarked up the slope that leads to the car park an odd thing happened. At the top of the slope, and as though guided by some unseen hand, everyone stopped and turned to take a last look at the abbey, now washed by the light of the evening sun. Had they found what they had been seeking, I wondered, and were they now loath to break the thread that bound them to it? If so, would the benison bestowed be lasting or, as with Boswell, transitory? A hundred years ago on Dover Beach Matthew Arnold had given his answer.

> The sea of faith
> Was once too at the full, and round earth's shore
> Lay like the folds of a bright girdle furl'd;
> But now I only hear
> Its melancholy long withdrawing roar,
> Retreating to the breath
> Of the night-wind down the vast edges drear
> And naked shingles of the world.

And so Boswell and Johnson crossed to Mull, still accompanied by Sir Allan Maclean. They spent that night at the home of the local minister the Revd Neal MacLeod who the doctor said was 'the clearest-headed man' he had met in the Western Isles. At breakfast next morning Sir Allan ventured that Scotland had the advantage over England by having more water. If meant to provoke, it could not have succeeded better. 'Sir,' said the doctor, 'we would not have your water, to take the vile bogs which produced it. You have too much! A man who is drowned has more water than either of us.' Not content to leave it there, he went on: 'Your country consists of two things, stone and water. There is indeed a little earth above the stone in some places, but a very little, and the stone is always appearing. It is like a man in rags, the naked skin is still peeping out.'

After breakfast the three set out eastwards on what Boswell called 'a very tedious journey across the most gloomy and desolate country I had ever beheld' – a description which anyone who has traversed the wastes of Mull on a gloomy day will amply confirm – and dined en route with a Dr Alexander Maclean, a local doctor ('In this country', commented Johnson, 'every man's name is Maclean'). So struck was the doctor by Johnson's conversation that he called him '*a hogshead* of sense'.

That evening they arrived at the house on Mull's south-east coast of the Laird of Lochbuy and his wife who was Sir Allan Maclean's sister: both were very old, indeed Sir Allan described them as 'antediluvian'. Before their arrival the travellers had heard Lochbuy described as 'a great, roaring, braggadocio, a kind of Sir John Falstaff, both in size and manners', while Col, contrariwise, had called him 'quite a Don Quixote'. They recognized neither description: 'a bluff, comely, noisy old gentleman' Boswell called him, while to Johnson he was 'rough and haughty and tenacious of his dignity'. Warned by Sir Allan of Johnson's deafness, at dinner Lochbuy shouted at him, 'Are you of the Johnstons of Glencro or of Ardnamurchan?' 'Dr Johnson,' said Boswell, 'gave him a significant look but made no answer; and I told him that he was not John*ston* but John*son* and that he was an Englishman.'

There was a comic scene at breakfast next morning when, before Dr Johnson came down, Lady Lochbuy proposed offering him for breakfast a cold sheep's head. 'Sir Allan,' wrote Boswell, 'seemed displeased at his sister's vulgarity and wondered how such a thought could come into her head.' Boswell, out of mischief, took his hostess's part, saying it would be only fair to offer it. ' "I think so," said the lady, looking at her brother with an air of victory. Sir Allan, finding the matter desperate, strutted about the room and took snuff.'

When Johnson appeared he was offered the sheep's head but declined it, according to Boswell, 'with a tone of surprise and anger'. Lady Lochbuy then said, 'It is here, sir,' thinking he had refused it to save the trouble of fetching it. 'Thus,' said Boswell, 'they went on at cross purposes, till he confirmed his refusal in a manner not to be misunderstood; while I sat quietly by and enjoyed my success.' After breakfast Lochbuy took them to the family castle, now unoccupied, but in whose dungeons he had some years before imprisoned several malefactors; and it may have been the sight of them that led Lady Lochbuy, the matter of the sheep's head now forgotten, to describe Dr Johnson (in contrast to a hogshead of sense) as 'a *dungeon* of wit'. Having, along with the other Highland lairds, lost his rights of heritable jurisdiction after Culloden, Lochbuy had no business imprisoning anybody and had been heavily fined for it by the Court of Justiciary (among whose judges, he reminded Boswell, was his father Lord Auchinleck). Sir Allan then whispered that his brother-in-law could not accept that times had changed.

Later that day Johnson and Boswell took passage in the ferry from Mull to Oban where they found a Glasgow newspaper which announced that the doctor was confined by tempestuous weather to the isle of Skye. 'Such a philosopher', said the report, 'detained on an almost barren island, resembles a whale left upon the strand.' If Johnson took exception to this, he would surely have smiled at the concluding passage which saw him adrift in Skye yet 'charming his companions and the rude inhabitants with his superior knowledge and wisdom, calm resignation and unbounded benevolence.'

# CHAPTER 9

## *Journey's End*

ALTHOUGH THEIR ARRIVAL AT OBAN MARKED THE END OF BOSWELL'S and Johnson's tour of the islands, their journey south to Glasgow and Edinburgh before the doctor took the stagecoach to Newcastle was not without incident.

Their first port of call was the inn at the charming small town of Inveraray, recently rebuilt by John Adam and Robert Mylne after the ravages of Montrose and one of the two best preserved eighteenth-century towns in Scotland (the other is Haddington in East Lothian). The doctor declared the inn to be as good as any in England and after supper, in happy mood, called for a gill of whisky – the first time on the tour, said Boswell, that he had tasted liquor. 'Come,' he said, 'let us know what it is that makes a Scotchman happy!' When it had been brought, said Boswell, 'he drank it all but a drop, which I begged leave to pour into my glass that I might say we had drunk whisky together.'

Just outside the town lay Inveraray Castle, the seat of the dukes of Argyll and recently rebuilt in the neo-Gothic manner; and now the pair plotted how best to attract the attention of the duke in the hope of being invited to a meal. Boswell had met the duke before who, he said, had always treated him with civility but he was less sure about the duchess, a daughter of the Duke of Hamilton against whose family Boswell had appeared for the family of Douglas in a famous lawsuit. The doctor, always a scourge to those less learned than himself, was not far behind Boswell when it came to attracting the notice of the quality. 'He was secretly not unwilling to have attention paid him by so great a chieftain and so exalted a nobleman,' said Boswell; and when it was agreed that Boswell should call on the duke, Johnson urged him not to do so until after dinner (then served in mid-afternoon), 'as it would look like seeking an invitation.'

Accordingly Boswell pottered up there, 'just about the time when I supposed the ladies would be retired from dinner,' was received by the duke 'most politely' and invited to bring the doctor to dinner the following day. As Boswell was leaving, the duke invited him to stay to tea and led him to the drawing-room to be introduced to the duchess, her daughter and other ladies. The duchess, said Boswell, 'took not the least notice of me,' a slight which he said would have mortified him 'had I not been consoled by the obliging attentions of the duke'. My guess is that he was mortified anyway.

Next day Boswell presented his travelling companion to the duke who showed them round the house with its fine collection of pictures, firearms and furnishings and in the course of which Boswell admitted to being much struck (and doubtless aroused) by 'some of the ladies' maids tripping about in neat morning dresses', after which the duke took them for a drive in the park. At dinner the duke placed Dr Johnson next to him, while Boswell, though aware he was out of favour with the duchess, yet felt it incumbent on him to try and make his mark:

> I knew it was the rule of modern high life not to drink
> to anybody; but that I might have the satisfaction for once
> to look the duchess in the face, with a glass in my hand, I
> with a respectful air, addressed her, 'My Lady Duchess, I have
> the honour to drink your grace's good health.' I repeated the
> words audibly and with a steady countenance. This was, perhaps,
> rather too much; but some allowance must be made for human
> feelings.

Not afraid to record his own social unease in the presence

of rank, Boswell was equally quick to observe it in others.

> A gentleman in company, after dinner, was desired by the duke
> to go to another room for a specimen of curious marble which
> his grace wished to show us. He brought a wrong piece, upon
> which the duke sent him back again. He could not refuse; but
> to avoid any appearance of servility, he whistled as he went out
> of the room to show his independency. On my mentioning this
> afterwards to Dr Johnson, he said it was a nice trait of character.

After dinner the duchess continued her indifference towards
Boswell but had an animated conversation with Johnson on whether
between death and resurrection there was a 'middle state' or limbo to
which Christ may have been conveyed on his way to Hell – a fancy
propagated by the Revd Archibald Campbell, the duke's kinsman.

The two returned to the inn, well pleased with their visit,
and in the evening were joined by the minister of Inveraray, the
Revd John Macaulay, the same John Macaulay who with his father
the Revd Aulay Macaulay, the reader will recall, had attempted
to shop Prince Charles when he was on the run in Benbecula
twenty-seven years earlier and so claim the £30,000 reward. It
was no doubt knowledge of this incident and as a reward for
his initiative that had persuaded the previous Duke of Argyll,
the prince's arch-enemy, to grant him the living of Inveraray.
If this past incident in John Macaulay's life came to the ears
of the two travellers (and Macaulay may have thought it best to
conceal it) neither makes mention of it. At any rate at the inn that
evening the doctor and Macaulay had a row, Johnson asserting that
it was possible for a man to be of good principle but bad practice
and Macaulay denying it; to which, said Boswell, the doctor grew
warm and accused Macaulay to his face of being grossly ignorant of
human nature.

Next day the pair set out for Glasgow. Johnson, having complained that the little Shetland pony on which he had ridden from
Oban was too small for him, was mounted on a magnificent horse
provided by the Duke of Argyll and which made Boswell's servant
Joseph say, 'He now looks like a bishop'. The road from the head of
Loch Fyne, where today are farmed the delicious, small Loch Fyne
oysters, leads upward through Glen Kinglas to a 3,000 feet summit
where beside the road Dr Johnson observed a seat with the inscription

REST, AND BE THANKFUL — the name without the comma by which the mountain is known today.

On the far side the travellers descended to the shores of Loch Lomond where they spent a couple of days with Sir James Colquhoun of Luss, sailing on the loch and visiting several of its islands, many of which he owned. In Glasgow they put up at the Saracen's Head where Johnson was delighted to find a coal fire, having seen nothing but peat fires (never so warm) for the past two months. Next day over breakfast, tea and dinner, he met several of the university's professors, and while praising their system of one long academic term and one long recess instead of the three maintaining in England, he was at his most pompous when assessing the talents of the graduates. 'Men bred in the universities of Scotland cannot be expected to be often decorated with the splendours of ornamental erudition, but they obtain a mediocrity of knowledge between learning and ignorance, not inadequate to the purposes of common life . . .' Less pompously he might have rephrased that '*more than adequate* to the purposes of common life', for the strength and glory of teaching in the Scottish universities was in its breadth, not depth; and one of Scotland's complaints today is that a curriculum which has served its sons so fruitfully in England and throughout the world has been increasingly amended to conform with English educational practices.

Nor were his spirits raised when the Foulis brothers, the Glasgow printers, came to dine. Boswell found their conversation tedious, saying that instead of listening to what the doctor had to say, 'they teased him with questions and doubtful disputations' — an attitude born of nervousness which I have seen many Scots adopt in the presence of those more self-assured — and, bored, he left the dining-room to write a letter. Presently the doctor 'came in a flutter to me and desired I might come back again, for he could not bear these men.' 'Oh ho, sir!' said Boswell, making the most of the doctor's discomfort, 'you are flying to me for refuge.' Johnson, with equal repartee, replied that he was the lesser of two evils.

From Glasgow they set out for Ayrshire, dining en route with the Earl of Loudoun and his mother who was ninety-five. The reader will recall meeting Lord Loudoun when he was in command of the government garrison in Inverness during the '45 and of his abortive attempt to capture Prince Charles at Moy when the only casualty had been the MacCrimmon, MacLeod's piper. Since then he had served a term as Governor of Virginia but was not considered a success. But Boswell liked him, spoke of his humanity to the vanquished, in contrast to Cumberland after Culloden, and said that he had given more service to Ayrshire than any man. 'His mind was never soured, and he retained his good humour and benevolence to the last.'

Another ancient *grande dame* was waiting at Eglinton Castle, their next port of call, in the shape of a remote Kennedy forbear Susannah Countess of Eglinton, then eighty-five and whose hobby, according to Peter Levi, was taming rats. Her son Alexander, the tenth earl, had died four years earlier in a curious manner. An excise officer named Mungo Campbell from Saltcoats, having been observed previously shooting a hare on Lord Eglinton's estate, was again seen walking with a gun on his land. Told of this, the earl, who happened to be passing in his carriage, alighted and asked Campbell to hand the gun over. Campbell refused. The earl advanced as though to enforce his demand, Campbell, retreating backwards, stumbled on a stone, the gun went off and the earl was shot. Taken to the castle, he died at two o'clock in the morning. Campbell was arrested and tried in Edinburgh for murder, his defence being (contrary to what the earl said before he died) that the shooting had been accidental. Campbell was found guilty and condemned to death, but cheated the executioner by hanging himself in his cell the day after the trial.

Boswell had been saddened by Eglinton's death, for it was when both were living in London that the earl, as one of the representative peers of Scotland, had introduced Boswell to what he called 'the circle of the great, the gay and the ingenious'. Eglinton had liked Johnson too, though at times was embarrassed by the doctor's often bearish manner. Boswell wrote that the doctor was much taken by the old Countess. 'Her figure was majestick, her manners high-bred, her reading extensive, and her conversation elegant.' When she learned that the doctor had been born the year after her marriage, she said that he might have been her son and now adopted him as such. 'And when we were going away', said Boswell, 'she embraced him, saying "My dear son, farewell."'

From Eglinton the pair travelled in a post-chaise hired from Kilmarnock to the eponymous estate of Boswell's father, Lord Auchinleck. The estate lies between the villages of Auchinleck and Ochiltree in one of the less attractive parts of Ayrshire, and today is approached along a road that runs under a chute from an abandoned coal mine, through a pair of lodge gates and up a longish drive to Auchinleck House. The house itself, an elegant Palladian mansion with four pillars, a flight of steps and a quotation from Horace running along the top, is still standing, though behind the façade the rooms are derelict; the Boswell Society, I understand, is hoping to raise sufficient funds for restoration. The house commands a fine view over fields bordered by woods and rhododendrons.

Boswell was taking a risk in inviting his companion to Auchinleck for his father was a man well set in his ways. 'His age, his office and his character', wrote his son, 'had long given him an acknowledged claim to great attention in whatever company he was, and he could ill brook any diminution of it.' The same could be said of Johnson. Boswell said of his father that he was as sanguine a Whig and Presbyterian as Dr Johnson was a Tory and Church of England man; 'and as he had not much leisure to be informed of Dr Johnson's great merits by reading his works, he had a partial and unfavourable notion of him, founded on his supposed political tenets; which were so discordant to his own that instead of speaking of him with respect, he used to call him a Jacobite fellow.' What Boswell didn't know was that on first hearing of the trip to the Hebrides, Lord Auchinleck's only comment was, 'Jamie's gone clean gyte [crazy], pinning himself to the tails of an auld dominie [schoolmaster]'. The visit contained all the seeds of conflict; and to ensure as much harmony as possible, Boswell urged his companion to avoid three topics: Whiggism, Presbyterianism and Sir John Pringle whom Lord Auchinleck and his son admired and Johnson thought slightly mad; to which Johnson conciliatingly replied, 'I shall certainly not speak on subjects which I am told are disagreeable to a gentleman under whose roof I am; especially I shall not do so to your father.'

At first all went smoothly. When it rained, as it often does in those parts, Johnson made use of his host's library, and when it cleared Boswell took him on a walk round the estate, past the old family castle, now in ruins and along the banks of the river Lugar. It has been said often enough, and it is true, that the Scots are obsessed about their family histories and in the course of their walk Boswell told Johnson of his pride in an ancestor Thomas Boswell 'who was highly favoured by his sovereign James IV of Scotland and fell with him at Flodden'.

Next day the pair dined with the local Presbyterian minister, the Revd Dun, and it would seem that the presence of other ministers there led the doctor to make some unfavourable comments about Presbyterian practices. This led one of the company to make disparaging remarks about the narrowness of views among Anglican dignitaries, with particular reference to 'fat bishops' and 'drowsy deans' which prompted Johnson to exclaim testily, 'Sir, you know no more of our church than a Hottentot'. Boswell was sorry that he had brought this exchange upon himself.

It could have been this incident which helped to trigger off what Boswell called 'the collision' that occurred between his father and Johnson next day. What began it is not known, and indeed Boswell was so embarrassed that he subsequently refused to enlarge on it. 'They became exceedingly warm and violent,' he wrote, 'and I was very much distressed by being present at such an altercation.' In the course of it, he said, their Whiggism and Presbyterianism, Toryism and Episcopacy, were terribly buffeted. There was one compensation. 'My worthy hereditary friend, Sir John Pringle, never having been mentioned, escaped without a bruise.' In the course of time the incident became quite famous, and twelve years later the satirical artist Thomas Rowlandson made a sketch of it. The following day was a Sunday when, not surprisingly, Johnson declined to accompany his host and his friend to the Presbyterian service conducted by the Revd Dun.

When the travellers left Auchinleck, said Boswell, 'notwithstanding the altercation that had passed, my father . . . was very civil to Dr Johnson and politely attended him to the post-chaise which was to convey us to Edinburgh.'

In Edinburgh the doctor was the guest of Boswell and his wife in James's Court, as he had been at the beginning of the tour. There and elsewhere in the town there was much entertaining, Margaret Boswell finding herself having to pour out numerous cups of tea for the doctor and his visitors while Boswell was on duty in the Court of Session. Although always ready to play the part of a dutiful wife, Margaret regretted her husband's relationship with Johnson as keenly as her father-in-law, indeed used much the same imagery in describing it. She had often seen a bear led by a man, she said, but she had never before seen a man led by a bear.

One evening, exhausted by so much entertaining, Johnson said to his host, 'Sir, we have been harrassed by invitations,' but when Boswell agreed, the doctor reflected how much worse it would have been if they had not received any. Both were tickled by the compliments paid on their safe return. 'We are addressed,' said Johnson, 'as if we had made a voyage to Nova Zembla and suffered five persecutions in Japan,' when in fact there had been no danger. Boswell reminded him that there *had* been danger during the storm off Col, but that he, being below deck, had been unaware of it: 'he was like the chicken that hides its head under its wing, thinking itself safe.'

They visited the Court of Session where they found Lord Auchinleck on the bench; but did not hear him describe Dr Johnson to a fellow judge as 'Ursa Major' – the Great Bear. There was talk of the importance of the oath, the doctor's religious beliefs obliging him to say what few would say today, that a man would feel a necessity to tell the truth on oath when he might not do so without it. Shown Edinburgh castle, he said it would make a *good prison* in Edinburgh; and declined to visit the room at Dunfermline where Charles I was born. Did he envy us, asked Boswell naïvely in his diary, having the birthplace of a king?

Known in Scotland as well as England for his anti-Scottishness, Johnson was again at his loftiest when summing up his stay in Edinburgh:

> The conversation of the Scots grows every day less unpleasing to the English: their peculiarities wear fast away; their dialect is likely to become in half a century provincial and rustick, even to themselves. The great, the learned, the ambitious and the vain, all cultivate the English phrase and the English pronunciation, and in splendid companies Scotch* is not much heard, except now and then from an old lady.

But now the great adventure was over and on Saturday, 20 November 1773 the pair set off south. On the way they visited Roslin chapel, still owned today by the earls of Rosslyn, with its unique and delicate carvings in stone and then, further along the same glen, Hawthornden Castle, once the home of the poet Drummond of Hawthornden. The English poet Ben Jonson had paid Drummond a visit there in 1618 and it pleased Boswell's

*Lowland Scot.

fancy that he should now be taking *Sam* Johnson to the same spot.

They had accepted an invitation to dine and stay the night with an historian called Sir James Dalrymple, Bart. at his house at Cranston, but by the time they left Hawthornden it was growing dark. 'Dr Johnson,' wrote Boswell, 'did not seem much troubled at our having treated the baronet with so little attention to politeness', doubtless because it had come to their ears that the baronet, along with other Scots, had been highly critical of the doctor, saying that he could not see how any gentleman of Scotland could keep company with him; and one must assume that his invitation to have their company was to boast of it to friends. For his part Johnson had a low opinion of Dalrymple, saying that the sort of history he wrote was nothing but Romance, being unsupported by evidence. And when Boswell spoke of the baronet's disappointment at their not arriving in time to eat a vintage sheep he had promised to kill, Johnson made fun of the disappointment and parodied Dalrymple's style as he might have recounted it.

Arriving at the baronet's seat, they found him 'not in very good humour'. Conversation was sticky, after which 'we went to bed in ancient rooms which would have better suited the climate of Italy in summer than that of Scotland in the month of November'.

Next day they left Cranston for the inn at Blackfields where they spent the night. After breakfast the stagecoach from Edinburgh to Newcastle pulled in. Among the passengers was Dr Hope, professor of botany at Edinburgh University who was as delighted to find he was to have the doctor's company as the doctor was to have his. Before the coach departed Johnson told Boswell (and on many future occasions reiterated it) that their tour of Scotland had been the pleasantest of his life. And the one went south to London and the other north to renew his duties at the Court of Session.

Despite its rigours and occasional differences of opinion, the trip for both men had been a huge success. 'Boswell will praise my resolution and perseverance,' Johnson wrote to Mrs Thrale on his return home, 'and I shall in return celebrate his good humour and perpetual cheerfulness. He has better faculties than I had imagined . . . It is very convenient to travel with him; for there is no house where he is not received with kindness and respect.'

For his part Boswell wrote that Johnson had completed the

trip with his anti-Scottish prejudices much lessened and with very grateful feelings for the hospitality he had received. Yet in his book on the jaunt, *A Journey to the Western Islands of Scotland*, his attitude towards Scotland and the Scots was often one of typically English condescension; of a superior being taking the measure of a people less enlightened than his own; although the one distinguished Scot who was more enlightened than himself, David Hume, he dismissed with contumely. Equally dismissive and offensive were his remarks, past and present, that the Scots loved Scotland more than truth; that oats were food for horses in England but for people in Scotland, that the knowledge acquired by students at the universities in Scotland was mediocre, that 'the conversation of the Scots grows every day less unpleasing to the English', that it was Cromwell by bringing shoes and cabbages to Aberdeen who had 'civilized' the Scots and, though deeply religious, his refusal to attend a Presbyterian church service.

No wonder that many Scots felt outraged by his comments and he was vigorously attacked in the Scottish (and some English) press. So angry were some writers that they spread scandalous stories about him: that he had challenged James Macpherson to a duel for falsely claiming that his poem *Ossian* was an ancient Erse manuscript, that the Highlanders had made him drunk, that he had caught the pox from a female mountaineer. For Johnson this was so much water off a duck's back. Of one Scottish critic, later a judge, who had published what Boswell called a ludicrous imitation of Johnson's style, he said that he could have caricatured it better himself;* while of what Boswell called 'a scurrilous volume, larger than Johnson's own, filled with malignant abuse . . .' Johnson said, 'This fellow must be a blockhead. They don't know how to go about their abuse. Who will read a five shilling book against me? No, sir, if they had wit, they should have kept pelting me with pamphlets'. But that some of the shafts against him had struck home is evidenced in a self-excusing letter he wrote to a friend in Norfolk. 'None of us would be offended if a foreigner who has travelled here should say that vines and olives don't grow in England' – a reference to his remarks about the paucity of trees on the Scottish east coast. But he knew he had said much more: he was one of the first of a whole

---

*Some years ago there was a competition in the *New Statesman* magazine for the best parody of Graham Greene. Graham Greene entered under an assumed name and won it.

regiment of Englishmen to point out to the Scottish people, and in an often demeaning way, some of their alleged inadequacies.

Boswell, now three-quarters anglicized himself, could not see this; he spoke of the rancour of the critics as coming from 'shallow, irritable North Britons' and wrote too of 'the extreme jealousy of the Scotch and the resentment of having their country [*his* country!] described as it really was; when to say that it was a country as good as England would have been a gross falsehood.' To bolster his view he published letters of three Scotsmen (a Mr Dempster, a Mr Knox and a Mr Tytler) all as anglophile as himself, saying there was nothing in the book that a Scotchman need take amiss, and more or less hinting that those who did were being unnecessarily sensitive.

It was left to a Scottish aristocrat, the 11th Earl of Eglinton, successor to Boswell's friend the 10th Earl, and as self-assured as any Englishman, to stand up for his country where Boswell had failed to. 'Damned rascal!' Eglinton said of Dr Johnson, 'to talk as he does of the Scotch.' When Boswell repeated this to the doctor, it seemed (he said) to give him pause. No wonder, for with Johnson's veneration for rank, it had never occurred to him to receive criticism from such a quarter. 'It presented his extreme prejudice against the Scotch,' Boswell was obliged to admit, 'in a point of view somewhat new to him.'

For Boswell the magnet of London never faded. Four years later he recorded a conversation with Johnson in which he said,

> I had long complained to him that I felt myself discontented in Scotland as too narrow a sphere, and that I wished to make my chief residence in London, the great scene of ambition, instruction and amusement; a scene which was to me, comparatively speaking, a heaven upon earth.

They talked about the matter for a while, Johnson saying he never knew anyone who had such a gust for London as his friend, yet pointing out that that would probably mean abandoning Auchinleck. Whereupon Boswell expressed his own reservations:

> I suggested a doubt that if I were to reside in London, the exquisite zest with which I relished it in occasional visits might go off, and I might grow tired of it.

It was this that led to what is probably the most famous of all the doctor's sayings: 'No, sir, when a man is tired of London he is tired of life; for there is in London all that life can afford.'

How many would subscribe to that today?

# INTERLUDE

I WAS STILL IN SKYE WHEN I HEARD THAT HITLER HAD INVADED Poland, so set off south to join up. It was, as I have recalled before, a lovely summer's day, the same that Nancy Mitford was experiencing as she and her mother drove to the ferry across Mull, with a light wind stirring the roadside grasses and moving the shadows of the clouds over sunlit heather and bracken. All the way south, across blue water at Lochalsh and over the moors to Invergarry, down to Ballachulish and its ferry, then across to the great dark cleft of Glencoe – a sombre reminder of the shameful massacre of the Macdonald hosts by their Campbell guests in 1692 – and so through to the bare uplands of Rannoch; criss-crossing the tracks of Bonnie Prince Charlie, Boswell and Johnson, Montrose and a score of others, I observed that marvellous country with heightened awareness, almost as though seeing it for the first time – because, I suppose unconsciously, I knew it could also be the last. Passing through Stirling at dusk I saw the shape of things to come. Not a light showed anywhere. The war had begun.

It was close to midnight when I reached my grandmother's flat in Belgrave Crescent, Edinburgh (my grandfather had died five years earlier), and heard that my father had flown south from

Islay a day or two earlier to take command of the armed merchant cruiser HMS *Rawalpindi*, then refitting in London's Albert Docks. Next morning the air-raid sirens sounded for the first time and my grandmother and I crept down to the cellar where we sat petrified for half an hour, fully expecting the annihilation of Belgrave Crescent, if not of all Edinburgh. When the All Clear sounded, I wrote a letter to the Admiralty, offering my services. Their reply reached me several months later, when I was at sea, regretting there were no vacancies at present and advising me to apply again in six months' time.

But I was lucky, and as an Oxford undergraduate was processed into the Navy as a sub-lieutenant through the Joint Universities Recruiting Board; and after five months' training in the south, found myself on my way back to Scotland to join a destroyer at Greenock on the Clyde. We sailed within a few hours of my arrival and in the early morning when I came on watch I saw that we were threading our way through familiar waters, past Islay with its seven years of memories and Skye with those more recent. Then the smudge of the outer Hebrides, where Prince Charles had so nearly been nabbed (and where a latter-day Prince Charles, then a pupil at Gordonstoun, was caught drinking cherry brandy in Stornoway), showed up to the north-west and I asked the first lieutenant, with whom I was keeping watch, a question that had been puzzling me ever since I had joined him on the bridge:

'Excuse me, sir, but where are we actually going?'

'Has no-one told you?'

'No.'

'How very remiss. Why, Scapa of course. Where else?'

We rounded Cape Wrath and headed for the Pentland Firth.

And so I came to the last of my Scottish islands, the Orkneys, and to the great naval base of Scapa Flow which was to be my home, on and off, for three out of the next five years. It was a natural harbour if ever there was one, a sheet of enclosed water some 10 miles by 8, the perfect refuge for sea- and war-weary ships. The Picts discovered it first, then the Vikings on their terrible raids south, and gave to the ring of islands that protected it their lovely Norse names – Hoy and Fara to the west, Switha and Hoxa and Flotta to the south, Burray and Ronaldsay to the east and, to the north, the long southern shore of Mainland. For the British too it was the ideal forward base in any war with Germany, for it guarded the entrance to and exit from the Atlantic to the North Sea and any enemy warship or blockade runner would have to pass between Shetland and the coast of Norway, only a hundred miles away. It was from Scapa that Admiral Jellicoe's Grand Fleet had sailed on a May evening in 1916 to do battle with the German High Seas Fleet off Jutland; here too that the High Seas Fleet had been brought in chains at war's end, to lie rotting in the Flow until Midsummer's Day 1919 when at a signal from their admiral, their crews opened the sea cocks and they all guggle-guggled to the bottom. (A party of Stromness schoolchildren on their summer outing in a pleasure boat thought this had been arranged for their benefit and gave three hearty cheers.)

And here, twenty years later, my father had come in his *Rawalpindi* preparatory to going out on his first patrol; and was present that October night when Gunther Prien, captain of the German submarine U47, found a gap in the defences of the eastern islands and crept into the Flow, silent and unobserved. Had the fleet been at anchor off Flotta as it usually was, the consequences for the British war effort might have been devastating, but fortunately they had put to sea a day or two before – all but the old battleship *Royal Oak*, acting as a guardship in Scapa Bay. A literally sitting target, she was sent to the bottom with the loss of more than 800 lives, then Commander Prien crept out as invisibly and silently as he had come. A month later the Germans scored another triumph when their fast battleships *Scharnhorst* and *Gneisenau* passed unobserved up the Norwegian coast, sighted the *Rawalpindi* off south-east Iceland as it was growing dark and after an hour's chase shelled her until she was ablaze from end to end: my father and 263 of his crew were not among the handful of survivors.

Admiral Beatty called Scapa the most damnable place on earth and few in the Navy disagreed. The islands were treeless, part heather part grass, home for seabirds and sheep, and across the bare face of the Flow tempests blew, often for days on end. There were no women, shops, restaurants, only a couple of canteens which dispensed warm beer, a hall for film shows and the occasional concert-party and a couple of football fields invariably too sodden for play.

For most of my shipmates this was depressing, but I came to love the place. Firstly because it was Scotland, even if its origins were Scandinavian, also because if one was going to commit oneself to a war, I preferred to do it without distractions. Admittedly it was a desolate place to return to in winter, though there were compensations in the way of duty-free drink and filmshows and flotilla parties. But in the summer, when the hills of Hoy were touched with purple and green and the Flow sparkled blue in the morning sun, at night too when the northern lights wove pale patterns in the sky, the place had a rare beauty. Sometimes I would take my fishing rod ashore and try for sea trout off the shore or climb a hill beyond which lay Loch Heldale and its mottled trout and there would spend many a contented hour with only skuas and curlews for company.

Yet in all my years at Scapa there was one place we could never visit because of always being at short notice for sea, and that was the mainland of Orkney and Kirkwall its capital. One day, I promised myself, I would return there and in the course of time I did. On the first visit I took my mother because she wanted to see where her husband had been in the First World War and her son and husband had been in the Second. It was a strange experience to motor down the east coast of Hoy to the base at Lyness and observe in Gutter Sound, which I remembered crowded with destroyers swinging at their buoys, only empty water: while ashore the prefabricated huts which had housed the accounts and medical offices were now long abandoned, windows removed or broken, rotting doors swaying and creaking in the wind.

Next time I took my wife, staying at the Standing Stones hotel near Stromness (one of the most literate small towns in Scotland) and fished in the lochs of Harray and Swannay. Two things struck me then about Mainland Orkney which I had not expected: unlike the islands in the Flow, the exceptional greenness of the land, evidence of age-long fertility for crops and cattle, and the amazing quality of the light, as pure as that of Arabia Deserta. Then came the making of a BBC documentary film on the Flow in which we brought over from Germany the engineer officer of Prien's U47 who gave us a rundown on how they had penetrated the eastern defences to sink the *Royal Oak* before returning to a triumphant welcome by the German fleet and a banquet with Hitler in Berlin.

The *Royal Oak* is now designated a war grave, not to be raised or disturbed. Above the wreck a buoy marks its position, and sometimes on a clear day you can see from the window of the plane about to land at Kirkwall the outlines of the battleship lying on the sandy bottom. We filmed other relics of the wars: the great monument on the cliffs of Marwick Head to Lord Kitchener and all but twelve of the men of the cruiser *Hampshire*, sunk by a mine on a wild night in 1916 while taking the Field Marshal to Archangel for talks with the Russians; the naval cemetery at Lyness where are buried the naval dead of both wars, among them some who died at Jutland, others who perished when the battleship *Vanguard* mysteriously blew up in the Flow in 1916; the graves of some German airmen, brought down by anti-aircraft fire in the early days of the second war and that of a lone Lascar fireman whose tombstone proclaims his name: HAM FAT. We also filmed the charming little Italian chapel, made with the scantiest of materials by the Italian prisoners of war captured in North Africa who, after Prien's exploit, built a long causeway linking the islands on the eastern side to prevent any further attempts at penetration. The Catholics of Orkney keep the chapel in repair and once a month Mass is said in it.

# PART 3
## *War in the North*

# CHAPTER 10

## *Orkneyinga Saga*

ON FURTHER VISITS IT WAS THE ANCIENT RATHER THAN THE MODERN
THAT I sought and found in abundance: artefacts more than 5,000
years old, evidence of the presence of Orkney's oldest known inhabitants and of whose existence when in Scapa Flow I had never dreamed.

In his *Portrait of Orkney*, the island's famous poet and chronicler,
George Mackay Brown, has written about them:

> As I came home from Sandwick
>     A star was in the sky
> The northern lights above the hill
>     Were streaming broad and high
> The tinkers lit their glimmering fires,
>     Their tents were pitched close by.
> But the city of the vanished race
> Lay dark and silent in that place.
>     As I came home from Sandwick
>     A star was in the sky.

On the west coast of Orkney's Mainland, close to Sandwick

and between the heights of Yesnaby and Marwick Head, lies the crescent-shaped Bay of Skaill, fronted by cliffs on its southern side and by a long spur of tidal rock at the other. Its beach is of soft sand and sea shells. Behind the beach are a line of dunes and behind them green fields where in early summer can be seen the white and yellow of daisies and marsh marigolds and, close by, roseate banks of sea pinks.

In the winter of 1850 a fierce storm swept along Mainland's west coast and in the course of it ripped the turf off the dunes at the southern end of the bay. This revealed a huge midden or congealed refuse dump and beneath it, though covered in sand, the almost perfectly preserved remains of a prehistoric village, now known as Skara Brae. Here from about 3100 BC, that is from before the building of the Pyramids, even before Stonehenge, lived the people of George Mackay Brown's 'vanished race'. Over the years the settlement was excavated and cleared of sand and today, the property of Historic Scotland, it has the reputation of being the best preserved prehistoric village in Northern Europe.

It consists of a number of semi-subterranean rooms with interconnecting passages. It was roofed at the time of its occupancy but is no longer. Yet what makes it so exciting and for the visitor brings it immediately to life is that *all the furniture is still in place*. The average room measures just over 6 metres by just over 4. The walls are of midden fronted with flagstones quarried locally, and in the centre of each room stands a square fireplace formed by four adjacent stone slabs. Either side of the fireplace and set against the walls are spaces for beds, lengths of flagstones forming the three outer sides: on the beds themselves were placed dried bracken or heather with the skins of sheep or deer as blankets.

Above most of the beds are recesses in the walls for storing things, while against the wall are stone dressers on two levels supported by stone legs and in front of them, like any lady's boudoir of today, stone seats. It is thought that on these dressers the inhabitants kept their personal possessions, artefacts that have been found on the site such as bowls made of stone and bone, some containing red ochre, tools fashioned from the bones of animals, birds and mammals (especially whales and walrus), stone axes, flints, curiously shaped small objects of stone for seemingly religious purposes, puffballs (now fossilized) for possible use against blood-clotting, jewellery in the forms of bone beads and pendants and pins, and what look like primitive dice. In the corners of the rooms stand square stone containers, their sides bound by clay to make them watertight; it is thought that these contained fresh water in which limpets were soaked for use as bait for fishing. Beneath some of the houses drains have been laid, one of the earliest systems of indoor sanitation.

It is estimated that some twenty families or upwards of seventy people lived in this community of underground rooms, and it is impossible to walk through them, or so I found, without becoming, so to speak, one of them. So graphic and stark are the items of furniture that they call out for one to imagine daily life there: lighting a fire of seaweed and dried dung in the morning and cooking on it during the day; the taking of tools from the dresser for the cutting up of meat or fish or to fashion the simple clothes they made from the hides of animals; people going out and returning, some to plant seeds of wheat or barley and later to harvest them, some to fish, others to gather precious driftwood from the shore (for there was no wood in Orkney), yet more to tend the cattle or pick berries and herbs; and then in the evenings perhaps the women would put on their jewellery and gather with their families round the fire for the telling of tales and the singing of songs before falling into the big wide beds whose flagstone sides would be proof against draughts and whose bracken and hides would keep them warm. Yet few lived beyond thirty.

By all accounts Skara Brae was occupied for some 600 years – 200 years longer than the time the Romans occupied Britain, 200 years longer than the time that separates Queen Elizabeth the First's day from that of Queen Elizabeth the Second. What happened in 2500 BC to lead to Skara Brae being abandoned no-one knows.

Yet Skara Brae is not the only evidence of prehistoric life on Orkney. A few miles to the south lie a whole collection of ancient artefacts: the standing stones of Stenness and those in the Ring of Brodgar, erected in roughly the same period as Skara Brae and similar to those at Avebury in Wiltshire, Callanish in Lewis and Carnac in France, though for what purpose nobody can say for sure. Not far off lies the jewel of them all, a huge circular mound like some female giant's breast, the prehistoric burial chamber of Maes Howe, said to be the finest of its kind in northern Europe.

Ten years after the storm that tore the grass from the dunes at Skara Brae, an amateur archaeologist by the name of J. Farrer broke into Maes Howe. He found a long passageway roofed and walled with stone, leading into a central chamber some 4.5 metres square, with smaller chambers leading off it. The stone slabs that formed the main chamber were found to weigh up to 30 tonnes which make one question, as one does with the stones at Avebury and Stonehenge, how the people of that time managed to position them. Disappointing for Mr Farrer was not to find any evidence (apart from part of a human skull and some bones of a horse) of the use of the chamber for burial.

But then Mr Farrer was not the first to break into Maes Howe. In the twelfth century or 4,000 years after Maes Howe was built the Vikings entered it by digging a hole through the top, and if there were human remains there in any number, they may have removed them. Equally Maes Howe may not have been used as a burial chamber but as a religious centre where offerings were made to gods or ancestors. This view is strengthened by the curious fact that the entrance to the chamber was built to face due west so that when the sun is setting on midwinter's day, a thin shaft of light penetrates the passageway and chamber.

Maes Howe may also have been used as a burial place for treasure. The Vikings believed this, for they left scrawled graffiti or runes on the walls which can still be seen today. One says: *It is surely true what I say that treasure was taken away. Treasure was carried off in three nights . . .* while another by Simon Sirith is more detailed: *To the north west a great treasure is hidden. It was long ago that a great treasure was hidden here. Happy is he that might find the great treasure. Hakon alone bore treasure from this mound.* All very emphatic, though other runes are of a more domestic nature, along the lines of Ron loves Mabel: *Ingigerth is the most beautiful of women*; *Thorni bedded Helgi*; *Benedikt made this cross.* Another rune says: *Jurusalem* [sic] *farers broke into Maes Howe*, while the one about the treasure being hidden says: *Lif the earl's cook carved these runes* thus pinpointing the time of the break-in to the time when Vikings led by Earl Hakon went on their pilgrimage to Jerusalem. There are also drawings in the chambers; a lion, a dog, a walrus and a serpent.

Of all the Norsemen who came to Orkney, first to pillage and plunder, then to settle as farmers and fishermen and marry Orcadian girls, the best known today must be St Magnus to whose memory the exquisite red and yellow sandstone cathedral in Kirkwall is dedicated. In the twelfth century Orkney was part of the kingdom of Norway, and one of its early and most successful governors was the mighty Earl Thorfinn, a cousin of Scotland's King Macbeth, and described in *Orkneyinga Saga* as 'of all men the tallest and strongest; he was ugly . . . had black hair, a large nose and a rather dark complexion'. After his death his sons Erland and Paul took over as joint earls, and when they died, the earldom passed jointly to Paul's son Hakon and to Erland's son, Magnus. Because of altercations between their followers it was agreed that the two earls should meet on the little island of Egilsay to reconcile their differences, and that each would bring only two ships and a small number of men.

Magnus arrived first with his two ships, carrying a dove and, being a pious man, spent the time waiting for Hakon in prayer. Then to his distress he saw Hakon arrive, not with two ships but eight and a large body of men. Facing the inevitable, he pleaded for his life but Hakon's followers, jealous of Magnus's increasing influence and the veneration in which he was held in the islands, insisted that he die. And Hakon complied.

> Hakon commanded his standard-bearer to kill him, but the man indignantly refused. Then Hakon laid the unwelcome duty on Lifolf his cook. Lifolf began to sob, and Magnus said: 'Stand thou before me and hew on my head a great wound, for it is not seemly to behead chiefs like thieves. Take good heart, poor wretch, for I have prayed to God for thee, that He be merciful unto thee.' So Lifolf took up the axe, and Magnus received his death wound on the head.

Despite this callous murder of his kinsman and rival, Hakon proved to be as good a governor as his grandfather Thorfinn. Yet after Magnus's body had been taken for burial to the church on the little promontory of Birsay, such was his reputation for piety and goodness that people visited his tomb, as they might go to Lourdes or Walsingham today, to seek cures for their ailments and deformities.

In time and by popular acclamation Magnus was sanctified, and his nephew Kali, described as an accomplished poet, musician and athlete, was granted by the King of Norway his uncle's half share in the earldom of Orkney. Kali took the title of Earl Rognvald or Ronald and vowed that during his governorship he would build a cathedral in the little market town of Kirkwall in honour of

Magnus. The master masons who built Durham Cathedral came up from the south; the first stones were laid in 1137 and over the next two decades this beautiful building, composed of locally quarried red and yellow sandstone, began to rise. When it was completed and consecrated as part of the archdiocese of Trondheim, Magnus's coffin was brought from Birsay and interred within it. Here his body remained undisturbed for nearly eight centuries until 1919 when, in the course of renovations, the coffin was found in one of the piers in the south arcade of the choir. Inside it was the 800-year-old skeleton of Magnus, the gaping cleft in his skull caused by Lifolf's axe proof of his ancient murder. In 1472, after Orkney had become part of Scotland, the cathedral was transferred to the see of the Archbishop of St Andrews. Like St Giles in Edinburgh it has retained the title of cathedral even though since the Reformation it has been a presbytery of the Church of Scotland.

There are some interesting things in the cathedral; a plaque in memory of the *Royal Oak*'s dead; statues placed on niches in the wall of Earl Ronald's father Kol who supervised the building of the cathedral, holding a plumb-line and architectural designs; of the Earl himself, holding a model of the cathedral. Elsewhere are plaques to three of Orkney's greatest sons, the novelist Eric Linklater, the poet and critic Edwin Muir and the Queen's painter and limner, Stanley Cursiter. In time, no doubt, a plaque to George Mackay Brown will join them.

More surprising are the inscriptions on some of the seventeenth- and eighteenth-century tombstones set into the walls. 'Whether sooner or later, we all hasten to one place. This is the last home of fate. Death levels all. Remember Death!' On another is written, 'Death is the end of all things'. Yet this is a concept quite alien to the Christian Churches whether Catholic or Protestant, who have always regarded death not as an end but a beginning, a stepping stone to eternal life. So what are such heretical proclamations doing on the walls of one of the oldest churches in the country?

Having entered the cathedral by the west door and walked the 230 feet length of it, past its fourteen massive roseate pillars, seven on either side, you come to two of the most incongruous memorials imaginable. One is of Dr John Rae, the Arctic explorer who was born in the Hall of Clestrain across the bay from Stromness and who between 1846 and 1854 made four expeditions to the Arctic to find out what had happened to the *Erebus* and *Terror*, the ships of Sir John Franklin's voyage to discover the north-west passage: their last port of call had been Stromness since when nothing had been heard of them; and on his final trip Rae had learned from an Eskimo that the two ships had been crushed by ice and was shown forks and coins taken from the pockets of the dead, deep-frozen sailors.

On top of Rae's tombstone has been carved a recumbent effigy of him in stone, as was the practice with knights in medieval times. But whereas the knights were carved lying on their backs with folded hands and eyes directed at heaven, Dr Rae, who is wearing a long cloak and long laced-up boots, has his arms folded behind his head and his eyes shut in the manner of one enjoying a light doze after a delicious picnic lunch. This impression is enhanced by the presence of a carved shotgun lying beside him, suggesting that at any moment he may be roused by a companion to pursue the chase. The butt of the gun appears to be resting on a book, presumably the Bible, a useful standby if game prove scarce.

The other tomb, which is not embellished by statuary, is of William Balfour Baikie:

> Born at Kirkwall 27th August 1825. Died at Sierra Leone 27th December 1864. The explorer of the Niger and Tchadda. The translator of the Bible into the languages of Central Africa. He devoted life, means, talent to make the heathen, savage and slave, a free and Christian man. For Africa he opened new paths to light, wealth and liberty. He won for Britain new honours and influence . . . a brave example of humanity, perseverance and self-sacrifice to duty. But the climate from which his care, skill and kindness shielded so many, was fatal to himself, and when relieved at last, though too late, he sought to restore his failing health by rest and home, he found them both only in the grave.

George Mackay Brown says there are some in Orkney who think that the cathedral could do without the tombstones of Rae and Baikie, presumably because of the bathetic obituary of the one and the ludicrous statuary of the other. They may be right. And yet such statuary is as typical of its time as recumbent knights in mail armour are of another. Both men typify those thousands of Scots who as soldiers, missionaries, sea captains, engineers, teachers and adventurers went out from Scotland in the nineteenth century to govern and people the Empire. Many, like Baikie, died in their thirties or even younger, as a visit to any British cemetery in India will confirm. They had courage, resilience and an urge, generated by a strong sense of morality, to bring the benefits of western enlightenment and progress to, as they saw it, people less fortunate than themselves. In some of the things they did and said and in some of their values, they may have been misguided; but they were as much prisoners of the mores of their age as Hakon was of his, and as we are of ours. Baikie and Rae R.I.P.

# CHAPTER 11

## *The Hammer of the Scots*

IN 1263, OR A CENTURY AFTER THE CONSECRATION OF THE CATHEdral, one of Norway's greatest kings, Hakon IV, came to his earldom of Orkney with a great fleet of ships. He had heard that another part of his kingdom, the western isles of Scotland and the Isle of Man, were being increasingly encroached upon by Scotland's king, Alexander III, and the bands of marauding Scots. To restore the *status quo ante* was the purpose of his mission, and he took his fleet out of Scapa Flow, past Cape Wrath and down the Minches to engage the enemy. But the enemy and the weather were more than a match for him and on 2 October, between the little seaside town of Largs in Ayrshire and the island of Bute, Hakon's fleet met its nemesis; the event is annually celebrated in Largs today. By now a sick and dispirited man, Hakon turned what remained of his ships round and came back to Scapa Flow.

Intending to pass the winter in Orkney Hakon took up residence in the Bishop's Palace, whose ruins, close to the cathedral, still stand. At first he was well enough to hear Mass in the Bishop's chapel and to visit the cathedral to pray by the shrine of St Magnus. Then he took to his bed, aware that life had begun to ebb from him. He gave instructions for the payment of his troops and made bequests to his personal staff. During the day and at night when sleep escaped him, his staff read to him, both the Bible and the chronicles of all the Norwegian kings. The bishops of Stavanger, Hamar and Orkney gave him extreme unction. Two days later he lost the power of speech and at midnight on the 15–16 December 1263, according to his Saga, 'Almighty God called King Hakon out of this mortal life'.

> On Sunday the royal corpse was carried into the upper hall and laid on a bier. The body was clothed in a rich garb with a garland on the head and dressed as became a crowned monarch. The Masters of the Lights came with tapers in their hands and the whole hall was illuminated.

The body was temporarily buried in the choir of the cathedral, close to the steps leading to St Magnus's shrine; when the spring came, it was taken to Norway and interred in Bergen Cathedral.

Three years later Scotland and Norway signed a peace-treaty whereby Norway was to cede all claims to the western isles and the isle of Man, but to retain Orkney and Shetland. And the future of both countries seemed assured when Alexander's only daughter, Margaret, became betrothed to the new king of Norway, Eric, in 1281. But as Burns was later to remark, even the best-laid schemes gang aft agley. On a dark night in March 1286 Alexander fell from his horse near Kinghorn in Fife and died without a male heir.

During the latter part of the twelfth century and almost all of the thirteenth century Scotland enjoyed a period of peace, especially with England, that was almost unique in its history; one reason was that Alexander III had married a daughter of England's Henry III and the two families were on excellent terms. Yet Alexander had to bear a succession of family losses. In 1275 his wife died, and in the next few years so did both his sons, either of whom would have become king of Scotland, and his daughter, the queen of Norway. To try and produce a male heir Alexander married again in 1285 and his French wife, Yolande, was five months pregnant when he was killed; but she produced no heir. His only legitimate heir therefore was his grand-daughter Margaret, 'the maid of Norway', the only child of the union between his daughter Margaret and King Eric. But she, when he died, was only three years old.

What to do? The so-called 'Guardians' of Scotland, consisting of the Bishops of St Andrews and Glasgow, two earls and two barons, met at royal Scone to assess the situation and decided to approach Edward I of England. It was a fateful decision that was to affect the relationship between England and Scotland for centuries. For Edward had his eye on Scotland. At a conference at Birgham on the Tweed in 1290 it was agreed that Edward's son and the maid of Norway should create a new dynastic union. Scotland would remain an independent country with its own Parliament and laws, but at Edward's insistence, until the little queen achieved her majority, Bishop Bek of Durham would act as Scotland's governor.

Such was the position when in 1290 the little maid of Norway, now aged seven, set sail from Norway for Scotland:

The ship rode at anchor in the calm of a little voe. The ship had limped out of the North Sea the day before, late; salt-encrusted, sail-torn.

Some of the islanders had come down to the shore, mostly women. The men were more cautious; they could see the foreign heraldry of Scotland on the stern. Strange ships meant, usually, trouble. The men waited round the crofts, ready to take to the hills.

But one man stood at the shore, slightly apart from the women. He was the farmer from The Bu, the chief man in the island.

From the shore they could see men on the ship, going about their business, but slowly, as if they were sailors in a gray sea dream. The sailors paid small attention to the island and the people on the shore.

A man in a gray cloak had stood since dawn at the helm: slowly he gestured here and there; slowly the sailors obeyed him. Needles were put into the torn sail. The salt scabs were scrubbed and washed from the handsome oak of the vessel.

Once the skipper at the helm turned his face shorewards. He raised his hand. The farmer, the laird, raised his hand in reply.

The women formed a circle then. They broke the long silence. Their faces were here and there. Their voices were sharp with inquisition.

The sun rose higher.

There was a dead child cradled in the ship, in a little oak-panelled cabin. Her hair was tangled like storm-beaten corn.

The dead girl lay on a narrow bed in the middle of the ship-chamber. She was clad in white linen. The sun came in at the cabin window and shone four-square across her.

The cabin smelt still of spindrift and flung weed, but country airs too came in at the window now. All was in order, except that one of the lamps had been half-wrenched from its wall-bracket. It hung, twisted, just above the door.

The women in this death-room began to move. They moved even slower than the sailors outside on rigging and forecastle. It was as if they bent and turned to unheard harps.

One gathered the wild hair of the child and made a bright knot of it and tied it in a white ribbon. The other two took from a carved chest under the bed a long gown: it was blue satin, it was sewn about the bodice with hundreds of little pearls, it had silver clasps at shoulder and waist. After they had raised the small stiff body they sheathed it in the magnificent fabric. Then, once more, they crossed the thin hands one upon the other.

The dead child was as remote as a star: a first star in the new darkness of autumn, at harvest-time, that glitters magnificent and cold in a pool.

One of the women took a crystal phial from the sea-chest. She shook drops on to her long fingers. She touched, here and there, the face and broidered hair of the dead child.

The second woman smiled.

Late in the afternoon the skipper of the ship had himself rowed ashore in a small blue boat.

He walked up the beach to the farmer who stood, still, on the sea-bank above. The women hovered around, like gulls about a half-broken crust.

The skipper said to the laird: 'You are wondering no doubt what brings a strange ship into your bay. Sir, I ought to have informed you sooner. Other concerns prevented courtesy. We have come from Bergen in Norway. We are bound for Leith in Scotland. Between Norway and Scotland we ran into a storm, one of the worst I have experienced, and I am an old sailor. *We carried the Queen of Scotland across the North Sea to her people and her throne.* It was foreseen that some day she would be Margaret, Queen of Scotland and of England and of Norway also. Sir, she was a tender child of seven years, and the storm that made me gray in the face was the end of her.'

The laird shook his head in wonderment.

The women covered their heads. The wailing was spun from mouth to mouth: a thin gray web of grief.

The harbour to which the ship carrying the body of the seven-year-old Margaret came is still called today St Margaret's Hope.

Now the field for claimants to the Scottish throne was wide open, for there was not a single, direct, male heir living from among the past three generations of Scottish kings. Of thirteen who put themselves forward the two strongest candidates were John de Baliol and Robert de Brus or Bruce, both descended through the female line from the youngest son of David I. Baliol's father had founded Balliol College, Oxford (an act of penance for having assaulted the Bishop of Durham), while his rich mother, who had brought his father half of Galloway, founded Sweetheart Abbey in memory of him. Baliol's sister had married John Comyn, lord of Badenoch and one of the six Guardians.

Robert Bruce came of an Anglo-Norman family, was lord of Annandale, had married a daughter of the Earl of Gloucester and been sheriff of Cumberland and governor of Carlisle. He had also been, briefly, England's Lord Chief Justice. His son, the seventh Robert Bruce, married the widowed Countess of Carrick and, according to custom, acquired her late husband's title and inheritance.

The Scots have always been inclined to unworldliness in their dealings with the English, and nowhere was this more evident than in the action of the Bishop of St Andrews in inviting Edward I to help to decide which of the two claimants should be awarded the Scottish crown. A hundred and fifty years of peace may have lulled him and the Guardians into a false sense of security, but Edward's appointment of Bishop Bek as governor of Scotland, coupled with demands (rejected by the Guardians) that English troops should garrison the castles of southern Scotland, should have given them warning.

Edward I, like his sister Margaret the wife of Alexander III of Scotland, was a child of Henry III of England and of Eleanor of

Provence. Though handsome, brave and ambitious, he had developed an inclination for cruelty even in a cruel age: the chronicler Matthew Paris records how once and without provocation he horribly mutilated a young man who he happened to meet and which made many of his subjects 'look forward with dread to the time when he should become king'. On a crusade to the Holy Land in 1271 he captured the town of Nazareth and 'slew all that he found there'. Two years after his coronation in 1274 he began a campaign against the rebellious Welsh whom he finally subdued six years later, removing to London their two most precious possessions, the crown of Arthur and a fragment of what was considered to be the true cross. After the death of the Welsh leader Llewellyn, his brother David ap Gruffyd was captured, taken to London and there subjected to an agonizing death: that of hanging, drawing (being cut down and, while still alive, disembowelled) and quartering (i.e. the severance of all four limbs). In 1278 he ordered the arrest of all Jews in the country and, anticipating Hitler, hanged 267 of them; the remainder were banished.

For Edward the invitation to come to Scotland was all he could have wished, for after the subjugation of Wales, Scotland, as he told his nobles, was next in his sights. So his first action on arriving at the convention at Norham on Tweed to decide on the Scottish crown was to ask the Scottish barons whether they recognized him as their superior lord. They said they didn't. He gave them three weeks to change their minds which, on reconvening, they did. The eight remaining claimants to the throne were also required to accept him as 'sovereign lord of the land'. After protracted negotiations in Norham and at Berwick, then Scotland's principal seaport, Edward announced that Baliol would be king but on conditions: he was to pay him homage, appear in London to answer charges brought against him and join him on an expedition to France.

This was too much for the Scottish nobles who themselves opened discussions with Edward's arch-enemy the King of France and took a force over the border to ravage Cumberland. Hearing of it Edward mustered his own army and marched north. After receiving homage from Robert Bruce and some eighty Scottish barons at Wark, Edward took his army to Berwick and demanded its surrender. When it was refused, he sacked the town and massacred hundreds of its inhabitants, including the Flemish wool merchants based there. 'The whole affair', wrote one historian, 'made the deepest impression on

Scotland. Edward implanted that bitter hatred for all things English which was to be nourished so consistently by English policy during the next three hundred years'. Not for nothing did he call himself The Hammer of the Scots.

From Berwick Edward and his army made a triumphal progress northwards, first capturing Dunbar, then the castles of Roxburgh, Jedburgh, Edinburgh and Stirling. At Montrose King John Baliol surrendered to him and for his pains was stripped of his royal trappings – tabard, hood and girdle – punishment a knight might expect when found guilty of treason. Thus humiliated, he was taken to the Tower of London, leading Edward to remark in his delicate way, 'A man does good business when he rids himself of a turd'. Edward and his army meanwhile marched on to Aberdeen, Banff and Elgin, receiving everywhere the homage of the nobles.

His over-running of Scotland complete, he returned to England, taking with him the archives and regalia of Scotland and the Stone of Destiny on which traditionally Scottish kings had been crowned at Scone: and the Great Seal of Scotland was broken up. Edward believed that Scotland would trouble him no more; but he did not know the Scots.

Angered by the presence of English garrisons in all the principal Scottish towns and by the continued incarceration of their king in the Tower of London, Andrew Murray, the son of a baron in the north, and William Wallace, son of a Clydesdale laird in the south, became leaders of a Scottish revolt, self-styled 'commanders of the army of Scotland and the community of that realm' and consisting of people of every class from nobles to peasants. The revolt was triggered off by the murder of an English sheriff at Lanark. The commander of the English forces in Scotland marched against Wallace and Murray who soundly defeated them at the battle of Stirling Bridge.

Murray died of his wounds after Stirling Bridge, but Wallace, now sole Guardian of the realm, adopted guerrilla warfare, making lightning raids across the border to ravage the northernmost English shires. But retribution was on its way. Enraged by what he regarded as an act of treason, Edward went north once more and at Roxburgh took command of a huge army, mostly Irish and Welsh. Having learned that Wallace's army was encamped at Falkirk, he took his own army to Linlithgow where they spent the night on the open heath. Next day they fell upon the Scots whom they greatly outnumbered and did terrible execution, much of it from the archers' arrows.

Edward returned home, once again thinking he had finally put paid to his northern neighbour, once again to find himself disillusioned. During the next seven years he launched more punitive expeditions against them, none ultimately successful; for his policy always fell half way between conciliation and conquest. However, in 1304 William Wallace, since Falkirk no longer sole Guardian, was taken prisoner, sent to London in chains and there put on trial for treason. In answer to the charge he said it was impossible for him to be a traitor as he had never given homage or fealty to any king of England. Despite this he was judged guilty, and England bestowed on him the same brutal and disgusting death as on David ap Gruffyd. It was a barbarous and uncalled for act of public humiliation on a courageous leader of a great country and neither then nor at any time since have the Scots forgotten it. William Wallace will always be our first hero.

Meanwhile King John Baliol had been released from the Tower and crossed to France where he went into retirement; and with the defeat and capture of Wallace there was a vacuum in Scotland's kingship. Two men wanted to fill it. One was Baliol's nephew, the Red Comyn, the other Robert Bruce's grandson, the Earl of Carrick, but like his father and grandfather best known to history as Robert Bruce. The two were the most powerful and influential Scottish leaders at this time, both of whom had been made Guardians in 1299, yet both of whom had pledged loyalty to Edward. They had quarrelled before at Peebles and it was only the intervention of the Bishop of St Andrews that temporarily healed the rift. Matters came to a head in 1306 when both were attending a conference in Dumfries, when it is believed that each thought the other was plotting with Edward against him. Whatever the reason, the two were together in Greyfriars Church when without warning and in disregard of church sanctity, Bruce drew his sword and killed the Red Comyn.

In London Bruce had seen the head of William Wallace stuck on a pole and the Stone of Destiny removed to Westminster; and had come to recognize, as no previous Scottish ruler had, the concept of a Scottish nation; indeed the depredations of Edward I had forced it on him. Within weeks he had had himself crowned King of Scotland at the abbey of Scone by the Bishop of St Andrews, with other bishops and nobles in attendance. For Edward, as for the Pope, this was the last straw. At Carlisle a papal bull was read out, excommunicating

Bruce for his crime. Then in a series of minor battles Bruce was defeated and fled to the west. Here, according to legend, he hid in a cave and watching the perseverance of a spider fixing its web concluded that if at first you don't succeed, try, try again.

Meanwhile Edward wreaked his vengeance. Bruce's wife, sister and daughter were taken prisoner and sent to London. The Bishops of St Andrews and Glasgow and the Abbot of Scone were also sent south and suspended from office. Bruce's youngest brother Nigel was beheaded at Berwick, his brother-in-law Christopher Seton at Dumfries, Alexander Seton at Newcastle; while another Bruce supporter, the Earl of Atholl, a cousin of Edward, was hanged on a gallows 30 feet higher than the pole on which the head of Wallace still stood. Bruce's older brothers, Thomas and Alexander, taken in Galloway, were executed at Carlisle. And a little earlier Wallace's brother John was sent to London to undergo the same hanging, disembowellment and quartering as William. Notwithstanding, wrote one chronicler of the time, 'the large number of those who wished Bruce to be confirmed in his kingship increased daily!'; while another said, 'Every class in Scotland, nobles and gentry, clergy and commons' had had the baseness and brutality of Edward's true character fully revealed to them. 'Life and limb, land and liberty, were all in peril and common danger taught the necessity, not felt in the time of Wallace, of making common cause'.

In July 1307 while on his way north, Edward's long and violent reign came to an end when he died aged sixty-eight at Burgh on Sands. In looks and physique the son who succeeded him, Edward II, was strikingly like his father; in other respects quite different. 'He never showed any inclination for a warlike life or even for the tournament,' says one report. 'He avoided fighting as much as he could and when compelled to take the field his conduct was that of an absolute craven. Lack of purpose blasted his whole career: his only object was to gratify the whim of the moment'. He was an alcoholic and bisexual who preferred the company of grooms and labourers to those of his own class and, whereas his father had ruled a united England, he stirred up nobles and prelates against each other. Captured and deposed at the instigation of his queen in favour of their son, he was taken to Berkeley Castle and there subjected to the sort of ill treatment and torture which his father had practised on others. When he was finally put to death, at the age of forty-three, his screams could be heard throughout the castle:

some say that because of his homosexuality the instrument of his death was a red-hot poker inserted into his anus.

With this weakling on the English throne and the English nobles at sixes and sevens among themselves, Bruce was in a position to return from the west and, with the help of his brother Edward, reduced one by one the English garrisons; and had so consolidated his power as leader of the Scottish people that at a general council of the Church at Dundee in 1310 and despite the earlier excommunication, bishops and clergy declared him to be their rightful king. By 1313 the only garrisons left to the English were Stirling and Berwick, and some of the English nobles persuaded a reluctant Edward that if Scotland was not to be lost to England for ever, he must emulate his father by taking an army north.

This army, consisting of some 20,000 foot soldiers, cavalry and archers, reached Falkirk, scene of so many battles between Scots and English, on 22 June 1314. Bruce, encamped with his army nearby, saw the leading patrols of the English army cross a sizeable stream called the Bannock Burn. Not yet expecting battle he was unarmoured and riding on a pony instead of his charger but wearing his gold coronet. An English knight, Sir Henry de Bohun, observing this, set his lance and charged him. Bruce side-stepped the lance and, rising in his saddle, felled Sir Henry with a single blow of his battleaxe. Looking down on his opponent's corpse, his only comment was, 'Alas, I have broken my good battleaxe'. Concern among his men at seeing him expose himself to such danger before the armies met was forgotten in their admiration for his courage and leadership and what it did for their morale.

The site of the Battle of Bannockburn today is a green field of 60 acres, purchased for the National Trust for Scotland in 1932 as a permanent memorial; in the centre stands a rotunda containing a flagpole and cairn to commemorate the battle and extending from it a pathway to where the statue of Robert Bruce in chain mail and armour, with battleaxe in hand and astride his royal charger, stands proudly on top of a great chunk of local white sandstone.

Generals who win battles are often those who have chosen the terrain and dictated the moves by which they hope the battle will be fought. Bruce was one such, as great a military leader as he was a king. Until now his success had been in guerrilla warfare, striking at the enemy when they least expected it, withdrawing as quickly afterwards. On this occasion and against the advice of many of his supporters he had decided on a pitched battle; it might be said that unless he wished to avoid action altogether he had no alternative. He divided his army of some 8,000 men into four divisions and positioned them on high ground; if the English were to attack they would have to cross either the marshy ground through which the 50-foot-wide Bannock Burn flowed and which gave no foothold for horses, or across firmer ground on the right in which the Scots had dug potholes. At first the English archers had some success, but soon ran out of space in which to manoeuvre so that some of their arrows were hitting their forward troops in the back. Their cavalry too gained some early advantages but later came to grief in the marshes or among the potholes on the right.

The Scottish troops, so close together they were likened by an observer to 'a dense wood', repelled with spears those that did get through, after which the handful of Scottish bowmen began to create havoc among the English. Then – a pre-arranged plan – a reserve division of lightly armed and untrained Scottish farmers, labourers, burgesses, craftsmen, known as 'the small folk', who had been keeping out of sight behind a hill, showed themselves on the crest of it; and the English, mistaking them for serious reinforcements, panicked and fled. The whole of their baggage train, stretching for some 60 miles, was captured and for the return of their captured nobles, lucrative ransoms were extorted. It was, says Michael Lynch, a humiliation of English arms unparalleled since the loss of Normandy over a century before. For the Scots it was the triumph of David over Goliath; a victory then and ever since to be recalled with pride, just as 200 years later their terrible defeat at Flodden in which James IV and his nobility were decimated, has, to this day and with the same heightened degree of feeling, always been remembered with grief. Other kings of England were to invade Scotland in the years ahead, but not one after Edward I would overrun it.

Bannockburn marks the culmination of the process by which Bruce, over the preceding years, had ended the warring factions of his fellow countrymen and made them conscious of Scotland as a nation; and to ensure the continuance of his own line he called a Parliament to approve of the succession; firstly his own male issue, then that of his brother Edward and failing that, the male issue of his daughter Marjory. In the event Bruce's son David succeeded first and, after a long reign, was himself succeeded by Robert II, the son of Marjory by Walter, the Hereditary Steward of Scotland; and so began the long line of Stewart or, as they became, Stuart kings and pretenders, the last to reign being Anne.

After Bannockburn there was no let up in Bruce's activities. His victory had not only inspired the Scots but the Irish, from whom the Scots had sprung. 'All the kings of lesser Scotland', wrote Donald O'Neil, the Celtic chief of Ulster, 'have drawn their blood from greater Scotland [i.e. Ireland] and retain in some degree our language and customs', and he begged Bruce to help his fellow countrymen throw off the English yoke. Bruce's reply was to send his brother Edward with 6,000 men to Carrickfergus. Edward fought a brilliant campaign all the way to the south of Ireland and in its latter stages was joined by his brother. But in the end the Scots over-reached themselves, Edward was killed at Dundalk and the army retreated to Ulster.

On return to Scotland Bruce engaged in a series of guerrilla raids into northern England (reciprocated by English raids into southern Scotland) and captured the last English garrison at Berwick in which he installed as governor his son-in-law Walter the Steward. He also instituted reforms in Scottish civil law, particularly in regard to land rights and the speeding up of justice. One statute urged the people to show love and friendship to one another, forbade the nobles to do injury to them and promised redress if they did. These laws were promulgated by the Scone Parliament of 1318 and remained in force for the next 300 years.

At this time of Scottish unity and consolidation, there remained one issue to be resolved. The influence of the Roman Catholic faith and of the Pope himself was then paramount throughout the western world. Now that Bruce had been accepted by the Scots as their undisputed king, had not the time come for the Pope to recognize him and annul his excommunication; and to bring his influence to bear in dissuading the English from further attacks on Scotland? In 1320 a group of leading Scottish nobles and clergy, meeting at the Abbey of Arbroath, agreed on a letter to be taken to the Vatican. The Declaration of Arbroath is an astonishing document, written in the same sort of simple, forceful language as the Gettysburg Address or the wartime speeches of Sir Winston Churchill, and as much cherished by Scots today as those other remarkable statements of faith by Americans and English.

The Declaration (translated from the Latin by a former Keeper of the Records of Scotland, Sir John Fergusson) opens with a statement of filial submission and reverence to the Supreme Pontiff by the nobles and freeholders of Scotland – among them the Earls of Fife, Moray, Annandale, March, Strathearn, Lennox, Ross, Caithness and Orkney, Sutherland and many others that included the Hereditary Steward of Scotland, Butler of Scotland, Constable of Scotland, Marischal of Scotland, and the sending of devout kisses of the Pope's blessed feet. Then this:

> Most Holy Father and Lord, we know and from the chronicles and books of the ancients we find that among other famous nations our own, the Scots, has been graced with widespread renown. They journeyed from Greater Scythia by way of the Tyrrhenian Sea and the Pillars of Hercules, and dwelt for a long course of time in Spain among the most savage tribes, but nowhere could they be subdued by any race, however barbarous. Thence they came, twelve hundred years after the people of Israel crossed the Red Sea, to their home in the west where they still live today. The Britons they first drove out, the Picts they utterly destroyed, and, even though very often assailed by the Norwegians, the Danes and the English, they took possession of that home with many victories and untold efforts; and, as the historians of old time bear witness, they have held it free of all bondage ever since. In their kingdom there have reigned one hundred and thirteen kings of their own royal stock, the line unbroken by a single foreigner.

And then, after a passing reference to Scotland's patron saint Andrew, 'brother of the blessed Peter', the petition comes to the heart of the matter:

> The Most Holy Fathers your predecessors gave careful heed to these things and bestowed many favours and numerous privileges on this same kingdom and people, as being the special charge of the Blessed Peter's brother. Thus our nation under their protection did indeed live in freedom and peace up to the time when that mighty prince the King of the English, Edward, the father of the one who reigns today, when our kingdom had no head and our people harboured no malice or treachery and were then unused to wars or invasions, came in the guise of a

friend and ally to harass them as an enemy. The deeds of cruelty, massacre, violence, pillage, arson, imprisoning prelates, burning down monasteries, robbing and killing monks and nuns, and yet other outrages without number which he committed against our people, sparing neither age nor sex, religion nor rank, no one could describe nor fully imagine unless he had seen them with his own eyes.

But from these countless evils we have been set free, by the help of Him Who though He afflicts yet heals and restores, by our most tireless Prince, King and Lord, the Lord Robert. He, that his people and his heritage might be delivered out of the hands of our enemies, met toil and fatigue, hunger and peril, like another Maccabaeus or Joshua and bore them cheerfully . . . To him, as to the man by whom salvation has been wrought unto our people, we are bound both by law and by his merits that our freedom may be still maintained, and by him, come what may, we mean to stand.

This is followed by a caveat and the caveat is followed by the Declaration's most famous and most quoted passage:

Yet if he should give up what he has begun, and agree to make us or our kingdom subject to the King of England or the English, we should exert ourselves at once to drive him out as our enemy and a subverter of his own rights and ours, and make some other man who was well able to defend us our King; for, as long as but a hundred of us remain alive, never will we on any conditions be brought under English rule. It is in truth not for glory, nor riches, nor honours that we are fighting, but for freedom – for that alone, which no honest man gives up but with life itself.

Finally came a plea for papal influence to cool the ardour of the English:

Therefore it is, Reverend Father and Lord, that we beseech your Holiness with our most earnest prayers and suppliant hearts, inasmuch as you will in your sincerity and goodness consider all this, that, since with Him Whose vice-regent on earth you are there is neither weighing nor distinction of Jew and Greek, Scotsman or Englishman, you will look with the eyes of a father on the troubles and privations brought by the English upon us and upon the Church of God. May it please you to admonish and exhort the King of the English, who ought to be satisfied with what belongs to him since England used once to be enough for seven kings or more, to leave us Scots in peace, who live in this poor little Scotland, beyond which there is no dwelling-place at all, and covet nothing but our own. We are sincerely willing to do anything for him, having regard to our condition, that we can, to win peace for ourselves.

Although the brave affirmation that so long as a hundred of us remain alive, we never will be brought under English rule was to be contradicted by future events – the union of the Crowns in 1603 and of the political Treaty of Union in 1707 – it stands as an aspiration of the time in which it was framed, later to find expression in the risings of the '15 and the '45; and for many Scots today it remains an aspiration and inspiration, a lodestar which after 670 years of war and peace and amalgamation, still and forcefully beckons.

Sadly the petition failed, for the Pope of that time, John XXII, was pro-English; but nine years later the Papal attitude softened sufficiently to allow future kings of Scotland to be anointed with holy oil at their coronations.

By 1327 however, the year which saw the deposition of Edward II, the English were ready to negotiate; for in terms of men, money, cattle and crops the Scottish wars had exhausted them, and if they were to renew hostilities with the French they needed to conserve their resources. Accordingly in 1328 a treaty of peace between the kings of England and Scotland was signed at Northampton, the Scottish copy of which is still preserved in Edinburgh:

It is settled and agreed that the kings and their heirs and successors shall be true friends and loyal allies and that the one shall help the other properly, as a good ally, saving on the part of the king of Scotland the alliance made between him and the king of France [an acknowledgement by the English of the existence of the 'auld alliance' which dated back to 1295].

By the treaty the English formally recognized Scotland as an independent country and Bruce as its rightful king; and to emphasize the new-found amity of the two nations Bruce's son David, aged five, was married to Edward II's daughter Joanna, aged seven.

In addition the King of Scotland agreed to pay the King of England £20,000 in three instalments over the next three years (and did) and to receive from the King of England those records and documents, mostly English but including Scottish, regarding England's claim to Scotland. It was also agreed that the Stone of Destiny on which the kings of Scotland had traditionally been crowned at Scone should be returned there.

To confirm this, Edward II was persuaded to issue an edict commanding its return, and it was contained in a royal writ of 1 July 1328 addressed to the Abbot of Westminster in whose keeping the Stone now lay. 'Whereas', the writ ran, 'it was formerly agreed by us, our council and our last Parliament held at Northampton that the stone on which the kings of Scotland used to sit at the time of their coronation, and which is in your care, should be sent to Scotland . . . we have ordered the Lords of our City of London that they should receive from you the stone as above written and that they should carry it to the Queen of England, our very dear dame and mother.'

The instructions were clear enough. The Stone was to be delivered to the Queen for safekeeping and thence to be returned to Scotland. But it never was. And thereby hangs a tale.

# CHAPTER 12

## *The Recovery of the Stone**

FOR SCOTTISH PATRIOTS THE STONE OF DESTINY HAS BEEN CHERISHED as an ancient symbol of Scottish nationhood, in much the same degree of attachment with which the American people, more exaggeratedly than those of other countries, regard their national flag; and because the English did not return it as they promised, indeed put it on permanent display in Westminster Abbey as a trophy of war, there are many in Scotland who regard the seizing and keeping of it as an act of theft.

Unlike the Scots the English have little or no sense of nationhood, expressing what feelings they have in terms of an all-embracing Britishness. Many Scots find Britishness an alien concept and are apt to wince when English people talk about 'we Brits' as though we were all part of some homogenous entity. Yet England itself which as an Anglo-Scot I love next to Scotland is not an alien concept but, like Scotland, a word of a thousand emotional connotations of war, peace, majesty, beauty, memory, mystery, myth.

If we in Scotland have a heightened sense of our nationhood, it is

*This chapter is based on *The Taking of the Stone of Destiny* by Ian Hamilton.

because we are no longer self-governing; it is why we are so prickly about such events as the establishment of E II R pillar-boxes when we never had an E I R and the continued refusal of the English to return the Stone of Destiny: both examples of English contempt for other people's sentiments. Will the English ever regain their own sense of nationhood? Only when the first and last satrapies of their domestic Empire have recovered at least some of their national autonomy. Northern Ireland is already on the way: Scotland will follow; and when Scotland goes, can Wales be far behind?

Before the Second World War, a young boy by the name of Ian Hamilton grew up in a semi-detached in Paisley. Two newspapers were taken in that house, the *Glasgow Herald* and its sister journal *The Bulletin*. One day Ian, who had a lively mind, noticed a picture in *The Bulletin* of a tartan-clad woman parading down Edinburgh's Royal Mile in a sandwich board. This was Wendy Wood, a great though eccentric Scottish patriot and campaigner for Home Rule. A little time before this, and as a result of pressure from the Scots, the English had returned to Edinburgh various Scottish archives which they had seized over the course of the years: and on the sandwich board was written, ENGLAND DISGORGES SOME OF THE LOOT, BUT WHERE IS THE STONE OF DESTINY? Ian asked his mother what this meant and she told him what she knew of the legend of the Stone, how it was supposed to be Jacob's pillar on which he had rested his head when he dreamt of the angels ascending and descending the heavenly ladder; how the forefathers of the Scots had lugged it all the way across Europe, first to Spain, later to Ireland and then, before Columba's time, brought it to Dunstaffnage in Argyll whence Kenneth Macalpine had taken it to Scone for the crowning of future Scottish kings. She also recited to him a verse taken from the Gaelic:

> Unless the fates shall faithless prove,
> And prophets voice be vain,
> Where'er this sacred Stone is found,
> The Scottish race shall reign.

Why, Ian asked his mother, was the Stone kept by the English after peace had been made between the two nations? Because, she said, although the English had promised to return it, they had broken that promise. 'A promise is sacred to a child,' Ian was to write years later. 'I remembered that broken promise all through my childhood. Something should be done to redress that old wrong.' And the something he decided to do was break into Westminster Abbey and retrieve from the English the Stone they had stolen from the Scots. Indeed they had done worse, for just as the kings of Scotland had regarded the Stone as a sacred ingredient of their coronation ceremony, so Edward I decided that it should be used in a similar function for the coronation of future kings of England: and he had ordered to be built a special oaken Coronation chair with the Stone nestling in a box-like compartment at the base of it. On this chair the kings and queens of the United Kingdom have been crowned to this day.

Ian Hamilton was not the first Scot to dream of retrieving the Stone. In the past other Scottish patriots, notably Compton Mackenzie and Wendy Wood, had discussed it, even planned it but in the end their schemes had come to nothing. On any reading it was a bold, some would say foolhardy venture, but Ian was driven by a fierce sense of injustice, a belief that a country such as Scotland with a history as a self-governing nation longer than that of England and with its own unique culture, religion and laws, should yet be subservient to England in so many ways. He also harboured a deep-seated resentment against the continued anglicization of Scotland:

I still had dreams of Scotland and the dreams I dreamed were of a new Scotland, alive, full of ideas and, above all, full of self-confident young people unashamed of their birthright; not trying to be a sub-species of the English, but being themselves . . .

We had lost our sense of community. English customs, English pronunciations, English table manners, were the mark of success. You were nothing if you did not speak proper, and proper was to speak with a south of England accent, or as near to it as the inherited muscles of the Scottish lips and tongue could manage. People even tried to think as the English did, and if there is one thing a people cannot do, it is to use the thought processes of another people.

It was after the war, when Ian was a law student at Glasgow university, that he decided to put his scheme into action. Two of the first people he took into his confidence were the poet Hugh MacDiarmid and, later, the University's Lord Rector, and a fervent Home Ruler, the much revered John MacDonald MacCormick.

And what qualifications did Ian think he had for embarking on his daring enterprise? 'My prime qualification was that I did not know my place. I never have. So many Scots, forgetting that one of the great features of our history is the mobility between the classes, have lapsed into the English habit of thought best expressed in the words, "I wouldn't presume. I hope I know my place". I always presume. I have never known my place. I am the second son of a tailor from Paisley . . . and it was in my father's house there that I first read Disraeli's great words, "Learn to aspire".'

In Glasgow's Mitchell Library Ian studied books relating to the Stone and the Coronation Chair. These were housed, he learnt, not in the main body of the Abbey but in the chapel of Edward the Confessor, the last English king before the Norman conquest. The chapel lay on the far side of the High Altar and was separated from it by a stone screen. When there was a coronation, Chair and Stone were taken through a door in the screen to the centre of the nave for the ceremony of the crowning. The Stone itself was rough-hewn, of a dirty grey colour, 3 feet long, a little over a foot broad, a little under a foot deep, and believed to weigh around 3 hundredweight − an underestimate that was to make things awkward later.

Next Ian travelled to London to see the Stone for himself; and found something offensive in a Scot having to pay a shilling entrance fee (today £3) to see his own country's most treasured possession. He mounted the half dozen wooden steps that led to the chapel which housed not only the Coronation Chair and Stone, set against the screen beyond the High Altar, but also the Confessor's huge elaborate shrine, dominating the room as its centrepiece, and below it and to one side the tomb of the depredator of the Stone, Edward I. He saw no great difficulty in removing the Stone from its resting-place, though this would mean cutting away a bar of wood protecting the front of it. More of a problem was how to manhandle the Stone down the wooden stairs: a more practical exit would be through the door in the stone screen that led past the altar and into the sanctuary. That night he returned to the Abbey, walked the streets surrounding it until 5 a.m. and was gratified to find only one patrolling policeman.

Back in Scotland Ian recruited the team that was to go with

him: Kay, a teacher from the Highlands; Gavin, an engineering student and very strong; and Alan, only twenty but contributing to the operation his own car; this would be in addition to one that Ian had hired, a twelve-year-old 8 horse-power Ford, which was all they could afford.

On the evening of 22 December 1950 the four set off south, Ian and Alan in the Anglia following Gavin and Kay in the Ford. Driving through the night to London at this time of year was a bitterly cold, hazardous journey, for in those days cheap cars had no heaters to warm the occupants or unfreeze the windscreen: the main road south was a thin two-way ribbon beaded by numerous villages and along which snow and ice were frequent hazards; even a powerful car could not expect to average more than 30 mph so that most drivers made a practice of spending a night on the way.

These had not the funds for that and in any case were impatient to reach their destination. They stopped for a meal at Gretna, then pushed on to Carlisle, taking turns to drive and doze. As they followed Prince Charles's route south the windscreen froze up so that the wipers were useless and they had to chip away the ice with their nails; dabbing the windscreen with rum from a bottle they were carrying also helped. It began to snow as they ascended Shap and soon the cars were slithering from one side of the road to the other. 'Several times we helped to pull drivers out of the ditch and more than once had the same assistance given to ourselves.' By daybreak they were into Nottinghamshire where they had breakfast and reached London by mid afternoon.

After a brief visit to the Abbey for the newcomers to see the lie of the land, the party made their way up Whitehall to Lyons Corner House in the Strand. Over a meal they debated whether, tired as they were after their long journey, to make an attempt on the Stone that night or, refreshed by a good sleep, the next night. Not being in a position to spend a penny more than they had to and with all the exuberance of youth they decided to go ahead that evening.

The plan was this. Just before closing time Ian would hide himself in some corner of the Abbey and remain there while the doors were locked. Secreted in or beneath his overcoat would be a complete burglar's kit: file, saw, screwdriver, wrench, torch, length of wire and large jemmy. At an agreed hour he would make his way to Poets' Corner where a door led to a little lane that ran along the south eastern side of the Abbey and came out opposite to where the statue of Richard Coeur de Lyon, black on his black charger and with uplifted sword, stands beside the Houses of Parliament. This door had an advantage over others in that it was made of pine not oak and therefore easier to shift. Outside it Gavin and Alan would be waiting. Ian would use his burglar's tools to open the door and let them in: the three would make their way to the Confessor's chapel, remove the Stone from beneath the Chair, take it through one of the doors in the stone screen, past the High Altar and into the nave and from there along the south transept to the Poets' Corner door. In the lane Kay would be waiting in one of the cars. The three men with the Stone would all pile in and drive to a side street where the second car would be parked. Here the Stone would be transferred and Ian, with either Alan or Gavin, would take it to Dartmoor and hide it until the hunt had died down. Later they would return it to Scotland. Then, in case the other car had been spotted, Kay would drive it to Wales so that the police might mistakenly think there was to be a link-up with Welsh nationalists.

The plan misfired from the start. Soon after the doors of the Abbey had closed for the night and all seemed quiet, Ian took off his shoes for silence, then crept out from his hiding place beneath a trolley. He had not gone more than a few steps when he heard the jangling of keys, a light shone in his direction and a disembodied voice said, 'What the devil are you doing here?' This took some explaining but Ian noticed that the watchman, who he now saw to be a tall bearded man, was as nervous at the encounter as he was. Ian said he had been shut in and had taken his shoes off in case someone heard him and came after him. Happy to accept this implausible explanation, the watchman told Ian to put his shoes on, an operation he found almost impossible without losing hold of the jemmy. He managed it somehow, was led to the west door and went out into the night feeling slightly ridiculous. Later he was to write with gratitude of the watchman's kindness: 'A Presbyterian beadle would have kicked my arse all the way to the church door.'

Having joined up with his friends (more by luck than management for they had made no contingency plans) they returned to Lyons Corner House and decided to make a further attempt the following night, though not by the same method which was clearly too risky. Meanwhile, where to stay the night? Once again the need for economy proved paramount and, although it was freezing outside and they hadn't slept between sheets for two days, they agreed at Kay's insistence to save three pounds and sleep again in the cars. There was another reason, too.

> Murder might have been in our hearts as we turned on Kay, but underlying her economy was a strange truth. In the cars we lived as a sort of community of mutual support. Together in the cars we preserved our fragment of Scotland and our comradeship and our integrity of purpose, all of which we might have lost had we sought warmth and soft beds.

Next day was Christmas Eve, a Sunday. After breakfast they made their way to the baths in Waterloo station to bring some feeling back into frozen limbs, then returned to the cars in Northumberland Avenue to decide what to do. Hardly had they sat down than Kay, shivering, turned to Ian and confessed she had the flu. Ian insisted on taking her to a cheap hotel near St Pancras to get some rest, then rejoined the others. With the Abbey crowded with Christmas Eve visitors, they agreed that a daylight attempt was out of the question and that after dark they would have to try and force an entrance in one of the side doors, preferably the one at Poets' Corner.

In the evening they approached the Abbey once more, this time via Dean's Yard and the cloisters: and here had an unexpected piece of luck. An elderly divine, who they afterwards found out to be Archdeacon Stephen Marriott, approached them and suggested, it now being past ten, that it was rather late to be there. Alan agreed but said they were interested in the Abbey's stonework and why so much of it was peeling (as it still is). Fired by Alan's apparent enthusiasm, the Archdeacon guided the three round the cloisters, Alan keeping him plied with pertinent questions.

Reaching the north-west corner of the Cloisters, who should appear from his cubby-hole but the bearded night watchman. The Archdeacon said, 'I thought you went off at ten', to which the man replied, 'Eleven, sir.' The Archdeacon said, 'Yes. And then Dandy or Hyslop comes on.'

Ian, who had kept his face averted during this exchange, could hardly contain himself. Entirely by accident they had gleaned some priceless information: that there was only one night watchman who was relieved at eleven, and it was unlikely that he patrolled more than once every couple of hours. If they succeeded in breaking in at a time when he was in his cubby-hole, the door near Poets' Corner and the area round the Confessor's chapel was too far away for him to hear.

Luck stayed with them. Having wished a happy Christmas to the Archdeacon, they came out of the Abbey and made their way along the little lane that led to Poets' Corner door. Ten yards from the door a locked and well-lit gate barred the way. However, short of the gate was a wooden hoarding containing a padlocked door, obviously leading to a temporary workman's shed: if they could force this door, the shed might enable them to by-pass the gate and take them to their destination. Miraculously it did. 'There, brown and solid before us, was the door to Poets' Corner. We had successfully outflanked the bolted gate.'

It was too early to put their scheme into operation, for there were still people about and they had decided to wait until the early hours of Christmas morning, when most of London was asleep. So for an hour or two they walked about and sat in the car and smoked. Then it was time to collect Kay. They telephoned her hotel but, it being near to three in the morning, there was no answer. So they drove there in two cars and hammered on the hotel door. A sleepy voice answered. Ian said he had come to fetch Kay to take her to Scotland as his father was seriously ill. The voice said he would go and tell her, and Ian rejoined Alan in the car.

As they sat there, they saw a figure mount the hotel steps, pass inside and in a few minutes come out. The figure approached and Ian wound down the window. The figure flashed a card at them. 'I'm a detective,' he said. Ian realized that his repeated and unanswered telephone calls together with his sudden descent on the hotel with an unlikely story, had led the proprietor to summon the law.

The detective asked Ian the car's registration number which he couldn't remember. Who can, especially of a hired car? The detective blew a whistle and a police car emerged from a side street and drew up across the Ford's bonnet. Things were beginning to look nasty: if the detective took it into his head to search Ian, he would find the jemmy. Luckily Kay came down the steps and confirmed Ian's story. Ian, who knew his law, told the detective that it was not an offence for a driver not to know the registration number of his car but that if he wanted confirmation, the gentleman who had hired the car was sitting in another car round the corner, and he would show him the receipt.

Mollified but still suspicious and taking Alan with him as surety, the detective went round the corner and asked Gavin for his driving licence and car hire documents which were promptly given. Then he returned to Ian and Alan, satisfied and apologetic. To rub it in and affirm his innocence, Ian said, 'You very nearly made a terrible mistake.' The detective continued to apologize and with a wealth of detail instructed Ian on the way out of London to the north.

'He was the soul of politeness,' Ian wrote. 'No policeman would act like that nowadays. He would run us in and ask questions afterwards. We were lucky. But at that time the police, and especially the London police, were noted for their wonderful politeness, and English justice was the envy of the world . . .'

Because the police had taken Ian's name and address and the number of the Ford, it was decided to use the Anglia for the operation and leave the Ford in a nearby car park. As they heard Big Ben strike four o'clock, they took the Anglia up the little lane beside the Abbey, switched off its lights and turned it round to face the Houses of Parliament for a quick getaway.

Kay slipped into the driving seat and the other three made their way through the mason's yard to the locked Poets' Corner door.

> First we prised off the covering lath of wood and then with the sharp end of the jemmy we chewed away a sufficient space to allow us to force the blade between the two sections of the door. Then the three of us put our weight on the end of the jemmy and the door began to give a series of creaks, each of which sounded like the report of a shotgun. At each creak we expected a police car to sweep up the lane, summoned by the watchman.

Ian noticed that one side of the door was held by a bolt matching a hole in the stone floor, and when they prised up that side, the bolt came free. There was now a gap of 3 inches between the two sides which enabled them to see into the Abbey.

> We put the blade of the jemmy close behind the padlock, and together we all wrenched mightily. With a crash the door

flew open. In the car Kay heard the noise and shuddered. But the way into the Abbey was open.

There was no sign of any watchman, so they moved quickly down the transept and up into the Confessor's chapel. There, in the light of Ian's torch, stood the Coronation Chair and below it the Stone. They lost no time in removing the bar of wood which lay across the front of it, and then in the dark put their arms and shoulders to pushing the Stone forward. When this had little effect, they stopped and reorganized themselves, one holding the torch, one prising at the Stone with the jemmy, and one pushing from behind. Inch by inch it moved forward until finally they were able to lift it out. But they had miscalculated the weight, which was nearer 4 hundredweight than 3, and had to put it down.

Realizing they could not carry it by hand, Ian took off his overcoat and lay it on the ground. There was a ring on one end of the Stone and when Ian pulled on it to drag it on to the coat, a part of it, about a quarter, came away. Although this was unintentional, it obviously eased the problem of getting the Stone out of the Abbey, two smaller pieces being more manageable than one big one. Holding the smaller piece Ian hurried across the stone slabs marked Chaucer, Tennyson, Byron, Spenser etc., to the Poets' Corner door, passed into the darkened mason's yard and through the door in the hoarding where Kay was waiting in the car. She opened the car door and Ian rolled his piece of the Stone on to the back seat; then returned to help the others.

With the larger piece of the Stone cradled in Ian's overcoat they had made good progress down the altar steps, to the nave and into the transept. Reaching the door into the lane Ian heard the car start up, saw it slowly move forward. He dashed through the mason's yard and the door in the hoarding beside which the car was parked.

> I opened the nearside door. 'Get the car back,' I said. 'We're not ready yet.'
> Kay looked at me coolly. 'A policeman has seen me,' she said. 'He's coming across the road.'

In the circumstances Ian did the only thing he could – though it must have taken some quick thinking – slid into the passenger seat, put his arms round Kay and began cuddling and kissing her. In a few moments they were aware of the policeman beside them. 'What's going on here?' he said. Ian released himself from Kay, explained that they had arrived in London from Scotland on holiday too late to find a bed, had driven around for a while to look at the lights, then ended up here to pass what remained of the night. Ian sensed the policeman's attitude softening towards two young lovers, then to his horror saw him put his helmet on the roof of the car, light a cigarette and prepare for a long chat. 'All this time,' he wrote later, 'I had been conscious of a scraping sound coming from behind the hoarding' – Gavin and Alan trying to move the Stone towards the hoarding door. Fearing that any further noise would lead to discovery, Kay's and Ian's response was to engage the policeman in noisy and animated conversation. 'His slightest sally brought forth peals of laughter and when we made a joke we nearly had convulsions.'

Then came a thud, too loud for any of them to miss. At once the policeman stopped speaking, ears cocked, listening. Kay and Ian froze, believing discovery at hand. Then the policeman laughed, knowing the only person to be in the Abbey at this hour would be one of the staff. 'That was the old watchman falling down the stairs,' he said and Kay and Ian laughed even louder.

But their ordeal was not over. Out of the corner of his eye Ian saw the door in the hoarding slowly opening and Gavin's face, followed by head and shoulders, peering out. Then Gavin spotted the policeman and Ian watched him retreating inch by inch backwards, closing the door behind him.

The policeman replaced his helmet and told Ian and Kay they'd better be going. Thankful, they drove down the lane into St Margaret's Street and from there to the car park where they had left the other car. Because the car they were in, the Anglia, had been observed beside the Abbey by an officer who might have noted its number, Ian thought it imperative that Kay, with her piece of the Stone, should leave London in it as soon as possible. He would return to the lane in the Ford and pick up Gavin and Alan with the larger piece.

In the car park Ian searched his pockets for the keys of the Ford, then remembered with horror that he had put them in the pocket of his overcoat on which Gavin and Alan had placed the larger piece to take from the chapel to the lane. So, having moved the smaller portion from the back seat of the Anglia to the boot and put on Alan's overcoat which had been covering it, he set Kay on the way out of London, then hastened back to the lane on foot. Weeks later he was to learn that when the Anglia was moving off from traffic lights at Victoria, the boot flew open and the Stone fell out; and that Kay, with admirable presence of mind, had jumped out and, though its weight was almost equal to her own, heaved it back in.

The policeman had gone, so Ian opened the door of the hoarding and went in. 'There was no one there. The place was in black darkness. I stood for a moment stock still, listening to the utter silence. The Stone lay at my feet. I could feel it, but of Alan and Gavin there was no sign.' He whispered their names but there was no answer. Assuming they were hiding in the Abbey he went in by the door at Poets' Corner and risked a low whistle. Again no response. Back in the mason's yard he searched for his coat in the dark, but could not find it. Where was it and where were his friends? Had they by now made their way to the car park?

He ran back there. The Ford was where they had left it but there was no sign of the others. This meant, he reckoned, that they had not found the keys of the car, for if they had, they would have been in it. So the keys must still be somewhere in the Abbey. With a recklessness born of desperation he hurried back to the Abbey for the fourth time that night and let himself in. It was now nearing six o'clock, and he believed the night-watchman would soon be starting his rounds.

I had left my torch with Kay so I was sightless. On my hands and knees I groped along the route we had taken until I reached the altar steps. Then I remembered my matches and, by the flickering light of one held in my hand, I retraced my steps. In that vast darkness the light lit nothing but myself, but I persisted until the matchbox was nearly empty. Suddenly near the door I put my foot on something uneven. I bent down and picked up the keys.

Again he ran to the car park and opened the Ford's door. The battery was flat so he found the starting handle and fired it by hand, then revved it up several times so there would be no chance of it stalling. On his way back to the lane he saw two policemen outside the St Stephen's door of the Houses of Parliament and, ignoring them, swung the car into the lane, then backed up opposite the hoarding door.

> The Stone was still lying where the other two had left it. I caught hold of it by one end and dragged it to the car. I raised it up on its good end so that it stood near the car and then I walked it, corner by rocking corner to the car door and tipped one end in. The car came down with a crash on to its springs and I thought for a moment it was going to beetle over on top of me. I got hold of the end which was still on the ground and lifted it mightily . . . when it fell, with another fearful crash. I followed it in and lifted it bodily on to the back seat. Then I took off Alan's coat and covered it up and went back into the driving seat and drove away down the lane.

It was about this time, Ian was to learn later, that the night-watchman, Andrew Hyslop, having discovered the Stone missing, was telephoning the police.

Where to go and what to do now? Elated by his eleventh-hour success against all the odds, Ian reckoned that the police would soon be setting up barriers on roads leading to the north, and therefore he should go south and hide the Stone in the country until any hue and cry had died down. Where Gavin and Alan had got to, heaven knew, but no doubt they would be going north by train, defeated and despondent. He drove across Westminster Bridge and into the Old Kent Road, feeling exaltation and relief with every mile that passed. Then, without intending it, he left the Old Kent Road and became lost in a maze of side streets. It was here that the last of that night's extraordinary encounters took place. Walking ahead of him were Gavin and Alan. Overjoyed to see him and the Stone, they told Ian that as soon as the policeman in the lane was out of sight, they had hastened to the car park and reached it just as Kay was leaving but too late to stop her. They looked for the keys of the Ford in Ian's overcoat pocket and, not finding them, assumed that he must have them. Then they started walking aimlessly south until Ian had found them. They shared out their money, planned that Alan would accompany Ian to hide the Stone and that they would pick up Gavin at Reading Station at four that afternoon. Ian asked the others what they had done with his overcoat and they had to admit that they had left it in the car park. This was disturbing, for the coat had Ian's name in it and the address of his father who had made it. After hiding the Stone he would return to the car park in the hope of retrieving it.

On reaching open country they found a cart-track leading up a hill. Fifty yards along it and out of sight of the road they hoicked the Stone out of the car, pulled it up a little bank and let it roll down the other side. Although to its captors it looked quite conspicuous ('like a wart on a girl's face', said Ian) they knew that no-one else would give it a second glance. They put some grass over it and a piece of scrap metal, then drove back to London.

They were at the car park before nine. Thankfully the overcoat with its telltale evidence was still there, though in a filthy state. They popped it into the car and, anxious to be clear of London as soon as possible, headed west for Reading. There Gavin and Alan would hire another car and take the Stone to Dartmoor while Ian in the Ford, whose number might have been taken, would take the role formerly allotted to Kay of laying a false scent by driving into Wales.

Having dropped off Alan in Reading, Ian took the A4 to the west. But having twice been passed by police cars who showed not the slightest interest in him, he thought it pointless to go further and decided to return to Reading and help Alan and Gavin retrieve the Stone. It was as well he did for, although he and Alan met several trains, Gavin was not on any of them. So Ian and Alan, the only two left of the original four, headed back to London, parked the car in a side street off Piccadilly and went into a restaurant for a meal. Then, having no radio in the car, they heard from a quartet at the next table that their exploit had become public. Ian knew the establishment on either side of the Border would be fulminating, but these he said were ordinary English people, obviously much amused by what had happened. They telephoned their friends in Glasgow and, there being little other news on Christmas Day, were told that the removal of the Stone was the talk of Scotland.

Having retrieved the Stone from its temporary resting-place they drove another 20 miles into Kent and dumped it in an easy to find scooped-out hollow, beyond a fence which was only 10 yards from a main road. Then they set out for Scotland, taking half-hour turns driving and sleeping and, when they were both awake, shouting and singing, giving new meaning, said Ian, to some of the old Jacobite songs. At Grantham Ian made a sketch on the back of an envelope of the location of the Stone and posted it to a friend c/o Glasgow University Union, so that if both were killed in an accident on these treacherous roads, at least one person would know where to collect it. They had been told to expect road blocks near the border, but a long way short of it, just north of Doncaster, they were flagged down by a patrol car. Asking why they had been stopped, the police told them about the theft of the Stone. 'A very good show,' said Ian. 'Should have been done years ago.'

They reached Edinburgh at midnight and in the Waverley Station bought the early editions of the papers. The story of the Stone was on all the front pages and would continue to feature in them strongly for several weeks. 'The reports were not hostile,' wrote Ian, although 'English officialdom had risen to the bait and there was much talk of sacrilege . . . The Dean's Christmas had been ruined. That was a pity, but it would teach him to be more careful when he meddled with stolen goods.' Later they heard the Dean speak on the radio of 'this cunningly planned and carefully executed crime' and said how sorely troubled the King was at the loss. They drove through the night to Glasgow, Ian beginning to hallucinate from exhaustion; and in the early hours of the morning came to the house of Alan's parents in Barrhead where, after a warm welcome and whisky, they piled into soft beds for the first time in five days and quickly fell asleep.

At the University Union next day Ian met Gavin who explained why he had never arrived at Reading: Ian was also glad to hear that Kay was safely back, having left the Anglia with the smaller portion of the Stone still in the boot, at a friend's house in Birmingham: she had since returned to her home in Wester Ross.

The only Scottish paper to disapprove of what had happened was the strongly anglophile *Glasgow Herald* which saw the incident as anti-monarchical. This, and the report that the King was sorely troubled troubled Ian, for he was not only a monarchist himself but had an admiration and affection for this one. 'He had led us, Scotland as well as England, through one of the most dangerous times of our history. He personally symbolized us all . . . he was one with the nation.' So that any notion of disloyalty to him might be dispelled, he and his fellow conspirators drew up a petition.

Declaring that they were loyal and obedient subjects they stated that in removing the Stone of Destiny they meant no injury to the

Church nor disrespect to the King as Head of the Church. The petition went on to show

> That the Stone of Destiny is however the most ancient symbol of Scottish nationality, and having been removed from Scotland by force and retained in England in breach of the pledge of His Majesty's predecessor, King Edward II of England, its proper place of retention is among his Majesty's Scottish people who, above all, hold this symbol dear.
>
> That therefore his Majesty's petitioners will most readily return the Stone to the safekeeping of His Majesty's officers if His Majesty will graciously assure them that in all time coming the Stone will remain in Scotland in such of His Majesty's properties or otherwise as shall be deemed fitting by him.
>
> That such an assurance will in no way preclude the use of the Stone in any coronation of any of His Majesty's successors whether in England or in Scotland.

After more protestations of loyalty the petitioners ended on a less flowery note: a detailed description of Ian's watch which had been found inside the Abbey, so that people might know that the petitioners were genuine.

How and where to deliver the petition? The English papers referred to the Stone as The Stone of Scone because it was from Scone Abbey that Edward I had plundered it. But Scone Abbey was no more, its ancient stones having been used in the building of Scone Palace, traditional home of the Earls of Mansfield. At first Ian thought of nailing the petition to the door of Scone Post Office, but remembering how the then Earl of Mansfield, although the king's Lord Lieutenant for Perthshire, had come out publicly in support of what had been done, decided to seek his help.

'Let me congratulate you', were the first words of Lord Mansfield when Ian was shown into his room at Scone, 'on one of the most brilliant exploits in Scottish history.' This was a promising start, and the atmosphere improved further when Ian was able to assure Mansfield that he was neither a republican nor a communist but a Covenanter for Home Rule like himself who was angry at English mismanagement of Scottish affairs. Ian showed him the petition and he approved of every word. But when Ian asked him to accept it as an intermediary and pass it on, Mansfield had to decline; as Lord

Lieutenant he could not be seen publicly to be associating himself with the capture. But, he assured Ian, he would help him in a private capacity in whatever way he could.

Back in Glasgow the petition was entrusted to a friend who handed it in at a newspaper office. That night, the seventh since he had gone south, he had a full night's sleep only to be woken in the morning by Gavin and Alan. Alan was worried. His father, a director of a big west of Scotland engineering firm, had told him that a piece of sandstone that had lain for six centuries in a dry and constant atmosphere must have lost a great deal of its strength. If it were exposed to the elements for any length of time, there was a danger that it might suck up water like a sponge and split into fragments when the water froze. Ian had visions of the Stone crumbling into little pieces and their brave endeavour ending in farce.

There was no time to lose: they must go south at once to bring the Stone to Scotland. He recruited three others to help him: Alan who helped himself to another of his father's cars, this time a 14 horse power Wolsley; Bill Craig, one of the original conspirators who had only been prevented from accompanying the others because of his duties as President of the Union; and a heavily bearded Scots-educated Englishman, the son of an admiral, by the name of John Josselyn.

They left Glasgow that night and took up the same routine as on the previous trip; one driving, another to talk and keep him awake – a real danger in the comfortable, heated Wolseley compared with the rigours of the Anglia and Ford. Despite dreadful weather which at one point necessitated them buying chains for the tyres, they made good progress, reviving themselves with food and drink from a picnic basket, and reaching London the evening of the following day. In a café they read the day's papers and were amused to find that the police were looking for the Stone in the Serpentine and other stretches of water: less amusing was the headline STONE: ARRESTS EXPECTED SOON.

They left London at 8 p.m. and took the road to Rochester. Now occurred the last and oddest of the coincidences with which the whole operation had been plagued. On the grass verge beyond which they had placed the Stone were two gypsy caravans and two fires. Their way was barred as effectively as if the gypsies had been policemen. Bill went over and asked if he could have a warm-up by their fire. When they agreed, he talked to them about liberty, liberty for the gypsies to lead the kind of life they had always cherished, unharried by the authorities, liberty for the people of his own country too. Then he said, 'To keep our freedom we need something the other side of that fence. It's not wrong but it's illegal: we will go to jail if we're caught.'

One of the gypsies said to wait until a local man with them had gone home on his bike and then they gave permission. The Stone was where they had left it and, to Ian's relief, in one piece. When the gypsies saw the weight of it they helped carry it to the car. It must have seemed to them a strange object to be concerned about. Ian had discovered that the front passenger seat of the car could be removed, so they put the Stone there and placed an old coat over it. Bill, with another coat on his knees, sat on it.

They set off for home, running into heavy snow again in the Midlands and finding themselves unable to fit the chains. They slithered and crawled forwards, foot by foot, though fortunately, it being a Sunday, there was little traffic. All this time the front passenger seat was propped up on the back seat where they knew it would invite suspicion if the car was stopped and searched. So the bearded Johnny Josselyn volunteered to take it north by train, and on the outskirts of York left the car holding it in his arms. He watched the car disappear down the road, then turned to find himself facing a policeman who had emerged from a nearby box. The policeman asked Johnny where he thought he was going and Johnny replied, 'Mull.' The policeman asked why he was carrying a car seat on a Sunday morning, and Johnny said it was a replacement for one in Mull that had been crapped on by a pig. Such a bizarre explanation seems to have satisfied the policeman and Johnny and the seat made their way to the station and took the next train north.

Near Darlington, where the Wolseley filled up with petrol, they bought the Sunday papers and Bill, sitting on the Stone in front, read out titbits. 'The front pages were full of us,' wrote Ian, 'and there were very heavy and learned articles inside. The heavier the newspaper, the heavier the frowns and thunderings against us.' But Ian sensed that however disapproving the establishment, the ordinary people, English and Scots, had been highly diverted.

After Darlington they turned west, passed through West Auckland, Corbridge and Hexham, and so down to Longtown where a bridge spans the border Esk and one might expect a police roadblock.

There was none. They sped across the river and in a couple of miles passed the sign which said SCOTLAND.

> We gave a little ragged cheer and shook hands. We were most moved. Success is a strange thing, much closer to tears than laughter. We felt that some sort of rude ceremony was needed to mark the return of the Stone to the custody of its own people. We drew the coat back and exposed the Stone to the air of Scotland for the first time in six hundred years. From the provision basket we produced the gill of whisky and poured a libation over the Stone's roughness.
>
> Thus quietly, with no army, no burning of houses or killing of people, and for the expenditure of less than a hundred pounds, we brought Scotland back the Stone of Destiny.

A week later Ian took a train to Birmingham where he picked up the Anglia left by Kay with the smaller portion of the Stone and brought it to Glasgow. Before this he had found a safe haven for the larger portion in a warehouse near Stirling and there the two pieces were carefully joined together. But now what to do? This was a question to which, in the excitement of planning to capture the Stone they had not given much thought. They could keep it hidden almost indefinitely but, as Ian pointed out, what good would that achieve? Sir John (later Lord) Cameron QC, Dean of the Faculty of Advocates, called on its captors to produce it publicly and then campaign openly for its retention in Scotland. But the government had responded unfavourably to the petition (and to another which they nailed to the west door of St Giles Cathedral) and once it had appeared in public, Ian knew that the authorities would immediately seize it. The Stone, he said, was becoming a millstone round their necks. 'In retrospect it would have been better if we had been caught with it somewhere in Scotland and then the problem would have been the government's not ours. We were the victims of our own success.'

No-one likes a vacuum, and as the days and weeks went by Ian sensed that Scottish public opinion was demanding a resolution of the affair. Also English and Scottish detectives had grilled Kay in Plockton for five hours and himself, Gavin and Alan in Glasgow, all without result; and although Ian would in some ways have welcomed arrest and a trial where he could air publicly the beliefs that had motivated him and his friends, he had others to think of like John MacCormick who would inevitably be sucked up in the police net. So a little more than three months after the .return of the Stone to Scotland, Ian and friends took it to the ruined Abbey of Arbroath where, 630 years earlier, the famous Declaration had been signed, and placed it reverently on the remains of the High Altar.

The authorities, said Ian, could do one of two things. 'They could please the people of Scotland by leaving the Stone in Scotland, or they could please the English establishment by unceremoniously bundling it back over the border.' They chose the latter, being incapable, Ian said, of the grand gesture. They locked it up in a prison cell and then, at dead of night, and to the professed dismay of the Scottish people, rushed it south in the boot of a police car.

Lord Hope, the present Lord President of Scotland's Court of Session, and the country's most senior judge, has called the story of the recapture of the Stone one of romance and adventure which has had a lasting place in his memory.

But when the Home Secretary of the day, Sir David Maxwell Fyfe (later Lord Kilmuir) was asked a question about the taking of the Stone in the House of Commons, he replied that its captors were thieves and vulgar vandals. As a Scot who had become part of the English establishment and was something of a vulgarian himself, he might have known better.

# PART 4
*A Highland Diversion*

In the highlands, in the country places,
Where the old plain men have rosy faces,
And the young fair maidens
Quiet eyes;
Where essential silence cheers and blesses,
And for ever in the hill-recesses
*Her* more lovely music
Broods and dies.

O to mount again where erst I haunted;
Where the old red hills are bird-enchanted,
And the low green meadows
Bright with sward;
And when even dies, the million-tinted,
And the night has come, and planets glinted,
Lo, the valley hollow
Lamp-bestarred.

O to dream, O to awake and wander
There, and with delight to take and render,
Through the trance of silence,
Quiet breath;
Lo! for there, among the flowers and grasses,
Only the mightier movement sounds and passes;
Only winds and rivers,
Life and death.

*In the Highlands*, R.L. Stevenson

That old lonely lovely way of living
in Highland places,—twenty years a-growing,
twenty years flowering, twenty years declining—
father to son, mother to daughter giving
ripe tradition; peaceful bounty flowing;
one harmony all tones of life combining—
old, wise ways, passed like the dust blowing.

That harmony of folk and land is shattered,—
the yearly rhythm of things, the social graces,
peat-fire and music, candle-light and kindness.
Now they are gone it seems they never mattered,
much, to the world, those proud and violent races,
clansmen and chiefs whose passioned greed and blindness
made desolate these lovely lonely places.

*For the Old Highlands*, Douglas Young

What would the world be, once bereft
Of wet and wildness? Let them be left,
O let them be left, wildness and wet;
Long live the weeds and the wilderness yet.

*Inversnaid*, Gerard Manley Hopkins

# CHAPTER 13

## The Thane of Cawdor and
## the Laird of Pitgaveny

OUTWITH SCOTLAND I KNOW OF NO OTHER COUNTRY IN THE WORLD whose face has been so pock-marked by ruins ancient and modern. Go to the far north and west and you will scarcely find a glen which does not harbour the tumbledown relics of crofts put to the torch and whose families were evicted wholesale by the agents of the nineteenth-century landlords to whom people were less profitable than sheep. Go to the border towns of Kelso, Jedburgh, Melrose and Dryburgh and see what is left of their exquisite abbeys (Kelso and Jedburgh founded by King David I in the twelfth century, Melrose guardian of the heart of Robert Bruce, Dryburgh where Sir Walter Scott and Field Marshal Lord Haig lie buried) after their sackings by the English. Go to the bleak uplands around Newcastleton and see the great deserted keep of Hermitage to which Mary Queen of Scots rode the 20 miles from Jedburgh and back in a day to visit the wounded Earl of Bothwell. Go to what is left of the royal palaces of Linlithgow where Mary was born or to Dunfermline where the future Charles I was delivered. Go to sea-girt Dunstaffnage in the north-west or Dunnottar on its rock in the north-east. In the Lothians go to Dirleton, demolished by General Lambert in 1650 or to the shell of majestic, rose-coloured Tantallon that guarded the approaches of the Firth of Forth until General Monk tore the heart out of it. Go to the island fortress of Lochindorb, go to Craignethan, Craigmillar, Spynie and Corsgarff, go to Caerlaverock and Sweetheart Abbey on the Solway coast, go to Dunollie and Elgin and a score of other places and you will find the same thing: dismantlings in peace, sackings in war. The history of Scotland is largely a history of its ruins.

Happily there are many Scottish castles which today are still extant and wholly or partly occupied: palatial rose-red Drumlanrig in Dumfriesshire with its stunning collection of pictures and furniture, seat of the Dukes of Buccleuch and where, it will be recalled, Prince Charles and his troops made themselves at home on their march north from Derby; Duart, dominating the Sound of Mull, traditional home of the chiefs of the clan Maclean; in Aberdeenshire the lofty, fairytale castle of Craigievar (though it's a long haul to the top); in the far north and facing the Pentland Firth the Queen Mother's cosy castle of Mey; my own ancestral stronghold of Culzean on the cliffs of Ayrshire's west coast, another of Robert Adam's flowerings, and today the most visited of all the properties of Scotland's National Trust; the late Sir Nicholas Fairbairn's miniature castle of Fordell near Dunfermline, lovingly restored by himself.

My favourite, however, is Cawdor, home of the Cawdor branch of the Campbells, equidistant from Fort George and Nairn, and which Johnson and Boswell visited on their way to the west. It was the first castle I ever entered when taken there for tea at the age of seven or eight while holidaying at Nairn. At that age I thought it huge and impressive, particularly the drawbridge; and when later at Eton I read Shakespeare's *Macbeth* and the bloody deeds done at Cawdor, I told my fellows that I had actually been there and, I'm sure, boasted in the way boys do, of how I had seen Duncan's bloodstains in the hall and his bones mouldering in the dungeon. In fact, as I discovered later, Macbeth had never been there, his birth, life and death having taken place in the twelfth century and Cawdor Castle not built until two centuries later. Shakespeare had relied on two Scottish chroniclers, Andrew of Wyntoun and Hector Boece and one English one, Raphael Holinshed, for background material and *Macbeth*, like so many of his plays, was an imaginative blend of fact and fiction.

When I next called at Cawdor, it was as a grown man, and the castle which had seemed to me so vast and impressive as an eight year old now struck me as being agreeably compact; its tower a pleasing rectangle, its modest-sized rooms with family pictures, furniture and other artefacts on a scale easy to comprehend and enjoy, not overwhelming as I have found elsewhere; and the lush pastoral surround of woodland and garden in which the castle stands seemed to add to its enchantment.

A further bonus was getting to know and enjoy the company of the late Earl and 26th Thane, Hugh Cawdor, a black-haired, funny, buccaneering sort of Thane and his talented and attractive Bohemian wife, Angelika, who always generously invited me to look in if passing and, when I did, I invariably found the champagne chilled and waiting. An even greater bonus was Hugh's determination to make the visits of the tourists, as they traipsed round, entertaining as well as enlightening. Whereas most guidebooks of stately homes are deathly dull in their descriptions of what visitors see, Hugh's *Room Notes* (and these are not all of them), if at times inclined to facetiousness, strike me as one of the plusses of Anglo-Scottishness. No native Scot that I know would have either the imagination or the daring to indulge in such iconoclastic wit.

### The Flemish Tapestries in the Tapestry Bedroom

Ham shamelessly telling his brothers Shem and Japheth, that their father, having sampled the new wine, is naked in his tent in a drunken sleep; for which piece of cheek Noah cursed Ham's son Canaan, in a characteristic flash of Old Testament peevishness. The curse was not all that effective, considering that Canaan begat (as you will recall) eleven sons.

The Holy Family's flight into Egypt with the Virgin and child on horseback, while Joseph walks along with a flintlock gun on his shoulder, dressed in period costume of the 17th century.

The musical box is Swiss and plays See-Saw, Fairie Voices and similar soothing stuff.

### The Yellow Room

The layout of the room is peculiar. The fireplace is hopelessly off centre, the windows are irregular, the walls are out of square, the plaster is floated directly on to the rough masonry, the bold Restoration cornice is uneven, and yet for all that, it makes a rather charming sitting-room.

*Birnam Wood* painted in 1889 was dedicated to the star actor Sir Henry Irving who visited Cawdor in August 1887 with his leading lady Dame Ellen Terry 'to absorb the atmosphere' for their production of *Macbeth*.

The handsome lady in the saucy brown hat is Mrs Jane Philips, affectionately nicknamed 'Aunt Glum'.

### The Thorn Tree Room

The legendary tale goes that the Thane of Cawdor, who had a small castle about a mile away, decided to build a new, stronger tower. Following the instructions received in a dream, he loaded a coffer of gold on to the back of a donkey and let it roam about the district for a day: wherever the animal lay down to rest in the evening, there his castle should be sited and it would prosper for evermore. The donkey lay down under this tree . . . modern scientific dating of the wood of the tree by radiocarbon measurement gives the approximate date of 1372.

### The Small Dungeon

There are indications that the dungeon may have served as a hideout for women and children and even as a playroom, apart from its more obvious use as a place to store hostages and the ungodly. On 17 May 1482 King James III of Scotland wrote a shirty letter to the Earl of Huntly instructing him to 'cause' the Thane of Cawdor to release William Rose of Kilravock from the dungeon. The neighbouring houses of Cawdor and Kilravock were then engaged in a quarrel. Rose was duly released, ruffled but unharmed.

### Pet's Corner

Goat. The Cawdor family have always had a soft spot for goats. The late Lord Cawdor had a favourite goat called Albert which was virtually indestructible and had a great fondness for devouring ivy. On Sundays it was given as a treat a packet of Players Medium Navy Cut cigarettes; first it ate the cigarettes, then the packet, leaving the silver paper as a last special morsel. Sadly Albert passed away after drinking a gallon of red-lead paint primer and was given a simple but moving funeral.

Australian 'Magpie'. For many years this Aussie reffo lived in great state in a cage suspended from a branch of the big yew tree in the flower garden. It could talk, presumably in Strine and it liked the castle housekeeper Mrs Gowans. To her it yacked 'Hello Janet' but to strangers it shrieked 'Get out!' The bird is a type of shrike.

*Stones*

The round stone with a hole in it is a sandstone spindle-wheel . . . This one was found by Lord Cawdor while wandering aimlessly in a ploughed field.


Relations between the Cawdors and the Roses of nearby Kilravock Castle (pronounced Kilrawk) which Hugh Cawdor touches on in his account of the Small Dungeon have never been easy, as I found on a recent visit to both for a BBC radio programme. There have been Roses at Kilravock for almost as long as Campbells at Cawdor, but the present head of the Rose family, Miss Elizabeth Rose, is likely to be the last; for although she has a nephew to whom she could leave the property, she intends to endow it as a religious retreat. Indeed it would seem to be going that way already, several members of The Salvation Army being in residence when we arrived. Hugh Cawdor was saddened when I told him this, but not altogether surprised.

In June 1993 I had a letter from Hugh in his neat hand, enclosing a new edition of his *Room Notes*. He added, 'No new brochure from Kilravock as yet . . . However Madam Rose recently discovered that I had been smitten with cancer for several months, and let me have it with a salvo of quotes from the Book of Isaiah – most unsoothing.'

Before I had time to acknowledge the letter, Hugh was dead. He was only sixty-one, a cruelly premature end, I felt, for such a life-enhancing figure.

In the autumn came another surprise: a memorial service for him, which I attended, at the Roman Catholic Church of St James's Spanish Palace. He had been received into the Church just days before he died.

Later, back at Cawdor, I asked Angelika about Hugh's last days. 'It began with a pain in his right arm which grew worse. His GP sent him to a specialist and on his last visit I went with him. The specialist said he had lung cancer and had only a couple of months to live, though in the end he lasted for six. In all that time he never complained. He was so brave, it was amazing.'

'Were you surprised when he converted to Catholicism?'

'Yes and no. The Church of Scotland said nothing to him, and he used to tell me how much he envied what being a Catholic meant to me and the relationship I had with the monks at nearby Pluscarden. But it was his wish, not mine. Father Giles went down to London and heard Hugh's confession at the Princess Grace hospital. I know it gave him peace at the end.'

I said that Hugh had always struck me as half poet and half pirate, and was that a fair description?

'Very fair. He loved shooting and fishing on the Findhorn and he was devoted to the estate and its woods. He adored the English language. He had a wonderful eye and a great sense of proportion, and he loved the company of women. And yet he could also be fey and idle.' She laughed, 'I think of him, above all, as a Pict. I met him here at Cawdor when I was thirty-five and unmarried, travelling with a friend. He had been married and had five children. He was the first man I ever met who made me feel that if I didn't do what he wanted me to do, I might always regret it. I'm sure I would have done. We were together for fifteen years and there wasn't a day when he didn't cease to surprise and amuse me.'

Some 30 miles east of Cawdor and a few miles north of Elgin in the county of Moray lies the 5,000-acre estate of Pitgaveny which runs to the sea. (It was here and not at Cawdor Castle that Duncan met his fate at the hands of Macbeth, later dying of his wounds in Elgin Castle.)

In the centre of the estate and surrounded by woods stands a large Georgian house, built in the year of the Declaration of American Independence. When you mount the steps leading to the entrance and open the front door, an astonishing sight greets you. Hanging on the walls and up the staircase are the stuffed heads of 170 mostly African wild animals. These include not only almost every known species of deer and buck but those of a lion, rhino, hippo and giraffe on whose head hangs a tweed balmoral. Originally there were some 370 heads on display including that of a warthog and a baboon wearing a red tarboosh, but these are now in store awaiting a decision on their future.

A hundred years ago such displays, though perhaps not on such a scale, were common in many country houses in England and Scotland; but in today's greatly changed climate of conservation and the protection of endangered species from extinction, the exhibition of so great a slaughter seems (at least it did to me) literally shocking. Understandably the sportsman responsible for it was from another age: Captain James Brander-Dunbar who died in 1969 at the age of ninety-four. In his youth he had joined the Queen's Own Cameron Highlanders, was sent to Africa, and in places like Somaliland, Matabeleland (where he fathered a half-caste boy), Nyasaland and the Sudan he pursued the local fauna unceasingly. Although only five feet tall he became something of a bruiser. Once during the Boer War he responded to a sentry's challenge by shouting at him, 'I've forgotten the bloody password so you had better shoot me and if you miss, you blackguard, I'll have you on a charge for damned idleness.'

At the turn of the century when his father died, he returned home to administer the Pitgaveny estate which he did with success for nearly seventy years, planting trees, shooting, stalking, fishing and becoming a JP, County Councillor and Deputy Lieutenant. He married in 1922 when he was forty-seven and although his wife gave him two daughters the marriage was not a success and ended within two years.

Some people took to him, admiring his courage and single-mindedness and, to those he knew, great kindness. Finding a fifteen-year-old boy trespassing on Spynie Loch, and discovering his interest in natural history, he invited him to take the boat out on the loch whenever he wished. Another friend wrote that although he often went too far, his friendships were deep, and that none who knew him well failed to love him. He often began letters, 'Dear comrade' and ended with an invitation to call any time 'for a dram and a blether'.

The shoots he organized at Pitgaveny were famous for their lack of planning and general muddle. One day the Captain telephoned Cawdor to ask Hugh's father to come to one of them. Hugh, then a young man, said his father was away. 'You'll do,' said the Captain, 'and bring your own bloody lunch.'

Hugh's first sight on arrival was 'an amazing band of rough and ready beaters, disreputable-looking keepers and dogs – mainly vast, black, curly-coated retrievers the size of donkeys, and a tame stag . . . With colossal energy these dogs fought, were sick, rampaged, fell over, copulated, barged into people and passed copious water.

'The laird emerged from behind the stack-yard, buttoning his flies. He was short and square, with a bullet head upholstered in grey stubble; it transpired that his hair was dressed by the farm grieve with horse-clippers. He had a dilapidated jacket, baggy plus-fours, a darned shirt, gumboots and, somehow holding everything together, a wide belt with a hunting knife and pouches. Unlike his contemporaries he never wore a hat.'

The Captain gave Hugh what he described as a terse greeting and then turned to the head keeper:

'We'll do the north end first with the wind the way it is,' said the Captain.

'Pitgaveny,' said the keeper, 'ye'r daft. If you want to do it that way, ye'll do it yersel'. There's nae bleeding wind.'

'Very well,' the Captain replied, 'you're a thrawn ape.'

The rest of the day followed much the same pattern.

But there was another even less refined side to the Captain. Once, staying at a lodge for the grouse-shooting, he told a fellow guest, Alan Lascelles, the King's private secretary, that he often spent Sunday afternoon rowing a boat-load of terriers and a bagged cat into the middle of his loch and then hunting the cat like an otter. Lascelles, who recorded this, summed him up: 'A jovial scoundrel, bloodthirsty as a stoat and cruel but good company and a man'. On his tombstone he had inscribed, 'A fine natural blackguard who gave more justice than he ever got.'

The owner of Pitgaveny today is a distant cousin of the Captain, Alexander (Sandy) Dunbar who I first met when he was Director of the Scottish Arts Council and I Chairman of Edinburgh's Royal Lyceum Theatre Company. A stocky, athletic man with a great sense of fun, Sandy is not the least interested in the sporting pursuits so enjoyed by his kinsman, but a lover of art, literature, history and conservation. So why does he continue to tolerate on his walls this frozen zoo of dead animals' heads? First, he says, because they are an expression of the Captain's personality and one should not judge the values that were current a hundred years ago by those of today. Secondly they form a unique collection which financially are worth little, but fill a large area of wall space and are part of the house's history. I asked if other guests had commented on his displaying them and he said no, although admitting that those who didn't like them were probably too polite to say so. But he did agree that he and his wife were ambivalent about the heads and their future, and indeed about some aspects of his macho kinsman.

I asked Sandy how he had come to inherit the estate, and this is what he said. On the evening of Boxing Day 1958 when staying with his parents at Duffus which is 5 miles from Pitgaveny, he was dining at a house near Gordonstoun school where his friend Oscar Hahn (nephew of Gordonstoun's legendary founder, Kurt Hahn) and his wife Margaret were staying. Sandy greatly admired Oscar's drive and the flair with which he ran his father's metal business, despite polio at ten which later confined him to a wheelchair. 'I'm only a scribe at ICI', Margaret remembers Sandy saying, 'but my ancestors did great things', and he cited his Uncle Arbuthnott, called by his eight sisters The Bounder. In India Uncle Arbuthnott had gone to a regimental ball dressed as a woman and had been asked by his Colonel for a dance. Later when stationed at the Curragh he took a bet that he wouldn't run naked over a distance of 5 miles, did it under cover of darkness and won. As an undergraduate Oscar had himself won a wager for propelling his wheelchair from Trinity College Cambridge to Hyde Park Corner.

Tickled by the story of Uncle Arbuthnott's naked midnight run, Oscar bet Sandy £5 on the spot that he wouldn't run naked from his parents' house at Duffus to Pitgaveny, increased to £20 if it was accomplished in daylight before the end of the year – then only five days away. Sandy needed £20 for a pair of skis, so took the bet and told the Captain (though not his parents) what he intended.

Next day Sandy began to see things in a rather different light. What had seemed a great idea after a good dinner looked rather different in the light of post-Christmas winter weather. Also the country between Duffus and Pitgaveny was flat and open, there were several farms to by-pass and two public roads and a canal to cross. Against this he was a practised runner and if by chance he did meet someone *en route*, there was little they could or would do.

Sandy's parents were at home that day but on the morning after, the 28th, they were going into Elgin to see their man of business. Sandy telephoned the Captain to say he would be leaving Duffus at 11 a.m. and hoped to arrive at Pitgaveny by twelve.

'The start', he was to write later, 'was the worst part. I went upstairs and undressed in my bedroom. I put on my gym shoes and nothing else. Stark naked beneath an army overcoat, I told the cleaning lady I was going for a run and walked down the garden path to the front gate. Cautiously I peered right and left:

there was nobody in sight. I stepped into the drive, removed my overcoat, flung it over the garden wall and set off.'

At first, he said, he felt unnerved and very vulnerable. The sun was out but there was a cold wind blowing. In singlet and shorts he was used to the wind, 'but the wind on the loins was a new experience.'

At the end of the drive he decided to strike across the fields and risk barbed wire rather than take the nearest farm road. It was as well he did because a moment later he saw the village postman on the farm road. Later he heard that on arrival home the postman had told his sister that he had seen a naked man running through the fields, to which she replied that he had had too many Christmas drams along his route and was seeing things.

He avoided two other farms by steering a course between them, then came to the canal. He didn't dare risk the road bridge, not knowing who or what might be on the other side. So there was no choice but to wade. 'It was cold, it was muddy, it was deep'. He clambered out on the other side and entered a marsh.

Giving a wide berth to the field containing the Captain's Highland cattle ('so wild that even his own cattlemen could not handle them') he was faced with a final, fraught obstacle, crossing the Elgin–Lossiemouth road. He hid up in some young pines until both directions were clear, then sprinted across the road and on to a track. But he had miscalculated. 'At that moment a big, blue double-decker bus came along the road, full of housewives returning to Lossiemouth from Elgin with their New Year shopping.' He ran on, reflecting that even if they had seen him, they were unlikely to stop.

The ruins of Spynie Palace showed up ahead and when he had passed them and crossed the disused railway track he was into the Pitgaveny home woods. Before twelve he was on the front doorsteps sounding the bell. The Captain answered it. 'Come away,' he said and put a tweed coat round him. But a condition of the bet was that before getting dressed Sandy and the Captain must have a dram together. So they went into the sitting-room where Sandy stood in an alcove to hide himself from the Captain's secretary who was also there. Then Oscar arrived with his clothes and Sandy went upstairs to bath and change. He had won his bet and in the New Year bought himself a pair of skis.

But that is not all. In 1925 the Scottish author John Buchan published *John Macnab*, his famous gung-ho story about three professional men in London, a lawyer, a banker and an MP who coincidentally (and luckily for the plot) are all so bored with life that they are at a loss what to do. Buchan has one of their friends sow the seed of an idea. 'You remember Jim Tarras? He had a little place somewhere in Moray and spent most of his time shootin' in East Africa. Well, when his father died and he came home to settle down, he found it an uncommon dull job. So, to enliven it, he invented a new kind of sport . . . He used to write to the owner of a deer forest . . . and beg to inform him that between certain dates he proposed to kill one of his stags. When he had killed it, he undertook to deliver it to the owner, for he wasn't a thief.' Thus was born the story of *John Macnab* in which three professional men did kill a stag or a salmon undetected on three adjoining Highland estates and returned them to their owners.

Jim Tarras who owned a little place in Moray and had spent his youth shooting in East Africa was Captain Jim Brander-Dunbar who had, as a subaltern, bet a fellow officer, Lord Abinger, £20 that on a certain date he would poach a deer from his estate of Inverlochy Castle (now one of the most luxurious hotels in Scotland) undetected and return it to him afterwards. That is what he did; and included among other heads at Pitgaveny is that of the Inverlochy stag that the Captain shot and a photograph of the original cheque for £20 that Abinger sent him. When *John Macnab* was published the Captain wrote to John Buchan to tell him that he was Jim Tarras and not dead, as Buchan had stated – a mistake which Buchan readily recognized by sending the captain a copy of *John Macnab* inscribed 'John Macnab from John Buchan.'

As a betting man himself the Captain recognized in his youthful cousin Sandy and his naked run a kindred spirit. So, at the age of eighty-three and having no male heirs to leave Pitgaveny to, he sent this line to Sandy soon after the run:

My dear kinsman,
    In view of your naked run, I have decided to leave Pitgaveny to you. The estate is yours.

And that is how, when the Captain died twelve years later, Sandy Dunbar came into his inheritance; where he and his wife Susannah have lived happily ever after.

# PART 5
*Edinburgh*

I always liked Scotland as an idea, but now, as a reality, I like it far better . . . and who indeed that has once seen Edinburgh, with its couchant crag-lion, but must see it again in dreams waking or sleeping? My dear Sir, do not think I blaspheme when I tell you that your Great London as compared to Dun-Edin 'mine own romantic town' is as prose compared to poetry, or as a great rumbling, rambling, heavy Epic – compared to a lyric, bright, brief, clear and vital as a flash of lightning.

Letter, 20 July 1850, Charlotte Brontë

. . . And in Edinburgh, where the past is so strong, and the memory of Scottish history is perpetually reminding you, if you are a Scotsman, that this was once a capital, the half-meaninglessness of Scottish life overwhelms you more strongly than anywhere else.

*Scottish Journey* (1935) Edwin Muir

Edinburgh pays cruelly for her high seat in one of the vilest climates under heaven. She is liable to be beaten upon by all the winds that blow, to be drenched with rain, to be buried in cold sea fogs out of the east, and powdered with the snow as it comes flying southward from the Highland hills.

'Edinburgh' (1878) R.L. Stevenson

# INTERLUDE

In the uniqueness of its setting and architecture, the Old town contrasting with the New, and between them the railway to Glasgow running over ground where the old Nor' Loch used to be, high above it the massive fortress of the castle from whose battlements you can see the grey waters of the Firth of Forth from Queensferry to the Bass Rock and, beyond, the blue hills of Fife, Edinburgh is like no other city in the kingdom. Whenever I think of it, I think of that other native son and writer, Robert Louis Stevenson and of the first few lines of a sonnet he dedicated to his wife shortly before he died in far-away Samoa:

> I saw rain falling and the rainbow drawn
> On Lammermuir. Hearkening I heard again
> In my precipitous city beaten bells
> Winnow the keen sea-wind . . .

Anyone who has lived in Edinburgh knows of the rain (and the haar), the beaten bells (less now than formerly) piercing the Sabbath silence and the chill of the keen east wind. So vivid were Stevenson's memories of his early days in his native city – Heriot Row and Swanston, childhood nightmares engendered and allayed by his Calvinistic but comforting nurse Cummy, the University and the Law Courts, the taverns and the stews – that it was no accident that he should have chosen Edinburgh as the setting for his last, great unfinished novel, *Weir of Hermiston*: in his imagination it enabled him to return there.

Running like a thread through the city as also through my own life has been the Water of Leith, the gentle stream that rises in the Pentland Hills and empties into the port of Leith. My first acquaintance with it came as a boy staying in the house of my grandfather in Belgrave Crescent. Opposite the crescent are the gardens: beyond the river flowed through a deep gully before crossing under the Dean Bridge over which the traffic rumbled on its way to Barnton, Queensferry and the north. So deep was this gully and so dark that as a boy I didn't dare climb down the steep bank to it for fear of tumbling in. As an older boy I saw it in a friendlier, fresher surround, flowing through my Uncle Nevill Dundas's property of Redhall out at Colinton and whose chauffeur taught me how to prise trout from it. And then some seventeen years ago it swam into my life again when I bought a house in Upper Dean Terrace, a few hundred yards downstream from Belgrave Crescent Gardens and just round the corner from Raeburn's exquisite Ann Street, and found it flowing past my door. Even today it is still with me, for when I stay with my nephew, who is Keeper of the Scottish Gallery of Modern Art, at his house in Warriston Crescent, I find it carolling along at the end of his garden, that much nearer the sea.

Robert Louis had a relationship with it too, first when his family lived at Howard Place (just round the corner from Warriston Crescent) and Inverleith Row, later when he stayed with his grandparents at Colinton Manse, not far from Redhall. There the river curls round the house on two sides so that in the words of one Stevenson biographer, 'it was the sound of the rushing waters as they went over the dam and into the mill race that pervaded the Manse and never left the ears of those who were brought up there.' One can imagine the effect that the sight and sounds of this must have had on little Robert Louis's own lively imagination. One can see him tossing homemade toy boats into the stream to compete with one another and wondering when they would reach the sea. One can see him too in later life when illness had temporarily put prose beyond him, remembering those halcyon, far-off Colinton days.

Dark brown is the river,
Golden is the sand,
It flows along for ever,
With trees on either hand.

Green leaves a-floating,
Castles of the foam,
Boats of mine a-boating —
Where will all come home?

On goes the river,
And out past the mill,
Away down the valley,
Away down the hill.

Away down the river
A hundred miles or more,
Other little children,
Shall bring my boats ashore.

That comes from his *A Child's Garden of Verses*, and there's another poem of his there I particularly cherish because what he saw in the Edinburgh of the 1850s I saw too in the 1920s. On winter evenings in Belgrave Crescent before the maid Helen brought in a gigantic tea (flapjacks, oatcakes, toast, drop scones, treacle scones, gingerbread, fresh butter, salt butter, heather-comb honey in a box, fish paste, strawberry jam, marmalade) and before we settled down to a game of Old Maid, I would stand in the drawing-room window listening to the organ grinder at the corner of the street and waiting for the lamplighter to come by. He carried a ladder and a pole with which he flipped open the little window on top of each lamppost, then ignited the gas jet inside. I was entranced when my mother used to read me this poem and imagined, as any boy would, that Leerie was the name, not just of any old lamplighter but of ours, the one who lit the lamps in Belgrave Crescent; and who Robert Louis must have known:

My tea is nearly ready and the sun has left the sky;
It's time to take the window to see Leerie going by;
For every night at teatime and before you take your seat
With lantern and with ladder he comes posting up the street.

Now Tom would be a driver and Maria go to sea,
And my papa's a banker and as rich as he can be;
But I, when I am stronger and can choose what I'm to do,
O Leerie, I'll go round at night and light the lamps with you!

For we are very lucky, with a lamp before the door,
And Leerie stops to light it, as he lights so many more;
And O! before you hurry by with ladder and with light,
O Leerie, see a little child and nod to him to-night.

I have written in my autobiography about life in Edinburgh as a boy, so here all I will say is that it was a full one: golf with my grandfather at Barnton and Muirfield, shooting with his brother-in-law Tom Boothby in East Lothian, fishing on Gladsmuir Loch courtesy of the other brother-in-law Nevill Dundas, skating at the Haymarket Ice Rink; Christmas holiday visits to the pantomime to delight in the comic genius of Tommy Lorne and Dave Willis; tram trips to the Leith Docks to satisfy my burgeoning curiosity about the sea and ships; and hours spent devouring the red volumes of William Hodge's Notable British Trial series which filled the top shelf of my grandfather's library and were the genesis of my lifelong interest in miscarriages of criminal justice.

I have been to Edinburgh many times since, later lived there, and like nowhere else have always found it to be an exclusive part of me, a much-loved blend of parent and mistress whose *persona* seldom disappoints. Returning to scenes of one's youth can often be a let-down in that many of them have changed out of all recognition. But not Edinburgh. In the seventy-odd years I have known it, its general lay-out seems hardly to have altered, although Princes Street, an elegant half-mile terrace when first built has been allowed to deteriorate into a tawdry mish-mash of utilitarian shops. Yet the general look of the place, the singular atmosphere and *feel* of it is always the same; on this foreigners as well as natives agree.

There have been enough guidebooks and anthologies about Edinburgh, God knows, without my adding to them; but open the doors of Edinburgh's best-known landmarks and you will find some of the riches of Scotland's past.

# CHAPTER 14

## *The Queen of Scotland*

Sir, never talk of your independency who could let your Queen
remain twenty years in captivity and then be put to death without even a pretence of justice, without your even attempting to
rescue her; and such a Queen too! as every man of any gallantry
would have sacrificed his life for.

Johnson to Boswell

In the United Kingdom are five 'Copyright' Libraries, that is the
repositories of books published in this country which are protected
by copyright. They are the British Library in London; the Bodleian
Library in Oxford; the Cambridge University Library; the National
Library of Wales in Aberystwyth; and the National Library of
Scotland on George IV Bridge in Edinburgh. In addition to its
collection of printed books, the National Library of Scotland houses
a rich store of archive manuscripts; among them the holograph letter
from Mary Queen of Scots to her brother-in-law the King of France,
written in the middle of the night before her execution.

\* \* \*

If ever there was a woman born for glory and fulfilment, one would have thought it would have been Mary; and in another incarnation she might have been. Already Queen of Scots when only a week old, then despatched to France to be first the playmate and then the wife of the Dauphin Francis, she blossomed into a lively, beautiful, intelligent and talented child. Later, tall with stunning red-gold hair and intensely feminine, she was loved and admired wherever she went. Francis's father, King Henry, said she was the most perfect child he had ever seen, the Cardinal of Lorraine that of all France's daughters, noble or commoners, she had no equal; while the poet Ronsard wrote:

> Just as we see, half rosy and half white,
> Dawn and the morning star dispel the night,
> In beauty thus beyond compare impearled,
> The queen of Scotland rises on the world.*

No woman could have asked for a more promising début, yet throughout her life misfortunes and misjudgements lay like little tigers waiting to pounce, some of her own making, some that of others. In 1558 the Catholic Queen of England, Mary Tudor, died. As Henry VII's granddaughter Mary in law, and lineage, had first claim on the throne, but her Protestant cousin Elizabeth, illegitimate daughter of Henry VIII, being on the spot assumed it herself. Whereupon Mary's father-in-law King Henry of France, unwilling to recognize, silly man, that possession is the greater part of the law, ordered the royal arms of England to be added to those of Scotland and France on Mary's equipage. Elizabeth was outraged, and the issue was to be an Anglo-Scottish sore between them, ending only with Mary's death.

Then came two further blows, both of God's making. King Henry of France died when splinters from a lance pierced his eye in a jousting tournament and Francis and Mary became king and queen. Yet only eighteen months later Francis too died, of an ear infection. Mary was disconsolate, mourned him in a darkened room, for during their young lives she had truly loved him. What was she to do now? She could have retired to the estates Francis had left to her and had she done so, and remarried, she might have led a

---

*Translated from the French by Maurice Baring.

happier life, though history would hardly have heard of her. But she was still Queen of Scotland where, during her thirteen years in France, her mother Mary of Guise had been acting as her regent. To Scotland and her destiny she knew she must go. But it meant leaving a country and a people which had given her the only home she had ever known for one smaller, colder, more primitive, whose people were entire strangers. On the ship that bore her across the North Sea from Calais to Leith she was seen weeping in the stern as the coast of France faded from view. 'Adieu, France. Adieu, my dear France,' she was heard to mutter. 'I think I shall never see you again.' Nor did she.

After the elegance and sophistication of the French court, the culture shock of less than bonnie Scotland with its nobles in a continual state of jealousy and feuding, must have been sharp. But the reception in her capital was as warm as she could have wished: bonfires were lit and in Holyrood that night a hundred fiddlers kept her awake, playing dreadfully out of tune.

On this wave of goodwill Mary was quick to capitalize, a task for which her apprenticeship as Queen of France had adequately prepared her. One tiger lying in wait was the radical, religious zealot and preacher John Knox who, having recently brought Protestantism to Scotland almost single-handed, feared that Mary, an ardent Roman Catholic, would attempt to put back the clock. But Mary, wise in her nineteen years, made it known that while she would celebrate Mass in her private chapel, she had no intention of challenging the newly established faith. This so impressed Queen Elizabeth's ambassador, Thomas Randolph, that he reported that since her arrival Mary's whole conduct had been accommodating and tactful, 'and never more so on the subject of religion'.

Others echoed him. Sir James Melville, who had been with her in France, said that she had conducted herself 'so princely, so honourably and so discreetly that her reputation had spread to all countries'. And the French ambassador reported that the Scots were delighted with their beautiful young queen and counted themselves lucky to be ruled by one of the most perfect princesses of her time.

Queenly duties apart, she entered with zest into those pastimes which Scotland and her own inclinations offered. She loved the countryside and open air, was a fearless rider, and on progressions through the kingdom would routinely break off for a day's hunting or hawking. Other outdoor pursuits were archery and croquet. She was fond of dogs too, not only hounds of the chase but little lap dogs which she dressed in blue velvet.

Indoors she took pleasure in music and is said to have played well on the lute; poetry (which she also composed), dancing (of which Knox disapproved), billiards, cards, backgammon, chess. She was a good embroiderer and read extensively in half a dozen languages. And being markedly feminine, she took a keen interest in clothes in which she showed exquisite but simple taste. Whatever she did, it was with an intense love of living and in the enjoyment of the company of those who shared her pleasures. Yet while many men were physically attracted to her she never incurred a whisper of impropriety. All in all at this time, she seemed almost too good to be true.

One thing she lacked and wanted, and her people even more, was a husband, for until she had remarried and produced a child, the kingdom was without an heir. Sadly, she was not the first woman in history of courage, beauty and good sense to be led astray when it came to matters of the heart. Henry Stuart, Lord Darnley, eldest surviving son of the Earl of Lennox, the man she chose to share her bed and throne, could hardly have been less suitable: four years younger than herself, he was vain, indolent, cowardly and vicious, a frequenter of taverns and brothels. But he had one attribute to which Mary succumbed, his physical presence: he was one of the few men she had met taller than herself, was very good-looking with golden locks, the waist of a girl and long, shapely legs ('more liker to a woman than a man' said one courtier). Mary, then twenty-three, healthy and lusty and, it is believed, still a virgin (it was thought that sickly Francis had never been able to consummate their union), experienced for the first time the turbulence of carnal love.

The union pleased nobody. Because Darnley was of the English blood royal (his grandmother on his mother's side was Margaret Tudor, daughter of Henry VII) Queen Elizabeth saw it as an added threat to her throne and tried to have it aborted. Mary's half brother, the bastard earl of Moray, left the court to join other nobles in rebellion. And as time went by, Darnley's arrogant attitude led Mary to regret her choice. Less than five months into the marriage, Randolph, once such a fan, was telling Elizabeth that he knew for certain that the queen had come to hate Darnley. More presciently he wrote: 'I know not, but it is greatly to be feared that he can have no long life among these people.'

For the moment though he was to have a breathing-space. In exchange for the promise of the crown matrimonial where they could manipulate him as they wished, the rebel nobles persuaded Darnley to join them in attempting to seize the queen from her apartments and murder the nobles loyal to her. But thanks to Mary's indomitable spirit the plot misfired, resulting only in the killing of her poor, little effeminate Italian secretary, David Riccio, a member of the Holyrood staff male voice quartet and who, the rebels wrongly thought, had become Mary's lover. Face to face, Darnley was putty in Mary's hands and, after convincing him that his fellow conspirators would discard him as soon as they had achieved their purpose, she persuaded him to desert them and help her to escape.

There was one thing to do before throwing him to the wolves. On 19 June 1566 Mary gave birth to her son James, the future king of Scotland and England, in a tiny room in Edinburgh Castle* where after Riccio's murder she had moved for greater safety. ('The queen of Scots is lighter of a bonny son,' said England's Elizabeth ruefully on hearing the news, 'and I am but of barren stock.') A few days later, before her husband and the court, and to assert his legitimacy, Mary held the baby up and addressed Darnley thus: 'My lord, God has given you and me a son, begotten by none but you. Here I protest to God, and as I shall answer to him at the great day of judgement,† that this is your son and no other man's son.' And she added, waspishly, 'For he is so much your own son, I fear it will be the worse for him thereafter.'

Ever mindful of Darnley's treachery and afraid that he might indulge in further plotting, Mary told a meeting of loyal nobles at Craigmillar Castle that she wanted rid of him, without asking or being informed how or where it was to be done, though she stipulated that it must not impugn her honour: in view of her known dislike of violence she may naïvely have thought that they might send him packing to England or else only capture and imprison him. The nobles, remembering his treachery to them, were only too ready to comply.

After the little prince's baptism (which he did not attend) in Stirling Castle, Darnley had slunk off to one of his father's

---

*Much visited by tourists today.
†Until recently this phrase formed part of the oath required of witnesses in the Scottish courts and was administered by the presiding judge.

properties near Glasgow where, realizing the antipathy not only of the queen but of the nobles against him, he intended to leave the country and take ship for France. Before he could arrange this, he fell ill with syphilis, no doubt acquired in an Edinburgh bordello. While he was recovering, and to pre-empt any further plots he might have in mind, Mary took a retinue to fetch him to Edinburgh to convalesce in a small house in the precincts of the church called Kirk o' Field, on the site of the present University's Old Quad and less than a mile from Holyrood. A week after his arrival the house blew up with an explosion that was heard all over Edinburgh. Darnley was not in it. Suspicious of something, he had fled in his nightgown to a nearby garden where his body was found strangled.

The rebel nobleman directly responsible for the explosion was the Earl of Bothwell, a very rough customer indeed with cruel, suspicious eyes. A fellow noble called him 'high in his own conceit, proud, vicious and vainglorious'. He was a bully too who had once kicked his servant in the stomach. He had been worming his way towards power and into Mary's affections for some time, and in allowing him to, she was making an even greater misjudgement than her submission to Darnley. Yet Darnley, four years younger than Mary, had been a kind of toyboy while Bothwell, six years older, was a man of action on whom, she deluded herself, she could rely for protection and advice; and to that end had given him a set of rooms in Holyrood.

Soon placards were going up in Edinburgh accusing Bothwell of Darnley's murder and claiming that Mary had been privy to it. Under duress Mary approved of a Parliamentary decision to put Bothwell on trial; but it was a farce and he was acquitted. Emboldened by the verdict, Bothwell advanced his cause a stage further by hosting a dinner-party in Edinburgh's Ainslie tavern to eight bishops, nine earls and seven barons, and persuading them (just how has never been explained) to sign a bond to the effect that the queen was in need of a new husband and that he was the best man for the job. It could be said that they were doing no more than recognizing the fact that (as the French ambassador put it) Bothwell's influence with the queen was now greater than that of all the other nobles put together.

Armed with the bond Bothwell put his suit to Mary and was refused. So a little later and with a force of 800 men he met Mary as she was returning to Edinburgh from Stirling after seeing her little boy for the last time. He told her there were dangers lurking in Edinburgh and he would take her instead to the castle she had given him at Dunbar.

For the queen this was the moment of truth, when she should have recognized Bothwell as the schemer he was and refused to fall in with his plans. But ever since an illness at Jedburgh the previous October from which she had nearly died, she had been a shadow of her self. Had she defied Bothwell and insisted on continuing to Holyrood, history would have had to be rewritten. But now, weak, confused and only too relieved that others should take decisions for her, she had become as much putty in Bothwell's hands as Darnley had been in hers. When they reached Dunbar Bothwell, brutal and resolute, did what he had to do as a means to his burning ambition: forced his way into the queen's bedchamber and ravished her, thus binding herself to him, for if she conceived, Mary could not run the risk and ignominy of bearing a bastard.

So they were married in the chapel at Holyrood according to the Protestant rites, an event which Mary regretted even sooner than her marriage to Darnley. During the next four weeks, which were all that was to remain of their married life, his treatment of her was worse than Darnley's. Bothwell used filthy and abusive language, made it plain he preferred the company of his divorced wife (to whom he remarked that he regarded the queen as his concubine), prevented anyone of influence talking to her unless he also was present. Mary was unutterably miserable, threatened suicide on more than one occasion, never passed a day without tears.

By now the same nobles who had joined with Bothwell in the plot to murder Darnley, angry at the manner in which he had seized power and manipulated Mary, repenting too of their own misjudgement of him, had unanimously turned against him. Fearful of his own life as well as that of the queen, he took her for safety to the castle of Borthwick, 12 miles away on a tributary of the Esk. Realizing the difficulty of defending it, he slipped away one night, leaving Mary to face the rebels alone. When they arrived, they called up to her to abandon the man who had abandoned her and return with them to Edinburgh. Here was the first of two opportunities to jettison her cruel husband. But she refused even to consider it: she was his wife and probably carrying his child and, as street girls need the pimps who bully and exploit them, she, a very different kind of woman, still desperately needed Bothwell. And when she gave her dusty answer to the insurgents gathered below they responded with jeers and insults. Then, disguised as a man, she too escaped from the castle and after joining Bothwell at another castle nearby, rode with him to the comparative safety of Dunbar.

The second chance to free herself came a few days later when a small royal army under Bothwell confronted a much larger rebel army at Carberry Hill. They stood facing each other for some time until the rebels sent the French ambassador du Croc to tell the queen that if she abandoned Bothwell, she could continue as queen and they would be her loyal subjects. At this Mary upbraided them. Was it not these same nobles who only recently had signed a bond approving her marriage to Bothwell, the man they now chose to revile? Yet he had been the only one to stick with her throughout and she utterly refuted any idea of not sticking with him. Poor Mary! She knew the vileness of Bothwell's character by now, but where else could she turn? With Riccio dead and her Secretary of State Maitland absconded, there was not a soul in the kingdom in whom she could confide.

To avoid bloodshed Mary arranged a safe conduct for her husband who galloped away to the safety of Dunbar: she never saw him again. *
Trusting in the clemency of the rebel lords, she rode over to their camp but could hardly have been prepared for the reception awaiting her. 'Burn the whore!' their soldiers cried, 'she is not fit to live.' Weeping piteously and wearing only a mud-stained red petticoat she had managed to pick up at Dunbar (her own clothing she had left at Borthwick) she was escorted on her horse into Edinburgh to cries of 'Kill her, drown her'. She was not taken to Holyrood or the castle but to a private house where, utterly disconsolate and exhausted and with guards at her foot, she lay fully dressed on a bare bed all night. In the morning she looked out of the window, spied her once faithful Maitland and called out to him, but he pretended not to hear. Then, unwashed, dishevelled, with hair uncombed, breasts hanging loosely out of the dirty, ill-fitting petticoat and in a state of near hysteria, she cried out to the people in the street that she

*Having tried and failed to rally support to rescue Mary, Bothwell, outlawed by the rebel lords, fled first to his uncle the Bishop of Moray at Spynie (which, the reader will recall, Sandy Dunbar passed in the course of his naked run), then to Orkney and finally to Scandinavia. Here he was arrested for an offence against his former Norwegian mistress many years before and confined in a series of squalid dungeons where he eventually died insane.

had been betrayed and was being kept a prisoner against her will. To many in the streets, especially the women, it was a shocking sight, to others an opportunity for more insults from those who, with some truth, believed that she, with the help of Bothwell, had conspired to murder Darnley.

Always resilient, Mary would in time recover from that ultimate degradation, but from now on there was to be little let-up in the long march towards her decline and fall; for her fate was in the hands of others. Fearful that their own participation in Darnley's murder be discovered and so as not to lose their grip on power, the rebel lords deemed it prudent to have the queen removed to some remote and well-guarded spot which would enable them to continue to blacken her name and keep their own misdeeds secret; and the place they chose was Lochleven Castle.

Thirty miles north of Edinburgh, Lochleven is a stretch of water some 3-4 miles across. Between the wars it was famous for its excellent trout fishing (each day's bags were recorded in the pages of the next day's *Scotsman*) though in recent years this has rather tailed off because of pollution. In the centre of the loch are four islands and on one, a quarter of a mile from the shore, stood (and the ruins of which still stand) Lochleven Castle. The island then was smaller than today, the water level having fallen, and extended little beyond the castle's walls and garden. It belonged to the Douglas family whose head, Sir William Douglas, was a half-brother of the bastard Moray, and therefore a reliable jailer. Also living in the castle were his mother and younger brother George Douglas, known as 'pretty Geordie' and described as a very handsome young man.

It was to this gaunt and isolated dwelling that Mary, at very short notice and without being told her destination, was removed after her return to Holyrood, and in such haste that she was given no time to pack clothes and forbidden to take any ladies in waiting with her. (The warrant for this outrage was signed by nine of the lords who had signed the bond approving her marriage to Bothwell.) On arrival she was shown to a bleak room, empty of furniture except a single bed on to which she collapsed. For two weeks, sick, pregnant, shocked and dispirited, she remained in a semi-coma so that at times her jailers thought she might die.

Informed by the rebel lords that if she agreed to divorcing Bothwell, she would be restored as queen, she refused even to consider it. For one thing she doubted whether they would keep their word, for another a divorce would make the child she was carrying by Bothwell a bastard. In fact there were twins in her womb and in July 1567 she miscarried them; and it was while she was recovering from this distressing experience which had resulted in much loss of blood, that one of the most disagreeable of the rebel lords, Patrick Lindsay, informed her that he had been instructed to demand her abdication in favour of her son.

Insulted by such effrontery, at first Mary gave short shrift to it, but when Lindsay compounded it by telling her brutally that if she did not do so, her throat might have to be cut, she had no choice but to accede, hopeful that a document signed under duress would be held to be legally invalid. Ill again with what would seem to have been jaundice, and dreadfully depressed by her confinement, Mary signed an instrument of abdication. And so history repeated itself: just as she had been crowned queen as a baby with her mother as regent to reign in her stead, so now her baby son was to be crowned king with her half-brother Moray as regent. On the day of the prince's coronation in a Protestant church in Stirling, Sir William Douglas ordered bonfires to be lit in the garden and the castle's guns to be fired. Mary, enquiring the reason and being told, retired to her quarters and wept.

Lindsay's successful overtures were followed by those of Moray. Apprised of his coming, she hoped for better news in the light of the many favours she had done him in the past which included a pardon for his earlier rebellion. But Moray, now in power, was not in conciliatory mood; and with similar veiled threats against her person, demanded Mary's confirmation of his appointment as regent. Almost more than deprivation of her crown, Mary minded what Moray did on return to Edinburgh. Already the rebel lords had plundered from Holyrood the queen's silver plate to be melted down into coin, as well as seizing her furniture and voluminous wardrobe. Now Moray took possession of her jewellery, which in her will she had left as a legacy to the crown of Scotland; some of it had been the gift of her first husband Francis and his father the King of France. Moray gave part of it to his wife and later and for his personal gain *sold* more of it, including beautiful black pearls as big as grapes, to the fashion-conscious Queen Elizabeth.

At this juncture the rebels, having achieved their object, might have brought Mary's imprisonment to an end; but they feared a popular movement might start up to restore her and thus curtail their power. The possibility of this was very real when it became generally known how deeply those who had imprisoned her had been involved in Darnley's death. Yet, although Mary continued to fret at her confinement, there was paradoxically a liberating element to it too. No longer a queen and freed of the responsibilities and demands that went with it, she regained much of her old spirit. Her health improved, she was permitted a basketful of fresh clothing and accessories such as soap, powder and perukes for her hair. With the approach of summer she enjoyed the air in the garden and boating on the loch, and took up her old loves of dancing and playing at cards.

Yet all through the months of her incarceration both as queen and ex-queen, she never passed a day without thought of escape. It seemed an impossible dream, for she had no allies on the island except the two maids who had been allowed to join her. In the past two of her greatest attributes, courage and charm, had stood her in good stead, and now they did so again. Among the many occupants of the castle were some who had come to love her: they included Sir William's daughter and niece aged fourteen and fifteen and a young, orphaned Douglas cousin by the name of Willy who, in return for her kindness to him, had smuggled letters in and out. But her greatest admirer was Sir William's younger brother, pretty Geordie. In confined spaces relationships are quick to blossom; and on this tiny island keep George Douglas, seeing and talking every day for months on end to a lively and attractive girl who also happened to be Queen of Scotland, was so utterly captivated he wanted to marry her. Although his feelings were not reciprocated, Mary was quick to see in George the means of escape. He readily agreed to help, and fate also played into their hands when he quarrelled with his brother and was ordered off the island. This enabled him to warn the lords loyal to Mary such as Seton what was proposed and to prepare for it.

Having spread it round the family that he intended visiting France, George was granted permission by his brother to return to the island to take farewell of them. Before returning to the mainland he was given a sign by young Willy Douglas, who was also in the plot, that all was ready: he then re-embarked. Mary meanwhile had dressed herself and one of her maids in a countrywoman's kirtle and hood, and together they crossed the courtyard to the main gate. Willy Douglas who had purloined the keys of the gate, opened it to let all three through, then disposed of the keys in the mouth of a nearby cannon. Unobserved, the little party embarked in the waiting boat and some ten minutes later had reached the mainland. There George was waiting with a pair of horses stolen from his brother's stables. Mary and Willy mounted and set off to the south. After ten and a half months of imprisonment Mary's captive body and spirit were free at last. How she must have revelled in being on a horse once more with the wind blowing in her hair; and after the humiliations of Carberry Hill and Borthwick, the cheers of country people who recognized her as she rode by must have been music to her ears.

She and Willy crossed the Forth at Queensferry and by midnight had reached Lord Seton's castle at Niddrie. At long last she was her own woman again. But how long would she remain so?

News of her return bushfired across Scotland so that less than a week after her escape she had reached Hamilton where nine bishops, nine earls, eighteen lairds and a hundred other supporters had declared for her, and an army of several thousand had flocked to her standard. Exhilarated by such backing, she revoked her unlawfully obtained abdication as queen, then set out for the royal stronghold of Dumbarton on the Clyde to await further developments and, if the rising failed to consolidate, take ship to succour help from France.

Unfortunately the Regent Moray stood in the way. He had a smaller army but better generalship and from the top of a hill overlooking the village of Langside she watched his forces overwhelm hers. With Dumbarton cut off, she decided to flee south to Catholic Galloway, there to regroup and replan. After three days and nights of hard riding, she reached the Maxwell seat of Terregles. Of her time at Lochleven and since, she wrote to a relation in France: 'I have endured injuries, calumnies, imprisonment; famine, cold, heat, flight (not knowing whither), 92 miles across country without stopping or alighting, and then have had to sleep upon the ground and drink sour milk and eat oatmeal without bread and have been three nights like the owls.' What to do now? Her advisers suggested either staying put in the hope of rallying further support or to find a boat in which to slip down the Irish sea to Brittany, but at all costs not to test the temper of England's queen by seeking sanctuary there.

But Mary overrode them: 'I commanded my best friends to

permit me to have my own way'. It was a brave and romantic decision but in the end a fatal one. Why she took it can be only speculation, but throughout her adult life, from that day in Paris so long ago (yet only ten years) when her father-in-law had foolishly ordered the royal arms of England on Mary's equipage to be added to those of Scotland and France, her relationship with Elizabeth had been fraught. As ruler of a country larger, richer and more powerful than hers, nine years older and dominant by nature, Elizabeth had always been a potent force in Mary's imagination; not unlike that of the headgirl of the third who worships, yet is in awe of, the headgirl of the sixth. If only they could meet face to face, she believed, then all the problems concerning the English throne and succession could surely be sorted out; after all, as queens and cousins they had much in common. Mary had asked for a meeting often enough, but Elizabeth had always backed off; perhaps under the spell of Mary's charm, she was afraid that she might concede something she would later regret. Was it in a belief that if she entered England now, the longed-for meeting and hope of friendship would at last take place, Elizabeth would recognize her claim to succeed her as queen and help restore her to the throne of Scotland? It was a risk of course, but one that in the future two other Scots, Montrose and Prince Charles, would be equally ready to take.

Having had her beautiful red-gold hair cut off to avoid recognition and put on a borrowed cloak and hood, Mary made her way westward to the handsome Cistercian Abbey of Dundrennan on the Solway coast (now another ruin) where she spent her last night in Scotland. Next day, on the 16 May 1568, she embarked in a little fishing boat with a score of attendants and followers and crossed over to England. Apprised of her arrival, the Deputy Governor of Carlisle sent a bodyguard of 400 men to escort her to the castle. She told him and everyone else she met that her purpose in coming to England was to solicit the help of their queen in quelling her rebellious subjects; and so confident was she that her wish would be fulfilled that on 20 May she was writing to my kinsman, Cassilis in Ayrshire, that she expected to be back in Scotland at the head of an army, 'French if not English', in about three months.

Her period of liberty, from the opening of the gates of Lochleven to the closing of those at Carlisle, had been just sixteen days.

Of all the lives of European monarchs, past and present, Mary's was one of the most singular, certainly the most diverse; twelve years of almost unalloyed happiness in France; seven years – by which she is mainly remembered – of turbulence and drama in Scotland; and nineteen years of frustration and misery in England; a journey from sunshine through storm to blackest night.

For nineteen years one sovereign queen, Elizabeth, kept another sovereign queen, Mary, incarcerated in a succession of castles in the English midlands, guarded by a succession of gentleman jailers, some castles and jailers better and some worse than others. For this Elizabeth had no legal justification; Mary's only offence, if it was one, being that of entering Elizabeth's kingdom without permission. As she frequently wrote to Elizabeth, her one object, indeed for the moment her only object, was to enlist Elizabeth's support in restoring her throne by force against her rebellious nobles. Reports of Mary's complicity in the murder of her husband had been a talking point at the English court, and until that matter had been investigated and resolved, Mary was informed, Elizabeth was not prepared to assist.

So Commissioners were appointed, English and Scottish, to meet first at York and later at Westminster to examine the evidence, which they did in the most perfunctory way. Part of it consisted of the infamous 'Casket' letters found under the bed (in a silver casket) of one of the minor conspirators in the Darnley murder and which purported to show that Mary had been privy to it: these had been supplied by the Regent Moray who, being now in power and determined to hang on to it, was set on blackening his half-sister's name irredeemably; for the last thing he wanted was an English invasion to restore her to Holyrood. In this he had the dishonourable support of Elizabeth who urged him 'to utter all he could to the queen's dishonour'. The bulk of the letters, however, were clearly forgeries, and in the event the Commissioners came to no conclusions: Mary had not proved the Scottish nobles had rebelled against her, and Moray and the nobles had not proved that Mary had had a hand in Darnley's murder.

Moray went home with a present from Elizabeth of £5,000 but Mary, with a verdict of Not Proven, was kept in prison. This was illegal, yet what was Elizabeth to do with her? She had ruled out any idea of forcibly restoring her, for that might mean war with Scotland; nor could she run the risk of allowing her to take up residence as a free woman; for so long as she was alive, whether in England, Scotland or France, she would always be a magnet for Catholics who wished to see her replace Elizabeth on the throne. What had begun with Mary's public assumption of that throne on the death of Mary Tudor had been a live issue ever since which, Elizabeth believed and with reason, Mary would never abandon. Persistently, unflaggingly and at times desperately Mary begged Elizabeth to grant her a meeting, and as persistently Elizabeth refused. One would have thought in such an intelligent woman curiosity alone – to see what her longtime rival looked and sounded like – would have led her to accept; but in the end she concluded it safer not. To accommodate Mary by granting a meeting could be seen as weakness; so long as she kept her distance, she could maintain a position of superiority over a supplicant. She may also have feared Mary's powers of persuasion, aware of what Sir Francis Knollys, Mary's first jailer, had said of her: 'A woman of innate intelligence, blessed with an eloquent tongue and full of practical good sense . . . also considerable personal courage'. He spoke glowingly of her charm, as did two of Elizabeth's envoys, Cecil and White, and a future jailer, Shrewsbury.

In the early years of her imprisonment and to whichever castle she was removed (except hated Tutbury with its cold and smell of middens) Mary did not fare too badly. She was allowed an ample personal staff (which included the last of her four 'Mary' ladies, Mary Seton, as well as her two faithful rescuers from Lochleven, George and Willy Douglas) and, especially under Shrewsbury, a degree of liberty. He permitted her to ride and go hawking, to exercise a greyhound, even to visit the baths at Buxton. Indoors she spent hours at embroidery which had always been a favourite pastime: some of the patterns she designed were remarkable and a few have survived to this day. She also carried on a large correspondence, especially to those whom she hoped might deliver her.

One possible escape route was marriage to England's only duke, the Catholic Norfolk, a dullish man to whom she became secretly engaged. 'You have promised to be mine and I yours,' she wrote him (in those formal times an unusual way of addressing a man she had never met). 'I believe the queen of England and the country should like of it'. But here Mary made another misjudgement, similar to her imagining that Elizabeth had approved of her marrying Darnley or that the nobles had approved of her marrying Bothwell. Once again Elizabeth was furious, seeing a threat to her throne and, for his pains, clapped Norfolk in the Tower.

At this time Mary's worries were mostly little ones, like the difficulty of obtaining clothes and the non-arrival of revenues from her French estates to pay her household staff. But there was one matter which greatly distressed her, the loss of all communication with her son James, now only a memory of long ago. When he was four, she sent him a pony and a saddle for it. 'Dear Son', she wrote, 'I send three bearers to see you and bring me word how ye do, and remember that ye have a loving mother who wishes you in time to know, fear and love God'. On another occasion she sent him some toy guns to play with, but Elizabeth forbade the delivery of all of these, so the little boy never even knew they had been sent. Throughout his childhood his mother was a stranger to him and became even more so when informed by his Protestant instructors that she had plotted with her lover Bothwell to murder his father so as to be free to marry him. Another blow for her was learning that the 'Association' of a joint Scottish kingship between her and James and which James seems to have accepted in 1584 he utterly rejected in 1585. The final straw came when she heard that James (now a young man of nineteen) and Elizabeth had concluded a treaty of alliance which excluded her altogether. A Stuart would succeed to the English throne but it would not be she who had coveted and claimed it from childhood; and she was understandably bitter.

Mary's life was dominated by two obsessions: sovereignty and Catholicism, and the two combined were to be her undoing. To those not of the faith the divisions in those days between Protestant and Catholic, often so rancorous as to lead to physical violence, seem incomprehensible. Yet the divisions of Christian denominations then had less to do with personal beliefs than what made societies cohere. Mary had been brought up in a society where Catholicism had been the cohesive force, and so for her it became a lifelong article of faith (in the same way as today democracy is our cohesive force and article of faith).

There were Catholics living in England who had known the old days under Mary Tudor and believed the same. Among them were the earls of Northumberland and Westmorland who, from their northern shires, planned to ride with their retainers to Tutbury and secure Mary's release. When this was known, Mary was hastily moved to Coventry, and Elizabeth decreed that if there were any possibility of her escape, she was to suffer immediate execution.

The Northern Rising, as it was called, soon fizzled out, but it was only the first of many attempts, all Catholic inspired, to give Mary her freedom and replace Elizabeth on the throne. Next came the Ridolfi plot, engineered by an Italian Catholic banker of that name whose plan was that the king of Spain's general in the Netherlands, the Duke of Alva, should invade England coincidentally with a Catholic rising there, capture Elizabeth and place Mary, with Norfolk as her consort, on the throne. There is little doubt that both Norfolk and Mary were privy to these plans, and when they were discovered, Norfolk, who had only recently been released from the Tower, was sent back there and executed (leaving England dukeless); the Commons voted for Mary's execution too, but at this stage Elizabeth declined to comply. Nor was Mary's growing unpopularity lessened by the news from France of the Bartholomew's Day massacre of the Protestant Huguenots by the de Guises in August of 1572. Indeed Elizabeth was so incensed by it that she suggested to Scotland's new Regent Morton (Moray, to Mary's delight, had been assassinated) that the Scots might consider disposing of Mary themselves. To this Morton replied that it would require Elizabeth's written approval which, not surprisingly, she declined to give. However, for the next five months Mary was guarded with special care and kept in close confinement in her rooms.

The Throckmorton plot was similar to the Ridolfi plot in that it was also Catholic inspired and envisaged a Spanish invasion to liberate Mary and put her on the throne. Once again it was apparent that Mary was privy to it, indeed had written encouraging letters to the Spanish ambassador, but in the event no proceedings were taken. However, Elizabeth's Secretary of State, Francis Walsingham, had by now convinced himself, and with reason, that Mary's continued existence posed a grave threat to Elizabeth's security, and one which would remain so long as Mary was alive. Indeed it had intensified ever since the Pope had excommunicated Elizabeth in 1570, resulting in an ever increasing flow of Jesuit missionaries into England from the Continent, hoping to re-convert the country to the true faith; and it was no secret that the Pope favoured Mary over Elizabeth as the rightful occupant of the throne.

In the light of the threat of this increased Catholic self-assertion, stern measures were taken. In 1581 the Commons passed a bill making it high treason to be reconciled to the Catholic faith, and four years later for a Jesuit to travel in England. They also, by the

Act of Association, voted for the death penalty not only against those found plotting against the Queen in favour of a usurper, but against the usurper too, even if he or she was not privy to what was being plotted, indeed was in complete ignorance of it: this was the net designed to trap Mary and it succeeded.

The final act in Mary's tragic life began in the autumn of 1584 when orders came for her to be taken from Chatsworth, where she had been under the care of the amiable Shrewsbury, back to the dreaded Tutbury where she arrived in the bitter January weather of 1585. Worse, on Walsingham's instructions, she now came under the guardianship of Sir Amyas Paulet, a new and very different sort of jailer to Shrewsbury; a Puritan bigot to whom Mary's charms meant nothing, he was determined to make her imprisonment as disagreeable as Shrewsbury had tried to make it pleasant. His first action was to remove from above her chair the royal cloth of state which expressed her queenly status. Next he put an end to Mary's outdoor activities such as riding and taking the baths at Buxton — to Mary, severe deprivations for she had always been an outdoor woman — stopped all private correspondence and ended her practice of giving alms to the local poor, for fear she might win their affections. And when she received a little package from London of rosaries and other Catholic artefacts, he ordered it to be burnt. To Elizabeth Mary protested vigorously, saying that Paulet was more fit to be the jailer of a common criminal than of an anointed queen. Elizabeth remained unmoved.

These restrictions had a deleterious effect on Mary's health. Of all the afflictions she had had to bear during more than fifteen years of imprisonment so far, her health had been the worst. In the past she had suffered from severe pains in her side, her right arm and legs, so that at times she was quite lame. In addition she suffered from bouts of gastric influenza and frequent attacks of vomiting. Recent researches have indicated that she may also have been a victim of the hereditary disease of porphyria which in time would be attributed to her descendant George III; there was evidence of psychosomatic symptoms too. Deprived of the fresh air and exercise on which she had depended all her life, and subject to the whistling winds and foul smells of Tutbury, her health once again suffered. Her face had become drawn and heavy and her once slim figure inclined towards the matronly; political pressures apart, she was already, at forty-two, a woman in physical decline.

# HOW I TOOK THE STONE
*A real life thriller more fantastic than fiction*

## Three men and a girl with flu

'FIRST ATTEMPT FAILS: I AM
CAUGHT RED-HANDED IN
THE LOCKED ABBEY'

Ian Hamilton (now Q.C.) 'I had dreams of a new Scotland, alive, full of ideas...'

The Coronation Chair, the Stone of Destiny nestling at the base of it.

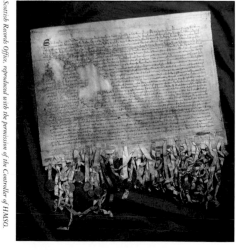

The Declaration of Arbroath, 1320. 'May it please you to admonish and exhort the king of the English, who ought to be satisfied with what belongs to him, to leave us Scots in peace...'

Captain James Brander-Dunbar, aka John Macnab. 'A jovial scoundrel, bloodthirsty as a stoat and cruel, but good company and a man.'

Hugh Cawdor, 5th Earl and 26th Thane. 'A black-haired, funny, buccaneering sort of Thane, half poet, half pirate.'

*Bridgeman Art Library/Scottish National Portrait Gallery.*

*Scottish National Portrait Gallery.*

The Queen of Scotland. 'Twelve years of almost unalloyed happiness in France; seven years of turbulence and drama in Scotland; nineteen years of misery in England; a journey from sunshine through storm to blackest night.'

Henry Stuart, Lord Darnley, Mary's second husband. 'I know not, but it is greatly to be feared that he can have no long life among these people.'

*Scottish National Portrait Gallery.*

BELOW: Loch Leven Castle, Mary's island prison for ten months. 'For two weeks, sick, pregnant, shocked and dispirited, she remained in a semi-coma so that her jailers thought she might die.'

The Earl of Bothwell, Mary's third husband. 'A very rough customer with cruel suspicious eyes...a bully who once kicked his servant in the stomach.'

*Still Moving Picture Company.*

David Hume, by Allan Ramsay, 1766. 'It is an absurdity to believe that the Deity has human passions and one of the lowest of human passions, a restless appetite for applause.'

The meeting in Edinburgh between Burns and Scott, aged fifteen, seated far right. 'The eye alone', wrote Scott, 'indicated the poetical character and temperament. It glowed (I say literally *glowed*) when he spoke with feeling or interest.'

Robert Louis Stevenson by John Singer Sargent. 'We are a race of gypsies and love change and travel for themselves. I travel not to go anywhere but to go. The great affair is to move.'

BELOW LEFT: Burns' Mausoleum in St Michael's churchyard, Dumfries. 'Light and airy, big enough to impress but not overpowering.'

BELOW RIGHT: Sir Walter Scott and dog seated in the Scott monument. 'That rare creature, a Scot who loved England almost as much as Scotland.'

Professor John Wilson (Christopher North), of whom Dickens said, 'A bright, mountain-looking fellow...as though he had just come down from the Highlands and never in his life taken pen in hand.'

BELOW: Register House Edinburgh by Robert Adam as it was until 1852 when a statue of the Duke of Wellington (above) went up which effectively blocked this view of it.

Henry Moore's statue of King and Queen at Glenkiln, Dumfriesshire. 'Majesty, authority, and in that desolate landscape, the loneliness and isolation of office.'

Parliament Hall, with Roubiliac's statue of Lord President Forbes, where advocates meet clients and each other. 'Intelligent men', said Stevenson, 'have been walking here daily for twenty years without a rag of business or shilling of reward.'

Mrs Thatcher addressing the General Assembly of the Church of Scotland, 21 May 1988, the Moderator presiding. 'She can use the most hackneyed language as if she had minted it that morning, and wears it like a badge of virtue.'

*Nick Garland/Daily Telegraph/Cartoon Collection, University of Kent/Ewan MacNaughton Associates.*

"... OUR BELIEF IN THE PRINCIPLE OF DEVOLUTION AND THE NEED FOR A DIRECTLY ELECTED ASSEMBLY REMAINS UNALTERED." ( MRS THATCHER)

*Nick Garland/Daily Telegraph/Cartoon Collection, University of Kent/Ewan MacNaughton Associates.*

*Peter Brookes/The Times/News International.*

English political leaders wake up to an awareness of the Scottish dimension.

Usually, when Mary complained of poor health her jailers dismissed it as a pretence to secure greater liberty, but on this occasion Elizabeth relented enough to allow her to be moved to the moated Chartley Hall, the nearby seat of the Earl of Essex. The journey was made on Christmas Eve, and even then was thought by some of Mary's staff to be too late, for she at once took to her bed and stayed there a month during which it was feared she might die.

It was while Mary was at Chartley that the last and fatal plot to rescue her and topple Elizabeth was formed. The chief of the plotters was a young, well-to-do, Catholic squire named Sir Anthony Babington, said by a contemporary to be good-looking with a quick intelligence, well read and well travelled and with enchanting manners and wit. He was born at about the time that Mary came to Scotland and so knew nothing and cared less of the claims against her for the murder of Darnley; indeed he might be said to be representative of all those English Catholics who regarded Mary as the rightful claimant of the English throne and her continued imprisonment by Elizabeth an outrage.

Once again the plot was to be similar in aim to those of Ridolfi and Throckmorton, the invasion of England by a Spanish force to coincide with a Catholic uprising; the assassination of Elizabeth to be carried out by six noble friends, while Babington himself with a hundred followers would storm Chartley to free Mary. Her correspondence having been stopped by Paulet, Mary had succeeded in setting up a secret method of smuggling letters in and out by bribing the brewer who brought the hall's beer supply. Unfortunately she had no idea that Walsingham had discovered this and that every message that Babington sent to her and she to him fell into Paulet's hands. So that when Babington wrote that the killing of the English queen was necessary for the plot to succeed and Mary in reply showed acquiescence, they were both signing their death warrants. In his determination that Mary should die, Walsingham went further: he forged a postscript to a letter from Mary to Babington asking the names of the six noble friends who had agreed to murder Elizabeth. When the news was brought to the Queen she was both frightened and angry. Writing to Paulet to thank him for his part in uncovering the plot, she referred to Mary as 'your wicked murderess' who would reap 'her vile deserts'.

Mary meanwhile, in blissful ignorance of the discovery, believed that deliverance was at hand, and when Paulet surprisingly offered her the opportunity of joining in a local deer hunt, and she saw a group of horsemen riding towards them, she believed for one delirious moment that they had come to free her. Disillusion came swiftly when the leader of the group announced that he had come to arrest her for plotting against the Queen and the state. Utterly taken aback, she was escorted to the nearby house of Tixall, still dressed in the pretty costume she had put on to impress the local gentry she had expected to meet at the hunt.

Mary remained at Tixall for two weeks, never leaving her chamber, during which her apartments at Chartley were ransacked for proof of further complicity, and many of her belongings and her small hoard of money taken. Babington and his fellow conspirators meanwhile had suffered a dreadful vengeance: their private parts were cut off, they were obliged to witness their own disembowelment, they were finally quartered. Knowing that her own fate could not long be delayed, Mary, on return to Chartley and her weeping servants, lived in fear of being secretly assassinated herself, either by a killer's knife or by poison. Had that happened, it would have defeated the martyrdom she sought. Happily for her it did not; and on 21 September she was taken from Chartley to her last place of imprisonment, the grim castle of Fotheringay in Northamptonshire.

Soon after her arrival Paulet informed her that she was to be put on trial for treason and advised her to confess her transgressions before the judges proved them. Mary greeted his request with the serenity which was to characterize her whole conduct from now until her death. 'As a sinner,' she replied, 'I am truly conscious of having often offended my Creator, and I beg him to forgive me, but as Queen and Sovereign I am aware of no fault or offence for which I have to render account to anyone here below. As therefore I could not offend, I do not wish for pardon. I do not seek, nor would I accept it from anyone living.' It was not the answer that Paulet expected.

The trial took place in a room above the great hall of the castle and was heard by a Commission of twenty-four peers and members of the Council. It was as much of a farce as the Inquiry held after Mary's arrival, being no more than an exercise to allow the Commissioners to announce the verdict they had already decided on. No witnesses were allowed to be called for prosecution or defence. Mary was not permitted a lawyer or even a clerk to advise her – her own two secretaries who had written the incriminating letters to Babington having been imprisoned in London. In any case, as Mary was not an English subject, how could she legally be tried for treason? How could she be tried by her peers when her only peer in England was England's queen? As she told a delegation of lords who saw her before the trial, 'I am myself a Queen, the daughter of a King . . . As an absolute Queen I cannot submit to orders nor can I submit to the laws of the land . . . For myself I do not recognize the laws of England nor do I know or understand them as I have often asserted. I am alone, without counsel or anyone to speak on my behalf. My papers and notes have been taken from me, so that I am destitute of all aid . . .' She ended with a dramatic flourish, 'Look to your consciences and remember that the theatre of the world is wider than the realm of England.'

But to Mary's objections as to the trial's legality the Commissioners remained blind. She had written to Babington, had she not, expressing agreement with his plan to murder their queen? She could deny it (and did) as often as she pleased, but there it was in black and white. Why had she assumed the English royal arms on the death of Mary Tudor? That was not her doing, she answered, but that of her father-in-law. She had not wanted nor attempted to claim the English throne while Elizabeth lived, but she did expect Elizabeth to recognize her right to it after her death. Despite all the disadvantages under which she laboured throughout the two days of trial, she put up the most spirited defence which even her accusers could not help but admire. Her last plea was to be allowed to present her case, in person, to Parliament. As Antonia Fraser says in her scholarly and compelling book, 'Throughout the trial she had shown herself unwaveringly regal, and not all the petty spite of Paulet could take this triumph from her'.* On her way out of the trial chamber she turned to her accusers and asked God to pardon them for treating her so rudely, adding majestically, 'May God keep me from having to do with you all again'.

At the end of October the Commissioners met again in the Star Chamber in London and declared Mary to be guilty of planning the death and destruction of their queen. Then the two Houses of Parliament presented an address to the Queen demanding Mary's execution for her own safety. But Elizabeth, when she had read the address, hesitated to confirm it. Could she really bring herself

*Mary Queen of Scots by Antonia Fraser.

to order the death of her own cousin, a woman she had kept imprisoned for nearly twenty years without just cause and whom she had consistently refused to meet? What would be the reaction in Scotland? In France? Was there not some better way, she asked the Lords and Commons, of ensuring her own safety so that Mary's life might be spared?

It seemed there was not; and yet when Paulet tried to extract from Mary the confession that Elizabeth so desperately wanted (so that she could then show magnanimity by granting her pardon?) she utterly rejected it; and when Lord Buckhurst told her that as she would have to die, she needed to repent, and who better to hear this than the (Protestant) bishop of Peterborough, Mary gave him the same unwelcome answer she had given Paulet. She was going to die, she said, in defence of her Catholic faith; and Paulet, Buckhurst and others were astonished by the extraordinary calm, even joy, of her demeanour. Dr Johnson was to say that when a man knows he is to be hanged in a fortnight, it concentrates his mind wonderfully, and it is a fact that when most human beings know with certainty they are going to have to die, a mechanism in the brain enables them to accept it: that is why, when hanging was in force in Britain, the great majority of those condemned went to their deaths unprotesting. Mary experienced this; she was also buoyed up by knowing she was dying a martyr. This impresses us less today than the composure with which she contemplated her end: truly for her death had no dominion.

The weeks went by; Christmas came and went: 1586 gave way to 1587, and still Elizabeth hesitated. Indeed it wasn't until the end of January that at last she put her signature to the warrant for Mary's execution. Even then she wondered if there was not some way in which she might avoid the obloquy that was bound to fall on her afterwards. Could not some 'loyal subject' do the deed instead? How about Sir Amyas Paulet, who was, so to speak, on the spot? But although Paulet had been a constant thorn in Mary's flesh, he was also a man of honour. When the idea was put to him, as coming from the Queen, he was forthright in his reply: 'God forbid', he wrote to her, 'that I should make so foul a shipwreck of my conscience . . . to shed blood without law or warrant.' Elizabeth called this 'daintiness', but he had shown far greater moral courage than she.

Elizabeth's conduct towards Mary during her lifetime, her refusal to meet her, her long imprisonment of her, had at least been debatable; but seeking an assassin to do her dirty work for her was contemptible; characteristic of the weak and feeble woman she admitted she was, and not one, as she wanted to be thought, with the heart and stomach of a king. Nor was Mary's death any longer necessary for Elizabeth's safety; for she was now a spent force, forty-four, ill, semi-crippled, bankrupt, heartily sick of all the intriguing and plotting and wanting only some days of peace in whatever time was left. Only recently, before the Babington plot, she had written to Elizabeth that all she desired was 'to retire out of this island to some solitary and reposeful place', as much for her soul as her body; and she had reiterated this at her trial: 'My advancing age and bodily weakness both prevent me from wishing to resume the reins of government. I have perhaps only two or three years to live in this world and I do not aspire to any public position . . .' Elizabeth did not have to have Mary killed, either by an assassin or the public executioner. Instead, and with no further threat to her, she could have had Mary deported to France, always her spiritual home, to spend her last days on one of the estates in Touraine or Poitou that Francis had left to her.

This option Elizabeth does not seem to have considered. Instead, having at last brought herself to sign the death warrant, she told her advisers that she did not wish to know anything further about the matter until the deed had been done. Not until the evening of 7 February did her former jailer Shrewsbury and another earl, Kent, together with Beale, the clerk of the Council, arrive at Fotheringay to tell Mary the news. They were informed that she had retired to bed. Told the matter was urgent, she begged leave for time to dress and then received them in a chair at the foot of her bed. Shrewsbury told her she had been condemned to death and Beale read out the warrant. When he had finished, Mary said, 'I thank you for such welcome news. You will do me great good in withdrawing me from this world from which I am very glad to go.' She was offered the services of the dean of Peterborough to prepare her for death, which she refused. She asked for her own chaplain to be with her, but even this humanity was denied her. Kent tried to explain. 'Your life would be the death of our religion, your death will be its life.' Hearing this, Mary's face shone with joy. Now she knew she would not be dying in vain.

Told that she was to die at eight the next morning, Mary spent her last night on earth in the company of her weeping servants (the rest of her staff had been taken from her), setting her affairs in order, allocating gifts to those close to her. Then she wrote her farewell letters, of which the last, written in French and now in the National Library of Scotland, was to her brother-in-law, King Henry of France. It is a strange feeling to handle and look at it today and to imagine Mary, more than 400 years ago, writing it in her room at Fotheringay by candlelight. It is a letter in which courage, dignity, pride and humanity shine uppermost. Here is its English translation:

Royal brother, having by God's will, for my sins I think, thrown myself into the power of the Queen my cousin, at whose hands I have suffered much for almost twenty years, I have finally been condemned to death by her and her Estates. I have asked for my papers, which they have taken away, in order that I might make my will, but I have been unable to recover anything of use to me, or even get leave either to make my will freely or to have my body conveyed after my death, as I would wish, to your kingdom where I had the honour to be queen, your sister and former ally.

Today, after dining, I was advised of my sentence: I am to be executed like a criminal at eight in the morning. I have not had time to give you a full account of everything that has happened, but if you will listen to my doctor and my other unfortunate servants, you will learn the truth, and how, thanks be to God, I scorn death and vow that I meet it innocent of any crime, even if I were their subject. The Catholic faith and the assertion of my God-given right to the English crown are the two issues on which I am condemned, and yet I am not allowed to say that it is for the Catholic religion that I die, but for fear of interference with theirs. The proof of this is that they have taken away my chaplain, and, although he is in the castle, I have not been able to get permission for him to come and hear my confession and give me the Last Sacrament, while they have been most insistent that I receive the consolation and instruction of their minister, brought here for that purpose.

The bearer of this letter and his companions, most of them your subjects, will testify to my conduct at my last hour. It remains for me to beg Your Most Christian Majesty, my brother-in-law and former ally, who have always protested your love for me, to give proof now of your goodness on all these points: firstly by

258

charity, in paying my unfortunate servants the wages due them – this is a burden on my conscience that only you can relieve: further, by having prayers offered to God for a queen who has borne the title Most Christian, and who dies a Catholic, stripped of all her possessions. As for my son, I commend him to you in so far as he deserves, for I cannot answer for him. I have taken the liberty of sending you two precious stones, talismans against illness, trusting that you will enjoy good health and a long and happy life. Accept them from your loving sister-in-law, who, as she dies, bears witness of her warm feeling for you. Again I commend my servants to you. Give instructions, if it please you, that for my soul's sake part of what you owe me should be paid, and that for the sake of Jesus Christ, to whom I shall pray for you tomorrow as I die, I be left enough to found a memorial mass and give the customary alms.

Wednesday, at two in the morning.

Your most loving and most true sister,

Mary R.

She passed what was left of the night on her bed but not sleeping. At six she rose and went to pray in a little alcove set aside for the purpose. Then she dressed in black except for a white veil which stretched to the ground and the white peaked head-dress which she had made her own. Carrying a crucifix and prayer-book and with two rosaries hanging from her waist, she entered the great hall where, it was said, some 300 people were waiting in awe for the dreadful spectacle to unfold. In the centre of the hall stood a 12-feet-square, raised dais, like a modern boxing ring, draped in black. Inside it were stools for Shrewsbury and Kent to witness the proceedings, the executioner's block, and beside it his huge axe. In silence and accompanied by six of her servants (Elizabeth, piling cruelty on cruelty, had decreed that Mary was to die alone, but in common humanity Shrewsbury and Kent had rescinded it) Mary moved towards the dais. She walked as a queen should, regally, calmly; mounted the dais to hear again the warrant, and with such an air of detachment, said one observer, that she might have been listening to a pardon instead of orders for her death. She said her prayers in English and Latin and gave forgiveness to all who had brought her to this pass. Then she sat on a little cushioned stool inside the ring to be disrobed by her ladies for death. When they had finished, the spectators noticed that her petticoat, bodice and sleeves were the colour of blood.

Jane Kennedy, her favourite woman of the bed chamber, took a small white cloth edged with gold, kissed it, wrapped it round Mary's eyes and withdrew. Mary knelt on the cushion in front of the block, laid her head on it. The executioner raised the axe. Mary cried, 'Into your hands, O Lord, I commend my spirit.' The axe fell, but clumsily, the blow, to the spectators' horror, striking the back of the head. It was hastily raised again and this time severed the neck from the shoulders. Such was the violent death of a woman who all her life had hated violence.

The executioner lifted the severed head by, as he thought, its auburn tresses to show the spectators his handiwork. But the tresses were a wig and as the head fell to the floor, Mary's hair was seen to be that of a grey-haired woman. Another strange thing happened. One of Mary's dogs, a little Skye terrier, had entered the hall unobserved. Whimpering, it stood between his mistress's severed head and body. Then Kent spoke up: 'Such be the end of all the Queen's and all the gospel's enemies.' But Shrewsbury beside him said nothing, for he had loved Mary and his face was wet with tears.

From this tragic story the only person to emerge with dishonour was the Queen of England. Informed of the execution and consumed with guilt, she put on a great show of grief, dressed herself in mourning and shed crocodile tears. Worse, she turned on the secretary of the Council, Davison, who, after she had signed the order for Mary's death, had activated it. Now she pretended that she had only signed it 'for safety's sake', had never intended it to be carried out, conveniently forgetting that she had discussed the execution of Mary in some detail, saying to Davison that it was not to be held in public but, as she had ordered, at Fotheringay. So the wretched Davison was made a scapegoat for Elizabeth's guilt, thrown into prison and fined £10,000. This was hardly the action of a woman with the heart and stomach of a king. She also sent an envoy to King James in Scotland with the same lie, that she had not authorized his mother's execution and was dumbfounded and grief-stricken when she heard of it; thus pre-empting the possibility of a Scottish rising. To placate James further, as well as her own sense of guilt, she authorized a magnificent funeral service in Peterborough Cathedral.

Even after her death Mary continued to influence the course of European history. In her will she declared that if James had not become a Catholic at the time of her death, the Scottish crown should pass to the man who had once been her brother-in-law, the Catholic King of Spain, Philip II. Every plot in recent years to depose Elizabeth and liberate Mary was posited on an invasion of England by Catholic forces to coincide with a Catholic uprising. All had come to nothing. But now Philip, to ensure that Mary's will was carried out, began to mount an invasion force. It sailed the following year and was called the Spanish Armada.

Sixteen years after his mother's death James VI of Scotland became James I of England, the first Stuart to inherit the English throne; and in 1618, he had the coffin of his mother brought from Peterborough Cathedral to its final resting place in Westminster Abbey. Over her coffin he had built a magnificent tomb of white marble, with Mary's effigy lying on top. Her eyes are closed, her fingers joined in prayer, she wears the peaked head-dress she wore at her execution, her body is enveloped in a cloak edged with ermine, the lion of Scotland rests at her feet. Composed and beautiful, she looks as she looked throughout her life, and especially at its end, every inch a queen.

Another of Mary's requests that Elizabeth frustrated was her desire to be buried in France, if possible at Reims in whose cathedral her husband Francis had been crowned. But given the choice of Reims and the Abbey, there can surely be little doubt as to which she would have chosen. All her life her great ambition had been to become what her son became, sovereign of England and Scotland, to be counted among the company of those who had preceded her, Normans and Plantagenets and Tudors and of others unknown who were yet to come. In life that ambition had been denied her. In death she achieved it.

# CHAPTER 15

## *The Great Infidel*

SCOTLAND CAN CLAIM MANY HEROES: WALLACE, BRUCE, QUEEN Mary, Montrose, Bonnie Prince Charlie; modern achievers too like Watt and Stephenson, Dunlop and Macadam, Baird and Fleming. My own favourite whom I came to look on as guide, philosopher and friend was none of these, a thinker not a doer; not a creative artist like Burns or Scott or Stevenson, but a meditator and Humanist, one of the world's greatest, whose name has appeared in these pages already; David Hume, of whom Einstein said 200 years later that his writings had contributed to his discovery of the theory of relativity. During his lifetime Hume occupied two residences in Edinburgh, the first an apartment in James's Court near the top end of the High Street and later in a street off St Andrew Square in the New Town.

Like many of my generation I was subjected at prep school and public school for ten years to a veritable barrage of Christian propaganda – in all, I reckoned, some 1,300 hours and would like to think that I regarded it all with a sceptical eye, but that would be to falsify the record. On all sides bishops, deans, chaplains and headmasters assured me that the story of Christ's birth, miracles, death and resurrection was all true, every word of it; and if my own critical faculties remained dormant, it was not because I disagreed with it, rather that I did not understand what the *cognescenti* were on about, what the whole package meant. So I accepted it in the way I accepted logarithms or Milton as something largely beyond my comprehension.

Most of my contemporaries at school who had undergone the same conditioning seemed unaffected by it. Like my parents they became so much Church fodder, who didn't know what they believed or disbelieved and would have been far too embarrassed even to discuss it, but thought that both God and their neighbours (and any staff they might have) would be glad to see them on their knees in church every so often: they believed their presence there helped to stabilize society. Being of a more critical nature, I wrestled with the problem of belief for many years. How could the supernatural claims of Christianity be justified, and why did so many eminent people support them? Was there something wrong with me that I couldn't?

It was during the war that I first came across two writers who were to change my thinking irrevocably. The first was the Englishman Tom Paine whose book *The Age of Reason*, published just before the beginning of the nineteenth century, demolished on grounds of common sense the allegedly supernatural aspects of Jesus's life. This led me on to the religious writings of my fellow countryman David Hume who preceded Paine by a number of years, but had approached the problem in rather greater depth.

David Hume spent his childhood, along with his elder brother John and sister Catherine, at the family home of Ninewells in the Scottish borders, overlooking the river Whiteadder and close to the village of Chirnside. At the local kirk the family occupied the dominant pew and had possession of the largest vault, and although they had little time for Covenanters and Evangelicals, they still underwent the rigorous Scottish Sunday schedule which, according to a contemporary Englishman was, in its strictness of devotion and resignation to the will of God, unequalled by any other nation on earth. 'They all pray in their families before they go to church and between sermons they fast. After the sermons everybody retires to his own room and reads some book of devotion till supper after which they sing psalms until they go to bed.' The effect of such practices on the mind of Hume in his formative years cannot have been all that different from the effects that similar though less rigorous practices had on me.

David's father Joseph died when he was still a baby, and in 1723 when he was twelve and his brother fourteen their mother took lodgings in Edinburgh's Lawnmarket and enrolled them at the university. Here David studied Greek, Logic, Metaphysics and Natural Philosophy but left without taking a degree. At the age of seventeen he was described as being almost six feet tall, speaking with a pronounced Scottish accent and being somewhat clumsy and ungainly in appearance. He also had a strange habit of staring fixedly at whoever he was listening or talking to, which many people found disconcerting.

For the next nine years he alternated between Edinburgh and Ninewells, studying all the great writers, Latin, French and English and making up his mind what career to pursue. Although interested in politics, he rejected it as being unsuited to his somewhat bashful manner, lack of ease in public speaking and physical awkwardness, 'of which', wrote one biographer, 'he was ever conscious'. He toyed with the idea of the law which his mother favoured, but in the end rejected that too. 'I had an unsurmountable aversion to everything,' he wrote at the end of his life, 'but the pursuit of philosophy and general learning, and seeking a structure on which to build a new system of truth'.

Truth was Hume's touchstone, as it is to every serious writer, and when he was sixteen he gave a delightful and singular example of it. The occasion was a dinner party given by Lady Dalrymple in her house in Edinburgh. When the company had gathered in an upstairs room, Hume farted, not noisily which would have identified him at once, but silently and, as is so often the way with silent ones, malodorously. Inevitably the other guests noticed it and assuming it to have issued from the family dog, name of Pod, chorused in dismay, 'Oh, the dog, the dog! Put out the dog! Tis that vile beast Pod. Kick him down the stairs!' But Hume, as brave and generous as he was truthful, cried out, 'Oh, do not hurt the beast! It was not Pod, it was me.' In relating this story to her grand-daughter, Lady Dalrymple remarked that few people would have had the moral courage to own up as the sixteen-year-old Hume had done when there was a convenient scapegoat handy.

Another example of Hume's attachment to truth was his decision, logical enough, to change the spelling of his name from Home (a well-known border family) to Hume to conform to its pronunciation. It was absurd, he thought, as well as inconvenient to others, to spell his name one way and expect people to pronounce it another.*

For a long time, and before submitting anything for publication, Hume worried about his ability to express his thoughts clearly, knowing what he wanted to say but unsure how to say it. 'I had no hopes of delivering my opinions with such elegance and neatness as to draw to me the attention of the world'. But he persevered, taking endless pains as his friend Boswell did, to remove all Scotticisms from his prose so that as his career progressed, readers came to admire its clarity and forcefulness. Boswell, the finest Scots writer of English of his day, said in 1762 that he considered Hume the greatest writer in Britain.

Like all philosophers, Hume's starting point was the nature and extent of human knowledge; and the more he applied his mind to it, the more he realized that we had a false notion of cause and effect. First: 'Nothing exists without a cause'. Then: 'All reasonings concerning cause and effect are founded on experience, and all reasonings from experience are founded on the supposition that the course of nature will continue uniformly the same. But the uniformity of nature can admit of no proof at all and which we take for granted without any proof. We are determined by custom alone to suppose the future comfortable with the past. 'Tis not reason which is the guide to life but custom'. In other words, although this spring and every previous spring we have seen flowers bud and trees blossom, that is not proof that they will do so next spring. Experience says they will but experience can be wrong, as for instance when the nineteenth-century Irish potato crop failed and widespread famine followed.

From here it was a short step to considering religion which Hume called a species of philosophy. If everything had a cause, what was the cause of the world we lived in? The popular belief was God, but to what degree could that be sustained? If God was the cause and if everything had to have a cause, what caused God? If something else caused God, what caused that something else? There was no end to this line of reasoning and it ended only in absurdity: logically a first cause could never be established.

Then there was the problem of suffering, not just the sufferings

*The dramatic critic Kenneth Tynan once wrote of a play called *Caro William*: William Douglas Home (pronounced Hume) has written a third act which made me foam (pronounced fume).

that men inflicted on one another, but those arising from natural causes such as famine, plagues, earthquakes, floods. Christians claimed their god was all powerful, all knowing and all good. If he was all knowing, said Hume, he was aware of the suffering in the world. If he was all powerful and all good, he could prevent the suffering, yet didn't. What kind of a god was that?

Then there were those who relied on the Design argument, that just as a watch had been designed by a watchmaker or a house by an architect, so the universe had been designed and governed by certain fixed laws to allow it to function as it did. Hume admitted the attractions of this argument but the more he examined it, the more he distrusted it, there being an insurmountable gap between the natural world, of whose origins we are ignorant and an object such as a watch or a house which we *know* to have been manufactured and by whom. Was not the universe more like an animal or a vegetable that regenerated itself than something manufactured?

In any case, he argued, why predicate that if the world was made by a god, it had to be by one god? Why not a collection of gods, indulging in teamwork as humans do, to build a ship or a city? Adherence to monotheistic gods bred superstition and fanaticism, conflict and war. Was not a world of many gods preferable to 'the implacable narrow spirit of Judaism', 'the bloody principles of Mahometanism', 'the grotesque intolerance' of modern Christianity? It was all very well to assume from the works of nature a Supreme Creator, but when you turned the reverse of the medal and surveyed the religious principles which prevailed in the world, 'you will scarcely be persuaded that they are anything but sick men's dreams . . . or the playful whimsies of monkeys in human shape'.

While it was on belief in the so-called Father rather than the Son that Hume concentrated his criticisms, he did not neglect to point out the absurdity of miracles:

> A miracle is a violation of the laws of nature. Nothing is esteemed a miracle if it ever happens in the common course of nature . . . But it is a miracle that a dead man should come to life; because that has never been observed in any age or country . . . When anyone tells me that he saw a dead man restored to life, I immediately consider with myself whether it be more probable that this person should either deceive or be deceived or that the fact which he relates should really have happened.

The same sort of phraseology was employed by Tom Paine when discussing the same problem fifty years later.

> When I am told that a woman called the Virgin Mary said, or gave out that she was with child without any co-habitation with a man and that her betrothed husband Joseph said that an angel told him so, I have a right to believe them or not: such a circumstance requires a much stronger evidence than their bare word for it.

Hume was equally dismissive of belief in the immortality of the soul. All sorts of arguments had been advanced in favour of it, but it was the gospels and only the gospels in which Christ pronounced on the subject, that had brought the belief into being. (I wished he had gone further and attempted to give some definition of the word 'soul' and what people thought they meant by it.)

Nor would Hume allow religion to be the source of morality and goodness. A thing was right or good because it was right or good, not because some authority such as the headmaster, the bishop, the king, the Bible, Jesus Christ, God, said so. Even if one allowed that a god or gods created the world, it was nonsense to claim for them human attributes such as mercy, justice, love. In what way, he asked, did the Deity's benevolence and mercy resemble the benevolence and mercy of man: 'Where does Divine benevolence display itself?' And if we allowed there to be a deity or deities, 'what trust or confidence can we repose in them?' The laws of nature were carried on by an opposition of principles, hot and cold, moist and dry, light and heavy. 'The truth is that the original cause of all things is entirely indifferent to all those principles and has no more regard to good above ill than to heat above cold or moisture over drought . . . We have no more reason to infer that the rectitude of the First Cause resembles human rectitude than his benevolence does'. And if one was going to equate the Deity with human attributes, why not bestow on him the human form – eyes, a nose, a mouth, ears, etc? After all, Epicurus had said that no man had ever experienced reason but in a human figure.

But was not some religion, he was asked, better than none? Could it not be said to regulate the hearts of men, humanize their conduct, encourage temperance, order and obedience? No, said Hume, and cited the clergy who were always lamenting the universality of human wickedness and yet in the same breath, as it were, claiming that without religion society would fall apart. 'It is certain from experience', he wrote, 'that the smallest grain of natural honesty and benevolence has more effect on men's conduct than the most pompous views suggested by theological systems and theories; and none but fools ever repose less trust in a man because they hear that . . . he has entertained some speculative doubts with regard to theological subjects.'

Popular religion, said Hume, was based on man's hopes and fears, what was going to happen to him in this world and the next. 'We incessantly look forward and endeavour by prayers, adoration and sacrifice, to appease those unknown powers whom we find by experience so able to afflict and oppress us'. Yet in those moments when man is happy and successful, it does not occur to him to thank his god for it, at least spontaneously; he only calls for him in times of distress and terror. Nor, said Hume, did man run any risk in using his reason to reject the terrors and with them the worship of God. 'It is an absurdity to believe that the Deity has human passions and one of the lowest of human passions, a restless appetite for applause.'

The worst effect of organized religion, he said, was its subversion of sincerity and self-knowledge. Popular religious belief was a form of make-believe which became a chain of hypocrisy leading to fraud, dissimulation and falsehood. 'Hence the highest zeal in religion and the deepest hypocrisy, so far from being inconsistent, were often united in the same individual character.'

'To all the purposes of life,' concluded Hume, 'religion is useless . . . No new fact can ever be inferred from the religious hypothesis; no event foreseen or foretold; no reward or punishment expected or dreaded beyond what is already known by practice and observation.'

Hume's writings have been known to us for nearly 250 years, so what I have been telling of him here may for many, perhaps for most, be old hat. But to a twenty-five-year old as I was when I first read him, the impact was electric. Almost overnight the burden of trying to resolve the conflicts in my mind concerning Christian belief was lifted, and as subsequent years have gone by, religious belief of any kind has increasingly seemed to me to be absurd, and the claims of Christianity preposterous.

What makes Hume's views so remarkable is the dispassion with which he sets them out, examining the phenomenon of Christianity as a scientist might examine a specimen under the microscope. He had no proselytizing desire to urge people to deny God which he himself was careful not to, admitting (his reasoning being all of a piece) that it was as impossible to prove that a god didn't exist as to prove that he did. His reasoning was entirely academic in the sense that he did not expect it to influence practice. He knew that whatever he said, people would go on believing that the order they sought in their own lives came from the same source that had created order in the universe. Indeed he advised one young sceptic who was in doubt about taking holy orders to go ahead, on the grounds that it didn't do to care whether the vulgar thought him a sceptic or not.

Hume was also quite indifferent to his critics, of which there were many, including those who were so shocked by his scepticism as to deny him the Chair of Moral Philosophy at Edinburgh University and of Logic at Glasgow University after his friend Adam Smith had vacated it. In his autobiography he tells of the Reverends and Right Reverends bringing out answers to his views two and three times a year, and that he could cover the floor of a large room with books and pamphlets written against him, 'to none of which I ever made the least reply, not from Disdain (for the authors of some of them I respect) but from my desire of ease and tranquillity'.

His wit too was another example of his detachment from his subject. A story is told of him attending the kirk at Inveraray with Lady Elizabeth Hamilton, where they were guests of the Duke at the castle. The minister announced that his sermon would be on the subject of unreasonable scepticism. Lady Elizabeth turned to Hume, 'That's you,' she said, as perhaps the minister had hoped she would. At the end of the sermon the minister said, 'And now, my friends, I will address a few words to the chief of sinners.' Hume turned to his companion, 'And that's to your ladyship,' he said.

All this dispassion led some people to assume that Hume was still at heart a theist and therefore, said the Revd Caleb Fleming, could not be an enemy to true Christianity. The same conclusion was reached by Sir James Macdonald of Sleat* who, writing to a friend in England after Hume's arrival in Paris aged fifty-two in 1763 as secretary to the English ambassador, said, 'Poor Hume who

---

*Elder brother of Sir Alexander Macdonald of Sleat who succeeded him in the baronetcy.

on your side of the water was thought to have too little religion, is here thought to have too much.'

This was a reference to a famous group of Parisian free thinkers who came to be styled Les Philosophes, the 'fathers' of the French Revolution, and who believed that by the end of the eighteenth century Christianity would have disappeared from Europe. Its leader was the Baron d'Holbach who was known as The Personal Enemy of God, just as Hume in Britain was known as The Great Infidel. The French philosopher Denis Diderot, who was another member of the group, described the first occasion when Hume dined with them. Hume was seated next to the baron and in the course of conversation told him that *he didn't believe in atheists and had never seen any* (my italics). D'Holbach replied, 'Count how many we are here. We are eighteen. Of these, fifteen are atheists. The other three haven't yet made up their minds.' Diderot himself was one of the most radical of the group. 'A people who think that it is belief in a god and not good laws which make men honest,' he once said, 'seems to me but little advanced.'

Not surprisingly Hume and Diderot got on famously, the latter despite his own bulk, likening Hume to a fat, well-fed Bernardine monk. Diderot had been educated by the Jesuits and had come to loathe them and their religion. He had suffered imprisonment in 1746 for his *Pensées Philosophiques*, but this had not stopped him forging ahead with his famous *Encyclopédie*. No letters from Hume to Diderot have survived but those from Diderot to Hume speak of great affection and admiration. 'My well-beloved and greatly honoured David,' he addresses him, '. . . you are of all nations and you will never demand from a poor wretch his baptismal certificate . . . Madame Diderot will kiss your two large Bernardine cheeks . . . I salute you – I love you – I revere you.'

A friend of Diderot was the German-born writer and philosopher Friedrich Grimm who also had come to admire Hume, having read his works before his arrival in Paris. 'As philosophers belong less to their native country than to the universe which they enlighten,' he wrote, 'this man . . . can be included in the small number of those who by their wisdom and by their works have benefited mankind.' He particularly admired Hume's *History of England*, saying that the writing of history belonged by right to the philosophers, 'exempt from prejudice and passion'.

Both within the circle of Les Philosophes and in the wider ranks of

Paris society, Hume found himself lionized, the French always having held serious writers in greater veneration than the English; and with the major contributions to his life's work behind him, Hume was in social demand everywhere. Duchesses, he wrote home, received him with open arms, and at court the children of the Dauphin (the future Louis XVI, Louis XVIII and Charles X), then aged from nine to six, had learned by heart polite little speeches to recite to him. Grimm wrote of the contrast between Hume's solid, expressionless face and those of the beauties of the salon, a scene which his mistress Madame d'Epinay elaborated on when she recalled the absurdity of Hume's appearance in a *tableau vivant* where he appeared dressed as a sultan with two of the prettiest girls in Paris in the guise of slaves standing on either side. 'He could find nothing to do', recorded his biographer Mossner, 'except to smite his stomach and repeat every quarter of an hour, "Eh, bien, mesdemoiselles, eh bien, vous voilà donc!" ' ('Well, well, ladies, here we are!')

None of the eulogizing seems to have turned his head, and in spite of his lack of finesse and social graces, the French were quick to appreciate his good nature, simplicity and shrewdness. 'Le bon David' they called him, and when he left for England in 1766 Grimm said of him:

> M. Hume ought to love France where he has received the most distinguished and most flattering reception . . . What is still more pleasant is that all the pretty women had a great run on him and that the fat Scottish philosopher was pleased with their society. This David Hume is an excellent man; he is naturally placid; he listens attentively, he sometimes speaks with wit, although he speaks little; but he is clumsy, he has neither warmth nor grace nor charm of humour, nor anything that properly appertains to the chirping of those charming little mechanisms known as pretty women. Oh, what a ludicrous people we are!

Everyone with whom Hume had come in contact during his years in Paris had observed his lifelong habit of staring relentlessly at those with whom he was engaged in conversation; and D'Alembert, an even greater friend than Diderot, warned him about it. 'I remember', he wrote to Hume at the time of his leaving Paris, 'when you were once talking to me and at the same time staring fixedly at me that I advised you in a friendly manner to break off as much as possible that habit because it might play you a nasty trick. It is not necessary to gaze intently at the people you are speaking to . . .'

Hume did not heed the advice. Towards the end of his time in Paris he was asked if he could help to arrange the temporary exile in England of the philosopher Jean Jacques Rousseau who was in trouble with the authorities for something he had written. Hume did so, and Rousseau journeyed to England. At the time Rousseau seems to have been suffering from a persecution complex, was convinced that Voltaire, d'Alembert and Hume were all conspiring against him and libelled them publicly. A sort of climax in their relationship was reached when, just before setting out for Derbyshire where the lease of a house had been obtained for him, Rousseau, according to one source, 'saw Hume's eyes fixed upon him with an expression that made him tremble'. This caused Rousseau to burst into tears, whereupon Hume did the same, and both embraced. However the quarrel had gone too far for it to be patched up, and Hume was eventually persuaded by his friends, both French and English, to write a truthful account of the affair, without bitterness. This was published towards the end of 1766 and is now in the archives of the Royal Society of Edinburgh.

It is at this juncture that our old friend James Boswell briefly enters the story. When Rousseau came to England he had not been able to bring with him his attractive mistress Thérèse le Vasseur. However, Boswell was in France at the time, and as he and Rousseau had become intimate friends, Hume asked him to companion Thérèse on the journey over. To ask Boswell to companion any woman, and especially an attractive one, was like handing the keys of one's house to a burglar and on the voyage from Paris to London Boswell lost little time in seducing Thérèse. The fact that Boswell had often discussed sex with Rousseau and confided in him past liaisons, could have given his possession of Thérèse an added spice. She told him however that he was not as good a lover as Rousseau: he had virility but he lacked art. Had he not discovered on his travels, she asked, what men could do with their hands? Clearly not. We know from his encounter with the fair Louisa that he was a stayer and indeed multiple performer, but of pleasure, if any, he had given to Louise or any other woman, he never speaks. One suspects that Boswell, like many Scots (and English) was ignorant of, or indifferent to, the need for arousal in women (and especially French women) leading to heightened pleasure for both.

Boswell told Hume of his *amitié amoureuse* with Thérèse, but promised not to reveal it to others until Rousseau was dead.

Three years later Hume returned to Edinburgh and moved into the apartment in James's Court with his sister Catherine who had acted as his housekeeper ever since their elder brother John had married. He was now quite well off as a result of the sales of his books and a generous pension, and was happy to spend his declining years in the company of old friends such as Adam Smith and Boswell, putting in appearances at the Poker club and other Edinburgh societies, always good-natured and enjoying the company of his fellow men and women (to whose presence, although he never married, he was particularly partial). He was painted by another friend the portraitist Allan Ramsay son of the poet; his large moon face giving nothing away.

In 1770 he started to build the house, off St Andrew Square (later named St David's Street after him) and one day, crossing from the Old Town to the New, fell into the bog which was the residue of the Nor' Loch after it had been drained. Unable to extricate himself unaided, and noticing a fishwife passing by, he begged her to help him out. Recognizing the man she knew as 'Hume the Atheist' she said that in view of his beliefs or lack of them she doubted whether she ought to help. 'But my good woman,' said Hume, 'does not your religion teach you to do good, even to your enemies?' 'That's as maybe,' the fishwife replied, 'but ye shallna get oot of that till ye become a Christian yoursel' and repeat the Lord's prayer and the Belief [the Creed]'. Hume did so, no doubt surprising the woman that he was able to, and she helped him out. Hume said that she had been the most acute theologian he had ever encountered.

In 1775, when sixty-four, Hume fell ill with what was thought to be cancer of the liver. It gradually worsened and in his autobiography written in April 1776 he said he expected a speedy dissolution. He suffered little pain, his spirits and love of studying were not affected and he told his friends that he did not regret the loss of a few years of infirmity. 'It is difficult', he added, 'to be more detached from life than I am at present.'

This philosophical approach to death was not what the pious thought proper or expected, the thoughts at this time of those dying being concentrated on what awaited them in the great beyond, and trusting that their lives had been an adequate preparation for it. Dr Johnson, when he heard of Hume's calm at the approach of death, refused to believe it. A few years earlier, when discussing with him the question of death, Boswell mentioned that Hume had told him that he was no more uneasy to think that he *should not be* after this life than that he *had not been* before it; to which the orthodox Johnson replied, 'Sir, if he really thinks so, his perceptions are disturbed; he is mad. If he does not think so, he lies'. Such was the wisdom of the times.

Friends came to say goodbye, among them another strong believer, the widow of Baron Mure. He gave her an inscribed copy of one of his weighty tomes on the *History of England*. She took it gratefully but could not resist expressing reservations about his other, slimmer but more controversial writings. 'Oh, David,' she said, pointing to the *History*, 'That's a book you may weel be proud o'. But afore you dee, ye should burn a' your *wee* bookies' (i.e. those criticizing the faith). Half in jest, half offended, Hume replied, 'What for should I burn a' my wee bookies?' but was not able to continue.

Then it was Boswell's turn. For all his philanderings he was as much a conventional believer as Johnson, and he has left a wonderful and much quoted account of his last visit to the Great Infidel:

> On Sunday forenoon the 7 of July 1776, being too late for church, I went to see Mr David Hume, who was returned from London and Bath, just a-dying. I found him alone, in a reclining posture in his drawing-room. He was lean, ghastly and quite of an earthly appearance. He was dressed in a suit of grey cloth with white metal buttons and a kind of scratch wig. He was quite different from the plump figure he used to present. He seemed to be placid and even cheerful. He said he was just approaching to his end. I think these were his words.
>
> I had a strong curiosity to be satisfied if he persisted in disbelieving a future state even when he had death before his eyes. I asked him if it was not possible that there might be a future state. He answered it was possible that a piece of coal put upon the fire would not burn; and he added that it was a most unreasonable fancy that we should exist for ever.

That immortality, if it were at all, must be general; that a great proportion of the human race has hardly any intellectual qualities; that a great proportion dies in infancy before being possessed of reason; yet all these must be immortal; that a porter who gets drunk with gin by ten o'clock must be immortal; that the trash of every age must be preserved, and that new universes must be created to contain such numbers. This appeared to me an unphilosophical objection, and I said, 'Mr Hume, you know spirit does not take up space' . . .

I asked him if the thought of annihilation never gave him any uneasiness. He said not the least. 'Well,' said I, 'Mr Hume, I hope to triumph over you when I meet you in a future state; and remember you are not to pretend that you was joking with all this infidelity.' 'No, no,' said he. 'But I shall have been so long there before you come that it will be nothing new.' In this style of humour and levity did I conduct the conversation.

Perhaps it was wrong on so awful a subject. But as nobody was present, I thought it could have no bad effect. I however felt a degree of horror, mixed with a sort of wild, strange, hurrying recollection of my excellent mother's pious instructions, of Dr Johnson's noble lessons, and of my religious sentiments and affections during the course of my life. I was like a man in sudden danger eagerly seeking his defensive arms; and I could not but be assailed by momentary doubts while I had actually before me a man of such strong abilities and extensive inquiry dying in the persuasion of being annihilated.

When Boswell reported to Johnson that Hume was quite easy at the thought of annihilation, the doctor, who was terrified of death, confirmed what he had said earlier. 'He lied. He had a vanity in being *thought* easy. It is more probable he lied than that so very improbable a thing should be as a man not afraid of death . . .'

On the day of Hume's burial, Boswell went along to inspect the open grave, and hid behind a wall to watch the mourners pass, fearful that the grave might be desecrated by religious zealots. That it was not desecrated was due, at least in part, to the presence of two guards whom the Ninewells family had hired to watch it.

Even then there was no ending to the controversy over Hume's beliefs. His friend Adam Smith wrote a tribute to him in a letter to William Strahan, which was subsequently published. 'Thus died our most excellent and never to be forgotten friend, concerning whose philosophical opinions men will no doubt judge variously, everyone approving or condemning of them according as they happen to coincide, or disagree with his own; but concerning whose character and conduct there can scarce be a difference of opinion.'

After praising Hume's gentleness, generosity, good humour, depth of thought, independence of mind, modesty and frugality, he concluded: 'I have always considered him, both in his lifetime and since his death, as approaching as nearly to the idea of a perfectly wise and virtuous man as perhaps the nature of human frailty will admit.'

Although this sort of fulsomeness was standard practice for obituaries of the time, it caused outrage among the devout. 'A single and, as I thought, a very harmless sheet of paper which I happened to write concerning the death of our late friend Mr Hume,' Smith wrote after publication of his great work *The Wealth of Nations*, 'brought upon me ten times more abuse than the very violent attack I had made upon the whole commercial system of Great Britain.'

But Hume's reputation continued to be enhanced as time went on. The biographer of his entry in the *Dictionary of National Biography* wrote of his influence on Kant, on Adam Smith, on Bentham, and concluded by saying, 'He may be regarded as the acutest thinker in Great Britain of the eighteenth century'.

It is good to know too that his dismissal of the idea of an external god or gods is now, 250 years later, at last beginning to gain popular acceptance.

# CHAPTER 16

## The Fornicator

WHATEVER ELSE THE CHURCH OF SCOTLAND MAY BE NOTED FOR, it is not for imagination or vision. And yet a few years ago it did something so out of its ordinary that one could only stand back and applaud. It commissioned a new design for the west window of St Giles Cathedral in honour of our national poet. The work is in three sections: the bottom five panels represent the farmer's world of green and growing things; the upper five symbolize the brotherhood of man ('It's coming yet for a' that/That man to man the world o'er/Shall brithers be for a' that') while at the top of the window a burst of creative sunlight represents the ideal of love. It was love and liberty, said Burns, that had been the two inspirational themes of his life.

When the project was first mooted, there were inevitably dissenters. A memorial in the national church to *Robert Burns*? Was he not an out and out atheist? Well, no actually, he was a deeply religious man, well versed in the Bible, whose early religious poems proved of great solace to many readers; what he could not abide was the cant and hypocrisy of the holier than thou brigade, as exemplified in *Address to the Unco Guid or the Rigidly Righteous* ('Oh ye, wha are sae guid yoursel,/Sae pious and sae holy/Ye've nought to do but mark and tell/Your neebour's fauts and folly'). Was he not then a promiscuous lecher, who had seduced countless innocent country girls and fathered innumerable bastards? Outside his marriage to Jean Armour, only four. It is true he was a fornicator, but then he adored the opposite sex and for much of his life was engulfed in a fever of lusty, loving longings for them. 'My heart was completely tinder', he wrote, 'and was eternally lighted up by some Goddess or other and, like every warfare in the world, I was sometimes crowned with success and sometimes mortified with defeat'. His near contemporary James Boswell was also a great womanizer, but with a difference: Boswell was a patron of prostitutes, Burns the romantic would have nothing to do with them. And whereas Boswell liked to enter in his journals the sexual details of his encounters ('I met with a monstrous big whore in the Strand whom I had a great curiosity to lubricate, as the saying is') on only one occasion to my knowledge did Burns, in a private letter, descend to the same level: 'I took the opportunity of some dry horse litter, and gave her such a thundering scalade that electrified the very marrow of her bones. Oh, what a peacemaker is a guid weel-willy pintle [penis].' But as the girl in question was his future wife, the passage wears a rather different aspect. It should also be remembered that Boswell's condoms of sheep's bladders and wetted linen had not yet reached rural Ayrshire, so that in country parishes the fruits of fornication were plain for all to see: one Andrew Noble noted in the Mauchline kirk minutes, 'Only 24 fornicators since the last sacrament'. Burns himself had to do public penance in the kirk at Tarbolton and pay a guinea fine for fornication with Betsey Paton who subsequently bore him a daughter, but even when undergoing the penance (and this is part of Burns's honesty and charm) desire rose up in him:

> Before the Congregation wide
> I passed the muster fairly,
> My handsome Betsey by my side,
> We gat our ditty rarely;                    [sermon]
> But my downcast eye by chance did spy
> What made my lips to water,
> Those limbs so clean where I, between,
> Commenced a Fornicator.

For most men at that time the fate of a child they had unintentionally fathered would have been of little consequence. But Burns looked forward to the event with a blend of curiosity and tenderness, always a feature of his character, whether towards humans or animals; and thus he greeted her arrival:

> Welcome, my bonie sweet, wee dochter,
> Though ye come here a wee unsought for,
> And tho your comin I hae fought for,
>     Baith kirk and quair                          [church and court]
> Yet, by my faith ye're no unwrought for —
>     That I shall swear.

Well, if he wasn't an atheist and wasn't a greater fornicator than others in the district, was he not a congenital toper, usually more drunk than sober? Despite the myths that have grown up around him, the evidence is otherwise. His brother Gilbert, a faithful chronicler of much of his early life, said that he had never seen him intoxicated and that he wasn't at all given to drinking; for one thing he didn't have the money, for another it was inclined to make him ill. Nor are there reports of him being other than sober while being lionized at parties in Edinburgh and elsewhere. It is true that when he was in the Dumfries area in the later part of his life he did go on one or two benders and wake in the morning with what he called 'a severe head-ach'. But in a hard drinking age there was nothing remarkable in this:

> I love drinking now and then. It defecates the standing pool
> of thought. A man perpetually in the paroxysms and fevers
> of inebriety is like a half-drowned, stupid wretch condemned
> to labour unceasingly in water, but a now-and-then tribute to
> Bacchus is like the cold bath — bracing and invigorating.

Because of my English education and early unfamiliarity with the Scots tongue, I came to Burns late in life, but welcomed him all the more for that. I think I have visited most places connected with his life, such as the little cottage in Alloway where he was born, the upstairs room of the Bachelors Club which he founded in Tarbolton and where once at a Burns supper I was an honoured guest, to his final resting-place in the churchyard of St Michael's

279

in Dumfries which he attended during his last years. The Alloway cottage, not far from the famous Gothic brig o' Doon, is low-lying, whitewashed, with a thatched roof. It has been preserved as near as possible to what it must have been in his day. At one end is a room for storing farm implements and machinery: there's a cart of the period there, a turnip sowing machine, a cheese press and a butter churn. Next is the byre with stalls for the beasts and, beyond, the parlour with a picture of the poet painted on wood and wearing a jerkin with blue and beige horizontal layers and carrying the inscription, 'The Airshire Poet'* (sic).

At the far end is the little kitchen, whitewashed, with a black fireplace and black pot and griddle hanging over it, and a black oven: a dresser with a plate rack containing pale blue plates; a stout wooden chair with two arms which belonged to the poet's parents. And then the two little box beds with floral coverlets set into the wall, so small you might think they were made for dwarfs and in one of which the poet was born. The date was 25 January 1759, the year before the accession of George III, and a day of storm as Robert later noted in the poem about himself that he called 'Rantin, Rovin, Robin'.

> Our monarch's hindmost year but ane
> Was five and twenty years begun,
> 'Twas then a blast o' Janwar win'
> Blew hansel in on Robin.                     [a New Year gift]

Here, after the cottage had been repaired from the storm damage, little Robert spent the first seven years of his life. Although poor, his father did everything possible to give his eldest son a good education, partly by his own efforts, partly in engaging an occasional tutor. From an early age Robert was a voracious reader, burying himself in whatever came to hand.

> The first two books I ever read in private and which gave
> me more pleasure than any two books I ever read again, were
> the life of Hannibal and the history of Sir William Wallace.
> Hannibal gave my young ideas such a turn that I used to strut
> in raptures up and down after the recruiting drum and bagpipe

*Copied from the painting by Alexander Nasmyth.

and wish myself tall enough to be a soldier; while the story of Wallace poured a Scottish prejudice in my veins which will boil along there till the flood-gates of life shut in eternal rest.

Here was the genesis of his great patriotic poem on Bannockburn, *Scots Wha' Hae* which did not come to flower until after he had visited the site of the battlefield twenty years later, and the French Revolution had further inflamed his nationalistic fervour. His wish to be a soldier, so often a characteristic of a creative writer's childhood, is reminiscent of Boswell at Fort George ('At three the drum beat for dinner. I, for a little while, fancied myself a military man, and it pleased me').* For a long time Robert entertained the idea of becoming a soldier and Boswell, it will be recalled, had it in mind to obtain a commission on his first visit to London.

But the greatest influence in his early childhood was his mother's helper in the house, an old crone called Betty Davidson. She had what Robert called 'the largest collection in the country of tales and songs concerning devils, ghosts, fairies, brownies, witches, warlocks, spunkies, kelpies . . . wraiths, apparitions . . . and other trumpery. It was Betty Davidson's tales, said Robert, that cultivated in him the latent seeds of poesy; and twenty-five years later he distilled them into another famous poem, 'Tam o' Shanter'.

When Robert was seven the family moved to a farm a couple of miles from Alloway, and here he combined further education, some of it dispensed by his former tutor who was now head of a school at Ayr, with helping his father plough and till the barren soil. Books that came his way were *A Geographical Grammar*, *A History of the Holy Bible from the beginning of the world to the Establishment of Christianity*, *Letters by the Most Eminent Writers*, *Durham's Physico and Astro-Theology*, *Titus Andronicus*, Richardson's *Pamela* and volumes of Smollett, Fielding, Hume and Pope. He also had access to *The Edinburgh Magazine* and *The Spectator*, and learned the rudiments of French. Such was the initial depository of knowledge on which he drew for prose and poetry.

When he was fifteen he discovered for the first of many times what was to become the lodestar of his life, the ineffable, insatiable joy of contact with female flesh. It happened at harvest time when boys and girls were paired off together to stack the sheaves:

*See p 112.

. . . my partner was a bewitching creature who just counted an autumn less [i.e. fourteen]. My scarcity of English denies me the power of doing her justice in that language; but you know the Scotch idiom. She was a bonie, sweet, sonsie lass. In short she altogether unwittingly to herself, initiated me into a certain delicious passion which . . . I hold to be the first of human joys, our chiefest pleasure here below.

I never expressly told her that I loved her. Indeed I did not well know myself why I liked so much to loiter behind with her when returning in the evenings from our labours; why the tones of her voice made my heartstrings thrill like an Aeolian harp; and particularly why my pulse beat such a furious ratann when I looked and fingered over her hand to pick out the nettle-stings and thistles . . .

Thus with me began Love and Poesy . . .

And continued, he might have added, for the rest of his life, resulting in many of the greatest as well as the simplest love poems yet which have the simplicity of genius. Most words are of one syllable, few more than two. It is that sort of simplicity that most of us have tried to cultivate when writing fledgling poetry of our own, but Burns apart, the only other poet who can be said to have at all succeeded in it is A.E. Housman. How true was Burns's remark that only on two or three occasions in his life had he composed from the wish rather than the impulse but had never succeeded to any purpose. The impression he gives, especially in the love poetry, is of verses gushing out of him already formed, that in a way he was their agent, not their originator. His brother Gilbert, speaking of the source of the poem 'To a Mouse', wrote how he was with him when the plough sliced into the mouse's nest and how, by the time they returned home, the poem was already half completed. The emotion, the humour of Burns's verses goes straight from his heart to that of the reader so that I gain most from them by reading them alone and aloud, and poems like 'Ae Fond Kiss', 'My Love is Like a Red, Red Rose' and 'John Anderson, my Jo' can reduce me to tears, while others like 'On Meeting with Lord Daer', 'The Lass that made the bed for me' and 'To a Mouse' often bring on an unconscious smile. Add to this such diverse poems as 'The Selkirk Grace', 'The Wounded Hare', 'To a Haggis', 'Tam o' Shanter', 'Scots Wha Hae', 'To a Mountain Daisy', 'A Parcel of Rogues in a Nation', the 'Holy Willie' diatribes and 'Auld Lang Syne' (the most sung song in the western world) and you have the full range and flowering of his genius. Few English-speaking revellers incidentally who sing 'Auld Lang Syne' have much idea of what it means.

Because Burns's poetry is concerned with the universal human condition, love, sorrow, grief, compassion, patriotism, there is hardly a country in the literate world where his works have not been translated. In the little house in Dumfries in which he spent the last years of his life there are volumes of his in Norwegian, German, Japanese and half a dozen other languages. A million copies of his poems have been sold in Russia in the last thirty years, 100,000 copies have recently been published in Beijing. Because the Scots have dispersed themselves across the world in even greater numbers than the Irish, the Greeks or the Jews, there is not a major city from Vancouver to Tokyo, Bangkok to Pretoria, without a Caledonian Society to host an annual St Andrew's or Burns Night dinner. I visited one in Copenhagen recently, attended not only by resident Scots but a score of enthusiastic Danes dressed in whatever clan tartans they happened to fancy and reeling and halloing with the best of them. And once, when returning from America to Britain in the Dutch liner *Nieuw Amsterdam*, her captain who spoke English with an atrocious accent, read to me a poem of Burns in almost impeccable Scots.

Yet there is one country which Burns has never penetrated and I guess never will. After he had visited Edinburgh to celebrate the publication of the first (Kilmarnock) edition of his verse, the critic Henry Mackenzie wrote: 'I have given Burns's poems to several English gentlemen who cannot discern their beauties'. Sadly, this is still true; that while no educated Scot could fail to recognize in Shakespeare the world's greatest classical playwright, few educated English would be prepared to acknowledge Burns as the world's greatest poet of the human emotions. One cannot blame them. Told that 'To a Mouse' is a funny, sad poem containing the famous line about the best laid schemes of mice and men, the Englishman starts off optimistically enough. In the first two stanzas he learns that the poet's ploughshare has destroyed the mouse's nest which he deeply regrets. Then comes the third stanza and at first all seems clear:

> I doubt na, whyles, but thou may thieve;
> What then, puir beastie, thou maun live!

So far, so good: the mouse's nest contains an ear or two of the poet's corn. But what comes next?

> A daimen icker in a thrave
>  'S a sma' request:
> I'll get a blessin' wi' the lave,
>  And never miss't!

The Englishman's jaw drops. If he perseveres, the glossary will tell him that a daimen icker in a thrave is the odd ear of corn in twenty-four sheaves, and that the poet, blessed with the remainder, will not miss it. But the Englishman is unlikely to persevere. Why should he waste time and effort having to decipher incomprehensible Scots when there are plenty of good English poets to hand such as Keats and Tennyson? The Englishman loses out on Burns only because he is not a complete foreigner. If he was, there would be no problem: for even if the poems lose something in translation, they are at least all of a piece.

When Burns died, of what is now thought to have been brucellosis at the age of thirty-seven, his funeral procession in Dumfries was attended by thousands. He was first buried in an ordinary grave in St Michael's churchyard, but in 1815 a square white mausoleum with a cupola was built for him, and his remains and those of his wife Jean Armour and some of their children were moved into it. The mausoleum is set in a little enclosed garden of white heather and other shrubs. Through a glass window we see an effigy of Burns with his left hand on a plough and the other holding a round cap, looking up at Coila the muse of poetry spreading a white drapery over him.

I find the mausoleum pleasing: light and airy, big enough to impress but not over-powering. I wish I could say the same of its surroundings: row upon hideous row of nineteenth-century tomb-stones blackened and decayed, some of the upright slabs leaning at an angle, many with fulsome and almost illegible eulogies inscribed on them, as used to be the fashion; monuments to the dead burghers of Dumfries who have lang syne been forgotten. What a service the Trustees of St Michael's could render to the memory of Burns and to Dumfries and Scotland, if they could seek permission to clear away the clutter, turn this junkyard of mould and decay into a garden of remembrance with little plaques to commemorate the names of

284

the vanished dead, and flowers and shrubs and a grass lawn with a pathway leading naturally and purposefully to Robert Burns in his mausoleum, standing white and shining at the end of it. He deserves no less.

# CHAPTER 17

## *The Obtrusive Duke*

LIKE MOST CITIES OF THE SAME SIZE EDINBURGH IS THICK WITH STATUES, though I guess that few of its inhabitants who pass them every day would be able to tell you where they were and who they represented. One exception is the weird Gothic extravaganza in Princes Street, a kind of frozen space rocket whose passengers are the seated marble figures of Sir Walter Scott and his dog; a monument which, like St Giles and the National Gallery, has been part of the Edinburgh landscape for so long (almost 150 years) that it has passed beyond criticism. Those of the amorous King Charles II in Parliament Square and of the puritan John Knox inside the interior of St Giles only a few yards away, are also outstanding; and almost everyone in Edinburgh knows where to find Greyfriars Bobby (at the top of Candlemaker Row), the little Skye terrier which every day after his master's death came to visit his grave in nearby Greyfriars churchyard and keep a vigil on it until his own death ten years later. Others are more elusive. Who in Edinburgh today can guide one unerringly to those monuments in bronze or stone that commemorate David Livingstone, Allan Ramsay, George IV, Henry Dundas, Alexander and his horse Bucephalus, Adam Black, Field Marshal Haig, Sir William Chambers, Admiral Lord Nelson?

For most people living in cities statues are invisible: they are dwarfed by their surroundings – buildings, railings, traffic, people, all of which combine to divert attention. At the east end of Princes Street moreover there is the curious situation of one notable artefact cancelling out another. I refer to one of the most distinguished buildings in the city, Robert Adam's superb Register House which holds the Scottish National Records, and the bronze statue of the Duke of Wellington on his prancing horse Copenhagen which stands in front of it. It would be difficult to think of a greater mismatch, the one a perfect example of the work of one of Scotland's and the world's greatest domestic architects, the other, though well enough executed, celebrating a great English military and political leader of a period considerably later. At the time that Register House was erected in 1772, a visitor standing on the North Bridge would have had an uninterrupted view of the whole of Register House and marvelled at its symmetry and elegance. But ever since the Duke and his charger went up, that view has vanished. The Duke too has been disadvantaged, being now dwarfed not only by Register House but by the General Post Office and the Balmoral (né North British) Hotel across the street.

Is it too late, I wonder, to invite the Edinburgh City Fathers, or whoever is responsible for the capital's statuary, to shift the Duke elsewhere? It is not my intention to belittle him, for he was one of the great generals of European history. Yet although he had many Scottish soldiers serving under him at Waterloo and elsewhere, he has never been specifically revered as a hero by the people of Scotland. In Elizabeth Longford's two-volume life I can find no mention of his coming to Scotland, although Sir Walter Scott was one of many who visited Waterloo soon after the battle and on the occasion of his meeting the Duke spoke of 'the sweetness and abandon' of his conversation.

Surely a more suitable locus can be found for the Duke than his present awkward position? Up at the castle perhaps where he would be at home with the other military relics, out at Gogarbank fronting the residence of the GOC Scotland or honouring the army barracks at Glencorse or Redford. And once that has been done, we can look at Register House again with opened eyes.

There is, however, one place in Scotland where the problem of making statuary invisible by placing it in the centres of busy cities has been overcome, although this is very special statuary and not the run of the mill depictions of mostly long-forgotten public figures. It is to be found among the bare hills and gated roads of one of the more remote parts of Dumfriesshire. Its name is Glenkiln.

In the year 1924 a young Anglo-Scot called Tony Keswick, son of the chairman of the great Far Eastern Trading Company of Jardine Matheson, was given by his father as a twenty-first birthday present the 3,000-acre Glenkiln estate which lies 8 miles to the west of the county town of Dumfries. Most of the estate consists of grassland and moor, and it supports quantities of sheep and birds, including wildfowl and grouse.

After the Second World War in which he rose to Brigadier, Tony Keswick worked in Jardine Matheson's London office, going at weekends to his country house in the village of Theydon Bois in Hertfordshire. One Saturday there he was in need of brass bath taps and hearing on the local grapevine that there was a craftsman who worked in bronze by the name of Moore living in the nearby village of Perry Green, motored over to see him.

At the time Mr Moore had visitors but he told Keswick that if he would care to take a stroll, he would be glad to see him on his return. Now far from being a manufacturer of bath taps, the Mr Moore that Keswick had come to see was Henry Moore the sculptor, and although at this time he had never heard of him (Moore's international fame did not come until later) he was not slow to recognize from the objects in his studio that he was in the presence of a major artist. Indeed, on his stroll his eye caught sight of a curious 12-feet-high elongated plaster cast which Moore called Standing Figure and an idea formed in his mind. Beside one of the roads on the Glenkiln estate stood a large, flat boulder, and for a long time Keswick had had the intention of putting some object on it by way of decoration. The Standing Figure was just what he had been looking for; and before he went home that afternoon, he reserved one of the four bronze casts that Moore was to make of it.

In time 'Standing Figure' was completed and taken to Glenkiln. None of the family was there when it arrived, so it was taken possession of by the estate gamekeeper, Mr Maxwell. Having peered inside its covering Mr Maxwell concluded that it must be a spare part for the tractor and sent it up to the farm. Ever afterwards he referred to it as 'Yon figure'.

After Standing Figure had been erected on its boulder plinth, one of the first visitors to see it was the art historian and collector,

'K' Clark. Clark had been a friend of Keswick at Winchester and was also a close friend and proponent of the works of Henry Moore. A brilliant scholar but deeply conventional, Clark was appalled by what he saw — city squares and art galleries were the proper places for sculpture, not a desolate Scottish hillside — and on arrival south he told Moore (but without telling Keswick that he was doing so) of his reaction and that he ought to have nothing further to do with Glenkiln.

Then Keswick invited Henry Moore to travel north to see his handiwork for himself. And Moore was bowled over. Like Clark he had previously associated sculptures with art galleries or city squares, but unlike Clark he saw at once how the environment dramatized the sculpture, emphasized in that vast landscape Standing Figure's essential loneliness. You could see it from any angle you wanted, uncluttered by people or passing traffic, its only background the empty hillside or sky; you could assess the strength and purity of it, its volume, flow and line. For Moore it was a revelation. 'Tony Keswick opened out a whole new outlook and direction for me', he said, 'and gave me an experience I'd never had before.' Even 'K' Clark on a future visit began to see the point of it. Yet the most realistic view of it came from the estate forester, Jock Murray: 'Seeing him in the headlights at night makes your hair stand on end.'

This was only the beginning. Fired by the success of Standing Figure, both Moore and Keswick wanted to add to it. One day, walking on the estate, they saw a shepherd silhouetted against the skyline on high ground, and agreed that this would be the ideal setting for what was to become known as The Glenkiln Cross. Described as 'a totem like, cruciform, semi-figurative bronze' twice the size of a man, it had originally been conceived as a centre piece of a triptych, but here it was to stand alone, looking out over the hills and glens towards England. Close to, it resembles another of Moore's figures but in the distance, as he himself said, it is more like one of the old Celtic crosses. On one part of it Moore drew pictures of a sun, a moon and a ladder, but asked in his old age what the purpose of these were, he said he couldn't remember.

Another Henry Moore to find its way to Glenkiln was his Two Piece Reclining Figure, originally a bronze lent by his daughter Mary but later withdrawn and another put in its place made of fibreglass coated with bronze dust. Just what this piece is intended to represent is unclear, but I find it expressive of great power and tension, the figure with the bullet-shaped head clearly dominating his smaller dog-like companion. Part of its strength may be due to Moore's insistence that the space between the solids is as important to the overall effect as the solids themselves.

But of all Moore's statues which decorate Glenkiln, the one that most art critics and he himself considered his finest work is the striking King and Queen, seated together on a bench overlooking the reservoir and, like the Glenkiln Cross, looking in the direction of England. Moore said that the idea for this came to him in 1953 which was not only Coronation Year but a time when he was reading bedtime stories about kings and queens to his daughter Mary then six. He began the work as a 10-inch wax maquette instead of a drawing so that it should be three dimensional from the start, and as he rolled the wax in his finger, he found a sort of crown taking shape on the head of the king. This led him to give the King a consort, and although hardly representational there can be no doubting the masculinity of the one and femininity of the other. His back is convex, hers concave: he modelled the hands of the King on those of the then Director of the National Gallery and those of the Queen on the hands of his secretary. Between the two solids one can see the 'leaf-shaped space' of which Moore was so fond. To me the statue says everything that is true about ancient kingship: majesty, authority and in that desolate landscape the loneliness and isolation of office; but at ease too, as the King's right hand resting loosely on the side of his bench clearly shows, the prerogative of aristocrats through the ages.

All of Moore's outdoor sculptures had to be larger than life if they were not to be dwarfed by the surroundings. If he had made any of them life-size, he once remarked, people would have said his models must have been very small people. One is aware of this when looking at the life-size statue of what seems a tiny George Washington outside the National Gallery in London. Equally one must not mount a statue so big that it dominates its environment, as with the 144-feet statue of Christ – the Corcovado – that squats on top of the Sugar Loaf Mountain in Rio de Janeiro and, to anyone of sensibility, looks grotesque. The key to Glenkiln, said Tony Keswick, was that 'the statues must possess the surroundings and the surroundings the statues'. Moore thought that even Rodin, the father of modern sculpture, sometimes made his statues too small and that one of the most famous, The Burghers of Calais, could have done with some enlargement.

In the world of twentieth-century statuary there are two names worthy to stand beside that of Henry Moore: Rodin and Epstein, who had once been Moore's master and a great help to him as a young man; and it was to these that Tony Keswick turned to complete his monumental zoo. He was not familiar with Rodin's works but his wife Mary had been impressed when she visited the Rodin Museum in Paris as a young girl. So he went there himself and was attracted to a bronze nude of John the Baptist, left arm at his side, the right raised as though beckoning people to come to him. Of this seemingly sunburned, wild, swarthy prophet the poet Rainer Maria Rilke said, 'This man's body is not untested; the fires of the desert have scorched him, hunger has racked him, thirst of every kind has tried him. He has come through all and is hardened.'

As he looked at it and what he called 'the best bouncing light of any statue I know' Keswick thought of a grassy knoll at Glenkiln on which to place it. So he entered into negotiations with the Museum's trustees and was able to buy it for £2,000. This was the most expensive of his Glenkiln purchases, for none of the Moores cost more than £1,000; and I remember 'K' Clark once telling me that he himself had seldom paid more than £50 for any painting or *objet d'art* when putting together his stunning collection between the wars; for in those days art had not yet become the sort of commercial investment that it is today. Like most of his purchases, Tony Keswick acquired the Epstein in an unusual way.

While visiting his studio to see if he had anything suitable for Glenkiln, three workmen turned up and asked Epstein where 'she' was, to which Epstein replied, 'Under the stairs'. Keswick asked who 'she' was and was told it was a bronze cast of The Visitation, a statue of the Virgin Mary of which the original was in the Tate Gallery. At the time Epstein was working on two busts of Sir Winston Churchill and being always short of money, was selling his own bronze cast of The Visitation for scrap. Hearing this, Keswick asked to see it and bought it on the spot.

At first Tony put The Visitation in a larch grove at the end of the reservoir, but when the local authority who owned the land objected on the grounds that people who came to see it were relieving themselves in the reservoir, he shifted it to the centre of a small group of Scotch pines. Here she stands today, often accompanied by the Glenkiln sheep, her gentle bowed head modelled on that of Epstein's Lebanese mistress. 'The trees guard her,' said Keswick, and they do. 'K' Clark thought The Visitation the best of Epstein's works.

For Henry Moore another excitement of Glenkiln was that his works could be studied in all kinds of weather (snow or darkness, he said, often seemed to enhance them). And because there is no law of trespass in Scotland, anyone who wishes may go there, wander about the estate and enjoy the statues for themselves.* They are an enduring monument to the most brilliant of twentieth-century sculptors and to a patron of the arts who had the gift of knowing how they could best be sited.

---

*As a result of which in March 1995 the heads of the King and Queen were cut off by vandals. They are to be replaced.

# CHAPTER 18

## *Dickens in Edinburgh*

AT THE EAST END OF PRINCES STREET AND A FEW HUNDRED YARDS eastwards from Register House, stands one of the odder of Edinburgh's architectural wonders, the bits and pieces that adorn Calton Hill and first led to the city being designated the Athens of the North. Among the neo-classical buildings erected here between 1776 and 1830 and still standing are the Old Observatory, a tower with Gothic windows; the New Observatory, Roman Doric and in the shape of a cross; a small circular Grecian style temple dedicated to Dugald Stewart; a column to Nelson, 100 feet high and allegedly in the shape of an inverted telescope; and beside it the shell of what was to have been a copy of the Parthenon, but after its foundations had been laid in 1822 and twelve columns had been erected, the money for completion ran out; and thus it stands today, to the Scots a monumental folly, to the unsuspecting Yankee a genuine antiquarian ruin. At the foot of the hill stands the old Royal High School, built between 1825 and 1829 and now designated as home for a future Scottish Parliament.

Five years after its completion, in September 1834, Earl Grey, recently Prime Minister, came to Edinburgh to receive the freedom of the city; and in the courtyard of the High School a large pavilion had been erected in which more than 1,500 guests were to attend a grand dinner in his honour. Covering the day's proceedings for the *Morning Chronicle* and on his first journalistic assignment outside London, was the young Charles Dickens, and in his account of the preliminaries to the dinner already exhibiting the unique comic gift that in a score of books was to make him famous:

It had been announced that the dinner would take place at five-o-clock precisely; but Earl Grey and the other principal visitors, as might have been expected, did not arrive until shortly after six. Previous to their arrival, some slight confusion and much merriment was excited by the following circumstance: – A gentleman who, we presume, having entered with one of the first sections, having sat with exemplary patience for some time in the immediate vicinity of cold fowls, roast beef, lobsters and other tempting delicacies (for the dinner was a cold one) appeared to think that the best thing he could possibly do would be to eat his dinner while there was anything to eat. He accordingly laid about him with right goodwill; the example was contagious, and the clatter of knives and forks became general. Hereupon several gentlemen who were not hungry, cried out 'Shame!' and looked very indignant; and several gentlemen who were hungry, cried 'Shame!' too, eating nevertheless all the while as fast as they possibly could. In this dilemma one of the stewards mounted a bench and feelingly represented to the delinquents the enormity of their conduct, implored them for decency's sake, to defer the process of mastication until the arrival of Earl Grey. This address was loudly cheered but totally unheeded; and this is, perhaps, one of the few instances on record of a dinner having been virtually concluded before it began.

Seven years later, with *Pickwick*, *Oliver Twist* and *Nicholas Nickleby* behind him, Dickens returned to Edinburgh, this time to receive the freedom of the city himself. He and his wife were given a set of rooms in the Royal Hotel facing the castle, and on his first morning he was taken to the Parliament Hall to meet some of the advocates, Writers to the Signet and others; among them one whom he described with his extraordinary eye for detail, as 'a tall, burly handsome man of eight and fifty, the bluest eye you can imagine and long hair – longer than mine – falling down in a wild way under the broad brim of his hat. He had on a surtout coat, a blue checked shirt; the collar standing up, and kept in its place by a wisp of black neckerchief; no waistcoat; and a large pocket handkerchief thrust into his breast which was all broad and open. At his heels followed a wiry, sharp-eyed shaggy devil of a terrier, dogging his steps as he went slashing up and down, now with one man beside him, now with another, and now quite alone, but always at a fast, rolling pace with his head in the air, and his eyes as wide open as he could get them.'

This was my three times great grandfather Professor John Wilson, alias Christopher North, Newdigate Poem prize-winner at Oxford, columnist and critic of *Blackwood's Magazine*, popular lecturer to crowded university classrooms, and whose portrait by Sir John Watson Gordon hangs above me as I write. He was to take the chair at the celebratory dinner in Dickens's honour. 'A bright, clear-complexioned, mountain-looking fellow,' Dickens continued, 'he looks as though he had just come down from the Highlands, and had never in his life taken pen in hand. But he has had an attack of paralysis in his right arm, within this month. He winced when I shook hands with him; and once or twice when we were walking up and down, slipped as if he had stumbled on a piece of orange-peel. He is a great fellow to look at, and to talk to.'

The day after the dinner Dickens wrote, 'The great event is over, and I am a man again. It was the most brilliant affair you can conceive . . . The room was crammed, and more than seventy applicants for tickets were of necessity refused yesterday. Wilson was ill, but plucked up like a lion and spoke famously.' Wilson gave the toast to Scottish literature, Dickens to the memory of the Scottish painter David Wilkie who had recently died. 'I *think* (ahem!),' he wrote, 'that I spoke rather well', and despite what he called the 'enthoostemoosy' (the enthusiastic reception given him), boasted of being as cool as a cucumber. Earlier that day he had been given the freedom of the city, and the parchment scroll on which it was recorded hung in his study until the day he died.

Dickens visited Scotland on several other occasions for performances of his famous readings; and when chairing a dinner in London to raise funds for the Great Ormond Street Hospital for Sick Children, he recalled an encounter with a sick child which he had had in the slums of Edinburgh's Old Town some years before. Dickens's gifts of comedy, pathos, vivid characterization and a strong narrative line were his outstanding qualities as a novelist. Here in Edinburgh and in real life not fiction he showed all of them, his comic account of the Earl Grey dinner, his acute observation of Wilson in Parliament Hall, and now the narrative skills and pathos of the visit to the sick child in the Old Town slums as recounted at the Great Ormond Street dinner:

> Our way lay from one to another of the most wretched dwellings, reeking with horrible odours; shut out from the sky and from the air, mere pits and dens. In a room in one of these places, where there was an empty porridge-pot on the cold hearth, a ragged woman and some ragged children crouching on the bare ground near it – and, I remember as I speak, where the very light, refracted from a high, damp-stained wall outside, came in trembling, as if the fever which had shaken everything else had shaken even it – there lay, in an old egg-box which the mother had begged from a shop, a little feeble, wan, sick child. With his little wasted face and his little hot worn hands folded over his breast, and his little, bright attentive eyes, I can see him now, as I have seen him for several years, looking steadily at us. There he lay in his small, frail box, which was not at all a bad emblem of the small body from which he was slowly parting – there he lay, quite quiet, quite patient, saying never a word. He seldom cried, his mother said; he seldom complained; 'he lay there seemin' to woonder what it was a' aboot'. God knows, I thought, as I stood looking at him, he had his reasons for wondering . . .

The dinner raised £3,000 for the hospital which Dickens later supplemented by funds from a public recital of his *Christmas Carol*; and from that moment, said one of his biographers, the Great Ormond Street hospital never looked back.*

*In 1988 a public appeal for funds for rebuilding and refurbishment brought in more than £54 million pounds.

# CHAPTER 19

## *The Sermon on the Mound*

AT THE TOP OF THE MOUND AND LOOKING DOWN FROM A GREAT height (as many think proper) on Princes Street and its gardens stands the Assembly Hall of the Church of Scotland, the national Church north of the border although not established as the Church of England is to the south of it.

If the Church of Scotland today no longer preaches the harsh asceticism of its founders, its chief characteristic, says its official guide, may still be classed as the Scottish one of reserve. Until this century Christmas and Easter were not even recognized, while today neither Boxing Day nor Easter Monday are public holidays, while the New Year, with its promise in a cold climate of rebirth and renewal, is thought a more appropriate time for temporal if not spiritual celebration.

An Anglican visitor to a Scottish kirk would be startled to find how distant is the form of service to which he is accustomed. No prayer-books are issued for the simple reason that the congregation is not required to make responses, and in music it is only within the last 150 years that hymns have been permitted to take over from the metrical version of the Psalms. At one time organs were forbidden;

and the Eucharist which in John Knox's time and for long after was celebrated only once or twice a year is now in most churches celebrated once a month.

There are no bishops and at baptisms no godparents. There is no kneeling, only a little leaning forward, a custom which used to lead the Episcopalian street urchins in the last century to shout at Kirk congregations, 'Presby, Presby, never bend. Sit on your seat on Man's chief end!' and for Church of Scotland boys to bawl at Episcopalian congregations, 'Pisky, Pisky, Amen. Down on your knees and up again!'

Any comparison therefore between a Kirk and Anglican service results in this paradox: that while the Church of Scotland prides itself on its democracy (the cause of the famous 1843 walkout of ministers to form their own Free Church was their objection to the rights of local lairds, as in England, to appoint ministers to livings) the conduct of its services is quite autocratic; the minister is the shepherd, his flock (hymns apart) dumb sheep. By contrast an Anglican service seems more democratic, the priest inviting the congregation to respond to his prayers and to join with him in turning to the altar (or Table as the Scots call it, feeling no doubt that 'altar' is too suggestive of fatted calves and burnt offerings) and saying with him one of the creeds that are the core of his beliefs. Against this though the Kirk has been at a loss to understand why the Church of England has been tearing itself apart in the matter of women priests. Women ministers in Scotland have been ordained since 1968, and of the new elders who are ordained each year, 40 per cent are women.

For most of the year the Church of Scotland makes no use of its Assembly Hall, letting it out for conferences and seminars and, during the Edinburgh Festival, for plays. It was here, in one of the early festivals, that Sir David Lyndsay of the Mount's famous play, *Ane Satyre of the Thrie Estaites*, was first put on to much critical acclaim.

But once a year in May the Hall comes into its own when it hosts for a week the Church of Scotland's General Assembly. This, in its modest way, is quite a grand affair. Because the Kirk is officially recognized, the reigning monarch invites some prominent, establishment-minded Scot to represent her as that year's Lord High Commissioner to the Assembly, to take over the Palace of Holyroodhouse for the week, entertain Scottish and other notables to lunch or dinner and a bed for the night and then attend with him, or her,* some of the next day's proceedings in the Assembly Hall. He goes there in some state, with a police escort, and is greeted first by a guard of honour and trumpeters; and then by the Moderator, dressed up in eighteenth-century court costume: lace ruffs, breeches and buckled shoes, the Kirk's annually elected chief representative. Having arrived at the hall, he is not permitted to enter the body of it. As observers he and his party must troop upstairs to the gallery, as in the Houses of Parliament, where God might sit if he were invited to attend. Below him on a raised dais sit the Moderator and his staff, some in robes and wigs, and on three sides facing them on green leather benches sit the 600 ministers and 600 elders who are the delegates or Commissioners to the Assembly.

Many Scots today will tell you that the annual meetings of the General Assembly have become an anachronism, and that while they are to be cherished as an officially recognized expression of Scottish nationhood, the Assembly is a poor substitute for a Scottish Parliament which many, perhaps most Commissioners, feel to be in the offing. Most of the Assembly's debates are centred on purely Church affairs, but one full day is given over to political debates organized by the Church and Nation Committee: these could be about the desirability or otherwise of nuclear weapons on Scottish soil, the economics of the Highlands and Islands or some topic of wider concern such as Britain in Europe or Aid to the Third World. Yet however topical and sometimes passionate these debates may be, it has to be said that the General Assembly has no power to give effect to its conclusions and has no more influence than any other non-political body. But for many ministers and elders and their wives it is a happy social occasion, giving those who have shifted parishes the opportunity to renew old friendships and create new ones.

It was to this gathering, in May of 1988, that the Prime Minister of the day, Margaret Thatcher, dressed in a sky-blue two-piece outfit, delivered an address to the Assembly which has since come to be known in Scotland as 'The Sermon on the Mound'.

'I am greatly honoured', she began, 'to have been invited to attend the opening of this 1988 Assembly of the Church of Scotland and

*In 1970 Margaret Herbison became the first woman Lord High Commissioner.

I am deeply grateful that you have now asked me to address you.'

The Moderator of that year's General Assembly was the Very Reverend Dr James Whyte, then Professor Emeritus of Practical Theology and Christian Ethics at the University of St Andrews. 'That opening sentence of the Prime Minister', he was to write later, 'was a little naughty. It gave the impression that it was the Church which had issued both the invitation to attend and the invitation to speak. This was not the case. She was there of her own choice. The invitation to speak was the Church's courteous response to her presence.'

The facts were these. The Prime Minister was then having a rough time in the opinion polls, particularly in Scotland where, at the general election the year before her party had been reduced to a rump of nine seats out of seventy-two, their lowest number since 1910. Nor, because of the strident Englishness of her manner, had she ever been a popular personality in Scotland. I had better declare an interest here and say that that has been my view too. Although she has the reputation of being privately charming and considerate (as I once experienced*), I have always found her public persona almost totally repulsive – pretentious, raucous, humourless, vain.† 'She can use the most hackneyed language', wrote Jonathan Raban, 'as if she had minted it that morning [and] wears it like a badge of virtue.' No doubt it was this trait – her very ordinariness, combined with gutsiness – which the common or garden of the electorate recognized in themselves, and led them to return her to Downing Street for eleven and a half years. Yet her tendency to bestow Prime Ministerial patronage on those she considered 'one of us' and deny it to others better fitted for the job was akin to the political jobbery of the eighteenth century. No other Conservative Prime Minister in my lifetime has been so far removed from the Disraelian concept of One Nation, no other Prime Minister of modern times has better exemplified Lord Acton's dictum about the corrupting influence of power.

Apart from her personal unpopularity in Scotland, there were two political reasons why she and her government were resented there: first the news that the ill-fated community charge or poll

---

*See *On My Way to the Club*, pp. 354–355.
†To which I would add, having seen the three television programmes on her premiership mounted by the BBC after her fall from power, histrionic, self-pitying and partly deranged.

tax was to be foisted on Scotland a year before the rest of the country (why Scotland?); and secondly cuts in welfare benefits which had been severely felt in the poorest parishes of the Lowland Belt. With the Conservatives then holding only nine of Scotland's seventy-two Parliamentary seats, the time had come to retrieve the situation. First, arrangements were made for Mrs Thatcher to watch a Glasgow football match, a pastime for which she had never shown any previous enthusiasm and which must have bored her rigid. Her next ploy was more devious. A message was passed from her office in London to the Lord High Commissioner of that year's forthcoming General Assembly, Captain Iain Tennant (now Sir Iain, KT), a North of Scotland landowner. The message was this: that she would very much like to attend the opening session of the Assembly and to speak at it; and Captain Tennant duly passed this on.

Dr Whyte and those who arranged the Assembly's business found themselves in a dilemma. While the Church of Scotland, like that of England, had always felt itself free to criticize government policy and would do so on Church and Nation Day later in the week, the opening session of the Assembly had always been free of controversy. The Lord High Commissioner would make some anodyne remarks to which the Moderator would make a suitably anodyne reply. But Dr Whyte and his colleagues were no fools and as aware as anyone in Scotland that if the Prime Minister (or rather *this* Prime Minister) was allowed to address the Assembly, it could only be to make political capital.

So what was Dr Whyte to do? He could not have been unaware that a few years earlier, when the question arose of Oxford University granting her an honorary degree, the members of the Hebdomadal Council, smarting from her government's cuts in university funding, had voted against. If he were to ask the Assembly, as by the rules he had to, to vote as to whether they wanted to hear her speak or not, they might want to debate the matter and then she might be given the same and even more humiliating (because more public) dusty answer. What was the alternative? 'We could have avoided the problem,' he wrote later, 'by pretending she wasn't there. But that would have been a discourtesy to her office and unworthy of the Established Church.'

So there was nothing for it but to go ahead and hope for the best. When Captain Tennant and Mrs Thatcher had taken their places in the gallery and the Convener of the Business Committee had drawn

301

formal attention to their presence, Dr Whyte posed the question, 'Is it the will of the Assembly that the Prime Minister be invited to address the Assembly?' Although at that moment no one could be sure of how things would go, the shock of seeing this creature from outer space among them and even more their curiosity as to what she had to say (for there had been no press handout) swayed even those Commissioners to whom she and her works were anathema. The motion was agreed to, but also in accordance with the rules, Dr Whyte invited those who disagreed to show their dissent. There was a great rumbling of feet on the floor, and a large number of ministers and elders from those parishes most hit by the cuts came forward. When they had retaken their seats, sky-blue Mrs Thatcher came down from the gods to address them.

With her superficial knowledge of theology, it says something for Mrs Thatcher's effrontery, not to say insensitivity, in thinking she had something of value to say to an audience of theologians and divines, many as far to the left politically as she was to the right, and who had been steeped in the teachings of the Bible for most of their adult lives. What she did say was a weird amalgam of fundamental Conservatism and simplistic Sunday school homilies.

She cantered off by declaring that most Christians would consider it their duty to help their fellow men and women and to regard the lives of children as a precious trust, but that a number of people (number not stated but assumed to be a minority) not Christians would also go along with that − a statement of such blinding obviousness that, as one commentator put it, without acting on such beliefs society would collapse. What then was so distinctive about Christianity? For her the buzz word was choice, God allowing us to choose between good and evil, Christ choosing to die for our sins rather than live. But, as Dr Whyte was to point out afterwards, there were thousands of very poor people in Britain who had very little choice; and surely as Christians we could not wash our hands of them.

In her next passage Mrs Thatcher said that 'in my early life we all agreed that if you try to take the fruits of Christianity without its roots, the fruits will wither.' No-one to whom I have shown this passage can tell me what it means. Perhaps Mrs Thatcher, having discovered that 'roots' and 'fruits' rhymed, felt she ought to make something of it. Jonathan Raban, who devoted a whole booklet, *God, Man and Mrs Thatcher*, to analysing Mrs Thatcher's speech, called it 'a Mystical Conundrum, an Impenetrable Mystery'. He does however pick up the bombastic phrase 'In my early life' where most people would say 'in my childhood' or, if a woman, 'when I was a girl'. Raban says that this is Mrs Thatcher seeing herself, as during the Falklands affair, in a heroic light, *My Early Life* being the title of one of Winston Churchill's books.

She concluded her remarks on Christianity by saying that one reason Christians go to church is because they accept the sanctity of life. This from a woman who during her time in Parliament had consistently advocated and voted for the killing of those who killed.

She moved on to biblical exegesis, explaining to those divines who were unaware of it that the Old Testament taught us to love our neighbour and obey the law and that the New Testament was a record of the Incarnation, the teachings of Christ and the coming of the kingdom of God. From these two books combined, she said, 'we gain a view of the universe, a proper attitude to work and principles to shape economic and social life'. What our view of the universe was or should be, she didn't say. *A proper attitude to work* was a dig at the scroungers and idlers who shirked work and who St Paul had in mind when he told the Thessalonians that a man who didn't work wouldn't eat. Not a word about the two million plus unemployed most of whom were desperate for work which was consistently denied them. The Bible tells us to work hard to create wealth, said Mrs Thatcher, and the spiritual dimension came in deciding what to do with the wealth. In her book it was to 'answer the many calls for help, invest for the future and support the wonderful artists and craftsmen whose work also glorifies God'. The inference was that to spend money on non-spiritual things was deplorable and doubtless she hoped that her Church of Scotland audience with its long tradition of self-denial would agree. Dr Whyte thought otherwise. 'To sum up the social teaching of the Bible as "Create wealth" is a grotesque distortion. It ignores all the hard teaching of the prophets and almost everything said about money in the New Testament.'

During her time in office Mrs Thatcher was always banging on about 'our heritage' and the importance of history, largely I fancy because she lacked any sense of them herself, and turning to religious education she spoke of the importance of children being given a good grounding in the Bible. 'It is quite impossible to understand our literature or history without grasping this fact'. Then, giving the impression of assuming her audience to be as well acquainted with Shakespeare and Sir Walter Scott as herself, she asked how anyone could make sense of their works without a knowledge of the Bible. One could in fact make sense of them all; so that one begs to doubt whether Mrs Thatcher has ever turned more than a page of either Shakespeare or Scott in her life, and that even if she had, that she would have progressed very far with either.

She moved on to immigrants and how they had always been welcomed here and assured of equality under the law. 'There is absolutely nothing incompatible between this and our desire to maintain the essence of our own identity.' Emphatic negatives, wrote Jonathan Raban, always suggest that what is being denied may be what is being asserted; for having the occasional stranger in the house doesn't normally threaten the essence of the host's identity. Yet, although Mrs Thatcher was aware of the fears of many people of being overrun by Asians and West Indians and had said so in an interview with Kenneth Harris, she was seemingly quite unaware that this was an English and not a Scottish problem.*

Yet her two crassest remarks Mrs Thatcher kept to the end. The first concerned the Gettysburg Address, President Lincoln's ringing tribute to the dead of the American civil war, delivered on one of its bloodiest battlefields. I once heard Mrs Thatcher read this on a recording which should never have been allowed, for with every word she uttered in her pedestrian, unfeeling way, it was clear that the beauty and substance of Lincoln's simple words had entirely eluded her. Here she referred to it as Lincoln's 'famous Gettysburg *speech*', as an uneducated person might, and described it as 'a neat definition of democracy which has since been widely and enthusiastically adopted' – language that a twelve-year-old might express in a school essay. The triviality of this interpretation was compounded when she went on to say that what Lincoln enunciated as a form of government ('of the people, by the people, for the people') was not in itself specifically Christian, '*for nowhere in the Bible is the word democracy mentioned*'. Lincoln, said Raban, was *not* giving a neat definition of democracy but pointing to the brute injustice of the rule of the South and to the moral ascendancy of the North. 'He is treated by Mrs Thatcher as a fringe-bearded simpleton. Yet at

*Of the 3 million blacks and Asians resident in the United Kingdom, 2.9 million live in England (Office of Population Statistics).

Gettysburg he was offering something far more explicitly Christian than anything said by Mrs Thatcher in Edinburgh.'

Nevertheless, said Mrs Thatcher, even if the word democracy was not in the Bible, she was an enthusiast for it because it safeguarded the value of the individual 'and, more than any other system, restrains the abuse of power by the few'. Later Dr Whyte spoke for many Commissioners when he said, 'That of course has not been exactly the experience of the Scots in recent years', for in Scotland it was the few – the nine Conservative MPs – who represented British power and abuses, while it was the electorate in the other sixty-three seats who, to no effect, had voted against them.

Then came her conclusions, prefaced by her claim which caused a lifting of eyebrows among the Commissioners, that the politician's role was a humble one, humility never having been one of Mrs Thatcher's strong points. The whole debate about Church and State, she said, had never yielded anything comparable in insight to that beautiful hymn, 'I vow to thee, my country'. This was a complete non-sequitur. She quoted the first two lines of the hymn ('I vow to thee, my country, all earthly things above/Entire and whole and perfect, the service of my love') which she described as 'secular patriotism – a noble thing indeed in a country such as ours' (why only ours?). The faces of some Commissioners looked baffled, as well they might, for no-one on Mrs Thatcher's staff had thought to tell her that this very English hymn, so popular in country churches during the Great War in its call to England's young men to enlist, is virtually unknown in Scotland.

Yet again she compounded one piece of ignorance with another. The second of the hymn's two stanzas begins with the line 'And there's another country I heard of long ago/ Most dear to them that love her, most great to them that know', which of course is Heaven, the final resting-place of those who, having answered the call to arms, were killed. The last two lines of this stanza are 'And soul by soul and silently her shining bounds increase/And her ways are ways of gentleness and all her paths are peace.' I have always found those lines, especially when sung by a massed choir, very poignant, but its effect on Mrs Thatcher was to launch her into a flight of fancy so dotty as almost to make one gasp. What the author of the hymn, Cecil Spring-Rice, saw as something mystical and moving, Mrs Thatcher interpreted as a reassertion of her belief in rampant individualism. 'Not group by group, or party by party, or even church by church,' she told the astonished Commissioners, '*but soul by soul*'.

Now she was ready for the *coup de grâce*. 'That, members of the Assembly, is the country which you chiefly serve.' Did she really mean that? The country of the dead? Did the Commissioners not also and rather more chiefly serve the living – the poor, the dispossessed, the sick, those in need of spiritual comfort? Apparently not. 'You fight your cause under the banner of an historic church. Your success matters greatly . . .' To Mrs Thatcher all causes had to be fought but the Commissioners, by now quite bulldozed, didn't *look* like fighters and I doubt if that is how they regarded themselves. And to wish *success* to an historic church – a word more applicable to a business about to launch an export drive – was also a rum way of viewing things. But then, outwith politics, Mrs Thatcher has always had a woolly way with words. In anyone less cocksure, it could have been part of her charm.

Apart from the approval of Lord Hailsham the speech had an almost universally bad press, the general consensus being that it is not the business of politicians to mix politics with religion, especially when they knew so little about it. To *The Sunday Times* it was an unedifying spectacle; to Jonathan Raban an audacious piece of work, 'in which historical ignorance turns into a kind of precious freedom, a dismal paucity of phrase is recast as vibrant simplicity and the inert cliché as a warrant of the homely common touch'. Dr Whyte called it 'quite bizarre'.

Some Commissioners had hoped that the Church and Nation Committee might have found room to debate it on the Thursday, and thus give those most resentful of it the opportunity to tell the Assembly and the country what they thought. But the Committee declined. It had been bad enough having to sit and listen to the wretched thing. To allow it any further lease of life by debating it would have given the impression that it was worth debating. In their view it was not; the sooner it died a death the better.

There was no evidence afterwards that the speech had helped to retrieve Mrs Thatcher's unpopularity in Scotland in any way.

# CHAPTER 20

## The End of an Old Song

OPPOSITE ST GILES, ON THE SOUTH-WEST CORNER OF PARLIAMENT Square, are the Scottish Law Courts, i.e. the Court of Session and the High Court of Justiciary, and within their precincts stands an ancient building that was once the beating heart of a living Scotland and is now, like much else in Edinburgh, part of the dead museum of Scotland's past.

I mean the Parliament Hall which Charles I ordered to be built in 1632 to provide new accommodation for Parliament, the Court of Session and the Privy Council. Completed in 1639, it was opened in a ceremony as lavish as that of the annual opening of the Westminster Parliament today. What was called 'the riding of Parliament' (and by some 'The Splendid Display of Haberdashery') began when a mounted procession of members of the new Parliament set off from the Palace of Holyroodhouse up the Canongate and High Street. The burgesses of the Royal Burghs led the way followed by the shire commissioners and the nobility. Next came the regalia of Scotland followed by Lord Lyon King of Arms with trumpeters, pursuivants and heralds, and after them the King's Commissioner in Scotland and attendants. At the entrance to the Parliament Hall the Commissioner was received by the Lord High Constable and the Earl Marischal who escorted him to the throne before which the regalia had been laid. The Commissioner declared the Parliament open and the three Estates got down to business.

Parliamentary business, during the first sixty years in its new home, consisted of the great events of the day such as the revolution against Charles I, the Solemn League and Covenant, the Irish Rebellions of 1641, the campaigns of Montrose, and in addition the routine matters with which all Parliaments are concerned: Supply and Excise, sea-fishing and salt, Quartering of Soldiers and Defence of the Realm. It had other functions too. In 1650 it tried the captured Montrose for treason and sentenced him to death and quartering. Eleven years later it did the same to the Marquis of Argyll who was executed by the Maiden, the Scottish forerunner of the French guillotine. The Hall was also used for entertaining royalty; among those who attended banquets in it were Charles II, his brother James when acting as his Commissioner, George IV and, in 1994, the King and Queen of Norway. But above all it was a place for parliamentary business; and as the troubled seventeenth century gave way to the eighteenth century, the Estates had to consider an Act greater in every way than any that had gone before; an Act for their own abolition; that, following the union of Crowns in 1603 whereby Mary's Protestant son James had become king of England as well as Scotland, there should now be a union of Parliaments.

The idea was not a new one. When James told the English Parliament in 1607, 'Here I sit and govern Scotland by my pen, I write and it is done . . . which others could not do by the sword', he knew as well as anyone the disadvantages of having one of his Parliaments a stone's throw from his residence and the other 400 miles to the north. Perhaps if he had ever fulfilled his promise of visiting Scotland once every three years, the problem would have been less acute: but he only returned once in his entire reign and that against the wishes of his Privy Council. When in the same year a bill for Parliamentary union was laid before the English Parliament, it was rejected decisively, members fearing not only a massive incursion into England of Scots on the make, as well as hordes of beggars, but England being flooded with cheap Scottish goods. Nor was the Scottish Parliament any more keen, its members fearing that their country would become what one called 'a conquered and slavish province governed by a Viceroy or Deputy'.

James's ideas were before their time which, because of the turbulent religious conflicts in England and Scotland during the reign of Charles I followed by Cromwell and the civil war, had to wait until the century had almost ended. What paved the way to eventual Union was the so-called Glorious Revolution of 1689; the abdication of the Catholic James II and VII and the accession of the Protestant William of Orange and his wife Mary, who was James's daughter. Protestantism was once again the common religion of both countries (and our secular age should not underestimate its then importance) just as English or variations of it was increasingly becoming the common language.

In the last decade of the seventeenth century a number of events occurred which accelerated the move towards union. The first in 1692 was the famous massacre in the pass of Glencoe, in which Wagnerian setting government-led troops butchered thirty-eight members of the clan Macdonald and put their barns and dwellings to the torch because their chief Maclain had not signed his oath of submission to the king until the deadline for it had passed. Next came the two ill-fated Darien expeditions in which an organization called the Company of Scotland, recognizing the possibilities for overseas expansion and trade such as the English had pursued since the days of Drake, planned to establish a colony on the isthmus of Darien in Central America. When they heard of it the English, jealous of any competitor to their own East India Company, persuaded the merchants of Amsterdam and Hamburg not to invest in it. So the bulk of the capital was raised from private sources in Scotland (representing, it was said, a quarter of Scotland's wealth). A further embarrassment for the king was that Darien belonged to Spain, the ally of his enemy France. Both expeditions ended in disaster: in the first, one in four of the hopeful settlers died of fever or from attacks by natives; those of the second surrendered to the Spanish. The investors lost everything.

To add to Scotland's economic plight the failure of the harvest in 1698 and 1699 led to an estimated 5–7 per cent of the population dying of starvation.* The English Navigation Act and tariffs against

---

*'Many stories were handed on for generations afterwards; about men dropping dead with grass or raw flesh in their mouths; about sons vainly trying to carry their father's corpse to be buried and falling from hunger by the way; about respectable tenants forced to buy bread for their children from pitiless neighbours who themselves succumbed later to the Wrath of God' (T.C. Smout, Union of the Parliaments).

certain Scottish goods had further depressed the Scottish economy so that their desire for union was, as one historian put it, not because they were poor and saw no way to riches but union, but because they were poor and rapidly getting poorer. They knew they were caught in a vice; that any union agreeable to the English would have to be on their terms; and that if these were refused, war would probably follow.

The English, however, still remained lukewarm — apart from the King who saw it as the only means of controlling Scotland and, before he died in 1702, he urged his heir, sister-in-law Anne, to think the same (which she did). But now a new problem arose. With the death of her eleven-year-old son, the Duke of Gloucester, it looked as though Anne would die childless. If so, who would be *her* successor? Without consulting or even informing the Scottish Parliament, the English Parliament decided it would be issue of Sophia the Electress of Hanover who was descended from Elizabeth of Bohemia, a daughter of James I and VI. The response of the Scots to this was the Act of Security and Succession, the inspiration of a formidable East Lothian laird, the much respected Andrew Fletcher of Saltoun. By it Scotland refused to ratify a Hanoverian succession unless Scottish government was severed from 'English or any other foreign influence' while a further Act gave Scotland the option of contracting out of English foreign policy, including wars, that was not in Scotland's interest (as the current one, with France and Spain, certainly wasn't). This posed a threat to England's security, for an independent Scotland could, if it wished, make peace with France, even revive the Auld Alliance. So in March 1705 the Westminster Parliament passed the Alien Act by which, unless within nine months the Scottish Parliament had agreed to negotiate for an Incorporating Union, all non-naturalized Scots in England would be treated as aliens, all Scottish estates in England would be seized and all Scotland's major exports to England (cattle, linen, wool) would be barred. The angry response of the Scots was for agents of The Company of Scotland to arrest the English ship the *Worcester* on a bogus charge of piracy and summarily execute the captain and two of his crew.

But by now the die was cast, and when tempers had cooled, the Scots agreed to the establishment of a Commission of thirty-one members each of English and Scots to meet in Whitehall to hammer out an agreement; such an agreement to be voted on separately by their two Parliaments. On the evening of 1 September 1706 the Duke of Hamilton, ostensibly against Union but always with an eye to feathering his own nest, proposed to the Estates that the appointments of the Commissioners should be left to the Queen. A snap vote was passed by four votes with the result that all the Scottish Commissioners were pro Union with the exception of Lockhart of Carnwath, a Jacobite who had no idea why he had been chosen.

Another Scottish duke whose services the English sought to further the Union was Argyll, at this time serving as a colonel under Marlborough on the Continent. He was an arrogant, pushy young man whom Marlborough cordially disliked, and this is how he replied to a request from the English Lord Treasurer to return to Scotland and bring his influence to bear. 'My Lord, it is surprising to me that my Lord Treasurer, who is a man of sense, should think of sending me up and down like a footman from one country to another without ever offering me any reward.' Sore at his name having been omitted from the recent promotions, he added, 'My Lord, when I have justice done me here and am told what to expect for going to Scotland, I shall be ready to obey my Lord Treasurer's commands.' Whereupon he was given immediate promotion and a promise of further rewards for promoting Union when it came to be debated in the Scottish Parliament.

Ideally the Scots would have liked a federal union which would have let them retain their own Parliament, but the *realpolitik*, they recognized, was that it was to be an Incorporating Union or nothing. This having been established, the Commissioners in Whitehall met in separate rooms and communicated only in writing. Despite or perhaps because of this, they agreed within ten days of first meeting on the broad outlines of an agreement and in a further ten weeks they had completed all twenty-five articles.

Of these the most important were the four which decreed that the kingdoms of England and Scotland would henceforth become the United Kingdom of Great Britain, that the succession would be Protestant, that the Westminster Parliament would be that of Great Britain, and that after the Treaty had come into effect, all the subjects of the United Kingdom would have full freedom of trade and navigation to and from all ports in the kingdom and those of the Dominions and Plantations belonging to them. And Britain itself would be a free trade area of seven million people.

In some ways Scotland was given a poor deal; in the matter of Parliamentary representation, for instance, she was allocated only forty-five seats, or one more than rural Cornwall, to England's 513, while only sixteen elected Scottish peers would join the 190 English in the Lords; and for the sake of uniformity Scottish regulations concerning Trade, Customs, Excise, Taxes, Coinage, Weights and Measures, etc., were to be abolished in favour of existing English ones. On the credit side, however, Scotland was to receive what was called The Equivalent, a sum of nearly £400,000 to compensate partly for the losses to the investors in the two Darien schemes and partly to fund the Scottish national debt. Even more important it was agreed that Scotland was to keep her own Presbyterian Church, system of education and legal system. This meant that England lost her sovereignty in theory but not in practice but that Scotland lost in both; that Scotland would be the only advanced country in the world that had, as it still has today, its own law and law courts but not its own legislature; that English nationalism would become British nationalism and that while Scottish nationalism might remain in abeyance, it would never die.

Because it was known that ratification of the Treaty by the English Parliament would go through almost on the nod, it was agreed that it should first be debated by the Scottish Parliament where strong opposition was expected. So on 3 October 1706 the Estates – representing the nobles, the shires and the burghs – assembled in Parliament Hall to go through the Treaty clause by clause. The proceedings would be conducted by the Queen's Commissioner in Scotland, the Duke of Queensberry, described as short and swarthy, much disliked by the Queen but with the reputation of being the most persuasive politician in Scotland. His chief supporter and Secretary of State, the Earl of Mar, a Jacobite, was described as a skilled private negotiator.

Just three weeks after the debate had opened, Daniel Defoe, the author of *Robinson Crusoe*, who was attending both as observer and English agent, wrote that when about to return from Parliament Hall to his lodgings the night before, he

> found the whole city in a most dreadfull uproar and the High Street full of the rabble. In this posture things stood about 8 to 9 o-clock and the street seeming passable, I salleyed out and got to my Lodging. I had not been long there but I heard a

great noise and looking out saw a terrible multitude come up the High Street with a drum at the head of them, shouting and swearing and crying out all Scotland would stand together. No Union, No Union, English dogs and the like.

A little later the Earl of Mar had the same experience. 'I am not very timorous,' he wrote, 'and yet I tell you that every day here we are in hazard of our lives. We cannot go on the streets but we are insulted.'

The only person not to be insulted, it seemed, was the Duke of Hamilton, described as ambitious and haughty, of middle stature and with a black, coarse complexion, playing his game of double bluff. Lord Leven, governor of the castle, observed the mob not only escorting him to the Parliament with repeated cheers 'but gave such loud huzzas when his grace entered the House as were heard by all the members when sitting on their benches.'

Such demonstrations were replicated in Glasgow, Dumfries, Perth and other places, exhibiting the very real depth of feelings of ordinary people at the imminent prospect of – as they rightly thought – Scotland surrendering to her age-old enemy. Throughout Scotland, Defoe reported, there was a general aversion to Union: Sir John Clerk of Penicuik said that three-quarters of the population were against it: addresses and petitions urging Parliament to reject it came from the General Assembly of the Church of Scotland who feared the spread of Episcopacy, the Generality of Freeholders, the magistrates. And yet in some quarters opinion was divided. The Convention of Royal Burghs voted 24 in favour, 20 against, with 22 abstentions; and as Professor Smout points out, three-quarters of the burghs and two-thirds of the shires sent no petitions at all.

The hard fact was that some merchants and the bulk of the aristocracy knew what the populace did not know: the dire straits of the Scottish economy, with no revenue coming in to pay off accumulating debts. Truthfully, if characteristically bluntly, the Duke of Argyll dismissed the addresses and petitions as 'only fit to make kites of' while Mar told the House that Parliament was the only proper judge to consider the terms offered. Defoe, the great democrat who had earlier championed the people of England in respect of *their* Parliament, was equally dismissive. 'They are meddling with what they have no right to be meddling with.' Autocrats Argyll and Mar and Defoe may have been but they

313

were right. The Earl of Roxburgh spoke for his peers when he wrote that the factors that had led them to support Union were, for most, increased trade, for some the Hanoverian succession (and an end to Jacobitism), for others 'ease and security together with a general aversion to civil discords, intolerable poverty and constant oppressions'.

Within Parliament Hall during the three months the debate ran, the atmosphere was often tense. Members complained of the long hours they were obliged to sit and of being unable to assuage their hunger; and of the dangers outside, without troops to protect them. According to Rosalind Mitchison 'the most crucial debates were fought by gentlemen with hands at their sword hilts, late into the night, with lighted candles burning under the painted timbers of the Parliament Hall'. It must have been a dramatic sight.

Of all the speeches against Union the most virulent were those of Andrew Fletcher of Saltoun, described as a 'short, thin man, of a brown complexion, pock-marked, full of fire, wearing a brown pen wig, and with a stern, sour look'. David Hume called him a man of signal probity and fine genius, though all agreed his temper was often his undoing. Earlier in his career he had joined Monmouth's rebellion and in the course of it shot dead a man called Dare in an argument about a horse. Later he went to Spain, then Hungary where he fought in the war against the Turks. In his absence abroad he was sentenced to death in Scotland and had his estate forfeited, but in James II's general amnesty of 1686 he was reprieved. Two years later he joined William of Orange at the Hague and was with him when he landed in England to assume the throne.

In the light of Fletcher's sustained opposition to Union in the final session of the Scottish Parliament, he has achieved sainthood in the canonization of Scottish patriots. It is therefore strange to discover, as Professor Smout has done, an event that took place after William's arrival. At this time a Scottish Convention was preparing to make overtures to the English Parliament for a full Incorporating Union (which the English Parliament subsequently ignored). With this Fletcher expressed himself in agreement. In a letter from London to a friend in Rotterdam dated 8 January 1689, he described a meeting of the new king with a group of Scottish nobles. In regard to Scotland's future he wrote, 'For my own part I think we can never come to any true settlement *but by uniting with England in Parliaments and Trade*' (my italics) adding that there never could be unity in matters of church and law.

What caused Fletcher to adopt such a diametrically opposed view fourteen years later is not known though it was probably disillusion with the English on several counts: their part in the scuppering of the Darien scheme, the French war, the tariffs on Scots goods. Whatever the reason he now threw himself into the case against Union with his customary passion. On one occasion Mar records him being 'in a vast heat' and running out of the House in a rage. Twice the House had to intervene to prevent him fighting duels with the Duke of Hamilton and Lord Stair. Although Mar personally liked Fletcher, he hoped they would still be on speaking terms when the debate was over. Fletcher complained bitterly that the Scottish Commissioners in London had betrayed their trust, 'and so much the more because those who pretended to carry it on were certainly against it in their minds'. 'A damned villainous union', he concluded. 'The whole nation has become rogues' – a phrase that Burns was to pick up seventy years later:

> O would, or I had seen the day
> That treason thus could sell us,
> My auld grey head had lien in clay,
> Wi' Bruce and loyal Wallace!
> But pith and power, till my last hour,
> I'll mak this declaration:–
> We're bought and sold for English gold –
> Such a parcel of rogues in a nation!

Another opposition speaker was Lord Belhaven who argued against a deal that was to leave one of the parties with all its institutions, laws and regulations intact and those of the other subject to amendments or annihilation. 'Good God! What is this?' he exclaimed. 'An entire surrender?'

The most effective speech pro union was that of Seton of Pitmedden. If Scotland was to keep her own Parliament, he said, then in foreign policy she could never please at the same time both England and France, and in any war must eventually succumb to one or the other. As for a federal union which Fletcher and others wanted, how could there be such a thing when one of the two nations involved was so much superior in riches, numbers of people and commerce? In any case England had flatly refused to consider it.

But of all the speakers none could exceed the eccentric behaviour of the Duke of Hamilton. In a flowery speech opposing Union which is said to have brought tears to some members' eyes, he said, 'Shall we in half an hour yield what our forefathers maintained with their lives and fortunes for many ages?'

Then what happened? According to the memoirs of Lockhart of Carnwath, Hamilton planned an armed rising with Jacobites from the north and Presbyterians from the south-west joining forces in the town of Hamilton and marching on Edinburgh to 'raise the Parliament'. When it was well under way, Hamilton reneged on it.

His next proposal was that all those entitled to vote should assemble in Edinburgh to move an address to the Queen to request her to call a new Parliament and General Assembly. Again at the last moment he killed it by proposing a clause approving the Hanoverian succession to which many voters were strongly opposed.

Finally he proposed that a Protestation should be prepared and supported by all members of the House who were opposed to Union who would then march out of the House and not return. Relying on addresses that had been presented to the House showing 'an utter aversion to any such union', the Protestation concluded that the Union was contrary to the Constitution 'by which the people of this ancient kingdom are joined together in a society amongst themselves'. It was strong stuff, but when the time arrived for the Duke to submit the Protestation to the House, toothache kept him at home.

After this opposition crumbled. With comfortable majorities the Articles were passed one by one, and amendments to certain financial provisions which the House asked for were all accepted by the English. When it came to the final vote, it was Mar's words that the House remembered most, that if they failed to approve the Treaty he did not see what they could possibly do to save the country from ruin.

On 16 January 1707 the deed was done and Queensberry touched the Treaty with the royal sceptre. Seafield, who had done so much to push it through, remarked, 'There's an end to an old song', and Fletcher said that Scotland was now only fit for the slaves who had sold it. Queensberry set off south, was met at Barnet by ministers and nobles and escorted into London by forty-six coaches and several hundred horsemen. By 4 March the Treaty had been approved by both Houses, and on the 6th received the Royal Assent. On 1 May the nation states of England and Scotland ceased to exist and the Queen went to St Paul's to give thanks for what only an Englishman could have called 'the greatest of all the victories with which God had blessed her reign'. In Edinburgh the bells of St Giles pealed out, 'Why should I be sad on my wedding-day?'

And Burns's parcel of rogues received their English gold, or offices in lieu of it. They have been much criticized for it yet who can blame them, for many, perhaps most, believed that the Union was as much in their country's interests as their own, and in the long term it was. Queensberry was given a pension of £3,000 a year from the revenue of the post office, became a British peer with the title of the Duke of Dover and appointed joint keeper of the Privy Seal. Mar was also given a pension and made Keeper of the Signet. Hamilton, who had so skilfully ridden with the fox and hunted with the hounds, received the Garter and was appointed British ambassador in Paris (but was killed in a duel before he could take up the post). Argyll, having already been promoted to Major-General, was granted an English peerage in the House of Lords and his brother was created Earl of Islay. And £20,000 was made available to lesser of the Scottish nobility who had helped to push the Union through.

Queensberry did not enjoy his pension for long, for he died in 1711, two years after his duchess. In a vault of Drumlanrig's little hillside parish church of Durisdeer, there is an astonishing memorial to both. On a floor of black marble and beside four fluted black marble pillars stands a sort of raised bed. On its nearside lies the supine effigy in white marble of the beautiful duchess resting on a marble pillow, dressed in her coronation robes, high heeled shoes peeping out from beneath them. Beyond and slightly above her lies the duke, also in white marble, reclining on his right side, with his hand under his head, dressed in the robes of the Garter, wearing a long wig, left leg lying over the right. A contemporary account suggests he is looking at his duchess mournfully; but to me the similarity of his position to that of a recumbent player in a photograph of a Victorian cricket team is striking.

The door to the vault is always open, so that anyone travelling north of Thornhill on the A75 could find a visit to this remarkable

317

and unexpected piece of statuary in the Dumfriesshire hills well worth the five-minute detour.

Before the signing of the Treaty the ever optimistic Daniel Defoe had assured the Scots that they could place every trust in it, that for them a new dawn was about to break. He could not have been more wrong. 'Every interest of Scotland', wrote one historian, 'was treated purely and simply with reference to the exigencies of political parties in England. There was not a class in Scotland which did not have reason to complain of a breach of the Articles of Union and to regret that it had ever been accomplished.' Scottish institutions in need of reform remained frozen in the state they had been in before 1707: trade continued to languish, agriculture was moribund, poverty widespread. The presence of busybody English revenue officials was widely resented, while the abolition of the Scottish Privy Council in 1708 left Scotland even more leaderless than before.

Such was the unrest that Mar, now in the Lords, wrote to Queen Anne in 1708 that 'the generality of this country is still as dissatisfied with the Union as ever and seem mightily soured'. In 1711 he wrote to his brother that he saw no solution to Scotland's hardships but an Act of Parliament to dissolve the Union, yet wondered how this could be brought about without civil war.

The minds of his fellow countrymen in the Lords were moving in the same direction and in 1713, after the Westminster Parliament had imposed the English Malt tax on Scotland (which by the terms of Union they had promised not to do until the present war was over), a motion to dissolve the Union was debated in the Lords. The mover was Lord Seafield, now the Earl of Findlater, and so strong were the feelings of the Scottish representative peers that it failed by only four votes.

Mar then proved himself as inconsistent as others of his former Parliamentary colleagues. George I having succeeded to the throne on the death of Anne in 1714, Mar, to disguise his Jacobite leanings, wrote a flowery letter to the king assuring him he was 'as faithful and dutiful a subject and servant as any of my family have been to the crown or I have been to my late mistress the Queen', adding that he had received documents from many of the most powerful Highland chiefs containing similar tokens of loyalty. Then, having attended a court levee at which the king snubbed him, he changed into the clothes of a workman, boarded a collier sailing to Fife and, within a week of arrival, having gathered the nucleus of a Jacobite army, raised the standard of the Old Pretender, the putative James VIII and III, then about to sail from France. Having recruited a mixed force of some 12,000 men, he set off south. But his way was barred by government forces under the command of his fellow peer and former Parliamentary colleague, Major-General the Duke of Argyll. The duke, although having at his disposal a force half the strength of Mar's, proved more than a match for him, and by the time James landed at Peterhead, the campaign to put him on the British throne had collapsed. After a stay of only six weeks he re-embarked for France: Mar went with him, never to return.

For the whole of the first third of the eighteenth century the Scottish economy remained stagnant, and as late as 1742 Lord President Duncan Forbes was reporting to the Scottish Secretary of State that the revenue was in such decline that the expenses of government could hardly be met. After the failure of the '45 things gradually improved. The introduction of modern methods of agriculture copied from the Dutch led to richer pasture land and increased crops, the black cattle trade from the Highlands into England was expanding, the linen trade too found new markets in the south. Yet almost the most important development was the widening and deepening of the river Clyde in Glasgow, the port that offered the shortest sea route to the American colonies; and west coast merchants were quick to take advantage of it by monopolizing the American tobacco trade and conveniently 'forgetting' the duty they were supposed to pay. West Indian cotton was also imported for refining in the newly built cotton mills at New Lanark and elsewhere. An iron works was established at Carron and there was an increased demand for Scottish coal to service the new industries. The age of Watt and Stephenson was just over the horizon when water power would give way to steam power and Scotsmen would gain a worldwide reputation as engineers.

These enterprises were reflections of a radically changed national attitude of mind. Religious beliefs and differences which had so obsessed the Scottish (and English) peoples during the seventeenth century gave way to a healthy secularism which freed the mind to engage in practical and imaginative ventures, and on an intellectual level found expression in the philosophies of Hume and Adam Smith and the poetry of Allan Ramsay. Less than fifty years after the execution of the Edinburgh student Thomas Aikenhead for publicly doubting the truth of the Trinity, less than thirty years after the last execution for witchcraft, Edinburgh debating societies, of which there were a growing number, were discussing not whether Presbyterianism had the edge over Episcopalianism or vice versa but such metaphysical questions as the existence of a Creator and the immortality of the soul. 'Absolute dogmatic atheism is the present tone,' declared Dr John Gregory, Professor of Physics at Edinburgh University, and in France Voltaire praised the onward march in Scotland of the human spirit.

Edinburgh, the second biggest city in the United Kingdom, was sloughing off the deep conservatism to which it had long been in thrall. The advances of the university's medical school became the envy of those in England. The law continued to develop and, despite dogmatic atheism, the General Assembly held its own. Theatres which had been repressed for decades opened their doors and in the exuberant reception given to John Home's patriotic play *Douglas*, a voice was heard shouting, 'Whaur's yer Wully Shakespeare noo?' Balls, under the guidance of a sister of Lord Mansfield, were held in the New Assembly Rooms, and there was a rich social life in both Old and New towns. The living conditions of the poor however, remained as squalid and cramped as ever.

And yet, despite the opportunities for employment which so many new ventures offered, Scotland, and especially the Highlands, still had a surplus of population. Some came south to find work in England as they do today, others took up posts on the Continent or joined as mercenaries the armies of foreign powers. And while the emigrant ships continued to take the poor and dispossessed across the sea to new lives in Canada and America, others signed up with the East India Company, Royal Navy or one of the newly formed Scottish regiments to play their part in conquering, garrisoning and administering the greatest empire, now long forgotten, the world had yet seen.

After the Union, Parliament Hall reverted to what it had always been in part: an assembly hall for the courts of law, especially for the Court of Session, established in 1532 as the supreme court in Scotland for civil cases, as it is today; and later, for criminal cases, it accommodated the High Court of Justiciary. In the eighteenth century pleadings and arguments were made in writing, not spoken.

'Ours is a court of papers,' said Boswell, 'we are never seriously engaged but when we write.' Lord Cockburn echoed him: 'Every statement, every argument, every application was made in writing. Eight out of every twelve hours of the lives of these men [counsel] were spent over inkstands'. The judges came to resent the burden, encouraging advocacy. 'My dear Sir,' one said to Boswell, 'give yourself no trouble in the composition of the papers you present to us, for it is casting pearls before swine.'

A curious development that took place before the Union and was allowed to continue long after it was the establishment of shops in the Hall: a hardware merchant's, a hatter's, a jeweller's, a cutler's, a bookseller's. There was also a coffee house 'with partitions made of the slimmest materials, some of them of brown paper.' Lord Cockburn recalled the shops when as a boy he bought his first pair of skates there. 'I remember my surprise', he wrote, 'at the figures with black gowns and white wigs walking about among the cutlery'. When he came to practise, the shops had disappeared.

After the business of the courts had removed to quarters in the adjacent buildings, the Hall was still used, as now, for advocates to confer with clients and each other, walking up and down or sitting on one of the benches at the side. Robert Louis Stevenson, himself an advocate, left this impression:

> A pair of swing doors give admittance to a hall with a carved roof, hung with legal portraits, lighted by windows of painted glass and warmed by three vast fires. This is the *Salle des pas Perdus* of the Scottish Bar. Here, by a ferocious custom, idle youth must promenade from ten till two. From end to end, singly or in pairs or trios, the gowns and wigs go back and forward. Through a hum of talk and footfalls, the piping tones of a Macer announce a fresh cause and call upon the names of those concerned. Intelligent men have been walking daily for ten or twenty years without a rag of business or a shilling of reward. In process of time they may perhaps be made the Sheriff Substitute and Fountain of Justice at Lerwick or Tobermory.

Today Parliament Hall is one of the jewels of Edinburgh, and although listed in most guide books, it is strange how few people go there. It is 143 feet long, 42 feet wide and 40 feet high, its most striking feature is its original hammer-beam roof, built between 1637 and 1639 of oak from the Baltic and with trusses spaced at alternate broad and narrow intervals; on the stone base of the trusses have been carved corbels showing tiny castles and grotesque faces. At the south end where in Parliamentary days the throne of the king's Commissioner used to stand, is a huge stained-glass window, created in 1868, to commemorate the founding of the Court of Session in 1532. In the centre of the picture the king, James V, enthroned, is seen presenting the Charter of the Court to its first Lord President who is kneeling before him. Beside the Lord President the Archbishop of Glasgow, who was also Lord Chancellor, is giving a blessing. On the king's extreme right is his mother Queen Margaret, widow of James IV, and on his extreme left, a small child helps himself to a bowl of fruit. The faces of the onlookers, court and clergy, are said to have been copied from photographs of those connected with the Court of Session at the time the window was commissioned. At the bottom of the picture are five stained-glass panels of coats of arms, in the centre the Royal Arms of Scotland with its motto, NEMO ME IMPUNE LACESSIT (Nobody provokes me with impunity) encapsulating what Neal Ascherson has called the Scottish characteristics of self-assertion and self-distrust, first cousin, you might say, of the apocryphal toast, 'Here's tae us/Wha's like us?/Gey few/And they're a' deid.'

Around the four walls are paintings of long dead Lords President, Lords Justice General, Lords Justice Clerk, Deans of the Faculty, Lords Advocate, as well as Scots-born Lord Mansfield, England's Lord Chief Justice. Some, like the Raeburns, are better than others, but collectively all are impressive. The fine array of statues include those of Lord Cockburn whose *Memorials of His Times* gives a fascinating picture of life in nineteenth-century Edinburgh, and the Chantrey statues of Henry Dundas, Viscount Melville, the 'uncrowned king' of Scotland and of his nephew Robert Dundas of Arniston, head of the Court of the Exchequer. Sir Walter Scott is here, as he was for much of his working life, dividing his time between duties as one of the principal Clerks of Session and writing the Waverley novels. He is shown seated in what his son-in-law John Gibson Lockhart called a characteristic pose, wearing a long frock-coat, waistcoat and cravat and holding a stick loosely between his legs. But the finest and oldest piece of marble statuary in all Scotland is that of Lord President Duncan Forbes of Culloden by the French sculptor Roubiliac. Forbes had shown his humanity by the leniency with which he prosecuted the rebels of the 1715 rising and as Lord President did what he could to prevent the '45. Seated, he is wearing the formal dress of Lord President, robes, breeches, buckled shoes and a full length wig to set off his lean, ascetic features. In his left hand he holds a scroll while with his raised right hand he appears to be questioning or perhaps correcting or even silencing whoever is pleading before him. The overall impression is of a man of great authority giving his entire concentration to the matter in hand.

Yet to me the Hall is peopled by even older ghosts: those of the 314 lords, knights and burgesses who signed away the last Scottish Parliament; Queensberry as Commissioner, sitting patiently on his throne at the southern end; Hamilton cravenly apologizing for the toothache which had conveniently kept him at home, Fletcher of Saltoun in a rage, threatening Hamilton with a duel, Mar at the end of a long session in candlelight afraid to go home for the rioting in the High Street, Argyll only there because of favours promised and bestowed. And then in the darkness and frost of the early New Year, the proceedings finally ended, the benches on either side emptied, the fires damped down, the candles snuffed out, the doors closed; the end, as was said, of an old song.

# INTERLUDE

ONE DAY I LUNCHED AT THE CASTLE WITH THE OFFICIAL IN CHARGE OF the approved guides. After the firing of the one o'clock gun, I asked what sort of questions the public asked of the guides. He thought for a moment, then said:

I'll tell you a story. There was a woman from an American television network here the other day, researching for a programme they were planning to make on the castle. She asked one of the guides, an old fellow he was, what were the silliest questions that American tourists asked.

'I can think of one,' he said, 'but I couldny tell you it.'

'Why not?' she asked.

'Because it's so daft,' he said, 'you wouldny like it.'

'Nonsense. Come on, let's hear it.'

He shook his head. 'I'd best not. You wouldny believe it.'

After further prevarication the woman became impatient. 'I was told you would help me with my researches,' she said. 'Are you going to help me or not?'

'I will.'

'Then what is the silliest question that American tourists ask?'

'You'll not mind?'

'Of course not.'

' "What time is the one o'clock gun fired?" You'd be surprised at the number of Americans who ask me that.'

There were tourists in plenty when I went on a guided tour of Holyrood. Our guide was a middle-aged woman wearing a green tartan skirt with red and yellow lines who seemed to me a blend of Jean Brodie and Joyce Grenfell. Having shepherded us together at the foot of the stairs she showed us two portraits of the Queen, one of her looking like a ferret, the other, more recognizable, of her receiving the Honours of Scotland in day clothes and carrying a handbag. Then she came to Prinny and in a schoolmistressy way addressed us as the ignoramuses we undoubtedly were. 'This is a portrait of King George the *Fourth* when he made his state visit to Edinburgh in 1822, and it's the work of *Sir* David Wilkie who was a *very* important Scottish *painter*. Now *unfortunately* when the king arrived here, it was found that his *kilt* was four inches *too short* for him – it *could* be said it looked a *wee bittie* like a mini-skirt. He was *also* seen to be wearing flesh coloured *tights* which of course are *never* worn with a kilt – I'm afraid his *tailor* was very *remiss* in not advising him. However, in the end *all* was *well* as Sir David painted the kilt at its *proper* length, and he also took the *liberty* of painting in the *stockings* the king *ought* to have been wearing. And now, if you'll follow me, please, we'll *move* along to the spot where Mary Queen of Scots's favourite courtier was *murdered*. *His* name was David Rizzio [*sic*]. *David*, as I'm sure you know, is a good *Scots* name. Rizzio is *not* a Scots name but *Italian* and there are those who say that *that* was the *reason* he was murdered – a very *racist* view which I'm sure *none* of us would wish to subscribe to today.'

# CHAPTER 21

## Who are the Scots?

WHO AND WHAT ARE THE SCOTS? WELL, FOR A START THEY ARE NOT THE English. Here, translated from the original, is what the anonymous author of *The Complaynt of Scotland* wrote in 1549:

> There are no two nations under the firmament that are more contrary and different as Englishmen and Scotsmen, although they be neighbours living in the same island and speaking the same language. For Englishmen are subtle and Scotsmen are facile. Englishmen are ambitious in prosperity and Scotsmen are humane in prosperity. Englishmen feel humiliated when they are subjected to violence and Scotsmen are furious when they are subjected to violence. Englishmen are cruel when they gain a victory and Scotsmen are merciful when they gain a victory. To conclude, it is impossible that Scotsmen and Englishmen can remain in concord under one monarch or prince because their natures and conditioning are as different as the natures of sheep and wolves.

This was written at the end of the Rough Wooing, when Henry VIII sent the Earl of Hertford and an English army to invade Scotland so as to bring about a marriage between the infant Mary Queen of Scots and England's Prince Edward; in the course of which Hertford reported, he had 'seven monasteries burned, four abbeys, five market towns, 243 villages', as well as sacking Holyroodhouse and its chapel, and devastating cattle and crops in the fields that lay between Edinburgh and the border. It was Edward I all over again, and the hatred the Scots felt towards the English was rekindled anew. No wonder that the author of the *Complaynt* felt that even had the wooing been successful it would have been impossible for Scots and English to live in harmony. Three hundred years later the English historian H.T. Buckle took a similar but more balanced view:

> An essential antagonism which still exists between the Scotch and English minds; an antagonism extremely remarkable, when found among nations, both of whom, besides being contiguous, and constantly mixing together, speak the same language, read the same books, belong to the same empire and possess the same interests, and yet are, in many important respects, as different as if there had never been any means of their influencing each other, and as if they had never had anything in common.

Another hundred years on in 1964 the Scottish writer Alastair Reid was telling the readers of the *New Yorker* much the same: 'The fact remains that the two countries are altogether distinct in temperament and manner, and their conjunction, although it is now a working one, has never been resolved to the satisfaction of either'. They differ, said Stevenson, 'in the very look of nature and men's faces.'

Today English executives who come to work in Scotland often speak of a culture shock. They become depressed by many things: the weather, the lack of English village life with its familiar church, vicar, cosy pub and the lusher, mellower countryside, by finding the law different and not knowing why, by the preponderance of Scottish (and therefore alien) news and sport on Scottish radio and television. A few, unable to come to terms with it, apply for transfer south. Yet there are others who not only do come to terms with it but appreciate a slower, less frenetic tempo of life and, after retirement, stay on.

What is it that the Scot sees in the Englishman which is so different to himself? Above all, aloofness, self-containment. 'His is a domineering nature,' wrote Stevenson, 'steady in fight, imperious to command, but neither curious or quick about the lives of others. He may be amused by a foreigner as by a monkey, but he will never condescend to study him with any patience.' Hence the deep desire of so many English today to wash their hands of Europe. 'His ignorance of his sister kingdom,' Stevenson went on, 'cannot be described. He takes no interest in Scotland or the Scotch and, which is the unkindest cut of all, he does not care to justify his indifference.'* The Scottish poet Maurice Lindsay put it another way: 'The leisured assurance of the southern English upper class, the easy superiority of a people who have never been conquered and who harbour the instinctive assumption that the Scots and the Welsh who submitted, are unimportant and slightly comic while the Irish who did not, are odd and troublesome'. Nor has it been only Scots who have marked the English attitude. William Cobbett, than whom no-one was more English, noted when visiting Edinburgh in 1832 'the absence of all foppishness and affectation of carelessness and that insolent assumption of superiority that you see in almost all the young men that you meet with in the fashionable parts of the great towns of England' — while of Edinburgh he said, 'Here all is civility, you do not meet with rudeness or even with the want of a disposition to oblige, even in persons in the lowest state of life.'

And how have English attitudes affected the Scots? Stevenson again: 'Compared with the grand tree-like self-sufficiency of [the Englishman's] demeanour, the vanity and curiosity of the Scot seem uneasy, vulgar and immodest. That you should continually try to establish human and serious relations, that you should actually feel an interest in John Bull and desire and invite a return of interest from him . . . puts you in the attitude of a suitor or poor relation. Thus even the lowest class of the educated Englishman towers over a Scotchman by head and shoulders'. In conversation too the difference between the two peoples is most marked. A Scot on meeting a stranger is often disputatious, sometimes tiresomely so, so as to get a response, but the Englishman's conversation tends to be vacuous,

*In 1886 John Stuart Blackie asked Benjamin Jowett, Principal of Balliol, 'I hope you in Oxford don't think we hate you.' Jowett replied, 'We don't think about you.'

about the weather and other trivialities ('How did you get here?'), so that in Stevenson's words, 'the contact of mind with mind is evaded as with terror'. One of the more embarrassing attempts of the Englishman who does try to be friendly to the alien Scot is either proudly to tell him that his wife's second cousin once removed is a Scot, or – which he would never dream of doing to a Scouse or Geordie – jocularly but embarrassingly imitate him to his face.

Where else do they differ? The English have always been as obsessed by class as Indians have by caste, each labelled according to his place. 'God bless the squire and his relations/And keep us in our proper stations' ran a nineteenth-century jingle, and despite the levelling effect of twentieth-century television, that is still more or less the way of it. It is true that in Scotland a border laird, a Dundee accountant, a Hebridean crofter and a Glasgow welder live very different lives on very different incomes. Yet none feels he is divided from the others *by class*, and as class in Scotland has never been a criterion of delineation, it rarely figures as a topic of conversation. Scott's son-in-law Lockhart wrote that people in Edinburgh visited each other with cordial familiarity, 'who, if they lived in London, would imagine their difference in rank to form an impassable barrier against such intercourse'. Stevenson pointed out how democratic student life was in Scottish universities compared with that of the élite of Oxford and Cambridge. 'At an earlier age the Scottish lad begins his greatly different experience of crowded classrooms . . . His college life has little of restraint and nothing of necessary gentility. He will find no quiet clique of the exclusive, studious and cultured. All classes rub shoulders on the greasy benches. The raffish young gentleman in gloves must rub shoulders and measure his scholarship with the plain, clownish laddie from the parish school.'

You find, or used to find, the same sort of equality in domestic situations, as I recall from the relationships that existed between my grandmother and her cook Bessie and maid Helen, who were with her for more than twenty years. Deference played no part in their make-up. Because my grandmother was the wife of a baronet, they addressed her as 'm'lady' as was the custom in those days; but this formal recognition of rank in no way inhibited either from saying whatever occurred to them, and there was no awareness on their part of any differentiation of status. Sometimes when a boy I used to play

329

cards with Bessie on the kitchen table and once, as she reminded me not long ago, she bawled me out for cheating. She and Helen were among my dearest childhood companions, and I kept in touch with both until they died.

Yet if they were free of deference, the same cannot be said of others in Edinburgh who, despite, or perhaps because of, Sassenach indifference, hold their southern neighbours in esteem. You notice it first in the eagerness with which doormen of the grander hotels home in on the fruity, unmistakable accents (which they do not think they have) of the English upper classes. You notice it too in the way in which the most genteel of the bourgeoisie regard the English as a cut above themselves and try, with dire results, to ape English speech. I have already mentioned their efforts to anglicize 'Bye-bye' resulting in 'Bay-bay' and sometimes they get in a real tangle as in 'Sarturday afternoon', while Moray McLaren once recalled a dance hostess saying to him, 'Do you perspaire? Ay do, frequently'.

Another illustration of the gentility of the Edinburgh bourgeoisie is the dearth of stimulating talk at some dinner parties. An air of eighteenth-century formality prevails. Few dare go out on a limb and say something provocative or even unexpected so as to introduce a little liveliness, for the Scots are terrified of giving themselves away. Once or twice when we dined out in Edinburgh, I would say something a little *outré* to my neighbour in the hope of arousing a response. It rarely happened. Too often I would be told, in the dullest tones imaginable, 'Oh, is that so? I must confess I had never looked at it that way before.' Once at a dinner party the woman next to me, having heard I was a writer, opened the conversation with 'And how fares the creative muse?' Never wholly at ease with the English language yet strongly Anglophile, the Edinburgh bourgeoisie feel safe in sticking with clichés. No wonder Boswell went to London for he had what he called 'the whim of an Englishman to make me think and act extravagantly, and the sense of a Scotsman to make me sensible of it'. When, if ever, will the Edinburgh bourgeoisie learn to think and act extravagantly?

Yet I suppose the most noticeable difference between English and Scots is that of English reticence and Scottish sentimentality. 'We are at bottom', said John Buchan, 'the most sentimental and emotional people on earth.' This sentimentality takes many forms, from the nineteenth-century kailyard (kitchen garden) school of writing, a sentimentalized view of Scottish small town life, to the extraordinary obsession with the use of diminutives which illustrate, says Maurice Lindsay, the ingrained Scottish habit of thinking small. My mother, an Anglo-Scot like myself, used to sing this nursery rhyme to her children and grandchildren:

> Dance to your daddie,
> My bonnie laddie,
> Dance to your daddie, my bonnie lamb!
> And ye'll get a fishie
> In a little dishie,
> Ye'll get a fishie when the boat comes hame.

W.A. Craigie (which itself sounds like a diminutive, as do Robbie, Gebbie, Reekie, Duggie, Lownie, Lambie, Gorrie, Smellie, Brodie, Snoddie, Lurie, Pirie, Naughtie and a hundred other Scottish surnames) also wrote on the subject:

> Hundreds of mothers throughout Aberdeenshire and Banffshire every night put their 'little wee bit loonikies' and 'little wee bit lassikies' to their 'bedies' while the infant of the household, described as the 'little wee eenickie', that is a 'teeny, weeny eenie' – lies in its 'cradlie'.

These diminutives, said Craigie (and he listed others such as sheepie, boatie, burnie, sheltie) 'are even employed by people who have sloughed off nearly every vestige of the vernacular, for the very simple reason that they cannot slough off the mentality which the diminutive represents and which it can evaluate as nothing else can do'.

For the poet Tom Leonard diminutives are a subject for satire:

> *The Voyeur*
> what's your favourite word dearie,
> is it wee
> I hope it's wee
> wee's such a nice wee word
> like a wee hairy dog
> with two wee eyes
> such a nice wee word to play with dearie

you can say it quickly
with a wee smile
and a wee glance to the side
or you can say it slowly dearie
with your mouth a wee bit open
and a wee sigh dearie
a wee sigh
put your wee head on my shoulder dearie
oh my
a great wee word
and Scottish
it makes you proud

The frequent use of 'dearies' and 'lambies' where the English would say 'darling' or 'sweetheart' was commented on by the writer Mary Symon when she said, 'Diminutives are our only emotional outlets. The tidal wave of passion swamps the Scot.' Which is why he uses the possessive pronoun for things rather than people, as in 'I'm awa' to ma bed' or 'It's time for ma tea', yet referring to his wife as 'the wife' or 'wifie' and to her face as his highest form of endearment, 'Hen'. Barrie touched on the general problem in his novel *A Window in Thrums*. The boy Jamie is fed up with the too obvious affection that his sister Leeby shows for him in the company of others.

'I wonder 'at ye dinna try to control yersel',' Jamie would say to her as he grew bigger.
'Am sure,' said Leeby, 'I never gie ye a look if there's onybody there.'
'A look! You're aye lookin' at me sae fond-like 'at I dinna ken which way to turn.'

Later, when Leeby asks Jamie directly if he loves her, he says love is a dreadful word to use and she shouldn't ask such annoying questions. Leeby says that if he will just *say* he loves her, she'll never let on again in public that he means anything to her at all.

'Aye,' says Jamie, 'ye often say that.'
'Do ye no believe my word?'

'I believe fine ye mean what ye say, but ye forget yoursel' when the time comes.'

'Juist try me this time.'

'Weel then, I do.'

'Do what?' asked the greedy Leeby.

'What ye said.'

'I said love.'

'Weel,' said Jamie, 'I do't.'

'What do ye do? Say the word.'

'Na,' said Jamie, 'I winna say the word. It's no a word to say, but I do't.'

With this legacy of inbuilt inhibitions, it's no wonder that the Scots have opened their hearts to Burns; for he, one of them and yet not one of them, says the things that they have always felt deep down but, like poor Jamie, have never dared to say.

And while on the subject of language, let us not forget how much easier on the ear is spoken Scots than spoken English. 'English', wrote an anonymous correspondent in *Blackwood's Magazine* of November 1870, 'bristles with consonants. Scotch is spangled with vowels as a meadow with daisies in May. English, though perhaps the most muscular and copious language in the world, is harsh and sibilant; while the Scotch is almost as soft as the Italian.' In the context of song, the writer goes on to praise the diminutive: 'English songs . . . however excellent they may be as poetical compositions, are not so available for musical purposes as the songs of Scotland. And the Englishman, if he sings of a "pretty little girl" uses words deficient in euphony and suggests comedy rather than sentiment; but when a Scotsman sings of a "bonnie wee lassie", he employs words that express a tenderer idea and are infinitely better adapted to music.'

In terms of softness and euphony the same may be said of Scottish place names, especially those of three and four syllables: Rosemarkie, Schiehallion, Acharacle, Dalmahoy, Benbecula, Locheilort, Inverurie, Altnaharra, Eriskay, Achiltibuie, Drumochter, Mingulay, Bracadale, Kinlochbervie, Craigellachie. The words glide over the tongue like a Highland burn singing its way to the sea. English place names have few such mellifluous counterparts.

Another Scots writer, R.B. Cunninghame Grahame once said,

333

'The Scots fornicate gravely but without conviction.' Short of being a regular voyeur, one wonders how he knew, though his general drift is clear: the Scot performs no differently from others but probably in silence so as not to seem to be enjoying it; not much bouncing around, one imagines, no spontaneous whoops of delight. I would say this is probably truer of the men than of the pretty, lively young women one sees in Lowland cities; and when they say through the nose 'Uh-ha' meaning 'I hear you', as in shops and offices many do, what my one time dentist, Dr R.A.F. Murdoch found deplorably vulgar, I find delightfully sexy.

It is in his native costume of the kilt (invented by an Englishman, according to Professor Hugh Trevor-Roper) which, unlike the philibeg, is of comparatively recent origin, that the Scot in my view comes into his own; not when employing it as a garment of everyday wear (except on moor or hill) and certainly not in England, but in the controlled abandon with which he executes the intricate steps of reels and country dances such as Hamilton House and the Duke of Perth. Here the sometimes graceless Scot shows grace abounding, here the often inhibited Scot gives vent to the joyous cries that are absent in the bedroom. Here Scots of both sexes find, as nowhere else, spiritual and aesthetic self-fulfilment.

In humour too the Scots and English have a quite different approach. A saying of the English savant Sydney Smith that it would take a surgical operation to drive a joke into a Scotsman's head has been much quoted and, in Scotland, much resented. What he meant, and should have said, was *an English joke*. English jokes, like the English, tend to be more sophisticated.

Most humour is based on human failings and Scots humour more than most. For instance, a golfer playing the first hole at St Andrews drove six balls one after the other into the notorious Swilcan burn. As he and his caddy walked forward to retrieve them, the golfer said, 'I'm going to drown myself in that burn.' The caddy said (another example of Scottish classlessness), 'You couldny.' 'Why not?' 'Ye couldny keep your heid doon lang enough.'

A similar story is told of an elderly gent sitting in a train at a station when he saw the porter he had engaged standing by his luggage on the platform. 'Why haven't you loaded the luggage?' he shouted at the porter. 'Yer luggage', the porter shouted back, 'is no sic a fule as yersel'. Yer in the wrang train.'

Much of Scottish humour centres on the macabre, not excluding death, and is delivered deadpan. At a dinner at one of Edinburgh's all-male dining clubs, the chairman said to a member at the far end of the table, 'Why is your neebour looking sae gash?' and the member said, 'He went to join his Maker a while back. I saw him step awa', but I didna like to disturb good company.'

Then there are the surreal stories which belong exclusively to Glasgow. A wee man the worse for drink, 'fou' as we say in Scotland, was running to catch a tram, observed by a relation of mine who was sitting on one of the cross-seats next to the platform. With a final spurt, he heaved himself aboard and, fixing my relation with an unsteady eye, said, 'Did ye see me get on the tram?' She said she had. He hiccupped loudly, resumed his gaze and said, 'Are ye quite sure ye seed me get on the tram?' Yes, said the relation, she was quite sure. Another hiccup and then, with a big smile and air of triumph he said, 'How did ye know it was me?'

In citing these examples, I am thinking in terms of the Lowlander. The only joke I ever heard tell about the Highlander was of a crofter in the outer isles who had just had a telephone installed. Soon after, it rang. The crofter picked up the receiver and heard a voice say, 'Long distance New York.' He paused. 'Aye,' he said. 'Aye. It is that. A vairy long distance,' and replaced the receiver.

The negative aspect of Lowland humour in its emphasis on the macabre is also reflected in the often negative view that Scots take of each other – both being the residue of nearly half a millennium of parish elders seeking to find fault with those they think may have transgressed. Denigration and disapproval come more readily to the tongue of the Scot than praise; and any praise must be qualified. On conclusion of an Annie Fischer recital at the Usher Hall, my friend Derek Hart heard one Edinburgh body say to another, 'She's awfy guid, don't you think?' to which the other replied, 'Well, so she should be. She's been doing it since she was eight.' A story is told of a honeymoon couple who, on return home, were showing an uncle their snapshots. 'What do you think of them?' they asked after he had studied them in silence. The uncle picked out one and said, 'That's the worst.' Fearing the worst is endemic in the Scottish character for, as one writer has said, too many good things happening on the same day make a Scotsman uneasy. Alastair Reid summed up the malaise in the last part of his poem *Scotland*:

Greenness entered the body. The grasses
Shivered with presences and sunlight
stayed like a halo on hair and heather and hills.
Walking into town, I saw, in a radiant raincoat
the woman from the fish-shop. 'What a day it is!'
cried I, like a sunstruck madman.
And what did she have to say for it?
Her brow grew bleak, her ancestors raged in their graves
as she spoke with their ancient misery:
'We'll pay for it, we'll pay for it, we'll pay for it'.

'The best people I have ever met in my life', Moray McLaren
wrote, 'have come from Scotland. And so have the most detestable.'
The detestable come in many guises. There's the pushy boastful Scot
who makes it plain that he thinks that you're a lesser man than he is;
the facetious jokey Scot who in England fancies himself as a raconteur
and manages to bore for Scotland; the cringing self-pitying Scot,
forever seeking your good opinion of him; and the sullen, taciturn,
Glaswegian Scot who speaks only when he has to and then in grunts
and glottal stops.

What these and other Scots share is a lack of any sense of
grace or beauty. How else could a people who produced in the
Adam family the eighteenth century's finest architects, creators of
Floors and Hopetoun, Mellerstain and Culzean, Charlotte Square
and Register House, have tolerated, let alone approved, the designs
of those hideous, chilling blocks of council houses in places like
Easterhouse and Galashiels. How could the same people have come
to patronize bars where, if there is no longer sawdust on the floor,
the furniture is functional and minimal, there is nothing by way of
decoration to please the eye, and an air of joylessness embraces all –
so unlike the cosy English pub where a customer may take his ease
in comfort.

And yet Moray McLaren was writing of the graceless Scot before
the war, before the graceless Englishman became a recognized and
recognizable national figure. Today, in the shape of the lager lout and
the yob, the graceless Englishman has caught up with his Scottish
counterpart and is, I think, even more graceless. Yet there is one
curious difference. The Scot may imbibe in austere surroundings, but
does not have the time or the wish, as the cosseted lager lout does, to
regale the company with salacious stories. This is not because of any

sense of delicacy, rather that for the Scot the sex act is something to be performed, albeit gravely, not ridiculed. Ridiculing it reduces it to the theatre of the absurd, and in that field a sense of the absurd has never been a Scottish characteristic.

What other facets characterize the Scot? 'We are a race of gypsies', wrote Stevenson, 'and love change and travel for themselves.' He himself was a prime example of it, declaring in a famous passage that it was better to travel hopefully than arrive. Here is another point of difference from the insular Englishman for whom traditionally wogs began at Calais and, in the hinterland beyond, food and water were always suspect and communication almost non-existent. That attitude has softened since Britain joined the Common Market, but in the minds of many English people distrust of Continentals still runs deep.

The Scots, on the other hand, from long before Stevenson's time, even before the Reformation, had gained a foothold in Europe. Poverty and a desire to improve themselves were two reasons for quitting Scotland, but that was never the whole of it. A love of adventure and exploration, a curiosity to see other peoples and other lands seems always to have been an element of the make-up of the Scot. In Europe from the Middle Ages on the wandering Scot rivalled the wandering Jew. There are records from that time of Scottish peddlers in Poland and Prussia travelling from town to town to sell their goods, cloth and pepper and saffron, some even settling there, so that several *Schottlands* are still to be found on contemporary maps. Later Scottish students enrolled at the universities of Leyden and Utrecht and as graduates brought home useful improvements to Scottish law. The kings of France formed a company of Scottish Life Guards to protect them, who on two occasions rescued Louis XI from imminent death. Mercenaries in their thousands joined the armies and navies of Russia, Sweden, Denmark, France, Holland, while those of the 'officer' class included James Keith who became Russian ambassador to Sweden and Governor of the Ukraine, his brother George the Earl Marischal who became Prussian ambassador to Spain and Governor of Neuchâtel, Patrick Gordon who became a Russian general and adviser to Peter the Great, John Law who founded the Bank of France, Macdonald, Marshal of France, Admiral Thomas Cochrane, commander in turn of the navies of Chile, Brazil and Greece. Some came back, some settled for what Muriel Spark has called the Scottish vocation of exile. Some, having shaken the dust of Scotland from their feet, seldom thought of it again: the minds of others, like that of Stevenson, were filled with thoughts of it all the time.

One can look back as we approach the millennium and, from the history of the Scot abroad, draw two conclusions. First there are now many more Scots or descendants of Scots living abroad than live in Scotland – some ten to fifteen million abroad, it is believed, and only five million in Scotland. (Comprising one tenth of the British population, it has been estimated that Scots fill one fifth of English professional jobs.) Secondly in many countries of the world and particularly in Europe the Scot is accepted in a way that the Englishman isn't. When my son Alastair was hitchhiking across France ten years ago, he found that when he put a tam o' shanter on his head, he was offered more lifts more quickly than when bare-headed – thus proving the longevity of the Auld Alliance!* As a result of our infiltration of Europe, the Scot has gained one priceless asset. Unlike other peoples on the Continent and in England, he has never been racist or anti-Semitic.

Yet it is probably as a British soldier that the ordinary Scot, both Highland and Lowland, has won most renown. Throughout the 300 years of wars between the two countries, the English were well aware of the Highlanders' fighting qualities, the savagery of their attacks with broadsword and dirk, their seeming lack of fear in any situation. William Pitt paid tribute to them in the House of Commons in 1766 on conclusion of the latest war with France. From the mountains of the north, he said:

> I drew into your service a hardy and intrepid race of men who . . . had gone nigh to have overturned the state in the war before the last. These men in the last war were brought

*The *Times* columnist Alan Coren reporting from the Café du Midi in Provence in 1994 just after Winnie Ewing had been declared MEP for the North of Scotland, said this:

> . . . the French for their part are beside themselves at this sudden doubling of the Caledonian Europresence; for while they are deeply suspicious of English suspicions over Europe, they are deeply convinced by Scottish convictions. And while they don't care a jot whether England is in or out, they care passionately that Scotland should be in. They love Scotland, as they always have, and when the French declare that they want to embrace Scotland within the EU, they do not use the metaphor lightly.

to combat on your side; they served with fidelity as they fought with valour and conquered for you in every part of the world.

It was the poverty of the glens combined with the Highlanders' skills in fighting that pushed them into enlisting in such droves. Although numbering only 3 per cent of the population, says John Prebble, they had by the end of the eighteenth century supplied the Crown with sixty-five marching and fencible regiments, as well as independent companies, militia and volunteers. In Skye during the first forty years of the nineteenth century, the island 'gave the British army 21 Lieutenant-Generals and Major-Generals, 48 Lieutenant-Colonels, 600 majors, captains and subalterns and 10,000 private soldiers'. And in the First World War, the casualties among the Scottish regiments were disproportionate to those of the English. In 1967 a former officer in the Cameronians, John Baynes, wrote a book about the valour of the men of his regiment on the western front.* In March 1915 it went into action at Neuve Chapelle, and when withdrawn a week later only 150 of the original 900 were left, commanded by a second lieutenant. But their morale was unbroken. Researching their origins, Baynes found that 70 per cent of them were Glaswegians from a social background so wretched as to constitute a kind of underclass; and the only explanation he could find for their courage and discipline was that for them, after the deprivations of life in the Gorbals, the regiment had been family, friend and home. Of the Highland regiments' kilts, friend and foe took differing views. '*Pour l'amour, oui*,' commented the French Marshal Joffre, '*mais pour la guerre, non.*' But the Germans found them unnerving. Watching these wild men in swishing kilts charging towards them with fixed bayonets, they dubbed them 'The ladies from Hell'.

Lastly, the dispelling of a myth. Between the two wars there was a running joke in Britain, propagated mostly by the Scottish comedian Harry Lauder, about Scotch meanness. It was a joke much enjoyed by the English and exemplified by comic dialogue on seaside picture postcards alongside the cartoons by Donald McGill of girls with protuberant breasts and balloon-like bottoms. A typical meanness joke was that of a golfer on the 18th green addressing another who was standing forlornly outside the clubhouse.

'Are ye no playing today, Sandy?'

'No, I canna,'

*Morale* by John Baynes.

339

'Why not?'

'I've lost ma ball.'

You do not hear meanness jokes today because they have outlived any humour they had and by now would probably be considered politically incorrect.

In any case the charge is a libel. When it comes to raising money for charities or the sick and deprived, Scots have always been outstandingly generous. What *is* a national characteristic, and understandably so in a country that has never been affluent, is thrift. The Scot has had to count his pennies and will never pay more for something than he has to; a sense of thrift is embedded deep in the national consciousness. Recently in Edinburgh I had an experience which I know others have had, and which I doubt could happen in England. I was in search of a clothes-brush and the elderly woman assistant showed me the only kind the shop had. When told the price, I said I thought it rather dear. 'Just what I think myself,' said the assistant. 'It's *ridiculous*. Now you take my advice and go down to Fraser's in Princes Street and I'll guarantee you'll find just what you're looking for at half the price.' Not a great advertisement for salesmanship, admittedly, but a touching example of neighbourliness, and another reason why Scottish thrift has made Edinburgh into one of the great savings and insurance centres in the country.

In this book I have concentrated mostly on Edinburgh and the Highlands and Islands because those are places with which I am familiar. I have said little or nothing about Aberdeen, Perth, Dundee and particularly Glasgow – Gles Chu as the Gaels called it, the dear green place, which once it was but not in my lifetime. I came to know it a little when I was investigating the case of the wrongfully convicted and imprisoned Patrick Meehan, an incompetent Gorbals safe-blower.* On visits then and since I have come to admire the amazing transformation of a city in industrial decline, its shipyards and heavy engineering plants derelict, and rife with crime, poverty and squalor to – thanks largely to the policy of an enlightened Lord Provost – the day in 1990 when it received the accolade of European City of Culture – the very idea of which at any previous

*Granted a free pardon after serving seven years of a life sentence for murder and awarded £50,000 compensation.

340

time would have seemed preposterous. While pursuing the Meehan case, I enjoyed the company of many Glasgow professional people as well as some of its villains, and found them one and all to be so different from their counterparts in Edinburgh – robust, earthy, jokey, independent-minded – that it was hard to believe they lived only 40 miles apart. Despite (or maybe because of) being of mixed stock, Glaswegians have always known who they are, and therefore have never experienced problems of identity in their relations with the English similar to their counterparts in Edinburgh.

# PART 6
## *The Past and the Future*

# INTERLUDE

In 1950 I had consolidated, as it were, my affinity with Scotland by marrying a Scots girl, the red-headed Dunfermline-born prima ballerina Moira Shearer, a principal member of the Royal Ballet Company at Covent Garden and star of the evergreen movie, *The Red Shoes*.* For the next sixteen years we lived in or near London, pursuing our twin careers of dancing and acting, writing and broadcasting; and bringing up four children to three of whom we gave Scottish names (Ailsa, Fiona, Alastair). The name of the fourth, Rachel, could be said to have been a concession to my father's English mother.

But Scotland was seldom out of our thoughts and we went there when we could, mostly on summer holidays; sometimes to new places like Shetland and Harris, Dumfriesshire and Aberdeenshire, sometimes to old ones like Islay and Nairn whose seemingly unchanged landscapes brought back a score of boyhood memories, some so intensely visual, like the fleet sailing into Invergordon or reaching the summit of Sgurr nan Gilean in Skye, that they appeared almost like photographic prints before my eyes. Then in 1966 a number of factors combined to lead us to move away from the London area,

*See *On My Way to the Club*, pp. 188–92.

345

Moira having retired from the stage and eager to give more time to the children, myself in search of time and space to complete a long book. So back to Scotland we went and found sanctuary in an old Manse in the Borders where we lived for the next fifteen years. It was lovely empty country and from my study window I could see beyond the orchard of Victoria plums and the wide valley of the Tweed the distant Cheviots, their winter tops capped with snow.

This was a country rich in historical associations, not only of perennial bloody battles across the border, but from which had sprung a whole host of self-made and successful Scots; Thomas Telford, engineer, son of an Eskdale shepherd, who built 1,200 bridges, 1,000 miles of road and the Caledonian Canal; John Broadwood, cabinet-maker from the Lammermuirs, who walked to London to build the famous Broadwood pianoforte; David Hume from Ninewells; James Cook, son of a Roxburgh farmer who mapped the South Seas as Britain's most famous navigator; another explorer, Mungo Park from Yarrow who met his death in the Niger; James Hogg, the Ettrick shepherd, author of *Confessions of a Justified Sinner*; James Thomson from Ferniehill who wrote *Rule Britannia* in celebration of the Union; and Walter Scott at the little farm of Sandyknowe in the lee of Smailholm Tower where he had stayed as a boy with his grandparents in the hope that fresh air and gentle exercise would help to cure his polio; and later at the great house of Abbotsford he built on the Tweed where he wrote his novels and speared salmon by torchlight.

Although we had moved to Scotland rather than, say, Devon, because I knew my roots to be there, I had not at this time considered the country in any political sense. But recently something had happened to alter that. During my time as a reporter for the BBC current affairs programme *Panorama* I and my colleagues had seen governors of colonies across the world standing to attention in feathered hats while on one flagpole the Union Jack was ceremoniously lowered and on another the flag of the newly liberated country – Cyprus or wherever – was with an even greater sense of occasion raised. And so the thought came to me that if these entirely new countries were thought fit to attain independence, had not the time come for Scotland, a country older, richer, with its own unique systems of law, education and religion, its own music and literature, its own face and *persona* – was not Scotland entitled to at least some degree of devolution in the running of its affairs? This belief was strengthened by the fact that the only British political party which then advocated Scottish devolution was the Liberal Party to which I belonged and for which I had fought two elections.

I now joined the Scottish Liberal Party (we lived in David Steel's constituency) and was invited soon after to join the Party's Council. Although Home Rule in a federal Britain was party policy, the issue never seemed to get discussed. Yet it seemed to me to be the most important political issue facing Scotland; and I became so frustrated by the Council's prolonged discussions on the drearier aspects of party policy, I proposed at the next Council meeting that in future all other Scottish domestic issues should be considered in relation to it. As I might have guessed, the proposal was passed unanimously and thereafter totally ignored.

The trouble was that, although the Council were prepared to pay lip service to Home Rule, their hearts were not in it and I realized there would have to be a parting of the ways. So I wrote out a letter of resignation but let it lie on my desk for four weeks, reluctant to leave a party to which I had belonged for twenty years. Then I received an invitation from Winnie Ewing, fighting a spirited campaign for the Scottish National Party at the Hamilton by-election, to join her on the platform for her eve of poll meeting, knew I could delay no longer and posted the resignation letter.* David Steel has since said there was no need for me to resign, as there was no Liberal party candidate standing, but I felt it would have been dishonourable not to. To my surprise it made front-page news in several papers: *The Times* called it startling and other papers sensational.

Winnie Ewing's victory at Hamilton marked the beginning of a whole string of further SNP successes. Although I never joined the party, I did speak on their platforms from time to time and also took part in a BBC television programme called *The Disunited Kingdom* in which I addressed the camera direct. 'Friends, enemies, Englishmen,' I began, 'hear now the claims of Scotland,' and for four minutes I spelled out what I thought they were. It caused something of a stir north of the border and was reprinted by the ultranationalist 1320 Club (1320 being the year of the Declaration of Arbroath), both in English and French.

*I rejoined the party a few years later.

Conservative friends naturally thought that what I was advocating was a retrograde step: narrow nationalism in an age of increasing internationalism. Nationalism yes, but not narrow; and a good deal more attractive than the fake nationalism south of the border of clapped-out English politicians urging the electorate to 'put the Great back into Great Britain again.' We believed with Burke in the virtues of the little platoon, in small being beautiful, in the greater the political unit (and the Common Market was then upon us) the greater the need for autonomy within that unit if those being governed were to feel any empathy with those doing the governing. As I wrote at the time, Scotland's affairs had once been ordered by her Parliament in Edinburgh; now most of them were ordered by the Parliament at Westminster; soon more would be dealt with in Brussels. A country which had once been central to itself was on the periphery; now it needed to become central again.

All this was much in my mind when I was invited by the Edinburgh Sir Walter Scott Society to be their president for 1969. This meant delivering a talk on some aspect of Scott at a grand dinner of Edinburgh notables at the North British hotel. My first instinct was to refuse, for apart from having won a Holiday Task prize at Eton on *Ivanhoe*, I knew little about him. My mother had tried to read *Rob Roy* to me when I was eight, but it being her, I professed to be even more bored than I actually was, thus provoking her into packing it in. ('If that's your attitude to our greatest Scottish writer, Ludovic, I see absolutely no point in going on.' 'Oh, good!' I said, which provoked her even more.) I tried one or two of the novels on my own later, but made little headway, finding the high-life scenes unreal and my ear not being sufficiently attuned at that age to Scottish low-life dialogue. It could also have been something more, an unconscious recognition that, as Edwin Muir put it, 'his picture of life had no centre because the environment in which he lived had no centre . . . He felt in one language and thought in another.'

I was aware, of course, of what Scott had done for Scotland in his writings by putting the country on the map, delineating its history and geography to visitors for the first time, encouraging them to see its manifold wonders; while his crowning achievement was to organize the visit of King George IV to Edinburgh, the first by any reigning British monarch for 170 years. Like Dr Johnson, he was both a Jacobite and a Hanoverian, and that rare creature a Scot who loved England almost as much as Scotland. His feelings on this score as interpreted by Allan Massie in his delightful, imaginative autobiography of Sir Walter, are ones I share. As a child he had been sent to Bath to take the waters which, it was thought, might improve his health:

> It gave me, young as I was, experience of a softer, more polite way of life and social intercourse than was to be found in our ruder Edinburgh. It was not wasted on me, and as a consequence I have never indulged in the folly of condemning our southern neighbours. On the contrary I have loved England ever since, second only to Scotland, and curiously this love was never shaken by what I learned of the long and heroic resistance which throughout more than two centuries my ancestral compatriots conducted against the threat of English dominance.

This was the man who John Buchan called 'the great reconciler' who strove to see an end to conflict between clan and clan, Highlander and Lowlander, Covenanter and Cavalier, Presbyterian and Episcopalian, Jacobite and Whig, Whig and Tory. If he were alive today he would, I am sure, bend his mind to find some compromise between those Scots who want self-government and those who are afraid of it.

In the end I accepted the Society's invitation, if for no other reason than that my grandfather had been President sixty-three years earlier and because I loved him dearly, felt that he would have thought the less of me for chickening out. The invitation specified white tie and tails, but after two years of wearing these in the thirties I vowed that after the war I would never wear them again. In their place, and knowing of Sir Walter's fondness for the plaid, I put on my Kennedy tartan smoking-jacket which I had recently had made; this led one of the female members of the bourgeoisie to lean across the table on conclusion of my speech and say, as only the bourgeoisie can, 'I enjoyed your peroration as much as I deplore your jacket.'

In preparing my speech, I thought to begin with a mention of some of his friends, among them my forbear, Professor John Wilson (Christopher North), whom Dickens has already described in Chapter 18; and from another joint friend, William Maguire, found this lively account of him:

> a sixteen stoner, a cocker, a racer, a six bottler, a twenty-four

tumbler, an out and outer, a true, upright, knocking-down poetical, prosaic, moral professorial, hard-drinking, fierce-eating,
good-looking, honourable and straightforward Tory.

Lord Cockburn in his *Memorials* had also praised him, saying
of his Noctes Ambrosianae column in *Blackwood's*:

the most singular and delightful outpouring of criticism, politics
and description of feeling, character and scenery, of verse and
prose and maudlin eloquence and especially of wild fun

while the *Oxford Dictionary of Quotations* credits him with two
sayings ('His Majesty's Dominions on which the sun never sets'
and 'Laws were made to be broken') which have been part of the
language ever since.

He was clearly a character, and so all the more surprising
that Owen Dudley Edwards and Graham Richardson should have
omitted Wilson – the man Dickens called 'a great fellow to look
at and to talk to' – from their anthology on Edinburgh on the
grounds that he was 'a sadistic and poisonous old fraud, unfit for the
company of our contributors, including McGonagall.' McGonagall
was a Scots-born Irishman who wrote execrable, unscanned verses
on Scottish themes, and fond though I am of Owen, I am surprised
that he thinks the poet's banal poem on Edinburgh ('Beautiful city
of Edinburgh/Where the tourist can drown his sorrow/By viewing
your monuments and statues fine/During the lovely summer-time')
more deserving of inclusion that the superior literary talents of John
Wilson.

From Wilson I moved on to Scott's childhood at Sandyknowe,
only a mile or so from my own house in the borders. Here he was often
to be heard spouting Border ballads, which stopped all conversation
and led the minister of nearby Smailholm to observe, 'One might as
well speak in the mouth of a cannon as where that boy is.' I went
on to illustrate from records of library borrowings the untruth of
the cliché that he was no longer read, and gave several examples
of his sense of humour. (He once likened the crassness of a Scottish
politician to a man in a sinking ship relieving himself over the side
to lighten the load), referred in passing to his absent-mindedness
(he lost the manuscript of *Waverley* for several years and found it
by chance when looking out some fishing tackle). I also spoke with

admiration and feeling of his discovery in a locked box in the castle of the ancient regalia of Scotland, the beautiful crown and sceptre and sword of state which had been lost after being used 160 years earlier at the coronation of Charles II at Scone. I was more of a monarchist then than I am now.

> Today the sovereign of the United Kingdom is crowned in Westminster by an English archbishop in an English coronation service ordered by the English Earl Marshal whose authority, like that of the Archbishop, stops at the Scottish border. Am I alone in this room, I wonder, in hoping that at the next accession there may also be a coronation in Scotland, that the regalia of Scotland be bestowed on the person of the sovereign by the Ministers of the Church of Scotland, according to the usages of the Scottish coronation service, long ratified by the Scottish law?

In the quarter century which has elapsed since, my views on that head have changed radically. But the idea behind the proposal, that Scotland be allowed to come into her own again, was one that I developed in the latter part of the talk. Scotland, I said, was beginning to wake again after a long sleep, to flex its muscles and question its identity, to rediscover the organic unity without which, as Edwin Muir had said in his brilliant essay on Scott, no nation could live.

> One of the bigger problems facing the world is that of reconciling the bigger unit with the smaller, nationalism with internationalism, centralization with devolution. Every day the world is shrinking before our eyes, getting to be what Marshall McLuhan in a famous phrase called a global village. More and more large businesses are swallowing up more and more little ones, so that in time our needs will be met by just a handful of international conglomerates. Audiences in Bangkok and Bournemouth and Bogota are gaping at the same internationally tailored films and in a hundred developed and underdeveloped countries James Bond has become the folk hero of our times. We are entering the age of common culture, where uniformity was all.

Earlier Scott had ridiculed the English attempts to impose uniformity on Scotland and I carried his reasoning further. One of the drawbacks of uniformity was that human beings were conservative by nature and cherished the patch of earth to which they belonged, and the friends and neighbours – those who Burke called the little platoon – with whom they shared it. Therefore the more uniform and standardized the culture, the more that each man and woman and country would want to assert their own individuality. 'This is what is happening in Scotland today', I concluded, 'and it is happening in other places in the world as well.'

# CHAPTER 22

## *The Long Road Home*

SEEN IN THE LONG VIEW OF HISTORY, THE PRESENT GROWING DEMAND FOR devolution in Scotland is a comparatively recent phenomenon. For if the creation of the political artefact of Great Britain had come into being to resolve the warring interests of Scotland and England, then the glue that held it together was the creation of another artefact, the British Empire; as prime an example as you could find of Proudhon's dictum that all property is theft. So long as it existed and prospered, the Scots prospered too.

It was the English who thought it might come unstuck first. In 1776, the year that saw both the triumph of the American colonists at Yorktown and the birthpangs of Irish Parliamentary independence, Horace Walpole wrote to Sir Horace Mann: 'I shall not be surprised if our whole trinity is dissolved, and if Scotland demand a dissolution of the union. Strange if she alone does not profit of our distress.' But Scotland had no wish to bite the hand that was helping to sustain her. 'Comparing the past with the present,' Lord Chancellor Loughborough had written in the *Edinburgh Review* some years earlier, 'we may clearly see the superior advantages we now enjoy, and readily discern from what source they flow.' Another cause of

Scottish tranquillity was the apparent willingness of Parliament to allow Scotland considerable licence in managing its own affairs.

Yet whenever the Scots believed England to be exceeding its powers they were quick to react. In 1779 the salaries of English judges were raised to £2,400 a year. No increase was made in the salaries of Scottish judges which had stood at £700 a year since 1759. Partly to rectify the anomaly, and partly to discourage placemen, in 1785 the government proposed a bill to subsidize a commensurate increase in the salaries of Scottish judges by reducing their numbers from fifteen to ten.

Scottish opposition was widespread and strident. Sir Adam Fergusson, MP for Ayrshire, told the House that the proposal was a violation of Article 19 of the Treaty of Union – that Scotland's Court of Session and legal system was to be preserved in all time coming – and the matter could not even be discussed without the king's assent. Boswell, as angry as anybody, said that the proposed increase for the full court would cost only £6,000 and could not that miserable sum be spared from some other corner of the establishment. Lord Fife echoed him: the sum involved was so small that it was 'degrading the dignity of the nation to raise it in so humiliating a manner'. Editorials in papers like the *Caledonian Mercury* and the *Courant* joined with sheriffs, magistrates and freeholders in fulminating against it; and in the face of such opposition the bill was withdrawn. This was one of the first of many occasions, stretching to the present day, of England treating Scotland like the poor relation she was instead of, as she also was, an equal partner under the terms of Union.

Forty years later history repeated itself. For some time past the Westminster Parliament had been endeavouring to bring Scottish ways of doing things into line with English ways. Some proposals, like the introduction of juries in civil cases, were welcomed. Others were not, and one of the clumsiest and least considered concerned the issue of Scottish banknotes. In 1825 there was a prospect of riches to be made in the burgeoning markets of South America; and some £200 million of English money was invested in a speculative boom which turned out almost as ruinous to English investors as the Darien scheme had been to the Scots. By the end of the year eighty independent English country banks had failed, and to stabilize the situation the government brought in a bill to prohibit the issue of paper money to the value of £5 or under.

Although this was a strictly English matter, for the sake of

uniformity the bill was extended to cover Scotland too. But the
Scottish system of banking was quite different from England's and
far more stable. Instead of a giant Bank of England at the centre
and numerous small, independent country banks, Scotland relied
on Edinburgh's five joint stock banks with country branch offices.
Unlike England, the Scottish currency was almost wholly in paper
money of which 63 per cent was in notes with a value of £5 and
under – the very ones the government was proposing to abolish.
Not only was the specie unsuitable for transporting across the wilder
regions of Scotland, but had the bill gone through, Scotland would
have suffered a massive, crippling deflation.

Once again all Scotland was outraged by the English ignorance
of Scottish affairs that lay behind the proposal, none more than Sir
Walter Scott who was as much angered by it as Boswell had been
in the matter of the judges; and under the pseudonym of Malachi
Malagrowther (descendant of a character in one of his novels) Sir
Walter wrote a polemic against it, published in consecutive editions
of the *Edinburgh Weekly Journal*.

After complaining of the absolute contempt with which Scottish
affairs were now being treated, he attacked in satirical vein the
government's insistence on extending the bill to Scotland for no
other reason than uniformity:

> In my opinion they might as well make a law that the Scotsman,
> for uniformity's sake, should not eat oatmeal, because it is found
> to give Englishmen heartburn. If an ordinance prohibiting the
> oatcake can be accompanied with a regulation capable of being
> enforced that in future, for uniformity's sake, our moors and
> uplands shall henceforth bear the purest wheat, I for one have no
> objection. But till Ben Nevis be level with Norfolkshire, though
> the natural wants of the two nations be the same, the extents of
> those wants . . . must be widely different. The nation which
> cannot raise wheat must be allowed to eat oat-bread; the nation
> which is too poor to retain a circulating medium of the precious
> metals must be permitted to supply its place with paper credit;
> otherwise they must go without food and without currency.

The Scottish system of currency had existed for 130 years and
the Treaty of Union had stipulated that it could not be altered
unless the alteration be to Scotland's advantage:

No advantage, evident or remote, has ever been hinted at, so far as Scotland is concerned; it has only been said, that it will be advantageous to England, to whose measures Scotland must be conformable . . .

But the gravamen of his complaint went beyond the matter of the currency:

There has been in England a gradual and progressive system of assuming the management of affairs entirely and exclusively proper to Scotland, as if we were totally unworthy of having the management of our own concerns. All must centre in London. We could not have a Caledonian Canal but the Commissioners must be Englishmen and meet in London . . . We could not be intrusted with the charge of erecting our own kirks or of making our roads and bridges in the same wild districts, but these labours must be conducted under the care of men who knew nothing of our country, its wants and its capabilities . . . Good Heaven, sir! to what are we fallen? – or rather, what are we esteemed by the English? Wretched drivellers, incapable of understanding our own affairs; or greedy speculators, unfit to be trusted? On what ground are we considered either as the one or the other?

He ended, true to character, on a note of reconciliation:

For God's sake, sir, let us remain as Nature made us, Englishmen, Irishmen, Scotchmen, with something like the impress of our several countries upon each! We would not become better subjects . . . if we all resembled each other like so many smooth shillings. Let us love and cherish each other's virtues, bear with each other's failings, be tender to each other's prejudices, be scrupulously regardful of each other's rights. Lastly, let us borrow each other's improvements, but never before they are needed or demanded.

The bill was never passed. Scottish banknotes continue to be issued to this day, a matter of great annoyance to English visitors who, on return to the south, find they have a fistful of them which few London cabbies are willing to accept.

The first move towards a loosening of the ties of the Treaty of Union came towards the end of the nineteenth century. In 1881 Lord Rosebery, then Under Secretary at the Home Office, said: 'The words Home Rule have begun to be distinctly and loudly mentioned in Scotland',* the reason being that with all the other business in hand, not enough time could be found for the proper consideration of Scottish affairs; and the Liberal Party leader, Gladstone, wondered if some sort of all-round devolution would not solve the problem of what he called 'an overweighted Parliament'. To lessen the weight, a Scottish Secretary was appointed in 1885. The following year saw the birth of the Scottish Home Rule Association. With a Liberal administration in power for the last decade of the nineteenth century and a big Liberal majority in Scotland, the Liberals might have been expected to push through a bill for a Scottish assembly. To have done so, however, would have meant depriving the national party of the support of the Scottish Liberals who had helped to put them in power – just the same argument as would be used in the twentieth century in regard to the Labour Party.† The only concession to Scotland having a greater voice in her own affairs came about in 1907 with the establishment of a Scottish standing Grand Committee. Successive Government of Scotland private members Bills were presented to Parliament in 1906, 1908, 1910, 1911, 1912, 1913 and 1914 but never progressed far. An Irish Home Rule Bill was *en train* at the same time, and it is possible that Home Rule for both countries would have reached the Statute Book had it not been for the Great War.

After the war, talk of Home Rule was again propagated, both in Scotland and at Westminster, but attracted little interest. Although the official Labour Party was formally committed to it, they did not see how the postwar Scottish ills of massive unemployment, slum housing and the decline of heavy industry could be remedied other than by gaining power at a British general election. However, in 1928 and as a sop to Scottish public opinion, the office of Secretary for Scotland was upgraded to that of Secretary of State, an appointment which, to ease the burden in Whitehall, led gradually to the removal

*By Home Rule is meant a Scottish Parliament to legislate for all domestic affairs but the Westminster Parliament to retain control over defence, foreign affairs and macro-economics.
†And the collapse of the Tory vote in Scotland today was mirrored by a similar collapse at the end of the nineteenth century.

of Scottish administration from London to St Andrew's House in Edinburgh. For a small group of Scottish patriots – among them R.B. Cunninghame Graham and Sir Compton Mackenzie – this was not enough and in the same year as the upgrading of the Scottish Secretary they formed the National Party of Scotland. Its guiding light was the legendary John MacCormick, regarded today as the principal founder of the modern Home Rule movement. Six years later they joined with the Scottish Party to form the Scottish National Party or SNP, dedicated to independence. The SNP chalked up its first victory at a by-election in Motherwell in 1945, but lost the seat at the general election six weeks later. Meanwhile, parallel to the political advancement and no less influential, Hugh MacDiarmid and others were staking their claims for Scottish independence in poetry and prose.

After the Second World War, Home Rule came back on the Scottish political agenda with a flourish, and has remained on it ever since with evidence of mounting internal support. In 1948 there were calls for a Scottish National Assembly to demand parliamentary devolution, and when this was ignored organized a National Covenant whose signatories pledged to work for the establishment of a Scottish Parliament within the framework of the United Kingdom. More than two million people signed (out of a population of five million) and even if, as alleged, some signatures were forged and others were those of children, it was a formidable display of public feeling. In 1950 Ian Hamilton and friends struck their blow for liberty with the capture and subsequent return of the Stone of Destiny (see Chapter 12). In the 1955 election the Conservatives reached the apex of their fortunes in Scotland when for the last time they captured half the seventy-two Parliamentary seats.

With Labour in 1958 reneging on their pledge to devolution, it was left to the SNP to sustain the momentum of the Home Rule movement and at the general election of 1966 they achieved their highest popular vote so far. Here was the writing on the wall, and in 1968 at Perth Edward Heath asked the Scottish Conservative Party Conference to seek some mechanism for devolution, which they signally failed to do. The SNP bandwagon rolled on. The second general election of 1974 saw them returned in eleven seats and at the same time the Labour Party, seeing the direction of the wind, became devolutionist again – though with some reluctance as it was on Labour seats in Scotland that they relied for their paper-thin majority, just as the Liberal government had done a hundred years earlier.

It now looked as though devolution could be only a matter of time, and in preparation for it the Labour government had the former Royal High School on Calton Hill, Edinburgh converted into a debating-chamber; and in 1979 a referendum was held to obtain the wishes of the Scottish people. Of those who voted 32.9 per cent were in favour, 30.8 per cent against; and 36.3 per cent of the electorate stayed at home – under the first past the post system a clear majority of 52 per cent but insufficient for victory under the amendment stipulating a 40 per cent minimum of the electorate to be in favour. Unexpected and disappointing was the large percentage of stay at homes. Obviously there were many who could not make up their minds as to whether Home Rule would be in Scotland's best interests or not; and these must have included Conservatives who, while remembering Edward Heath's call for devolution at Perth a decade earlier, yet were confused by the advice of the influential Alec Douglas Home not to vote in favour on this occasion but to wait for a future Conservative administration which would give them a better deal. Had a Conservative government been in office then and introduced a referendum of which Sir Alec had approved, it is possible that the necessary minimum in favour would have been obtained.

After the result Lord Home said that the question of devolution would remain on the political agenda. He was wrong; for soon after the referendum a little Englander in the shape of Mrs Thatcher swept into power and while ready to pay lip service to devolution, saw to it that during the next eleven years and despite the number of Conservative seats in Scotland dwindling to ten, it was kept firmly off the political agenda.

In the course of her premiership therefore, BBC Scotland put on a St Andrew's Day debate, the motion being, 'That devolution is dead and ought to be put to rest'. I was asked to speak on either side, and chose in favour of the motion, which puzzled the devolutionists opposite, who, understandably, thought I was betraying them.

Yet it could not be denied that as a matter of fact devolution was dead. 'Where', I asked, 'is the evidence otherwise?' The referendum, I said, had killed it, and we had been denied even the limited self-government that had recently been granted to the Cook Islands, Faeroe Islands and Cameroons. 'Stands Scotland where it did?' I asked, after Malcolm in *Macbeth*. ' "Alas, poor country, almost afraid to know itself." True in Macbeth's time and true today. For in the matter of self-government we have become a nation of political eunuchs.'

I ended on a note that pleased the devolutionists, though not the benches from which I was speaking. 'But because devolution is dead today, that does not mean that it will stay dead tomorrow. There has already been one recorded resurrection in history. Let us all hope that there will soon be another.'

And there was. In 1988 *A Claim of Right for Scotland*, a powerful pro-devolution polemic was published, the work of various hands, skilfully presented and edited by Owen Dudley Edwards. It led in turn to the setting-up of the Scottish Constitutional Convention, a body committed to the task of presenting detailed proposals for a Scottish assembly or Parliament and which could attract widespread support. The Conservatives, true to form, declined to take part, as did the SNP, bruised by the loss of half their Parliamentary seats; and it was left to the Labour Party and the Liberal Democrats, local Councillors, representatives of the Churches, Trades Unions and Universities, to hammer out an agreed set of proposals. They were moderate, they were just, they were wanted, but for all the notice the Conservative government took of them and the work that had gone into them, the delegates might have saved themselves the trouble. On the other hand, the proposals have not dated, and remain as a basis for negotiations when Home Rule, as it will be, is on the agenda again.

Indeed it might have been considered at the general election of 1992 had not a strange thing happened. Before the election a respectable opinion poll found that 50 per cent of the Scottish electorate wanted independence. In fact they didn't, they wanted Home Rule: people often mislead. But the poll enabled John Major, the Prime Minister, to say when he came to Scotland and mounted his little travelling soap-box that if the Scots wanted independence, they could have it. The very thought of shifting in one move from being a region of Britain to complete independence so terrified the bulk of the electorate that the number of Conservative seats in Scotland rose from nine to eleven while those of the SNP collapsed from five to three. But to make plain to Mr Major and other European leaders how much devolution was still coveted, a small army of 25,000 Home Rulers marched through the streets of Edinburgh at the time of the 1993 European Union summit.

# CHAPTER 23

## Birth of a New Song

As long as but a hundred of us remain alive, will we on any conditions be brought under English rule.

*Declaration of Arbroath 1320*

I am writing this in June 1996 when the present distribution of Scottish parliamentary seats is as follows: Labour 49, Conservative 10, Liberal Democrat 9, SNP 4. This means two things; that 62 of the 72 elected members are in favour of some form of Home Rule and only 10 are against; but because the 10 belong to Britain's governing party, that party can and does carry out policies in Scotland which are against the wishes of most of the Scottish people.

There is, however, some light at the end of the tunnel. The commitment of the Labour Party to Scottish Home Rule was recently reaffirmed by the new Labour leader, Tony Blair. If Labour was to find itself in power after the next general election, he said, a bill for a Scottish Parliament and a Welsh assembly would be laid before Parliament during the first session of its proceedings. Nothing is more unpredictable than political crystal-gazing, but if the unpopularity of the present government and its leaders is reflected in the voting patterns of the next election, now only two years away, then Scotland will have its own domestic parliament before the end of the millennium.

Today the reasons for Home Rule are what they have always been but even more pressing: that the further away from the seat of power a locality is, the less attention will be paid to it; that whatever domestic problems arise in Scotland, whether of health or housing, transport or education, urban decay in the Lowland belt or depopulation in the Highlands will have a greater commitment given to them by a Scottish Parliament working exclusively for Scottish interests than by a predominantly English parliament 400 miles away in London. If the lack of time at Westminster to introduce and debate Scottish bills which in 1883 caused Lord Rosebery to resign from the Home Office was thought to be acute then, it is even more so today.

In the past Conservative politicians such as the former Secretary of State for Scotland, Ian Lang, the present Secretary of State for Foreign Affairs Malcolm Rifkind, and the present Minister of State for Northern Ireland Michael Ancram, drew attention to this and the need for devolution to resolve it, but not enough to influence Conservative policy. In his Town and Gown address to the University of Strathclyde in November 1991, Sir David Steel, the former Liberal leader, spoke of the surprise and disgust of Scottish fishermen and teachers coming to the Commons to hear debates on fishing and education and finding them being held 'late at night at the fag end of a Parliamentary day', one such debate not concluded until after two in the morning. He went on:

> Let us take the procedure of Question Time. English members can table a question relating to their constituents on a farming matter on a Monday, on a housing matter on a Tuesday, an education matter on a Wednesday and a health matter on a Thursday. Scottish members cannot do that because the one member responsible [for all those departments] is the Secretary of State. We have to wait for our one chance a month when he comes to the Dispatch Box and hope to be lucky in the draw for the fifteen questions which will be reached in the hour.*

*Since the above was written a further Question Time has been introduced in the sittings of the Scottish Grand Committee.

Scottish Question Time, said Sir David, had been rendered even more farcical by the Speaker having ruled that both sides of the House must be balanced, even though there might be no more than four back-benchers on the government side and more than sixty on the opposition side from three different parties.

The result of this approach is that any English Tory who cares to wander in with a daft contribution will get called in preference to other elected representatives of the Scottish people who may sit through the whole hour and never get called. This practice is increasingly offensive to both the electorate and their MPs.

Sir David made two other points. Why had the government made a distinction in the matter of devolution between the province of Northern Ireland (as artificial a concept as that of Great Britain) and the nation of Scotland? Article 10 of the Anglo-Irish agreement referred to 'devolution which secures widespread acceptance in Northern Ireland.' Why not the same for us? (Presumably because we have not adapted the Irish practices of 'broken glass'.) Even more unjust in comparison was the status accorded to the Falkland Islands in 1982 when Mrs Thatcher decreed that in the future their constitutional wishes would be paramount – not consulted, not safeguarded but *paramount*. Why should the wishes of the 2,000 people of the Falklands, 8,000 miles away, be paramount but not those of five million Scots living just across the English border? More than £3,000,000,000 of British tax-payers' money had been spent on maintaining fortress Falklands, a sum, said Sir David, 'far in excess of the cost of establishing self-determination for Scotland'. His final point was that Westminster's refusal to take heed of the wishes of the Scottish people was an abrogation of the Treaty of Union; for the Lord President of the Court of Session, Lord Cooper, had ruled in a celebrated judgment in 1953 that while under Scottish constitutional law legislative sovereignty was vested in Parliament, political sovereignty lay with the people. His unspoken conclusion therefore was that if ever a majority of the Scottish electorate expressed a political wish for change (as they have done) not to grant them change would be a denial of their constitutional rights.

Whence then in Scotland does opposition to Home Rule mostly

come? From where you would expect it, society's upper and middle echelons, i.e. the lairds and the bourgeoisie who know that two-thirds of the electorate come from the lower echelons, and fear it; fear that a Labour-dominated Scottish Parliament, with its memories of William Gallacher and John Maxton and other Red Clydesiders, will bring in a punitive land or wealth tax, nationalization or re-nationalization of Scottish industries, state interference at every level of national life, leading to a reduced standard of living. It is, says Maurice Lindsay, the vested interests of the upper classes who have a long tradition of loyalty to the Crown (which is presumed to favour the status quo) that inhibits one stratum of society from giving support to the strengthening of Scotland's sense of nation-hood by political means. Others in opposition must include some of the 38 per cent of the electorate who were too apathetic to vote in the 1979 referendum and for whom, says Lindsay, the health of Scotland's nationhood is not of the slightest interest: they dislike the idea of any change and are quite content to continue their lives under a Great British government, whether Conservative (preferably) or Labour.

The fears of the lairds and the bourgeoisie are understandable but in my view are of the past. Labour's cloth cap image has long been discarded; so has nationalization and Clause 4; private ownership and market forces are now party policy. There is also emollience for the lairds and bourgeoisie in that the Scottish Constitutional Convention is not recommending the unfair Westminster voting system of first past the post (abandoned by almost every other western democracy) but some form of proportional representation (preferably additional list system) which should lead to a more equitable distribution of seats, and the inability of any one party to dominate.

There is a further reason for Home Rule which is based on the question of identity. So long as the empire and commonwealth existed, Scots were ready to clothe themselves in the mantle of Britishness in order to play a part in it. But now that empire and commonwealth have slipped down the plughole of history, the idea of Great Britain as a living entity to which love and loyalty can be given is, for most Scots and some English, fast disappearing. When the English use the word British, they do not have in mind the Scots or Welsh, for to them British means English. Britain and British are ugly words which already seem outdated. Singing 'Rule Britannia' and Britain never, never, never being slaves must have sounded fine in the heyday of empire but when played on the last night of the Proms, it sounds pretty tatty, like an old garment pulled out of the dressing-up box which is no longer in fashion. When Mr Colin Welland told a Hollywood audience on the night of the Oscars that the Brits were coming, it was difficult for most Brits not to feel a twinge of embarrassment.

No poet of consequence has celebrated Britain or Britishness in the past 200 years, as no philosopher in the same period has celebrated religion. But plenty have paid tribute to England, a word which as an Anglo-Scot I find as romantic and often moving as the word Scotland. We should be glad that Nelson signalled 'England expects' to his fleet before Trafalgar, and not 'Britain' despite the hundreds of Scots, Welsh, Irish serving under him. How much less attractive if Browning had written, 'Oh, to be in Britain, now that April's here', if Rupert Brooke had written 'Some corner of a foreign field that is for ever Britain', if the popular wartime song had been 'There'll always be a Britain'. The word Scotland and Scots arouses similar sentiments ('Scots wha' hae wi' Wallace bled'; 'I'll be in Scotland afore ye') and maybe Wales and Welsh does to the Welsh, though I never heard of any that were complimentary. The English *feel* English but use British out of political correctness. What I am saying is that a sense of Britishness is dying and the countries of the United Kingdom are psychologically in the process of returning to their constituent parts.

From time to time outsiders, mostly English and often persons of influence and authority, have encouraged us along the road to Home Rule or even independence. Here is what the Liberal candidate Winston Churchill said to the electorate of Dundee in 1911:

> . . . as to the future, we have to secure for Scotland a much more direct and convenient method of bringing her influence to bear upon her own purely domestic affairs. There is nothing which conflicts with the integrity of the United Kingdom in the setting up of a Scottish Parliament for the discharge of Scottish business. There is nothing which conflicts with the integrity of the United Kingdom in securing to Scotsmen in that, or in some other way, an effective means of shaping the special legislation which affects them and only them. Certainly I am of opinion that if such a scheme can be brought into existence it will mean a great enrichment not only of the national life

of Scotland, but of the politics and public life of the United
Kingdom.

and George Orwell, writing in 1947:

> Up to date the Scottish Nationalist movement seems to have
> gone almost unnoticed in England. To take the nearest example
> to hand, I don't remember having seen it mentioned in *Tribune*,
> except occasionally in book reviews. It is true that it is a small
> movement, but it could grow, because there is a basis for it.
> *In this country I don't think it is enough realized* – I myself had
> no idea of it until a few years ago – that Scotland has a case
> against England. On economic grounds it may not be a very
> strong case. In the past, certainly, we have plundered Scotland
> shamefully, but whether it is *now* true that England as a whole
> exploits Scotland as a whole, and that Scotland would be better off
> if fully autonomous, is another question. The point is that many
> Scottish people, often quite moderate in outlook, are beginning
> to think about autonomy and to feel that they are pushed into an
> inferior position. They have a good deal of reason. In some areas,
> at any rate, Scotland is almost an occupied country. You have an
> English or anglicized upper class, and a Scottish working class
> which speaks with a markedly different accent, or even, part of
> the time, in a different language.

And coming to our own times, a fellow Celt, the writer Jan
Morris, writing from Skye:

> How perfectly extraordinary, I thought, that any citizen of this
> singular and tremendous country would *not* wish it to control
> its own national destinies? In population Scotland is bigger
> than Denmark, Finland, Ireland, Norway or New Zealand. In
> ability it vastly outmatches countless members of the United
> Nations. In history it is proud and fascinating. In terrain it is
> self-contained and majestic. It contains two of the great cities
> of Europe, and some of the most glorious landscapes. How can
> any Scot stomach the fact that it is not a state in its own right,
> with its own voice?
> Skye is especially vulnerable, being of a supernal beauty
> and cherishing some of the most sensitive of Scottish heritages

from the Fairy Flag of the MacLeods in Dunvegan Castle to the lingering wistful cadences of the Gaelic language. But everywhere in Scotland one feels this country's inferior status. Its two grand cities . . . are still ancillary to London. Its famous fighting regiments are subject to British command, and probably British dissolution. Its most ambitious politicians can sit only in the London parliament, its most brilliant diplomats can serve only in British embassies. Officially this is still a kingdom, but whoever heard the Queen of England called the Queen of Scotland (or for that matter, the Queen of the United Kingdom)?

Breathes there a Scot who never says, his soul a' thrill, 'This is my own, my native land'? Yet five million Scots allow themselves to be subject, for most practical purposes, to the alien power of the south — a condition that seems, to one of my temperament, not merely degrading but inexplicable. For one cannot doubt that if the Scottish people demanded it, self-government could be theirs tomorrow — even independence, with their own star on the flag of Europe, and their own seat at the United Nations.

One of the odder paradoxes about Home Rule is the response of the English to it. Scottish life and affairs do not enter the average English person's head from one year to the next: we are as little known or thought about as if we were Turks or Portuguese. Yet whenever the question of Home Rule raises its head, and the English are faced with the possibility of our hiving off, partly or wholly, they take tremendous personal offence. Yet if, as they maintain, Scotland's living standards have to be subsidized by the English tax-payer, you would think they would be only too happy for that burden to be lifted, to allow us to paddle our own canoe.

But no, they become quite xenophobic. In February 1993 the *Independent*'s political columnist, Andrew Marr, himself a Scot, wrote a thoughtful piece about the problem of English identity entitled 'England's not the country nor the country England' (from a saying of Stanley Baldwin). 'You can be black and British but you cannot be black and English. In a multi-racial country this gives the word an explosive charge it never used to carry. For many English, and it is to their credit, their own label has worrying connotations of racism and xenophobia. "English nationalists" means fascists and anti immigrants.'

England is now a country, Marr went on, that exists on the sports field and in art but nowhere else. He asked whether the decline of England as a political or patriotic fact mattered, and said we should bear it in mind as a potential source of political instability:

> Nationalism can emerge in a foul temper when people feel their identity is threatened; and when the Maastricht rebels roar against the threat of 700 years of Parliament, we hear the authentic voice of English nationalism.
>
> National feeling matters, and should never be underestimated or ignored. Common sense suggests that English nationalism is buried too deep to influence modern Europe. But common sense, Einstein taught us, is merely 'the deposit of prejudice laid down in the mind before the age of 18'. *One day reformers may rebuild this country in a way that allows England to re-emerge in her own right.* (My italics)

In this intelligent and essentially moderate piece Marr was only exercising the plea of his fellow countryman Robert Burns to allow people to see themselves (in this case the English) as others (in this case a percipient Scot) see them. But English hackles were raised, and none more so than those of Mr Matthew Parris, the *Times* columnist and a former Conservative MP. Mr Parris is one of the sharpest, wittiest and most urbane of current political commentators: but, in reply to Mr Marr, wit and urbanity deserted him. Their place was taken by the sort of sarcasm you would expect from a twelve-year-old schoolboy and the sort of hysteria of which Mr Marr was complaining.

Marr, said Parris, 'offers us English his sympathies that we do not have that fully-fledged sense of nationhood that the three Celtic countries enjoy. Our Englishness is there, he suggests, but buried, inchoate. We, poor things, are in the closet and cannot parade or celebrate our nationalism. England is "the submerged nation".'

'It is always a pleasure to be patronized by the Scots,' Parris went on, 'but that really does take the biscuit . . . How shall we put this to Andrew Marr? You see, his concern that we take so little apparent satisfaction from being English arises from his observation that we don't talk much about it. But we don't talk about it much because we don't need to. And we don't need to, Mr Marr, because we *won*. We're on top. We're in control. The Celts lost. Your essay, we note, was not penned in Gaelic. We are the nation and on the whole we think it bad manners to rub it in. We realize you Scots are jumpy about your own nationhood and we think we can guess why. Our English nationhood goes without saying, because it's safe and we're secure in it.'

Mr Marr's critique must have struck deep, for the rest of Mr Parris's article continued in a rising crescendo of sarcasm and condescension:

> We know perfectly well who we are, hardly need to mention it and are terribly relaxed about names. Call us British if you prefer: we're happy to call you Scots, we promise to try to remember not to say 'Scotch' except for the whisky, and we really will make an effort not to address our postcards from Peru to Edinburgh, *Inglaterra* (though all the rest of the world does) because we know it upsets you.
>
> Or shall we go further? Would you like us to stop saying 'England, Scotland and Wales' and say 'Scotland, Wales and England'? Or shall we just call the whole of Britain 'Scotland'? As you please: we honestly don't care. The boss nation does not need to protest its nationhood: why, we go for whole days on end without even thinking about it.
>
> Oh, and would you like to have your road signs printed in your own language? We'd quite understand. Ah – you can't *read* your own language any more. So sorry. Well, what about a television channel in Welsh for Wales?* Fine, we'll gladly pay, for it seems to mean a lot to them, poor dears. Perhaps it would be nice to have 'border' signs erected and to rename British Rail 'ScotRail' in Scotland, so you can feel it's yours.†
>
> Tell us, too, how to be tactful about those long-ago victories, and we'll try. It was a good idea, wasn't it, to call it the 'treaty' of 'union' in 1707, though we know you had no choice. Anyway, we're terribly enthusiastic about your native customs and can't get enough of those bagpipes and Burns nights and haggis and people in delightful kilts: quite a money-spinner for you, down in England!

*A television channel in Welsh has been operating since 1982.
†British Rail in Scotland has been known as ScotRail since 1983.

What's that? Independence, you say?

D'you know, after careful thought: *yes*, if you really want it. The oil is running out now, isn't it? And fishing's not much cop, these days. Hang on a few minutes while we run through a checklist of what's in Scotland, but I don't think there's anything there we really need any more. We realize that most of you wouldn't want to go back and *live* there, but that's fine, too. We've always been relaxed about immigrants in England, as long as they do things our way: and you do, Andrew, you do. You can even come and be MPs here if you like. No rooted objection to independence, then. Shall you have a democracy, do you think – or something more tribal? Any chance of persuading the Welsh to go as well? Too much to hope for, I expect, but think of the saving! Oh, and when you do go, perhaps you'd take Northern Ireland with you – the colony for Scotsmen who could swim.

Are the Celtic satellites not colonies? We overwhelmed them, destroyed their governments, and relegated their languages. In our African possessions we whites seldom discussed our own nationhood, though the natives were always keen to tell us which tribes they came from . . .

. . . Britain? Humbug! England's the country, Mr Marr, and the country is England.

Another English journalist, the normally relaxed Mr Edward Pearce, joined Mr Parris in his contempt for the Scots when reporting on a by-election in Kincardine in 1991. Totally uncomprehending, he was offended by having to listen to what he called 'the whimper of nationalism' and by Scottish 'self-pity'; and he mocked the locals for pronouncing 'English' as 'Unglish' (which the Irish do too).

Why is it that Messrs Parris, Pearce and others get in such a lather whenever the question arises of Scots contracting out? My own view – and Messrs Parris and Pearce will no doubt find this as patronizing as what Mr Marr wrote – is that it is the buffer nations of Scotland, Wales and, to a lesser degree, the province of Northern Ireland together with their own three million blacks and Asians, that keep the English British. When Mr Parris says that the English don't assert their nationality because they don't need to, he is admitting to a defect rather than a strength. If the English are to rediscover their sense of nationhood, they can only do so when the need for it arises – for the present they can go on airily pretending that it doesn't matter. Mr Parris was near to recognizing this in a further *Times* article when he canvassed the idea of the English leaving the United Kingdom and setting sail on their own. When the break comes, it will be a traumatic but exhilarating experience, the pain of separation allayed by the prospect of new challenges and directions in both our national affairs.

You hear it said that if Scottish Home Rule comes about, it will be the slippery slope that leads to independence. That is what the Scottish National Party see as their goal, rejecting what Hugh MacDiarmid in a poem called 'the hauf-way hoose'. It is this reluctance to accept gradualism combined with an attitude that relies on economic arguments and has little cultural or sentimental base that, in my view, has led to a brake on the SNP's continued advancement. Their present leader, Alex Salmond, is a fluent and competent political activist but whether he is the commanding fig-ure to lead his fellow countrymen into the promised land remains to be seen. It is astonishing to me that he and his supporters have not cottoned on to the fact that, being the ultra cautious people we are, instant independence frightens the life out of most Scots while the hauf-way hoose, at least as a starter, is eminently desirable.

But there is one very big snag to the hauf-way hoose, and that is what has been called the West Lothian question, after the member for that constituency, Tam Dalyell, who first raised it. The hauf-way hoose, i.e. Scottish Home Rule, will mean that from the time it takes effect, Westminster will no longer be able to debate or legislate for Scottish affairs. In that case, asks the West Lothian question, why should Scotland, in addition to having its own MPs in Edinburgh, also be permitted to send other MPs to Westminster to debate and legislate for English affairs. My answer to that is quite simple. I cannot think of any self-respecting Scot who, with his own Parliament in his own country, would want to travel down to London to take part in the Parliament there: certainly not to contribute his voice to the twice-yearly defence or foreign affairs debates, in which, if his views differ from those of the government it is certain he will be outvoted. And what other interesting attractions are waiting to lure him there? The Charlwood and Horley Local Government Act 1974? The Regional Hospital Boards Act (England and Wales) 1994?

So, if the hauf-way hoose is necessary as a temporary measure, which I think it probably is, I cannot see it lasting as a permanent one. There are other cogent reasons to persuade one that sovereignty, either politically within the EU or, like Norway, outside it, is eminently desirable. Home Rule will give us control over areas like the Highlands where once people gave way to sheep and latterly sheep have given way to conifers; but in other vital areas we shall be powerless. Take fishing. Nine tenths of Scotland's borders are washed by the sea. Scotland's fisheries are very precious to it and at present they are being eroded by overfishing and pollution. The herrings I remember as a boy weighed a pound or more; today the average herring is half that. Russian factory ships appear in the Minch and off Shetland. Either we establish our own territorial fishing rights, as Iceland and Norway have done, or we renegotiate terms within the EU.

Then take the matter of oil, which the SNP declared was Scotland's oil when it was first discovered, but neither Scotland as a whole nor the Westminster Parliament took any notice. There was no broken glass. As I write, a vast new oilfield has been discovered in the Atlantic west of the Shetlands. At present it is British oil and under Home Rule will remain British oil, at least if precedents are to go by. But in a sovereign Scotland it would be Scotland's oil, and could help to activate the Scottish economy.

There's also the problem of the British nuclear deterrent, the huge Trident submarine which carries sixteen warheads and can devastate cities and regions 6,000 miles away. There are or will be four of these things based in a sealoch off the Firth of Clyde. In a Home Rule Scotland they would remain there; but a sovereign Scotland would surely order their removal. They cost a fortune, threaten nobody and there is no conceivable situation in which they can ever be used. Do Austria, Norway, Denmark, Holland, Belgium and Sweden feel any less secure because they do not possess them? If not, why should Scotland? The thing is a white elephant, an obscene anachronism, the last tattered remnant of a former imperial power still pathetically trying to reassert itself. The gesture – for it is no more – impresses nobody. The sort of navy that a sovereign Scotland would need would be half a dozen fishery and oil-rig protection vessels.

People say that the business, industrial and social ties between England and Scotland are now so intertwined that it would be impossible to unscramble them. Not if one had the will and if, as Sir Walter Scott pleaded, the English could bring themselves to accept it without rancour. After all, the Norwegians and Swedes once shared a single country, so did the Dutch and Belgians, the Spanish and the Portuguese and, ever more recently, the Czechs and the Slovaks, yet all successfully unscrambled themselves. In human affairs nothing is immutable and a time may come for England and Scotland to do the same. There are also those who fret about the financial position of Scotland in both a Home Rule and a sovereign Scotland. Opinion on this is divided. The SNP and some others claim that Scotland will be better off in either event, and have published some persuasive figures to prove it. The English and some Scots disagree. My own view is that if initially there is any shortfall (and I am not convinced of it) then a just share of the revenue from the new oil fields will give a boost to the economy on which to build; but more than that, the sense of exhilaration and pride in managing our own affairs again will release energies to create new enterprises, beget new inventions such as our people – Baird, Lister, Hunter, Simpson, Dunlop, Mackintosh, Fleming, Macadam, Watt, Stephenson and a score of others – achieved with such stunning success in the last 200 years.

And yet the financial aspect is not the mainstay. 'It is in truth,' said the Declaration of Arbroath, 'not for glory, nor riches, nor honour that we are fighting, but for freedom.' The patriotic Scot of today would endorse that, and add, beyond freedom, an even deeper sentiment, never more nobly expressed than by Sir Compton Mackenzie in his inaugural address as Rector of Glasgow University:

We now alive in Scotland, though not necessarily therefore living, are offered the grace of sharing in the rebirth of a nation . . .

Among the constant characteristics of all genuine conversions is the subject's suddenly heightened sense of ordinary life and an immensely wider perception of its richness. In a single instant of revelation he is made aware of the immortal substance of things; but his secret remains incommunicable.

The phenomenon of conversion, though usually accorded a religious significance, is not peculiar to religion. An artist may pass through a mental state analogous to conversion in the first moment of an imaginative conception, and when he does we call it 'inspiration'.

I have seen the phenomenon of conversion among those who have been wakened to a sudden comprehension of what true nationalism is. They are changed by some mystical experience, and in loving their country they love their fellow-countrymen. It is such a love which alone can justify the reformer. Too many attempts at reformation have been made either in a spirit of hate and destructiveness or, what is ultimately more deadly, in a spirit of constructive utility. Desire the good of your fellow-men, but desire it because you love them, not because a well-fed, well-clad, well-housed creature will be an economic asset to the state. Many of you present are filled with ambition to re-create a nation; but your immediate and predominant duty is to re-create yourselves, for only in re-creating yourselves will you re-create that nation . . .

Simultaneously sovereignty, in whole or in part, will free us at last of the crippling disability which has plagued us down the centuries: I mean the sense of inferiority instilled by our formidable neighbour, in relation to him and to no other; for as Isaiah Berlin says in quoting the German philosopher Herder: 'To be the object of contempt or patronizing tolerance on the part of proud neighbours is one of the most traumatic experiences that individuals or societies can suffer.' And he goes on, '. . . no minority that has preserved its own cultural tradition or religious or racial characteristics can indefinitely tolerate the prospect of remaining a minority for ever, governed by a majority with a different outlook or habits.' The shedding of that sense of inferiority will not happen overnight, it has been part of the Scottish psyche for too long, but the seeds of it will have been sown, the climate will be right for its dispersal.

In short it is time for the elephant to start moving out. Then and only then will we be able in love and friendship to face the English as equals, just as our emigrant ancestors learned to when they became Americans, Canadians, Australians, New Zealanders 200 and more years ago. Then and only then will Scotland be able to rejoin the comity of nations and come once again into her own.

# SOME BOOKS CONSULTED

Adam, Isabel, *Witch Hunt: The Great Scottish Witchcraft Trials of 1697* (London, 1978).

Anderson, A.O. and M.O., *Adamnan's Life of Columba* (London, 1961).

Atkinson, Eleanor, *Greyfriar's Bobby* (New York, 1929).

Barrow, G.W.S., *Robert the Bruce and the Scottish Identity* (Edinburgh, 1984).

Beattie, James, *Scotticisms* (Edinburgh, 1787).

Bell, Ian, *RLS: Dreams of Exile, a Biography* (Edinburgh, 1992).

Berlin, Sir Isaiah, *The Crooked Timber of Humanity: Chapters in the History of Human Ideas* [edited by Henry Hardy] (London, 1990).

Black, George F., *A Calendar of Cases of Witchcraft in Scotland, 1510–1727* (New York, 1938).

Boswell, James, *The Journal of a Tour to the Hebrides with Samuel Johnson* (London, 1785).

Boswell, James, *The Life of Samuel Johnson*, L.L.D., 2 vols (London, 1791).

Brown, George Mackay, *Portrait of Orkney* (London, 1981).

Brown, Peter Hume, *Scotland, A Concise History* (Glasgow, 1992).

Brown, Peter Hume, *Surveys of Scottish History* (Glasgow, 1919).

Buchan, John, *John Macnab* (London, 1956).

Buckle, Henry Thomas, *On Scotland and the Scotch Intellect* [edited and with an introduction by H.J. Hanham] (Chicago, 1970).

Burns, Robert, *The Complete Works* [edited by James Mackay] (Ayr, 1990).

Burns, Robert, *The Letters* [edited by Roy G. Ross] (Oxford, 1985).

Calder, Jenni, *Scotland in Trust* (Glasgow, 1990).

Carswell, Catherine, *The Life of Robert Burns* (Edinburgh, 1990).

Chitnis, Anand C., *The Scottish Enlightenment and Early Victorian English Society* (London, 1986).

Cobbett, William, *Cobbett's Tour in Scotland* [edited and with an introduction by Daniel Green] (Aberdeen, 1984).

Cockburn, Henry, Lord, *Memorials of His Time* (Edinburgh, 1856).

Colley, Linda, *Britons: Forging the Nation, 1707–1837* (London, 1994).

Cowan, Ian B., *Mary, Queen of Scots* (Edinburgh, 1987).

Cranston, Maurice, *The Noble Savage*, J.J. Rousseau, 1754–1762 (London, 1991).

Cruickshank, Andrew (ed), *The Scottish Bedside Book* (London, 1977).

Cullen, W. Douglas, the Hon. Lord, *Parliament House, A Short History and Guide* (Edinburgh, 1992).

*Culloden* (London, 1815).

Daiches, David, *Edinburgh* (London, 1978).

Daiches, David, *Robert Louis Stevenson and his World* (London, 1973).

Daiches, David, *Scotland and the Union* (London, 1977).

Daiches, David, *Sir Walter Scott and his World* (London, 1971).

Defoe, Daniel, *The History of the Union of Great Britain* (Edinburgh, 1709).

Defoe, Daniel, *The Letters* [edited by G.H. Healey] (Oxford, 1955).

Devine, T.M. (ed), *Improvement and Enlightenment, Proceedings of the Scottish Historical Studies Seminar*, University of Strathclyde, 1987–88 (Edinburgh, 1989).

Devine, T.M. and Mitchison, Rosalind (eds), *People and Society in Scotland: A Social History of Modern Scotland*, Vol 1, 1760–1830. (Edinburgh, 1988).

*Dictionary of National Biography* (London, various volumes).

Donaldson, Gordon, *Scottish Historical Documents* (Edinburgh and London, 1970).

Donaldson, Gordon, *The Auld Alliance, The Franco-Scottish Connection* (Edinburgh, 1985).

Dunn, Douglas, *Scotland, An Anthology* (London, 1992).

Edwards, Owen Dudley (ed), *A Claim of Right for Scotland* (Edinburgh, 1989).

Edwards, Owen Dudley and Richardson, Graham, *Edinburgh* (Edinburgh, 1983).

Elcho, David Wemyss, Lord, *A Short Account of the Affairs of Scotland: in the years 1744, 1745, 1746* [printed from the original manuscript at Gosford] (Edinburgh, 1907).

Feachem, Richard, *A Guide to Prehistoric Scotland* (London, 1963).

Ferguson, William, *Scotland's Relations with England: A Survey to 1707* (Edinburgh, 1977).

Fergusson, Sir James (ed), *The Declaration of Arbroath* (Edinburgh, 1970).

Fletcher of Saltoun, Andrew, *United and Separate Parliaments* (Edinburgh, 1982).

Forman, Sheila, *Scottish Country Houses and Islands* (London, 1967).

Gilmour, Ian, *Riot, Risings and Revolution: Governance and Violence in Eighteenth Century England* (London, 1992).

Goring, Rosemary (ed), *Chambers Scottish Biographical Dictionary* (Edinburgh, 1992).

Glover, Janet R., *The Story of Scotland* (London, 1960).

Graham, Henry, *The Social Life of Scotland in the Eighteenth Century* (London, 1937).

Grange, R.M.D., *A Short History of Scottish Dress* (London, 1966).

Halliday, James, *Scotland, A Concise History* (Edinburgh, 1990).

Hamilton, Ian, *The Taking of the Stone of Destiny* (Moffat, 1991).

Hanham, H.J., *Scottish Nationalism* (London, 1969).

Harvie, Christopher, *No Gods and Precious Few Heroes: Scotland since 1914* [The New History of Scotland] (London, 1981).

Harvie, Christopher, *Scotland and Nationalism: Scottish Society and Politics, 1707–1977* (London, 1977).

Holmes, Geoffrey (ed), *Britain after the Glorious Revolution, 1689–1714* (London, 1969).

Hume, David, *An Enquiry Concerning the Human Understanding: and An Enquiry Concerning the Principles of Morals* [reprinted from the posthumous edition of 1777 and edited with an introduction, comparative tables of contents, and an analytical index, by L.A. Selby-Bigge] (Oxford, 1894).

Hume, David, *Dialogues Concerning Natural Religion* (New York, 1948).

Hume, David, *The Letters* [edited by J.Y.T. Greig] 2 vols (Oxford, 1932).

Jenkins, David and Visocchi, Mark, *Mendelssohn in Scotland* (London, 1978).

Johnson, Samuel, *A Journey to the Western Isles of Scotland* (London, 1775).

Jones, Peter (ed), *The Science of Man in the Scottish Enlightenment* (Edinburgh, 1989).

Jones, Peter (ed), *Philosophy and Science in the Scottish Enlightenment* (Edinburgh, 1988).

Keats, John, *The Letters* [edited by Maurice Buxton Forman] (Oxford, 1952).

Keay, John and Julia, *Collins Encyclopaedia of Scotland* (London, 1994).

Kernohan, R.D., *Our Church, A Guide to the Kirk of Scotland* (Edinburgh, 1985).

Kidd, Colin, *Suberting Scotland's Past: Scottish Whig Historians and the Creation of an Anglo-British Identity, 1689–c1830* (Cambridge, 1993).

Knight, William Angus, *Lord Monboddo and some of his Contemporaries* (London, 1900).

Kybett, Susan Maclean, *Bonnie Prince Charlie: A Biography* (London, 1988).

Lindsay, Maurice (ed), *By Yon Bonnie Banks: A Gallimaufry* (London, 1961).

Lockhart, John Gibson, *Memoirs of the Life of Sir Walter Scott* (Philadelphia, 1838).

Lenman, Bruce, *The Jacobite Cause* (Glasgow, 1986).

Linklater, Eric, *The Survival of Scotland: A Review of Scottish History from Roman Times to the Present Day* (London, 1968).

Linklater, Magnus and Denniston, Robin, *Anatomy of Scotland* (Edinburgh, 1992).

Lynch, Michael, *Scotland: A New History* (London, 1991).

MacDiarmid, Hugh, *The Uncanny Scot* (London, 1968).

MacDiarmid, Hugh, *Complete Poems* [edited by Michael Grieve and W.R. Aitken] 2 vols (London, 1978).

Mackay, James, *Robert Burns: A Biography* (Edinburgh, 1990).

Mackenzie, Osgood, *A Hundred Years in the Highlands* (London, 1921).

Mackenzie, W.C., *Andrew Fletcher of Saltoun: His Life and Times* (Edinburgh, 1935).

Maclean, Sir Fitzroy, *Bonnie Prince Charlie* (London, 1988).

McLaren, Moray (ed), *The Shell Guide to Scotland* (London, 1965).

McLaren, Moray, *The Wisdom of the Scots* (London, 1961).

McLaren, Moray, *Understanding the Scots: A Guide for South Britons and other Foreigners* (London, 1956).

McWilliam, Colin, Gifford, John and Walker, David, *Edinburgh* [The Buildings of Scotland] (Harmondsworth, 1984).

McMillan, James, *Anatomy of Scotland* (London, 1969).

Magnusson, Magnus, *Treasures of Scotland* (London, 1981).

Maine, G.F. (ed), *A Book of Scotland* (London and Glasgow, 1950).

Marr, Andrew, *The Battle for Scotland* (Harmondsworth, 1992).

Marshall, Rosalind K., *Bonnie Prince Charlie* (Edinburgh, 1988).

Massie, Allan, *101 Great Scots* (Edinburgh, 1987).

Massie, Allan, *The Ragged Lion* (London, 1994).

Maxwell, Gordon S., *The Romans in Scotland* (Edinburgh, 1989).

Menzies, Gordon (ed), *The Scottish Nation* (London, 1972).

Miller, Karl, *Memoirs of a Modern Scotland* (London, 1970).

Mitchison, Rosalind, *A History of Scotland* (London, 1970).

Mitchison, Rosalind, *Life in Scotland* (London, 1978).

Mitchison, Rosalind (ed), *The Roots of Nationalism: Studies in Northern Europe* (Edinburgh, 1980).

Mosley, Diana, *A Life of Contrasts, The Autobiography of Diana Mosley* (London, 1977).

Mossner, Ernest Campbell, *The Life of David Hume* (Edinburgh, 1954).

Muir, Edwin, *Scott and Scotland: The predicament of the Scottish Writer* (London, 1936 and Edinburgh, 1979).

Muir, Edwin, *Scottish Journey* (London, 1935).

Nairn, Tom, *The Break-up of Britain: Crisis and Neo-nationalism* (London, 1977).

Neale, Sir John, *Queen Elizabeth* (London, 1934).

Notestein, Wallace, *The Scot in History* (Connecticut, 1970).

Paton, H.J., *The Claim of Scotland* (London, 1968).

Philipson, N.T. and Mitchison, Rosalind (eds), *Scotland in the Age of Improvement: Essays in Scottish History in the Eighteenth Century* (Edinburgh, 1970).

Piggott, Stuart, *Scotland before History* (Edinburgh, 1982).

Pope-Hennessy, James, *Robert Louis Stevenson* (London, 1974).

Pottle, Frederick A (ed), *Boswell's London Journal 1762–1763* (London, 1951).

Prebble, John, *Culloden* (London, 1961).

Prebble, John, *The Darien Disaster* (London, 1968).

Prebble, John, *The Highland Clearances* (London, 1963).

Prebble, John, *The King's Jaunt, George IV in Scotland, August 1822, 'One and twenty daft days'* (London, 1988).

Prebble, John, *The Lion in the North* (London, 1971).

Prebble, John, *Scotland* (London, 1984).

Pryce-Jones, David, *Unity Mitford, A Quest* (London, 1976).

Rait, R.S., *The Parliaments of Scotland* (Glasgow, 1924).

Ramsay, Edward Bannerman, *Reminiscences of Scottish Life and Character* (Edinburgh, 1859).

Ritchie, Anna and Breeze, David J., *Invaders of Scotland: An Introduction to the Archaeology of the Romans, Scots, Angles and Vikings highlighting Monuments in the Care of the Secretary of State for Scotland* (Edinburgh, 1991).

Sawyer, P.H., *The Age of the Vikings* (London, 1971).

Scott, P.H., *In Bed with an Elephant* (Saltire Society Booklet) (Edinburgh 1985).

Scott, P.H., *1707: The Union of Scotland and England* (Edinburgh, 1979).

Scott, Tom (ed), *The Penguin Book of Scottish Verse* (Harmondsworth, 1970).

Scott, Sir Walter, *Journals* (Edinburgh, 1890, 1891).

Scott, Sir Walter, *The Letters of Malachi Malagrowther* (London, 1826).

Scott, Sir Walter, *The Poetical Works*, 12 vols (Edinburgh, 1820).

Smout, T.C., *A Century of the Scottish People*, 1830–1950 (London, 1987).

Smout, T.C., *A History of the Scottish People*, 1560–1830 (London, 1969).

Steel, David and Judy, *Mary Stuart's Scotland: The Landscapes Life and Legends of Mary Queen of Scots* (London, 1987).

Stevenson, Robert Louis, *A Child's Garden of Verses* (London, 1888).

Stevenson, Robert Louis, *Edinburgh* (London, 1905).

Stevenson, Robert Louis, *Memories and Portraits* (London, 1911).

Stevenson, Robert Louis, *Virginibus Puerisque* (London, 1881).

Topham, Edward, *Letters from Edinburgh in 1774 and 1775* (Edinburgh, 1971).

Torrance, John, *Scotland's Dilemma: Province or Nation?* (Edinburgh, 1937).

*The War Dead of the British Commonwealth and Empire, 1939–1945* (London, 1959).

Webb, Keith, *The Growth of Nationalism in Scotland* (Glasgow, 1977).

Wordsworth, William, *The Complete Poetical Works* (Oxford, 1888).

Young, Douglas, *Edinburgh in the Age of Sir Walter Scott* (Oklahoma, 1965).

# ARTICLES/PERIODICALS

*Blackwood's Magazine*: 'The Poetry and Humour of the Scottish Language', No DCLXIL, Vol CVIII, November, 1870 and No. DCLXL, Vol CVIII, December, 1870 (Edinburgh, 1870).

Economic History Review: 'The Anglo-Scottish Union of 1707' by T.C. Smout, 2nd series XVI (London, 1964).

The English History Review: 'The Union of 1707 as an Episode in English Politics' by P.W.J. Riley, LXXXIV (London, 1969).

Historical Association: 'Scots Abroad in the Fifteenth Century' by Annie L. Dunlop, no. 124 (London, 1942).

House of Commons: Research Note 92/0

1. Scottish Constitutional Convention

2. The independent Option

3. Home Rule (Scotland) Bill, presented by Menzies Campbell MP (1992).

Scottish Historical Review: 'Lothian and the Early Scottish Kings' by Marjorie O. Anderson, vol XXXIX, no. 128 (Edinburgh, 1960).

'The Pioneers of Anglicized Speech in Scotland' by Marjory A. Bald, vol XXIV, no. 95 (Glasgow, 1927).

'The Making of the Treaty of Union, 1707' by W. Ferguson, vol XLIII no. 136 (Edinburgh, 1964).

'George IV and Highland Dress' by D.B. Horn, vol 47, nos 143–4 (Aberdeen, 1968).

'Some Scottish Writers of History in the Eighteenth Century' by D.B. Horn, vol XL, no. 129 (Edinburgh, 1961).

'Bruce versus Baliol 1291–1292' by George Neilson, vol XVI (Glasgow, 1919).

'Norse Settlement in the Northern and Western Isles' by W.F.H. Nicolaisen, vol 48, no. 145 (Aberdeen, 1969).

Scottish History Society: 'Sir John Clerk's Observations on the Present Circumstances of Scotland 1730' by T.C. Smout, Miscellany, vol X (Edinburgh, 1965).

Texas Studies in Literature and Language: 'Concepts of Enlightenment in Eighteenth Century Scottish Literature and Language' by John Valdimir Price, vol IX (Texas, 1967).

# INDEX

MISS McKIRDY'S DAUGHTERS WILL
NOW DANCE THE HIGHLAND FLING
Barbara Kinghorn

The compelling and heart-rending true story of an eccentric,
tragic and indomitable family.

Miss McKirdy, a teacher of Scottish dancing, lived with her
alcoholic husband and three talented daughters, Barbara, Annie
and Jilly, in a Dutch-gabled house on the outskirts of
Johannesburg in South Africa. Despite coming from a Calvinist
background, Miss McKirdy chose to teach in a Catholic convent,
for the very practical reason that her three girls could be educated
for the price of one. Scottish dancing dominated their lives.
An ambitious and powerful woman, Miss McKirdy believed
that winning was all and drove her daughters ruthlessly to
achieve her goals.

As the sisters grew up and coped with death, divorce, madness
and – unknowingly – with the realities of apartheid, the
indomitable strength and courage of an eccentric, funny, and
tragic family prevailed, proving that the ties of love,
sometimes irksome, can hold strong in the face of violent and
disruptive events.

Barbara Kinghorn's remarkable autobiography shows that she is a
survivor, and that out of grief and sadness have come great
understanding and peace.

'A WONDERFUL BOOK. FAITHFULLY AND WITH SUCH
RECALL BARBARA KINGHORN MAKES HER STORY
UNIVERSAL AS WELL AS FASCINATING. IT IS WRITTEN
WITH OBJECTIVITY AS WELL AS PASSION, SO THERE
ARE NO WINNERS, ONLY MEMORABLE AND
POIGNANT HUMAN BEINGS'
*Maureen Lipman*

0 552 99637 8

# A SELECTED LIST OF FINE WRITING
# AVAILABLE FROM CORGI BOOKS
# AND BLACK SWAN

THE PRICES SHOWN BELOW WERE CORRECT AT THE TIME OF GOING TO PRESS. HOWEVER TRANSWORLD PUBLISHERS RESERVE THE RIGHT TO SHOW NEW RETAIL PRICES ON COVERS WHICH MAY DIFFER FROM THOSE PREVIOUSLY ADVERTISED IN THE TEXT OR ELSEWHERE.

| 13182 2 | THE MESSIANIC LEGACY | Baigent, Leigh & Lincoln | £6.99 |
| 13653 0 | THE RELUCTANT JESTER | Michael Bentine | £5.99 |
| 99065 5 | THE PAST IS MYSELF | Christabel Bielenberg | £6.99 |
| 13337 X | THE PROVISIONAL IRA | Patrick Bishop & Eamonn Mallie | £5.99 |
| 13741 3 | LETTER TO LOUISE | Pauline Collins | £4.99 |
| 14093 7 | OUR KATE | Catherine Cookson | £4.99 |
| 13582 8 | THE GOD SQUAD | Paddy Doyle | £5.99 |
| 14239 5 | MY FEUDAL LORD | Tehmina Durrani | £5.99 |
| 13928 9 | DAUGHTER OF PERSIA | Sattareh Farman Farmaian | £5.99 |
| 99479 0 | PERFUME FROM PROVENCE | Lady Fortescue | £6.99 |
| 12833 3 | THE HOUSE BY THE DVINA | Eugenie Fraser | £6.99 |
| 13937 8 | THE FIRST FIFTY – MUNRO-BAGGING WITHOUT A BEARD | | |
| | | Muriel Gray | £8.99 |
| 14185 2 | FINDING PEGGY: A GLASGOW CHILDHOOD | | |
| | | Meg Henderson | £5.99 |
| 14164 X | EMPTY CRADLES | Margaret Humphreys | £6.99 |
| 99637 8 | MISS McKIRDY'S DAUGHTERS WILL NOW DANCE THE | | |
| | HIGHLAND FLING | Barbara Kinghorn | £6.99 |
| 14181 X | IRONING JOHN | James Leith | £4.99 |
| 13944 0 | DIANA'S STORY | Deric Longden | £3.99 |
| 07583 3 | NO MEAN CITY | A. McArthur & H. Kingsley Long | £4.99 |
| 13356 6 | NOT WITHOUT MY DAUGHTER | Betty Mahmoody | £5.99 |
| 13853 X | SOME OTHER RAINBOW | John McCarthy & Jill Morrell | £5.99 |
| 14127 5 | BRAVO TWO ZERO | Andy McNab | £5.99 |
| 14288 3 | BRIDGE ACROSS MY SORROWS | Christina Noble | £4.99 |
| 14303 0 | THE HOT ZONE | Richard Preston | £5.99 |
| 13935 1 | ULTIMATE RISK | Adam Raphael | £5.99 |
| 14275 1 | THE AUTOBIOGRAPHY OF A THIEF | Bruce Reynolds | £5.99 |
| 13950 5 | JESUS THE MAN | Barbara Thiering | £5.99 |
| 99638 6 | BETTER THAN SEX | Hunter S. Thompson | £6.99 |
| 99512 6 | NOBODY NOWHERE | Donna Williams | £6.99 |
| 14198 4 | SOMEBODY SOMEWHERE | Donna Williams | £5.99 |
| 99366 2 | THE ELECTRIC KOOL AID ACID TEST | Tom Wolfe | £7.99 |
| 13288 8 | IN GOD'S NAME | David Yallop | £6.99 |

All Transworld titles are available by post from:
**Book Service By Post, PO box 29, Douglas, Isle of Man, IM99 1BQ**
Credit cards accepted. Please telephone 01624 675137, fax 01624
670923 or Internet http://www.bookpost.co.uk for details.
Please allow £0.75 per book for post and packing UK.
Overseas customers allow £1 per book for post and packing.